A National Force

Studies in Canadian Military History
Series editor: Dean F. Oliver, Canadian War Museum

The Canadian War Museum, Canada's national museum of military history, has a threefold mandate: to remember, to preserve, and to educate. Studies in Canadian Military History, published by UBC Press in association with the Museum, extends this mandate by presenting the best of contemporary scholarship to provide new insights into all aspects of Canadian military history, from earliest times to recent events. The work of a new generation of scholars is especially encouraged, and the books employ a variety of approaches – cultural, social, intellectual, economic, political, and comparative – to investigate gaps in the existing historiography. The books in the series feed immediately into future exhibitions, programs, and outreach efforts by the Canadian War Museum. A list of the titles in the series appears at the end of the book.

Canadian War Museum
Musée canadien de la guerre

A National Force
The Evolution of Canada's Army, 1950-2000

Peter Kasurak

UBCPress · Vancouver · Toronto

21 20 19 18 17 16 15 14 5 4 3 2

Printed in Canada on FSC-certified ancient-forest-free paper (100% post-consumer recycled) that is processed chlorine- and acid-free.

Library and Archives Canada Cataloguing in Publication

Kasurak, Peter Charles, author
A national force : the evolution of Canada's army, 1950-2000 / Peter Kasurak.

(Studies in Canadian military history series, 1499-6251)
Includes bibliographical references and index.
Issued in print and electronic formats.
ISBN 978-0-7748-2639-6 (bound).– ISBN 978-0-7748-2640-2 (pbk.)
ISBN 978-0-7748-2641-9 (pdf).– ISBN 978-0-7748-2642-6 (epub)

1. Canada. Canadian Armed Forces – History – 20th century. 2. Canada – Armed Forces – History – 20th century. 3. Canada – History, Military – 20th century. I. Title. II. Series: Studies in Canadian military history

FC603.K37 2013 355.00971 C2013-904563-5
C2013-904564-3

Canada

UBC Press gratefully acknowledges the financial support for our publishing program of the Government of Canada (through the Canada Book Fund), the Canada Council for the Arts, and the British Columbia Arts Council.

This book has been published with the help of a grant from the Canadian Federation for the Humanities and Social Sciences, through the Awards to Scholarly Publications Program, using funds provided by the Social Sciences and Humanities Research Council of Canada.

Publication of this book has been financially supported by the Canadian War Museum.

UBC Press
The University of British Columbia
2029 West Mall
Vancouver, BC V6T 1Z2
www.ubcpress.ca

Contents

Acknowledgments

NO WORK OF HISTORY is written in a vacuum. We truly do stand on the shoulders of those who have gone before. This volume takes issue with the points of view of many of its predecessors but is nevertheless dependent on their scholarship. In particular, the works of Stephen Harris, Jack Granatstein, Douglas Bland, John English, and Sean Maloney have been extremely useful in establishing the narrative and pointing out sources.

It is equally true that history cannot be written without the work of archivists. Stephen Harris and his team at the Directorate of History and Heritage at the Department of National Defence provided both access and guidance to the use of National Defence holdings. Paul Marsden at Library and Archives Canada spent considerable time providing training and advice on using Library and Archives Defence files that had been received but not yet completely catalogued or organized. David Willis kindly guided me through the holdings of the Fort Frontenac Library at Canadian Forces Base Kingston, and Cathy Murphy helped me with the use of student papers and the library of doctrinal manuals of the Canadian Forces College in Toronto.

I was also assisted by numerous individuals in the Access to Information sections of both National Defence and Library and Archives Canada. Without exception, requests were processed as quickly as staff restrictions permitted, and the staff worked to ensure that I received all documents to which I was legally entitled.

Special thanks go to all those former members of the Canadian Forces or the Department who granted interviews, especially General Paul Manson (Retired), Lieutenant-General Richard Evraire (Retired), and Brigadier-General G.E. (Joe) Sharpe (Retired), who also shared personal papers with me.

I would also like to thank the anonymous reviewers for critiques that can only have improved this book, especially the second reviewer, who also suggested several leads that enriched the study. Thanks also to Dean Oliver at the Canadian War Museum, who provided comment on an early draft.

Any errors and omissions are entirely my own.

The author and UBC Press thank the *Canadian Military Journal* for permission to reproduce text that originally appeared in Peter Kasurak, "Canadian Army Tactical Nuclear Warfare Doctrine in the 1950s: Force Development in the Pre-professional Era," *Canadian Military Journal* 11, 1 (2010): 38-44. They also thank Sage Publications for permission to reproduce text that originally appeared as the final, definitive version of "Concepts of Professionalism in the Canadian Army, 1945-2000: Regimentalism, Reaction, and Reform, *Armed Forces and Society* 37, 1 (2001): http://online.sagepub.com.

Abbreviations

ABC	America-Britain-Canada
ABCA	America-Britain-Canada-Australia
ACE	Allied Command Europe
ADATS	Air Defence Anti-Tank System
ADTB	Army Doctrine and Tactics Board
AMF(L)	ACE Mobile Force (Land)
APC	armoured personnel carrier
ASW	anti-submarine warfare
ATGM	anti-tank guided missile
ATOB	Army Tactics and Organization Board
AVGP	Armoured Vehicle General Purpose (the wheeled Grizzly armoured personnel carrier and Cougar "tank trainer")
BMP	Boyevaya Mashina Pekhoty (Infantry Fighting Vehicle) (Soviet)
CAMRA	Canadian Advanced Multi-Role Aircraft
CAORE	Canadian Army Operations Research Establishment
CAR	Canadian Airborne Regiment
CARBG	Canadian Airborne Regiment Battle Group
CAST	Canadian Air-Sea Transportable (Brigade Group)
CD	Combat Development
CDC	Combat Development Committee
CDS	Chief of the Defence Staff
CDTDC	Combat Development and Tactical Doctrine Committee
CENTAG	Central Army Group of NATO
CFDP	Canadian Forces Development Plan
CFE	Canadian Forces Europe

CFHQ	Canadian Forces Headquarters
CGS	Chief of the General Staff
CIBG	Canadian Infantry Brigade Group
CIFV	Canadian Infantry Fighting Vehicle
CJFS	Canadian Joint Force Somalia
CLDO	Chief Land Doctrine and Operations
CMB	Canadian Mechanized Brigade
CMBG	Canadian Mechanized Brigade Group
COTC	Canadian Officer Training Corps
DCD	Directorate of Combat Development
DCDS	Deputy Chief of the Defence Staff
DFSV	Direct Fire Support Vehicle
DGMPO	Director General Military Plans and Operations
DMC	Defence Management Committee
DPMS	Defence Program Management System
DSR	Defence Structure Review
FSR	Field Service Regulations (British Army)
GBMC	Groupe-brigade mécanisé du Canada
GOC	General Officer Commanding
IFOR	Implementation Force (NATO)
KFOR	Kosovo Force
LANDCENT	Allied Land Forces Central Europe
LdSH	Lord Strathcona's Horse
MNF	Multi-National Force (Central Africa)
MRG	Management Review Group (Pennefather Committee)
NATO	North Atlantic Treaty Organization
NCBW	nuclear/chemical/biological warfare
NCO	non-commissioned officer
NDHQ	National Defence Headquarters
NIS	National Investigation Service
NORAD	North American Air Defense Command
NORTHAG	Northern Army Group of NATO
ODB	Officer Development Board
PPCLI	Princess Patricia's Canadian Light Infantry

R22^{e}R	Royal 22e Régiment
RBC	Régiment blindé du Canada
RCAF	Royal Canadian Air Force
RCD	Royal Canadian Dragoons
RCN	Royal Canadian Navy
RMC	Royal Military College
ROAD	Reorganization Objectives Army Division (US Army)
SAC	Strategic Air Command (US Air Force)
SACEUR	Supreme Allied Commander Europe
SACLANT	Supreme Allied Commander Atlantic
SCRR	Special Commission on the Restructuring of the Reserves
SFOR	Stabilization Force (NATO)
SHAPE	Supreme Headquarters Allied Powers Europe
SSF	Special Service Force
STF	Stationed Task Force
STOL	short takeoff and landing
TOW	Tube-Launched, Optically-tracked, Wire command data link anti-tank missile
UNITAF	United Nations Task Force in Somalia
UNOSOM	United Nations Operation in Somalia
UNPROFOR	United Nations Protection Force
UTTH	utility helicopter
VCDS	Vice Chief of the Defence Staff
VCGS	Vice Chief of the General Staff
V/STOL	vertical/short takeoff and landing

A National Force

Introduction

On a clear, cold March afternoon in 1995, the Canadian Airborne Regiment's twenty-seven-year history came to a close with a final march-past and the laying of its colours in the regimental museum at Canadian Forces Base Petawawa. The daylong ceremony had begun with a parachute jump by most of the regiment's 665 members, and the afternoon had featured troops rappelling from helicopters before charging through smoke to the sound of artillery and machine-gun fire. Their commanding officer, Lieutenant-Colonel Peter Kenward, told them, "You're the best," and stated: "I do not accept and will not accept that this regiment is disbanded in disgrace." Yet according to press reports, Kenward's head hung low and tears trickled down his face as he gave the final orders dismissing the regiment. It was "more a funeral than a parade."

Not everyone in uniform would have agreed with Kenward's assessment, and certainly the government did not. Defence Minister David Collenette had decided to disband the regiment after a series of incidents had publicly tarnished its reputation. The initial incidents during the regiment's 1993 deployment to Somalia as a stabilization force were the most serious, involving the shooting death of a Somali national who had infiltrated Airborne lines as well as the death in custody of a second Somali. As the court martial and Forces inquiry proceeded, the Airborne's reputation was further damaged when videotapes of its members making racist comments about Somalis and engaging in initiation rites that involved urine, vomit, and excrement became public. The press also reported that elements of the regiment sent to Rwanda on a second peacekeeping mission had shot up a convent they were supposed to be protecting from looters and that two soldiers had had to be repatriated because of self-inflicted cuts from a "blood brother ritual." Faced with adverse international publicity, both Collenette and Prime Minister Jean Chrétien agreed on the unprecedented step of disbanding the regiment. The press concurred. The *Ottawa Citizen* editorialized that the Canadian Airborne Regiment, "publicly disgraced and politically insupportable, has been properly disbanded."

The disbanding of the regiment was indeed a funeral – and not only for the Airborne. The inquiry ordered by the government into its deployment to Somalia illuminated both difficulties and deficiencies within the army, the Canadian Forces, and the Department of National Defence and created the conditions for significant change to institutional structures, army doctrine, and the military's concept of professionalism, changes that would eventually lead to a renewed relationship with the country's political leadership. The disbanding of the Canadian Airborne Regiment was therefore the beginning of the end of an army that had existed since the end of the Second World War. A new Canadian army would emerge that was more closely linked to political requirements and that would have broad popular support.

This book originated as an attempt to answer questions that had arisen in my mind during my career as the senior official in the Office of the Auditor General of Canada responsible for the audit of the Department of National Defence. Having become convinced of the centrality of doctrine to the success of a military force during my graduate education at Duke University, where many of my fellow students were serving US Army officers, I was perplexed by the relative unimportance of doctrine to the Canadian army. A frequently heard apocryphal story – sometimes attributed to a German officer during the Second World War and sometimes to a contemporary Soviet officer – was that while the Germans or Americans could be easily dealt with because they acted within a doctrinal framework, the Canadian army could not because it either had no doctrine or did not follow it, making its actions completely unpredictable. I was often struck by how many Canadian army officers believed that rank required visible privilege to be effective. Senior officers justified official residences on the basis that troops had to see that their commanding general was special. For their part, many junior officers were appalled that senior officers were compelled to use public transit in Ottawa and were not provided with staff cars – apparently vestiges of the Victorian social order still existed. The army, as well as the other services, also had a strong contingent within the officer corps that railed against "civilianization" and what they saw as the replacement of military values with "management." It was never clear to me how a multi-billion-dollar enterprise could be run without management techniques. As a legislative auditor, I had a front-row seat to the Somalia debacle and associated scandals. Clearly, something had gone badly wrong, but what?

This book is about the Canadian army as an institution and about its place in the Canadian state. It is not a history of operations except as they affected the institution itself. For the most part, this was mainly through the "war without battles" that was the Cold War, which the Canadian army prepared for from the end of the Second World War to the early 1990s. With the dissolution of the

Soviet Union and the Warsaw Pact, stabilization operations in the Balkans, Africa, and elsewhere put new pressures on the army. It is not my intention to analyze these missions in operational terms but rather from the perspective of how they led to change within the army itself. Thus, this book focuses on four main themes: the army's concepts of military professionalism and how they evolved during the last half of the twentieth century; the army's role in shaping Canada's national security policy; the army's planning of its future development through doctrine and force structure; and, finally, the Militia and the relationship between the Regular and Reserve army.

An explanation is required about what is considered to be the "Canadian army." The Canadian Army existed as an institution with a legislative mandate only before the three services were unified to form the Canadian Forces in 1968, four years after Defence Minister Paul Hellyer first integrated the armed services, creating a single chief of the defence staff and abolishing the individual service chiefs and the chairman of the Chiefs of Staff Committee. After integration, the land forces comprised several commands and national headquarters components under various titles. However, the failure to develop a truly unified force even after 1968 meant that the army continued to exist in everything but name. Service identities slowly reasserted themselves and "environmental commanders" emerged, heading a virtual navy, army, and air force. In this book, I consider all land forces, as well as the national headquarters staffs that set policy for or provided services to them, as part of "the Canadian army," and I use this term in discussing the post-1968 era regardless of the official nomenclature of the day.

The Canadian Army was created as a component of a British Imperial force and inherited many of its traits and preferences from its metropolitan parent. The outward style of the Canadian Army prior to unification of the armed services was British. In the early postwar period, its senior ranks were dominated by officers who had been trained in British staff colleges, and it borrowed British Army doctrine into the 1960s. The army fought in Korea as part of a Commonwealth Division and succeeded in getting itself assigned to the British-led Northern Army Group of NATO forces. The culture of the Canadian Army consequently was strongly oriented towards choosing officers based on character rather than knowledge and expertise. The army persisted in attempting to recruit the "right sort" of individual and did not share the rest of Canadian society's enthusiasm for university education during the postwar period. It also perpetuated a version of the British regimental system as a means of creating and preserving combat cohesion and morale. This book examines the effects of the Canadian army's culture on the types of officers recruited and retained, and on the relationship of the senior officer corps with political leaders and senior public servants.

The early postwar army had little capacity to develop – or even participate in developing – national security policy. These functions had not been required in an Imperial force led by the parent country and service. The Canadian Army nevertheless had strong policy views. It wished to perpetuate its Second World War type of force, one that was relatively large, heavily equipped, and prepared to fight a Great Power war in Europe. Peacekeeping forces were regarded as a lesser included capability within a "warfighting" army. The army's preferences would bring it into continuing conflict with Canada's political leadership, and its lack of policy development capacity would limit its ability to make its case to its civilian masters. After the Soviet Union's acquisition of strategic nuclear weapons, civilians became increasingly skeptical of the military value of any land force that the Canadian government could pay for in peacetime. The army that they preferred was generally one that reduced diplomatic pressure from allies to maintain forces in Europe and kept economic costs to a minimum. This book explores the interplay of military and civilian biases throughout the Cold War and its immediate aftermath.

Armies are complex organizations consisting of tens of thousands of individual members employing thousands of vehicles and a wide range of complex technology. In order to fulfill national objectives and work cohesively in the field, an army requires both a plan and an "operating manual" to provide soldiers with consistent information on how the various components are meant to work together. These publications are known as "doctrine." The NATO glossary defines doctrine as the "fundamental principles by which the military forces guide their actions in support of objectives. It is authoritative but requires judgement in application." The British Army put greater emphasis on the "judgement" than on the "authoritative" element of doctrine and relied upon the judgment of its senior commanders. Prior to and during the Second World War, its doctrinal development capability was weak. Once the Canadian army was on its own, it found that its ability to adapt to the challenge of tactical nuclear warfare was lacking. It eventually did build capacity and develop its own doctrine, only to have such capacity disrupted by unification of the armed services. After struggling for almost a decade, it managed to revive its doctrine and force development functions, but by the mid-1970s the atmosphere was so poisoned by the post-unification breakdown in civil-military relations and intra-service rivalries that the product was largely unusable. Tracing the development of doctrine is therefore essential for understanding what the army thought it was doing in building the type of force it sought, for understanding the level of institutional expertise it had attained, and for understanding civil-military relations.

The fourth theme explored throughout this book is the relationship between the Militia – the Reserve army – and the Regular Force. Prior to the Second

World War, the Permanent Force (that is, the Regulars) was envisaged as comprising a general staff and cadre force, with the main military muscle of the country coming from the Non-Permanent Active Militia. Relative to the demands of the war, however, neither force was sufficiently large or well trained. Well before the end of the war, senior army officials began planning for a large force supported by conscription, and they continued advocating such a force in the immediate postwar period. This policy was rejected by the civilian government, however, creating an impasse that endured for half a century. At no time did the government wish to pass legislation requiring, or even protecting, military service so as to permit the creation of a large reserve army. Nor did civilian governments wish to pay for the equipment and increased training that a large, effective reserve would require; they doubted the utility of even the Regular Force. For its part, the army produced one study after another documenting the poor state of readiness and training of the Militia, none of which resulted in material improvement. Solutions were either unacceptable to the politicians or would have led to a small reserve force, thereby undercutting the army's ambitions to expand someday. By the end of the twentieth century, relations between the Regular and Reserve armies had become vitriolic, and although some healing was achieved, the fundamental issues remained unresolved.

A fifth theme runs through this book – namely, the role of civilians in managing military policy and maintaining civil-military relations. This is a history and not a work of political science. It does not set out to establish or critique a theory of civil-military relations. Yet it is scarcely possible to write about civil-military relations without considering theory. To attempt to do so can result in implicitly adopting a theory that subsequently colours judgments about whether the actors are behaving appropriately. For the most part, the army officer corps and many military historians have accepted the ideal set out by Samuel Huntington in his 1957 book *The Soldier and the State.* Huntington argued that the military had three major responsibilities: to represent the claims of military security within the state machinery and to keep authorities informed of the minimum military security requirements of the state; to advise and report on alternative courses of state action from a military point of view; and to implement state decisions even if they run counter to military advice and judgment. Huntington based his model on the American military, and further claimed that the military had the right to present its views to public bodies that apportion resources, both executive and legislative. This part of Huntington's theory is largely non-problematic from a Canadian point of view, although Canadian officials (both civil and military) represent only their minister when testifying before legislative committees. More difficult to accept is Huntington's claim that the civil-military relationship is best served by what he called "objective civilian control." By this he meant that the civilian government should not attempt to make the military adopt values that are the mirror image of civil society, but should instead instill an ethos that both professionalizes the military and removes it from politics. Coincidentally, Huntington praised the military ethos and implied that it was superior to the grubby commercial liberalism of civilian America.[1]

Huntington's theory was no doubt very attractive to the military, including the Canadian army's officer corps, but it presents two problems. First, in attempting to create a distinct military professional sphere, it delegitimizes political considerations in the formulation of national security policy. Although this is not what Huntington intended, his theory has promoted a belief that military appreciations trump domestic political concerns and that civilian politicians are automatically wrong if they make security decisions based on political considerations. Second, the suggestion of military moral superiority further delegitimizes direction from the political level and fosters a belief that the military is justified in pursuing its own agenda. Huntingtonian thinking dominated the Canadian army during the 1970s and 1980s and contributed to the breakdown in civil-military relations.

More recently, Peter Feaver has proposed an alternative theory of civil-military relations in his book *Armed Servants*. Drawing on economic "agency theory," he argues that the relationship between the military and the state should be seen as one of principal and agent, where the political leadership is the principal and the military is its agent. According to Feaver, agents do what principals want when they are monitored (they "work") but follow their own agendas when not controlled (they "shirk"). The problem is therefore how to devise the best system of controls. Central to Feaver's approach is the premise that "in a democracy, civilians have the right to be wrong." They can ask for things that are not conducive to good national security, and while the military can advise against them, it should not prevent those policies from being implemented. According to Feaver, shirking by the US military has usually taken three forms: (1) the military has attempted to determine the outcome of a policy debate by giving inflated estimates of what a military operation would cost; (2) the military has attempted to determine policy by making an end run through public protest, leaks, or appeals to other political actors; and (3) the military has attempted to undermine a policy through bureaucratic foot-dragging and "slow rolling" so that the desired policy is never implemented. This book leans towards Feaver's theory. It is written from the perspective that civilians have the right to be wrong and is critical of the army when it is seen to be "shirking."[2]

That said, it should not be imagined that civilians are above criticism. Civilian direction to the army tended to be episodic, and grandiose when it was given.

Paul Hellyer's "mobile force" and Perrin Beatty's "Total Force army" are the two clearest examples of this. Neither Hellyer nor Beatty had adequate support in Cabinet to obtain funding for their plans, and both failed in implementation. Many ministers took inadequate steps to monitor and control the development of the army, allowing it to pursue its own agenda. Some actively colluded with the military to evade Cabinet direction. Just as the army lacked the capacity to contribute to the making of national security policy, so its civilian principals lacked knowledge of military capabilities and costs. What emerged was a relationship where neither the principal nor the agent played its role adequately.

This book is therefore a departure from most of the literature on the Canadian army. Over the years, a standard narrative of the army's history has developed. In this narrative, the army experienced a golden age between the end of the Korean War in 1953 and the beginning of Paul Hellyer's integration and unification of the armed services in 1964. Jack Granatstein calls this the period of "the professional army," after which professionalism came "under siege."[3] Douglas Bland, writing about the governance structure of the armed services and National Defence, divides history into approximately the same periods: a "Command Era" from 1946 to 1964, followed by a "Management Era" thereafter.[4] John English, in his *Lament for an* Army, takes a similar view. He argues that the post–Korean War Canadian Army suffered two blows from which it never fully recovered: emphasis on massive retaliation and air forces, which meant the end of the Militia as a mobilization force, and the 1964 *White Paper on Defence*, which placed top priority on peacekeeping and "ushered in a generation of professional decline."[5] In the standard narrative, the period that preceded integration and unification was vastly better than that which followed. The army was relatively well funded, fairly well equipped, and given its proper role in the development of national policy. Its British heritage and culture were intact. But beginning with Paul Hellyer's tenure as defence minister, military values were replaced by civilian management concepts and the army's British heritage was downplayed or discarded. Civilians determined missions and roles for the army but withheld appropriate resources. The Militia was ignored and allowed to deteriorate. The standard narrative places the onus for the Somalia incident on civilians. David Bercuson asks: "How and why did the Airborne get 'totally out of control,'" and answers his own question:

> [The answer] is rooted in the larger story of the crisis that [had] been developing in the Canadian army for at least a decade, and nobody in the press seems to care much about that. That crisis was caused initially by the deliberate bleeding of the defence establishment to death by successive, mostly Liberal, governments. It was made a great deal worse by unification and the imposition on the Canadian Forces

> of a structure designed to ease political and bureaucratic burdens rather than promote military effectiveness ... With NDHQ safely ensconced at the top of the defence structure, it was not long before soldier-managers took control of the army and soldier-warriors were shunted aside. We now have an army in which war fighting is of secondary or even tertiary importance. Which is absurd.[6]

This book challenges the standard narrative. The evidence presented here shows that the army's British heritage was problematic in that it created institutional deficits in the army's ability to contribute to national security policy and to develop military doctrine. Its cultural preferences for character over education and for regimental loyalty led to the army's further separation from civilian society and limited its ability to relate to its parent society. This book argues that for much of the last half of the twentieth century, the army "shirked." It followed its own agenda rather than that of the civilian government. The government responded by applying more controls through the Management Review Group (MRG) instituted by Defence Minister Donald Macdonald in 1972. The MRG reforms improved control but also increased resentment and reaction. The army pursued unrealizable plans and became increasingly insular. A final breakdown occurred during the stability operations of the post–Cold War period. The Somalia incident was the most notorious, but other incidents in the Balkans and elsewhere made it clear that the army required reorientation in terms of culture and doctrine.

Whereas the standard narrative accuses civilians of both starving and wrecking the army, this book asks readers to consider whether the army was not the author of its own decline. It asks readers to consider when the Canadian army became a national army implementing national policy rather than an Imperial or an alliance army. It also asks readers to evaluate whether the army's response to civilian direction with which it did not agree was appropriate. How these questions are answered is important for understanding the army we have today and in shaping tools to manage civil-military relations.

In writing this book I have attempted to "let the documents speak." That is not to say that I do not have a bias. I will, however, make my biases as explicit as possible and let the reader judge whether they are supported by the evidence presented.

This book was written from primary sources held in the archives at the Department of National Defence Directorate of History and Heritage and at Library and Archives Canada. Special attention was paid to the papers of Robert Lewis Raymont and Charles J. Gauthier, two officers who served in the central departmental secretariat from 1951 to 1989; besides maintaining an archive of policy documents, they also wrote unpublished histories of the central Defence decision-making process. I also attempted to obtain as many post-exercise reports, post-operation reports, and significant war game studies as possible. Many of these documents were still classified and required numerous Access to Information requests. The papers of the Canadian Land Force Command and Staff College contained useful information. I also relied upon Cabinet minutes and the papers of prime ministers from Louis St-Laurent to Pierre Trudeau as well as those ministers and senior public servants who left papers. Finally, I supplemented documentary sources with interviews of selected participants.

Despite these efforts, I would not describe this as the final or definitive work on the Canadian army. Some will believe that I should have not excluded operations to the extent I have, or that I should have included topics such as the movement towards linguistic, gender, and gender-orientation inclusiveness as an essential part of an institutional history. Because many documents are still classified, I was selective in what I asked for and received under Access to Information. There are also likely many documents in the custody of Library and Archives Canada for the 1980s and subsequent decades that await complete archival assessment. For lack of search tools, it is probable that much material of significance escaped untouched. Nevertheless, I believe that this account represents a step forward in its use of many sources that had been previously unavailable.

Canada needs an army. This army must be able to meet the goals of domestic and foreign policy. It must be able to deal effectively with security threats. It has to be built and maintained within the budget and policy framework established by Parliament. The army required by Canada may not be the one envisaged by those in uniform or that preferred by civilian politicians. It is important, however, that the army that is required is the one that is actually maintained. This book is an attempt to discern how close – or how far away – this goal was to being achieved during the last half of the twentieth century.

CHAPTER ONE

The 1950s: A Professional Army?

THE SECOND WORLD WAR was scarcely over when the Cold War began. In February 1946, Stalin stated that either communism would replace capitalism or war was inevitable. The riposte came a month later when former British prime minister Winston Churchill gave his "Iron Curtain" speech in Fulton, Missouri, to an audience that included President Harry Truman. Also in 1946, George Kennan, the American deputy chief of mission in Moscow, drafted his famous "Long Telegram," warning that the Soviet Union would not respond to normal diplomacy based on negotiation but was a repressive, expansive regime that had to be contained by force. In early 1950 – before the start of the Korean War – the United States set its foreign policy course in National Security Council Paper NSC-68, which stated that "the Soviet Union has one purpose and that is world domination" and was "unlike previous aspirants to hegemony ... animated by a new fanatic faith, antithetical to our own, and seeks to impose its absolute authority over the rest of the world." American goals were the reduction of Soviet power on the Soviet Union's periphery, the establishment of independent states in Eastern Europe, and the eventual fundamental change of the Soviet system. To achieve this, the authors of NSC-68 in the US State Department urged rapid rearmament and the strengthening of American allies.[1]

Canadians were reluctant to sign on to an aggressive foreign and defence policy. Prime Minister William Lyon Mackenzie King treated the revelation that the Soviets had an extensive espionage program in Canada as an unfortunate mistake perpetrated by junior Soviet officials, and he was prepared to give Stalin the benefit of the doubt. The Department of External Affairs was of the opinion that Soviet intentions were defensive, although the Soviets would not hesitate to attempt to divide and weaken the Western powers on an opportunistic basis. External Affairs did not think that the Soviet Union would intentionally start a major war, nor did it believe that the Soviets would be in any position to wage a major war in the near future.

The major concern of the Canadian government in the early Cold War period was "defence against help." During the Second World War, the United States had built extensive facilities to protect Alaska, including the Alaska Highway, airfields to stage aircraft from the lower forty-eight states to Alaska, about sixty weather stations, and the Canol Project, an oil distribution system between Norman Wells in the Northwest Territories and Whitehorse in Yukon. The United States had also acquired a lease to the Goose Bay, Labrador, air base. Given the technology of the day, this was the only location from which the US Air Force could bomb the Soviet Union with any reasonable prospect of the aircraft's return. The United States therefore pressed to retain and expand these facilities, especially Goose Bay. In addition, the Soviet Union's increased inventory of nuclear weapons and long-range aircraft led the Canadian government to construct three radar chains across the country – the Pinetree, Mid-Canada, and Distant Early Warning (DEW) Lines. Maintaining air bases and the radar chains to service US nuclear deterrent forces and air defences as well as providing a Canadian air defence force would become major claims on the Canadian defence budget.[2]

Despite the tense international situation, the domestic economy was booming. An initial spurt of postwar housing construction to meet pent-up demand was supplemented by Cold War rearmament. American corporations built or expanded branch plants to supply Canadians with consumer goods, and investment flowed to the oil and gas industry in Alberta. There were major investments in atomic energy, mining, and transportation infrastructure. By 1947 the baby boom was in full swing, increasing Canada's population by 2 percent a year. Population growth fuelled a demand for new schools, more teachers, and eventually colleges and universities. Immigration added to this. Between 1945 and 1957, a million and a half people came to Canada. About 500,000 came from the United Kingdom and 100,000 more from the United States, but the rest were from countries that had no links to either of the founding cultures or to the eastern European roots of the pre–First World War immigration wave. Canada was becoming more cosmopolitan, more urban, and more industrial.[3]

The army did not figure prominently in either foreign or domestic policy. The Canadian Army had emerged from the Second World War with a strength of 478,090 men and women, but within two years it had been reduced to only 15,852. Renamed "The Canadian Army" rather than "The Militia of Canada," the postwar army continued to be composed of both regular and reserve units. The original idea was to maintain the primary role of the Regular Force in providing training and administration of the reserves, who would provide the country's primary military muscle. However, the government sought economies and the general population was not interested in soldiering, full- or part-time. The field units of the Active Force (regulars) consisted of three infantry battalions training for parachute operations, two armoured regiments, and a regiment of field artillery totalling about 19,000. The reserves shrank to a total of 30,000 by 1947. As this army entered the 1950s, it faced unprecedented problems: it had to raise, deploy, and sustain one brigade to fight in Korea and another to meet NATO commitments while the country continued in peacetime mode; and it had to determine how to meet the challenge of nuclear weapons – in other words, adapt to a totally new technology and type of war. Both types of problems required decisions on the mission and structure of the reserves.

It can be argued that the Canadian Army met both these challenges well, generating the combat troops required to fulfill its commitments, and acquiring and integrating nuclear weapons into its force structure and exercises under what were assumed to be the conditions of the nuclear battlefield. Yet not all was well. Troop generation employed a number of schemes and produced field units of uneven quality. The development of nuclear warfare doctrine revealed weaknesses in the staff system. Fundamental problems in the reserve force were recognized but never dealt with. The army elected to lower officer educational standards to deal with its inability to recruit adequate numbers. More importantly, politicians and soldiers could not agree on the strategic role of the army within NATO. Civilians remained convinced that the brigade group in Europe was no more than an unreinforceable "tripwire" for nuclear retaliation, while the army saw it as the advance party of a division, or even a corps, prepared to fight a long war in Europe.

Rather than a golden age of military professionalism, the decade of the 1950s is more accurately seen as the beginning of a lengthy development phase of the army. A colonial fragment, it was struggling to stand on its own two feet. Not only was it incomplete but it had also inherited the culture of the British Army. British Army concepts of leadership, staff doctrine, and organization contributed to the difficulty it experienced in resolving military policy challenges. To be sure, by the end of the decade the army was much larger and had a much more dominant full-time component than at the beginning. Size, however, should not be confused with the apotheosis of professionalism.

Throughout the 1950s, two philosophies regarding the nature and purpose of the army became evident. Each was represented by one of the first two postwar chiefs of the general staff, Charles Foulkes and Guy Simonds.

Representing modernization and integration of the army into Canadian national security strategy in close cooperation with civilian decision makers was Lieutenant-General (later General) Charles Foulkes. Foulkes had attended the University of Western Ontario and completed the British Army's Staff

College, Camberley, in 1938, just in time for the war. He achieved senior command during the war and was one of Simonds's division commanders during the abortive Operation Spring in Normandy (the attack on Verrières Ridge), the bloodiest day of the war for the Canadian Army except for Dieppe. Simonds had considered sacking Foulkes, but allegedly could not because Foulkes was protected by H.D.G. "Harry" Crerar, the commander of the First Canadian Army. Foulkes, "dour, short, pudgy [and] unapproachable," was unpopular within the army. Nevertheless, he was appointed chief of the general staff (CGS) instead of Simonds in 1945, and later became the first chairman of the Chiefs of Staff Committee after playing an instrumental role in the organization of NATO.[4]

Simonds, on the other hand, had been deemed by Sir Bernard Law Montgomery to be Canada's only competent division and corps commander. While possibly true, Simonds – a Royal Military College (Kingston) graduate – was too anglophile and doctrinaire for the Canadian government, which parked him first at the Imperial Defence College and then at Canada's new National Defence College as commandant before he succeeded Foulkes as CGS in January 1951. Once appointed, however, Simonds would have the last word on internal army matters, as the chairman of the Chiefs of Staff Committee was a government adviser, not his superior officer. Throughout the 1950s, the two would disagree on many, if not most, important issues facing the army.

Growing up British

Summarizing a multi-volume analysis of the military effectiveness of combatants during the First and Second World Wars, Lieutenant General John Cushman of the US Army awarded the British Army a "D" in tactical performance in both wars, a "D" overall in operational performance in the First World War, and a "C" in operational performance during the interwar period and the Second World War.[5] Despite extensive studies, exercises, and field experiments during the interwar period, the British Army had made only limited progress in its ability to manage mechanized, mobile warfare. At the national level, the General Staff lacked the institutional capability to adequately direct innovation, develop operational and tactical doctrine, and integrate it into the field force. To be sure, a case can be made that the development of armoured forces was severely hindered by lack of funding during the interwar period and that the army's performance during the Second World War was damaged by the mistaken tactical ideas of radical reformers such as Percy Hobart. Nevertheless, it remains the case that the British Army did not develop the institutions to objectively test concepts, identify the useful ones, and implant them in its field force. What emerged was an "all-tank" concept of warfare embedded in the Royal Tank Corps on the one hand and the perpetuation of cavalry regiments and their historical roles of reconnaissance, screening, and exploitation on the other. Neither concept adequately addressed how best to combine armour with infantry and artillery, a situation that was exacerbated by the regimental system and the class structure of the army.[6]

Also contributing to operational weakness was the British Army's concept of doctrine itself. Its Field Service Regulations (FSR) and associated arms-of-service manuals stated only general principles and did not explain how these principles were to be applied. FSR (1920) stated that "no two situations are identical ... and the application of the principles cannot be made subject to the rules." Senior officers were supposed to figure this out for themselves. Senior officers shared a distaste for prescription and relied instead on "character" rather than abstract reasoning, which was considered to be a continental affliction. FSR (1924) asserted: "Above all it must be remembered that success in war depends largely on knowledge of human nature, and how to handle it to the best advantage." The expectation that senior officers could figure out each situation on the spot and then direct their tens of thousands of subordinates to implement their solutions meant that doctrine did not impose any common understanding of war throughout the army. Montgomery commented that the army as a whole had no clear doctrine, and that when you changed your commander, you changed your doctrine.[7]

Lacking such a common understanding of doctrine, the British were forced to rely on an autocratic command system that required junior leaders to obey not only the spirit but also the letter of their orders; in practice, they were encouraged to wait for orders rather than seize opportunities.[8] Unlike the German Army, the British Army could not delegate decision making far enough to exploit changing conditions on the battlefield. Instead, it preferred attritional, set-piece battles emphasizing infantry and artillery. Armour was used as infantry support rather than for exploitation.[9]

Canada's colonial status compounded these deficiencies. Maurice Pope described the Canadian Army during the 1930s as "British through and through with only minor differences imposed upon us by local conditions." All manuals and tactical training were British and, according to one observer, "learning about 'what was' at second hand from Britain left little time to think about what might be."[10] Canadian officers were committed to being British as a matter of national policy. Lieutenant-Colonel E.L.M. Burns, one of the more insightful Canadian officers of the period, wrote:

> It may strike the reader as rather presumptuous for an officer of a Dominion that has no military formation higher than a Brigade to propose reorganization [of] the British divisional system ... the British regular division is the prototype of all

> the divisions of all the forces of the Empire, it having been agreed long ago at Imperial Conference that organization and training should be uniform. Hence, a Dominion officer who feels it his duty to suggest improvements in military organization must argue the case for a change in all the Empire's forces, taking cognizance of the whole range of that army's duties, from first-class warfare to the suppression of religious maniacs in abominable deserts.[11]

Only a few officers, such as Burns, Simonds, and Ken Stuart, would venture to comment publicly on British practice and doctrine. The Canadian staff checked regularly with their British counterparts to ensure they were following the British model as closely as possible. Canadian innovations were abandoned and changes to training awaited the post from the mother country. The Canadian Army's problems were compounded by the instability of British manoeuvre doctrine as the Cavalry and the Royal Tank Corps fought for organizational dominance, and by the failure of the Canadian government to articulate a mission for the Canadian Army towards which officers could direct their thoughts.[12]

The intellectual development of the Canadian Army in the interwar period was also affected by the personalities of its leaders. For example, A.G.L. McNaughton, who became chief of the general staff in 1929, had a strong tendency to promote officers with good academic backgrounds and high marks in written, theoretical examinations. Because of this, a disproportionate number of engineer and artillery officers were sent to British or Imperial staff colleges, and officers who had passed staff college tended to be employed in headquarters rather than in field command. McNaughton assumed – much like his British counterparts, who considered it a matter of character – that military professionalism would simply develop if one had a sound education on which to build. Perhaps reflecting his own career and that of Sir Arthur Currie, a Militia gunner who rose to command the Canadian Corps during the First World War, he defined command simply as the ability to select experts and handle men, leaving out all reference to expertise in managing a battle. The army was not prepared to support the development of a unique profession of arms if it entailed full-time, lifelong, and concentrated study of the management of violence.[13]

The final dimension of the Canadian Army's British inheritance concerned how the army staff was organized. The Canadian Army directly imported the British staff organization. As late as 1963, the Canadian *Staff Duties in the Field* was an unamended version of the British Army manual, complete with references to the Military Secretary to the Secretary of State for War. In general, the staff was divided into three major components: (1) the General Staff branch, which dealt with all operational matters, including operations, plans, intelligence, staff duties, training, and support; (2) the Adjutant-General's Staff, or

A Branch, which managed all matters affecting the soldier as an individual (what we would today call Human Resources – allocation of manpower, reinforcements, and medical and personnel administration); and (3) the Quartermaster-General Staff, or Q Branch, which was responsible for materiel, maintenance, accommodations, and logistics.[14]

During the Second World War, when the Canadian Army was part of the "last great British imperial army," the adopted British staff system served Canada's needs. Canadian officers were trained to British standards in British procedures, and selected officers were sent to British staff colleges at Camberley and Quetta. The shared language and organization of field headquarters enabled Canadian formations to plan and carry out major military operations, and also to fit in with the British Army. Douglas Delaney has concluded that "the imperial system that trained [corps commanders] and provided them with both the staffs to organize their thoughts and the formations to fight their battles also implanted a connectivity that cut across oceans, ensuring that, when the time came, they could do what was asked of them in war."[15]

Reliance on the British Army, however, left the Canadian Army without a staff that could focus on national military strategy or the development of an "army of the future." The British themselves had not evolved a strong solution to these problems. During the early postwar period, there was in Canada only a small civilian analytical component in the office of the science adviser to the chief of the general staff at Army Headquarters. Only a few senior Defence Research Board officials were part of the headquarters, and the entire Canadian Army Operations Research Establishment (CAORE) never had more than fifteen professional staff throughout this period. Only two professional operations research positions were attached to 25 Canadian Infantry Brigade in Korea during that war.[16] Coupled with an inherited culture that relied on the personal insights of senior leaders, this would prove to be a significant shortcoming in the mindset and organization of Army Headquarters as it faced the challenges of the Korean War, the Soviet threat in Europe, and the prospect of nuclear warfare.

Generating Forces

Mobilizing for, and Learning from, Korea

The Korean War began on 25 June 1950 when North Korea's People's Army invaded the southern Republic of Korea. The Canadian government's first response was tepid and unenthusiastic; it sent only a naval contingent. But as the military situation worsened and the United Nations made a direct request for troops, Cabinet had to consider sending ground troops. The Chiefs of Staff Committee recommended against this. Canada had only enough soldiers to man the Mobile Striking Force, a brigade-sized unit committed to the defence of North America. However, pressure from the United States and the example set by Britain, Australia, and New Zealand in sending ground troops eventually overcame Canadian reservations and Cabinet decided to recruit an additional brigade, the Canadian Army Special Force, to meet the government's commitment.[17]

The expedient seized upon by the army was to recruit soldiers off the street for a short service engagement in Korea. Lieutenant-General Foulkes, then chief of the general staff, "felt it would be possible to recruit in Canada today, the personnel for at least a brigade from volunteer 'soldiers of fortune' if at enlistment there was a firm understanding given that they would be despatched for active service overseas. In case such a scheme was put into effect he would recommend engagement for one such term as eighteen months, inasmuch as the army would not wish to retain the 'soldier of fortune' type of personnel on a long term basis."[18] It is interesting to note that no one considered mobilizing the Militia to fill this requirement, and it is not difficult to imagine why (Militia readiness will be discussed below).[19] In the event, it proved easy to recruit the required number of Second World War veterans to fight on a short-service basis. Volunteers included an estimated 2,600 Militia soldiers as individuals within the complement of 7,000 recruited for the Special Force.[20]

The original Special Force fought in Korea from September 1950 to April 1951. After that, despite a change of heart regarding "soldiers of fortune" and attempts to re-enlist Special Force members, the army decided to rotate the Special Force "second battalions" and replace them with "first battalions" from the regular army in order to provide the regulars with operational experience and prevent a garrison mentality from developing. This rotation was itself replaced by another regular army set of "third battalions" a year later.

The army was able to meet its manpower requirements by improvising rotational and replacement systems, but it did less well in managing its organizational learning from the war. The first rotation was over before "Notes on Training from Korea" began to appear.[21] According to the most detailed and convincing history of the Canadian Army in Korea, *A War of Patrols* by William Johnston, the Special Force rotation was militarily the best. Under the leadership of John Rockingham, a Second World War brigadier, it developed tactics centred on aggressive patrolling and raiding of enemy lines. Unfortunately, the lessons learned were not passed on to the subsequent rotations. The regulars simply assumed that the Special Force soldiers had nothing to teach them, the real professionals, and there was no system in place to adjust doctrine based on experience and pass it on to the next group.

Johnston also makes it clear that army performance was highly dependent on the quality of senior leadership. As such, it followed the British Army model. Whereas Rockingham was aggressive and results-oriented, and frequently visited front-line units and personally adjusted defences, his successor was much more passive. Brigadier Mortimer Bogert had also commanded a brigade during the Second World War but, unlike Rockingham, was the antithesis of an "Errol Flynn" type. The regulars under him took great pride in fortification of battalion headquarters and rear-area road building rather than in patrolling and raiding. Spit and polish was highly regarded. During one visit to fighting trenches, Bogert was pleased to note that the brass base plugs of grenades were highly polished and that Brasso and polishing cloths were close at hand. Johnston also notes that when Jean Allard took over as commander of the third rotation, the focus on active operations was restored.[22]

In summary, the Korean War experience underlined the British parentage of the Canadian Army. Dependence on senior leadership to develop tactics and train troops was accompanied by weak institutional support for organizational learning. It should be noted, however, that the Canadian Army was not alone. The US Army concluded that its Korean War experience did not justify any real change to doctrine. A special bulletin originally called "Lessons Learned" was quickly renamed "Training Bulletin."[23]

Mobilizing to Meet NATO Requirements

The recruitment of the Special Force had been turbulent, to say the least. Foulkes's prediction that there would be sufficient volunteers proved to be a massive understatement. Recruiting centres were overwhelmed with applicants. The resulting logjam was bad enough to result in the personal intervention of Defence Minister Brooke Claxton. In addition, senior military staff and the public at large formed the opinion, based on widely publicized disciplinary incidents, that the Special Force had been poorly screened and contained a large number of misfits.[24]

Not surprisingly, when the government determined in April 1951 that Canada would contribute a brigade to NATO's new Integrated Force, Simonds, now the chief of the general staff, sought a different means of recruitment. He directed that a brigade group of 5,800 men and a replacement group of 4,000 be recruited on the framework of the Reserve Force. He also directed that the 27 Canadian Infantry Brigade being formed for NATO consist of composite highland, rifle, and line battalions drawn from Militia units. The men would continue to wear the uniforms and insignia of their parent Militia units. Simonds hoped that returning soldiers would provide a trained nucleus around which their parent units could build if general mobilization was ever required.[25]

Once again, the expedient employed produced the necessary numbers. However, use of the Militia revealed problems in training and readiness that could not be ignored.

Assessing the Challenge of Expansion

Overall, the Canadian Army did well in generating the numbers of troops demanded by the government's commitments to Canada's allies. Given the small size of the army after the Second World War, the deployment of two additional brigades (in effect tripling the size of the operational forces) was a considerable achievement. In part, the army had the good fortune to have a huge pool of experienced and willing manpower in the form of Second World War veterans. In addition, troop production was a "steady-state" affair. Units were trained and equipped to what was essentially a Second World War standard. New equipment types were few and introduced only gradually. The army had a known product and could run the factory that produced it reasonably well.

The difficulty lay in managing change. The Korean War showed that while units and formations could learn from their experience, there was no effective means of evaluating their responses or diffusing improvements throughout the organization. There were also signs that the Regular army was becoming fixated on spit and polish and considered garrison life rather than field operations to be the military norm. Dominick Graham, the biographer of Guy Simonds, the CGS throughout most of this period, concludes his judgment of Simonds's career by commenting:

> It must be asked what he achieved for the postwar army. Between 1939 and 1951 the army's prewar pomp and colour had been bleached to a utilitarian grey. Foulkes was not, at heart, a regimental soldier; Simonds, on the other hand, understood the importance of smart uniforms, efficiently run and colourful messes, bands, protocol, good food, physical exercise and recreation. He looked like an advertisement for his own policies. He restored regimental spirit and the morale of a drab and run-down army. The fear of losing all that had been gained was a prime reason why he fought unification after his retirement.[26]

It might have been better to have had a CGS more concerned with doctrine and force development.

The Search for Strategic Purpose

Carl von Clausewitz, the great nineteenth-century Prussian theorist of war, recognized that war was not only "the continuation of policy by other means" but also no longer merely the sport of kings. The mass armies of the Napoleonic era had led to the creation of the "remarkable trinity" of the state, the army, and the people. War had become such a massive event with so decisive outcomes that it involved whole societies. Based on this insight, he advanced the idea that all three sides of the triangle had to be involved and kept in balance for a war to succeed.[27] The Cold War presented fundamental challenges to Canada and its army – challenges that raised the basic questions of what armies were for, whether they had a place in the nuclear age, and, if an army was indeed useful, whether the population was prepared to support it. The failure to integrate the state, the army, and the people in a common purpose would result in decades of confusion, the waste of vast resources, and the near destruction of the Canadian Army. Although the army was not solely responsible for its struggle to define its strategic purpose, its professional weaknesses would play a significant role in the crisis.

Civil-military divergence had been obvious as early as the middle of the Second World War. The government, led by Mackenzie King, had strongly favoured an air and naval contribution to the war, with limited resources devoted to the army. A large army would likely require conscription to fill its ranks, and the King government was keenly aware of the explosive political impact conscription would have in Quebec and the generally lukewarm support it would get elsewhere. The army, on the other hand, not only favoured both a large land force and conscription during the war but also intended to continue this policy into the postwar period. Upon being appointed chief of the general staff in 1940, Major-General Harry Crerar penned "Observations on Canadian Requirements in Respect to the Army." He wrote:

> While the urgency of the moment forces us to utilize a Militia system and organization which looks to the past, rather than to the present and to the future, we must not lose a moment in undertaking a thorough analysis of Canada's probable post-war military requirements and in planning a defence organization which will produce our future Service needs with a maximum of efficiency and a minimum of expense. Unless this is done it will be impossible to ensure the progressive adoption of policies which will advance us in the desired direction. And we must be clear in our minds as to that destination, for the future Militia organization should be settled before demobilization of the present C.A.S.F. [Canadian Active Service Force] commences.

Crerar advocated conscription as a "reasoned plan for the organization of the Canadian Army" and informed the minister that "if, however, the defence of this country is to be dependent in large part on the voluntary or 'go-if-you-please' system, then it will be impossible to plan and develop the defence of

Canada in an ordered and economical way, and an uninformed public opinion pressing for 'action' may force our war effort into unproductive channels."[28]

Crerar, and his successor as CGS, Ken Stuart, steadily pushed the government to increase the size of the army and to extend conscription for home defence from four months to an indefinite period. The army assured the government that its increases could be achieved without conscription, but also designed formations that required a large number of overhead personnel. The proportions of Canadian Army headquarters and overhead were more than twice those of the US equivalents. The crisis finally arrived in 1944 when the army feared it would run out of infantry replacements and left the government with no alternative but to accept conscription for overseas service. There is considerable debate about whether the army had deliberately provoked the crisis by inefficient use of manpower and whether the Army Council delivered an ultimatum to Cabinet, threatening mass resignation if conscription was not instituted. In the end, the long-term effects were the same. Prime Minister King blamed the army for the crisis while maintaining political control. The generals were banished from the War Cabinet Committee in December 1944, and King noted that "the proceedings made it apparent that they were not needed and by their not being present the discussions were shortened."[29]

Before A.G.L. McNaughton, the minister, left Cabinet after failing for the second time to win a seat in the Commons, he had approved the army's postwar plan. The army view of the world was that lack of preparedness before the war had been costly and had to be avoided in the future. Although the army did not think that Canadian participation in a future Great Power war was likely, the weakened condition of Great Britain meant that Canada had to assume a larger role in the common defence. Army staff did not think that a large standing army would be acceptable to Canadians, but also did not believe that the country could safely revert to spending one-tenth the amount per capita of what Britain spent on defence. Their solution was a citizen reserve army, augmented by a volunteer regular force no larger than necessary to meet normal peacetime requirements and postwar strategic obligations. This army would consist of two corps with six divisions, four armoured brigades, and supporting corps troops. Such a force would require universal military training of one year, followed by three years of compulsory service in the reserve.[30]

The army correctly deduced that few of those who had served in the war would wish to remain in the service. They also did not think a voluntary reserve would attract sufficient numbers. Responding to questions from the minister regarding the necessity of universal military training, Lieutenant-General J.C. Murchie, the chief of the general staff, said that, on reflection,

> full strategic account shall be taken of the defeat of dictatorships, that the atomic bomb is completely controlled by the United States, Great Britain and Canada and, in consequence the World Security Council will have an effective weapon capable of immediate use, and so there is reason to believe that [the] World Security Council has something real for the prevention of any major aggression in the future, that the whole march of events has brought the Allies closer into harmony and there is real hope that harmony will continue long into the future.

Assuming that Cabinet would direct planning to be done using these assumptions, the army allowed that universal military training could be reduced from one year to four months.[31]

The government had no intention of imposing conscription, however. Canadians were so opposed to the idea that a major political crisis had erupted when conscription was instituted during the war. Defence Minister Douglas Abbott announced to the House of Commons on 16 October 1945 that although it was not yet possible to determine the requirements for the postwar army, the government proposed to set up a "basic military establishment" that could be developed as needed in the future. Pending determination of the final requirement, a limited number of personnel would be allowed to serve for a period of two years. The postwar army that the government intended to create was very much like its prewar predecessor: a voluntary reserve trained and administered by a full-time regular force.[32] By 1946 the government had decided that the operational element of the army would be a single airborne and air-transportable brigade to be known as the Mobile Striking Force. Its primary mission would be the elimination of enemy lodgements on Canadian territory, and it was designed to be capable of rapid expansion in the event of general war outside Canada.[33]

It was evident that right from the beginning that civilians and the military had different ideas regarding national strategy. The army was anxious not to repeat the unpreparedness and insignificance to which it had sunk in the interwar years. It saw Canada as a sort of associate Great Power, willing and able to pick up the slack left by British weakness in the Empire. The government, on the other hand, had to concern itself with national unity in a state where the francophone minority did not share the army's enthusiasm for overseas entanglements.

The Army and NATO

Canada's intent regarding NATO was to support the military organization but not be in the front lines. The Canadian proposal for the military organization was drafted by General Charles Foulkes, the chief of the general staff. He proposed that there be a centralized supreme commander, who would be an American. The supreme commander would be primarily concerned with the creation and employment of the strategic reserve. Reporting to the supreme commander would be a Strategic Reserve Group composed of representatives of nations that could provide uncommitted reserves of personnel and materiel. Canada was one of only three nations – with the United States and Britain – that met this condition. Foulkes also recommended the establishment of regional groups composed of countries possessing a "common vital interest which, if threatened, would call for *immediate military action*." Each group would be responsible for planning its own region's defences with regional defence committees advised by the group's chiefs of staff committees. In Foulkes's plan, Canada would be a member of the North American Group but not the Western European Group. When Britain's General Leslie Hollis received Foulkes's memo from a Canadian officer, he told the officer that "it must be a typographical error." It was anything but. Foulkes had recommended this structure based on three considerations: planning must be done by those who have a stake; it was necessary to compartmentalize to stop leaks from politically unreliable countries and to keep the strategic reserve and central planning in safe hands; and, finally, Canada should not be made to bear too great a share of the costs. Foulkes informed Brooke Claxton that

> it appears that they are attempting to work out a formula for the allocation of defence costs on the basis of equitable contributions in accordance with the proportion of the national budget spent on defence. I am a bit alarmed that the Western Union Powers may attempt to have this formula adopted by the Atlantic Pact, and I can see considerable trouble ahead for us if this is the case. The organization which I suggest in the attached paper would prevent such a thing and would keep the Western European Powers in their own bailiwick, attending to their own defence matters and not meddling too deeply in our affairs.

Arnold Heeney, the under-secretary of state for external affairs, objected to Foulkes's plan – but only because he thought it might backfire and result in Canada's having to assume disproportionate costs. Nevertheless, the Foulkes position was approved by Cabinet.[34]

Except for a few diplomats, no one in Canada believed that membership in NATO would require increased defence spending. However, the worsening international situation with a communist coup in Czechoslovakia, the Berlin blockade, the explosion of the first Soviet atomic bomb, and the growing realization that Western Europe was in no shape to defend itself resulted in a reversal of opinion by late 1949. By the fall of 1950, both the British and the Americans were pressuring Canada to send troops to Europe. Winston Churchill suggested in the British House of Commons that Canada could contribute two to three divisions. Although resistance appeared "unwise and unprofitable" to Canada's ambassador to Washington, Prime Minister St-Laurent publicly commented that it would not be "best value" for Canadian troops to be stationed in Europe.[35]

Chinese intervention in the Korean War was the decisive factor in changing the government's mind. NATO's Standing Group determined that Canada's contribution should be one-third of a division and 19 air force squadrons to serve in Europe, plus 28 anti-aircraft regiments, 7 additional warships with 16 crews, and 19 air force squadrons to serve in North America. On 5 October 1950, the Cabinet Defence Committee agreed that if the Special Force was not required for Korea, it would be sent to Europe, and on 12 October the NATO Defence Committee formally called on Canada to provide one-third of a division and 11 squadrons of aircraft. Claxton agreed that everything possible would be done to provide these forces, and the government announced the measure in the Speech from the Throne on 30 January 1951.[36]

Cabinet's decision to send troops to Europe created 27 Canadian Infantry Brigade and the Royal Canadian Air Force's Air Division in Europe. It was yet to be determined where these forces would be deployed within the NATO Integrated Force. Guy Simonds, the anglophile who had succeeded Foulkes as chief of the general staff, proposed that the Canadian Army be under British rather than American command. He also proposed that the army and the RCAF be grouped together. His main rationale was distrust of the United States. His paper to the minister stated:

> It was considered essential to foster and maintain with the Western democratic alliance a "balance of power" which could effectively restrain to some degree arbitrary unilateral action. The practical application of this concept in NATO at the present time would be to counter-balance the disproportionate and preponderant power of the US. This did not imply any unfriendliness to the United States but was simply facing the facts of the existing situation, viz., that the US with relatively limited experience in world affairs and because her policies were at times subject to unpredictable and emotional influences could conceivably, without some balancing restraint, carry the democratic nations into a Third World War.

Contrasting with this was the full confidence that the Canadian Army's officers and men had in British commanders. More pragmatically, the Canadian Army had trained and fought on British lines and was organized like the British Army.

The British, Simonds believed, would respect the need to maintain the national identity of Canadian forces, whereas the Americans would subordinate them. And although 27 Canadian Infantry Brigade was being equipped with American equipment, if an emergency should develop in the next eighteen months Canada would have to send two divisions overseas with British-type equipment in inventory from the Second World War. Simonds conceded that these reasons were more important to the army than to the air force. Finally, he argued that it would be no more expensive to group Canadian troops with the British than with the Americans.[37]

Foulkes, now the chairman of the Chiefs of Staff Committee, opposed these views. He regarded maintenance and supply as the dominant factors in a basing decision and did not believe that the British could support a Canadian brigade with American equipment on their lines of communication. The brigade had been proposed to the Cabinet Defence Committee as being under US command, with no Canadian maintenance group being required. Foulkes rejected the "balance of power" concept Simonds had put forward, and argued that the Canadian position within NATO must be to judge each case on its merits, not whether it supported or opposed the United States. If the US was dominant, it was only because it was the one country that could afford to assist others. In his mind, Canada should not align with any particular group but should always strive to assist and reconcile points of view.[38]

Simonds was supported by Arnold Heeney, who found his arguments regarding the balance of power "impressive." According to Heeney, the consensus at External Affairs was that, from a political point of view, it would be better to group Canadian forces under British command. A group of countries could be more effective than a single one in influencing the United States, given its "overwhelming" power. He also agreed with Simonds that it would be easier to maintain the troops' Canadian identity if they were grouped with the British. Norman A. Robertson, the secretary to Cabinet, remarked that since the brigade was essentially a token force, political considerations should win out. If two or three divisions were ever required, the logistics question could be examined in more detail at that time. The RCAF didn't care where the army went as long as the Air Division was located with the US Air Force. Air Marshal Wilfred Curtis even argued that this would make it clear that Canada was not aligned with any particular power.[39]

In the end, Simonds got his way, and the brigade was assigned to the Northern Army Group (NORTHAG) under British command. The Air Force units were deployed to 4th Allied Tactical Air Force, based first at Paris then at Metz after 1953. The decision to deploy forces to Europe caused problems that would bedevil the army and its political masters for the next forty-two years. First, it validated the army's view that it should be a large, conventional force designed on a Great Power pattern. The army continued to plan how to meet the commitment to field two divisions in Europe – a force of 50,000 to 67,000 men, not including the 20,000 additional personnel who would be needed to expand the training system. It believed that conscription would be necessary for over two years before a force this size could be fielded.[40] It also reinforced the British character of the army and enabled it to carry on with its British staff system, tactics, and culture without having to think overly hard about the effects or the alternatives.

The civilian concept of the army was also obvious. For the civilian decision makers, the purpose of the army was political and the brigade was a "token force." This fundamental divergence of opinion regarding national strategy went almost unnoticed in the deal-making atmosphere of the Chiefs of Staff Committee. Ironically, it was Simonds himself who had encouraged viewing the army as a counter in alliance politics rather than arguing from military requirements.

In tacitly cutting a deal with the RCAF by not opposing its desire to be under American command, Simonds also perpetuated the separation of tactical air forces from the army. As in the Second World War, any air forces the Canadian brigade would call upon for close air support would be under an allied air commander. The RCAF would never develop the capacity to provide effective tactical air support to the army, and the unified Canadian Forces would not acquire a close air support aircraft until 1968.

Finally, the decision to group the brigade with British forces in NORTHAG meant that 27 Canadian Infantry Brigade became a big fish in a small pond. As the British Army came under greater and greater financial stress, it found it more difficult to maintain the size and strength of its units. Smaller countries such as Belgium and the Netherlands had been hard-hit by the war and had trouble building effective units as quickly as Supreme Headquarters Allied Powers Europe (SHAPE) wanted. All the European states relied on short-service conscripts, which meant that their training levels were low. The 27 Canadian Infantry Brigade was a "brigade group," meaning that it had additional armour and support troops and was in some ways a small division staffed with long-service volunteer professionals. Not surprisingly, it came to be regarded as one of the strongest formations in NORTHAG, the weaker army group. This would severely complicate matters later on whenever the Canadian government proposed to change its role in NATO. Had the Canadian contingent been part of the much stronger Central Army Group (CENTAG), the government might have had greater flexibility in determining Canada's role in NATO.

Adapting to Nuclear War

Strategic Policy

NATO faced two very basic strategic problems. It could not afford, within budgets acceptable to the voters of its member countries, conventional forces large enough to defend itself. And, because it had pledged itself to defensive war only, any war would have to be fought on its own territory. These two factors created problems with no easy solutions for its military planners.

The NATO Ministerial Meeting in Lisbon in April 1952 concluded that a conventional force large enough to deter the Soviet Union without nuclear weapons was not feasible. It established a force goal of sixty-two divisions by 1954. This "shield" force itself was soon found to be unaffordable as it would have required the European states to quadruple their defence expenditures. The high cost of conventional forces pushed even the Americans to adopt a "New Look" strategy based on strategic air forces to avoid what President Dwight Eisenhower called "an unbearable security burden leading to economic disaster." Eisenhower believed that the Cold War could last decades and that defence could not come at the cost of weakening the US economy. The "New Look" rested on the doctrine of massive retaliation in response to any Soviet incursion. The role of ground forces was reduced to that of a postwar occupation force or maintaining order in the United States after a nuclear attack. Nuclear weapons appeared to be a substitute for armies while simultaneously creating a new set of tactical problems for them.[41]

The Soviets' growing military power in Europe and their emerging nuclear capability required a new strategy. The NATO solution was summarized in the Military Committee document MC 48 dated 22 November 1954. MC 48 stressed the defensive nature of NATO and stated that it would deter aggression by providing a credible forward defence of Europe. The position of NATO was to convince the Soviet Union that Europe could not be quickly overrun and that, if the Soviets should try, their forces would be "subjected immediately to devastating counter-attack employing atomic weapons." Even if the Soviets attacked with only conventional forces, NATO would use nuclear weapons in response. The paper envisioned a war in two phases: an intensive first phase of approximately thirty days during which each side would deliver a large portion of its nuclear arsenal as counterstrikes against the other's nuclear weapons; and a second phase, "the exact nature of which would largely depend on the outcome of the initial phase [!]." While the nuclear first phase was taking place, naval, land, and air forces would continue to conduct operations.[42]

NATO policy was further elaborated in a subsequent document, MC 14/2, designed to provide regional planning guidance to NATO forces. Accepted by the alliance in October 1956, it reiterated the essential strategy outlined in MC 48, but added a more detailed examination of threats on the NATO periphery and the possibility that the Soviets might begin operations short of a general war against NATO. It included forward conventional and nuclear defence of the NATO area as the first priority and strategic nuclear war as the second.[43]

Canada had been directly involved in the development of NATO strategy through the chairman of the Chiefs of Staff Committee, General Foulkes, as well as at a diplomatic and political level. Foulkes was in close touch with British and American senior military strategists and was consulted by them in the development of their nuclear warfare strategies.[44] NATO and Canadian strategy were essentially one. As Foulkes saw it, by accepting MC 48 the primary role of NATO became to avoid war by making surprise attack impossible. This meant that the greatest possible deterrent had to be created, and the centrepiece of such deterrent was the US Air Force Strategic Air Command. The role of tactical forces was to blunt initial enemy strikes until the full weight of strategic retaliation could be brought to bear. Governments also had to create effective civil defence forces to sustain civilian morale. To Foulkes, this was Canada's primary task in NATO and took priority over other endeavours.

As for Canada's army, MC 48 did mean that force structure could be rationalized, converting the Mobile Striking Force and the 25 and 27 Brigades into a single army of four interchangeable brigade groups capable of conventional and nuclear operations. However, Foulkes believed that MC 48 meant that there should be a thorough examination of the cost of maintaining the brigade group in Germany. In a June 1955 appreciation, he wondered whether this Canadian role might be considered uneconomical in the future as the Germans rebuilt their own land forces. He also questioned whether the reinforcement of the brigade group by the other two-thirds of a division as planned would even be possible in the first period of a possible war, whether it was vital to store heavy equipment on the Continent, and whether the Canadian Army was really the best contribution that the country could make to the defence of Europe. Foulkes thought that the army needed to examine the role, extent, function, and costs of its reserves in light of the conditions of thermonuclear war. He questioned whether army plans to reinforce a division in Europe were realistic, and concluded: "It therefore appears that this whole problem of the roles, extents, functions and costs should be given very close examination."[45]

Foulkes's appreciation cut the ground from under basic army plans and questioned the very usefulness of the brigade group in Europe. It would be several years before the army could pull together a riposte.

Exercise GOLD RUSH

The army's first effort to adapt to the nuclear age was at the tactical rather than strategic level. The nuclear battlefield posed obvious problems for conventional forces, and Army Headquarters recognized these first. The initial problem was how to support troops in the forward area of the nuclear battlefield. The use of nuclear weapons would require combat forces to be widely dispersed to avoid creating an attractive target. It also meant that the large numbers of ground vehicles in the logistic train presented just such a target.

In February 1955 Simonds initiated a study, called "Exercise GOLD RUSH," to determine how field forces at or below the corps level should be organized and what the logistic implications would be for a future war, conventional or nuclear.[46] He informed the minister that British and American studies did not extend far enough into the future and that it was therefore essential that the Canadian Army begin its own study of the problems presented to an army in the field by the new weapons of war.[47] In commissioning the study, Simonds overrode concerns expressed the previous month by Major-General H.A. Sparling, the vice chief of the general staff (VCGS), who had conducted a preliminary study of the feasibility of using fixed-wing aircraft in lieu of wheeled vehicles to support combat formations in the forward area. Sparling had cited the large number of aircraft that would be required and the need for continuous ground control and a landing area that would require support. This would be difficult to protect from enemy aircraft, costly to construct, and expensive to maintain. If helicopters were used, a considerable portion of the lift would be consumed simply in moving fuel for aircraft forward. This did not deter Simonds, who thought that since the British and Americans were already researching the use of helicopters, the Canadian Army should concentrate on fixed-wing aircraft. According to him, all previous studies had been done the "wrong way," and he was not convinced that there was any requirement for fixed air strips. He sought a radically different solution, essentially just-in-time delivery by air of logistic support to forward combat elements.[48]

GOLD RUSH was based on the concept of supplying infantry division and armoured brigade areas day and night by short takeoff and landing (STOL) and vertical-lift aircraft. An experimental helicopter unit was to be formed and a fixed-wing "flying truck" developed. The timetable was ambitious: the study phase was to be completed by December 1956 (less than two years) and the helicopter experiments by 1957; flying truck trials were to start in the summer of 1958 and overall conclusions to be reached by 1959. The study team was chaired by Brigadier R.W. Moncel, the deputy chief of the general staff, and included director-level representatives of all branches plus the scientific adviser. It was given a permanent staff and authority to draw on Army Headquarters, 1 Canadian Infantry Division, and the Staff College.[49]

The project soon ran into difficulties. The de Havilland company challenged the specifications for the flying truck as being beyond state-of-the-art. Simonds insisted on takeoff and landing within five hundred feet, but existing piston engines were insufficiently powerful, turbine engines too new a development, and propeller and wing designs immature. The Defence Research Board representatives expressed concern that industry was being pushed to produce something beyond its capabilities. Simonds agreed only to postpone the five-hundred-foot requirement until 1959 and to work towards an interim goal of twelve hundred feet by 1957.[50]

Simonds was equally dissatisfied with the output of a project working group on tactical concepts. He found that they had concentrated troops too closely and that consequently the troops would present too large a nuclear target. He lectured them, saying that he appreciated how difficult it was to divorce oneself from current concepts of war but that it would be necessary to make the exercise a success. He ended up virtually dictating the tactical concept to the team, including details of the distribution of armour. The working group was allowed to choose the types of guns needed.[51]

It was left to Simonds's successor as CGS to complete GOLD RUSH. In June 1956, the study team advised Lieutenant-General H.D. Graham that the tactical concept had been presented at the divisional study period and at command and corps conferences, and was the basis for the summer's divisional exercise at Camp Gagetown. The team recommended that he approve the tactical concept as the basis for staff discussions with Britain and the United States. Graham agreed to this and to further development.

The final concept at least partly reflected Simonds's early direction. A battalion group covering force was to occupy a front of 10,000 yards, much greater than the 1,600 yards originally proposed. The concept was that the forward zone of resistance would be set up on a major river obstacle. The covering force would detect the enemy and exert pressure on it during crossing so it would bunch up and present a worthwhile target for nuclear weapons. Planners expected congestion to ripple through enemy rear areas, creating additional nuclear targets. The Canadian main defensive zone would be sufficiently far back that it would not be harmed by the initial nuclear bombardment and it would be difficult for the enemy to locate the main units – perhaps ten to twenty-five miles behind the main obstacle. The corps reserve would consist of mobile armoured and infantry units of regiment/battalion size supported by self-propelled artillery.

Although the concept depended on air transportability and rapid cross-country land vehicles, the flying truck had disappeared.[52] Mobility was key to the concept, however, as was reduction in the size of units. The concept called for fully tracked amphibious reconnaissance vehicles with only limited fighting capability so that "every opportunity to use the nuclear weapon can be taken." Infantry were to be fully mobile in their own armoured personnel carriers (APCs), also with greater amphibious ability than those then under development. Fire support was to be provided by self-propelled weapons with nuclear shells, as well as ballistic rockets and guided missiles. Planners wanted a light anti-tank weapon effective up to tank gun range, which would probably be a guided missile. GOLD RUSH also called for tactical aviation under the control of army commanders, as well as logistic aircraft also under their operational control for certain tactical missions.[53]

Graham felt that what GOLD RUSH had come up with was sound, but he was in no hurry to implement significant force structure changes. He directed that the concepts not be used in exercises with troops, but agreed that they might be discussed with the British and Americans at an early date. Possibly with an eye on the army's budget, he noted that NATO political leaders did not think a major war was likely in the next ten years and that thinking should therefore focus on post-1966 requirements.[54] Following Simonds's example, he then exercised his prerogative as CGS and totally redirected force development efforts. He gave Major-General N.E. Rodger, the VCGS, six months to initiate and complete studies on the organization of an *air-transportable* brigade group, abandoning the mechanized heavy infantry force recommended by GOLD RUSH. He further directed that the organization be based on "threes" – that is, three battalions of infantry with one armoured regiment of three squadrons (but perhaps with a fourth for reconnaissance). Each battalion would be based on three companies of three platoons of three sections of ten men each. He wanted the GOLD RUSH team to continue working on this project under the name "FIRE-FLY,"[55] and informed the minister that he would be in a position to provide advice on re-equipping the army in early 1957.[56]

The objectives of FIRE-FLY were to develop a practical air-transportable field organization for the Canadian Army, to assess the date by which this might be achieved, and to determine how to phase in this new structure. The roles of this force would be the rapid reinforcement of NATO in Europe, the defence of North America, and engagement in peripheral wars and police actions as part of a larger international force. It was assumed that only part of this force would be air-transportable in the short term; the balance of its equipment would have to be positioned overseas or the force would rely on sea transport. Like the GOLD RUSH brigade, air-transportable units were to be capable of operations with or without nuclear weapons.[57]

The GOLD RUSH/FIRE-FLY working group struggled with this new direction. The main problem, lack of strategic airlift capability, would likely result in piecemeal commitment of forces that were too small to be effective. The team doubted that any unit smaller than a division would be viable on the battlefield. They also did not know how to do logistic analysis without a commitment or operation having been specified. Throwing up their hands, they commented that, provided the Canadian Army was well trained in combined arms tactics, "it appears that we shall have done as much as we can do." The staff had little or no idea of Canada's strategic airlift potential, but was pessimistic that there were sufficient resources to move anything but personnel and light equipment over modest distances. Moving armour by air was out of the question. The risk that there would be no airfields in the operations area meant that vertical-lift aircraft would be required. These did not exist, however, and helicopters could not lift heavy equipment. As this situation was likely to persist for some years to come, the team concluded that it would be "unsound" for the army to be structured entirely as air-transportable units. They were also pessimistic that Canada had the wherewithal to develop the new weapons and equipment required by the concept. Finally, the team rejected an organization based on "threes" and concluded that "fours" was superior. They conceded that the British Army had adopted "threes," but claimed that this was based on "national rather than tactical considerations."[58]

Shortly after Graham received the team's report, he turned the entire study over to Brigadier M.P. Bogert, the commandant of the Canadian Army Staff College at Fort Frontenac, Kingston, with instructions that by May 1957 Bogert should advise the CGS on the types of weapons and equipment that would be available to British and American forces, British and American tactical concepts, and the organization up to the divisional level that would enable such tactical concepts to be applied by the Canadian Army.[59] With that, GOLD RUSH/FIRE-FLY and the army's first attempt at thinking through a force structure for itself came to an end.

GOLD RUSH/FIRE-FLY was not a success, but neither was it a complete failure. Two field exercises had been held at Camp Gagetown in 1956 and 1957, although it is unclear how the headquarters staff exercises were related to the field exercises, since Graham did not approve the study for exercises with troops.[60] Staff had developed the main outline of the Canadian Mechanized Brigade Group that would appear in Europe between 1958 and 1965 with the advent of APCs and nuclear weapons.[61] Tactical employment was consistent with NATO plans to use river barriers.[62] However, there had been a lot of wheel spinning along the way. The army recognized the potential of air transport but had insufficient expertise to determine its best use. Simonds saw "flying trucks" and the elimination of the logistic tail from combat units. Graham wanted air-transportable strike units that major powers fifty years later would have difficulty maintaining. Neither had a good grasp of technological limits, and listened to expert staff only reluctantly.

The doctrinal product was consistent with British tactical preferences in that it was both defensive and attritional, although the substitution of nuclear weapons for artillery created certain qualitative changes. It is interesting to note that the army had developed its doctrine without apparent assistance from the air arm. Despite the huge air transport implications of both the GOLD RUSH and FIRE-FLY concepts, the army did not consult with the experts. And although nuclear weapons greatly expanded the battlefield, neither of the two staff studies addressed tactical aviation in any detail, except for transportation.

The process had also been too heavily driven from the top of the organization. There is a dividing line between inspired leadership and pigheaded dilettantism, and both Simonds and Graham had crossed it. Given the British Army culture of "doctrine is the opinion of the senior officer present" and the weaknesses of the British-style staff system, which did not, at the time, recognize the need for a separate, future-oriented development cell, perhaps this was only to be expected.

Staff had recognized that the GOLD RUSH exercise was both important and qualitatively different from previous studies. The working group itself had recommended that the study team be made permanent, and at the conclusion of the two studies, N.W. Morton, the scientific adviser to the CGS, recommended that a permanent planning cell be established. Morton believed that the pace of technological development had accelerated so rapidly that new equipment did not merely replace old types but also called into question operational concepts, organization, and logistic procedures. He saw this process continuing and felt that the army ran a major risk of "gross waste" if it did not create a planning cell that could look three to fifteen years into the future. Morton pointed to the US Army, which already had a combat development function at the top level of its staff.

The Rise of Combat Development

A more rational and systematic approach to planning the future army, along the lines of Morton's suggestion, finally emerged in the Directorate of Combat Development (DCD), which the army established in early 1958 to institutionalize the GOLD RUSH staff. The Canadian Army did not copy the American approach, in which a self-contained combat development function drove school and exercise programs. It adopted a more modest approach that grafted the combat development cell on the General Staff and gave it the task of "encouraging thought, study and work on the future but not monopolizing this activity," with a mandate to look five years and more from the present. This made "doctrine" the preserve of existing staff organizations, primarily the Directorate of Military Training. The DCD consisted of only a director and four other professional staff, plus support staff, but went on to complete more than forty staff studies.[63]

GOLD RUSH had left a number of important issues unresolved. The role of aviation has already been mentioned. The second was the lethality of tactical nuclear war. The army operations research staff continued to war-game the GOLD RUSH concept with various levels of nuclear strikes. By 1958 they had concluded that tactical nuclear warfare was impossible and that land battles as previously known would not develop. In their war games, as soon as conventional forces concentrated, they were overwhelmed by a nuclear strike or two. The staff concluded that "the force with no or low nuclear capability will survive but a short time and a clash between simultaneously alerted forces, both with nuclear plenty, will result in mutual annihilation." The best that could be hoped for was that a force would endure long enough to "make a contribution to success in other theatres."[64]

The army dealt with these studies by ignoring them. VCGS Major-General J.V. Allard merely forwarded the report to senior officers with a comment that it contained impressions and not conclusions and that it would be wrong to use it as the basis for new doctrine. He directed their focus to the apparent ineffectiveness of infantry in the forward zone: "They seem to be there only to become casualties."[65] No strategic rethinking was undertaken, however, and the army remained wedded to NATO's concept of tactical nuclear war, using the combat development process to refine it.

The Search for a Strategic Role Continues

The Army of the Future

The army had spent three years grappling with the tactical implications of nuclear weapons without addressing the issues Foulkes had identified soon after MC 48 had been accepted. Did a Canadian contribution to NATO ground forces actually make sense in light of the relatively small size of the force that could be fielded? And once a brigade group was there, could it be reinforced? And if not, what was the purpose of the army reserves? Graham's investigation of an air-transportable army that could quickly reinforce NATO and also fight brush-fire wars appeared to be aimed at addressing this dilemma by totally restructuring the army. NATO itself was divided on how to deal with the Soviet threat. The British favoured a small "shield" force that would permit them to continue their overseas policing role, and wanted to rely on massive retaliation. Other countries were not so sure that massive retaliation was credible and wanted a large conventional shield force. It was originally agreed that the shield force would consist of sixty-five divisions, but this proved impossible to sustain. In 1954 a lower target of thirty divisions was agreed to, but this also came to exceed the means of member states. Canadian diplomats believed that Canadian troops were in Europe mainly to assure the Europeans that the Anglo-Saxon countries would not leave the Continent to its fate. While a worthwhile goal, this did not require any particular size of force to achieve. NATO staffs were aiming at a thirty-division force with both nuclear and conventional capability. NATO's preference was to cut reserve forces and emphasize standing forces for thirty days of conflict.[66]

The army again attempted to deal with this issue in the fall of 1958. By then the cast of players had changed: John Diefenbaker had become prime minister in 1957, with George Pearkes as minister of national defence. Pearkes had won the Victoria Cross as an infantry major during the First World War. He stayed on a professional soldier, attended the Imperial Staff College, and rose to the rank of major-general during the Second World War. Sent back to Canada by Montgomery for being "no good ... [having] no brains,"[67] he subsequently served as General Officer Commander in Chief Pacific Command, where he oversaw the defences of the west coast. S.F. Clark, who had been chief signals officer of II Canadian Corps Headquarters and subsequently rose through senior staff and command positions, had succeeded Graham as CGS.

Pearkes asked Clark to review the role and organization of the army in light of new weapons and the changing concept of modern warfare.[68] In the fall of 1958, Clark challenged the members of the Army Council to rethink the role of the army. According to him "penetrating thinking" was required.[69] The first member to respond was Major-General J.D.B. Smith, the adjutant general, who drafted a paper called "The Nature of Future War." In it he noted the Joint Intelligence Committee's estimate that the Soviet Union had the capacity to strike at least fifty targets in North America with nuclear weapons, as well as the fact that the Soviets would soon completely phase out manned aircraft in this role. NATO's real deterrent, therefore, consisted of US second-strike forces. Purely defensive forces in North America (such as air defences and naval forces) were valueless. If there was to be a role for the navy, it lay in Polaris submarines. What mattered, according to Smith, were armed forces with offensive second-strike capability that could both deter war and destroy the enemy if attacked, and "survival forces" to resuscitate population centres after an attack.

Unless the Canadian Army was a second-strike force, Smith could see "no role ... [for it] in the prevention of major war." Moreover, he saw national resuscitation as "the primary role of the Canadian Army in the context of major war and ... of the highest national importance." Such a role would require maintaining six brigade groups in Canada, one of them committed to NATO. All the brigade groups would require their own air units.

For anything short of major war, Smith said, the Canadian army should maintain a Korea-type balanced, self-contained force consisting of highly ready, air-transportable forces. A brigade group would be the largest force of this type that Canada could be justifiably expected to provide. Although nuclear-armed, Canada would expect major allies to provide supporting infrastructure and heavy weapons.[70]

N.W. Morton, the scientific adviser to the CGS, thought that Smith had made some fundamental errors in his paper on the nature of future war. First, Smith had drastically underestimated the effect of a nuclear strike on North America. Estimates were that by 1967 the Soviet Union would have one thousand nuclear weapons of 80 percent reliability. If 25 percent of these were set as ground bursts, they would blanket the entire United States with deadly radiation for two months. Morton believed that there would be an air defence role for Canada for some time and that Canada could not afford to play the "big league" game of Polaris submarines. He asked: "Would it be better advised to pick a middle-power role of which the contribution will be in relation to the more probable everyday necessity of patching things up so that the all-out war is less likely to take place?" He agreed that for the purposes of fighting a total war in Europe, ground forces were no longer critical and could not be reinforced. However, the assignment of Canadian forces was a political and moral effort, not a purely military one, and he advanced a different conclusion than Smith: "The role par excellence of the Canadian Army, directly supported transportwise by both the RCN and the RCAF, is the provision of globally mobile forces up to the scale of a brigade group or equivalent for the purpose of less than total war. This will require one brigade group located in Canada at a high state of readiness."[71]

After further discussion but no evident staff work, the Army Council endorsed two papers that Clark sent to Pearkes. The first, "The Nature of Future War," followed Smith's views fairly closely. It contended that "strike-second" forces were the real deterrent and that these forces and a national survival force were key. Like the Smith paper on future war, it deprecated both air defence and anti-submarine warfare as not increasing the capability of second-strike forces. Neither the Canadian ground nor air forces in Europe were regarded as critical. Since Canada could make only a small contribution to a second strike, it should allocate a large portion of its effort to national survival. This effort should "equal or [be] even greater" than resources committed to the prevention of major war. Only the armed forces could do the job and "the Army is particularly suitable to carry out these tasks." "The Nature of Future War" also advocated a brigade-sized, highly ready, nuclear-armed force provided with airlift and rapid air and sea transport for United Nations duty, but its major conclusion was that "national survival must be the nation's prime concern for the future" and that the army should take the lead role in this.[72]

The second paper, "The Organization of the Canadian Army," elaborated the force structure necessary to respond to the army's vision of the future. Ignoring the conclusion that ground forces in Europe contributed little to Canadian defence, it called for the continuation of the brigade group in Europe, plus two more high-readiness brigades to round out a Canadian division on the Continent. An additional brigade "organized and equipped on a strategically portable basis" should be available to meet UN requirements. Finally, assorted units were required to meet miscellaneous Canada-US commitments and minor UN tasks. The high-readiness brigades were justified as "deterrent forces."

Regarding the national survival mission, the paper painted a grim future for Canada following a nuclear attack. It forecast 4.5 million casualties, with 3 million dead. The army estimated that every three survivors would require one person in the survival force. The paper recommended adjustments to the Militia "to make it effective in its primary role of survival operations." It also recommended that the Regular Force in Canada be provided with training and equipment for survival operations.[73]

George Pearkes found little to like in the army's proposal. He told Clark that NATO document MC 14/2 was based on both shield and retaliatory forces. The army's proposal made no reference to shield forces and Canadian policy had never been, and was not then, to contribute to retaliatory forces. Furthermore, Canada was not committed to providing troops to the UN and the Secretary-General had said that an international standing force was not required. With the Soviet Union having a veto on the Security Council, it was unlikely that there would ever be another Korea-type UN operation. As for the place of the Department of National Defence in civil defence, this was not a military decision but rather "a matter for the government." No decisions had yet been made. Regarding the organization of the army, Pearkes thought that while there might be a role for the Regular Force in national survival, "there is a limit to what can be done within the appropriations allotted by Parliament." Agreeing with Foulkes's long-standing opinion that Europe could not be reinforced once hostilities had commenced, Pearkes said that a thirty-day war was planned and that the brigade group in Europe should be self-sufficient for that period. There was little point in maintaining two additional brigades in Canada as it was anticipated that the ports would be destroyed. Moreover, if Canada itself was devastated, the two additional brigades would be required at home. In short, there was not much of a case that the brigades should be organized and equipped for the first phase of a nuclear war, and since there was no UN commitment, Pearkes could not agree to equip additional brigades to the same level of readiness as the one in Germany. In his view, it would be sufficient to have training equipment so each battalion could do a year's training prior to rotation to Germany. He concluded: "Any recommendations with regard to the composition and training of the Militia to make it more effective in the survival operations will receive serious and immediate consideration."[74]

Clark responded that the army was not questioning government policy, but rather was raising issues for the 1960-67 time period. He questioned the wisdom of a policy of non-reinforcement of Germany and non-support of troops in the field. According to Clark, Canada had already undertaken to provide a strategic reserve of two-thirds of a division to NATO, and in this context "strategic" meant a ready force capable of rapid deployment. Pearkes did not wish to debate the matter, however, and asked Clark to take it up with Foulkes, the chairman of the Chiefs of Staff Committee.[75] Three months later, Clark reluctantly accepted Pearkes's direction and informed him that the army would adopt the following posture:

- The brigade group in Europe would be trained and equipped to fight for thirty days.
- The brigade groups in Canada would be trained, equipped, and ready to undertake survival operations and police actions under the UN, but would have limited fighting capability because of equipment shortages. They would degrade progressively as equipment aged.
- The National War Reserve of thirty days of war stocks for the brigade in Europe would be the only war reserve held in Canada.
- The Militia would be trained and equipped for survival operations only.[76]

The entire affair was another demonstration of the army's inability to deal with development issues, this time at the strategic level. The most senior level of army leadership had attempted to develop a master plan that would have greatly increased the army's combat power and cost as well as expanded its overseas mission. The assumptions of the plan called into question the primary roles of the Royal Canadian Air Force and the Royal Canadian Navy. The plan had been developed as sort of a senior class writing project without any visible preparatory work done by staff; indeed, the assumption was that staff need become involved only once the big decisions had already been made. It had foreign and defence policy implications, yet none of the higher National Defence officials outside the army had been consulted. Indeed, the only outsider consulted was the scientific adviser, and he had been largely ignored.

Overall, the army had shown little or no institutional capacity to develop higher-level military concepts or policy. The assumptions inherited from the British Army that senior officers would have innate personal capacity to engage in problem solving appeared to be what the Canadian Army of the 1950s relied upon. Policy was therefore unstable as it was almost totally dependent on personality. This deficiency would become more significant as time went on and the problematic nature of the army's NATO assignment became increasingly evident, resulting in even greater divergence between civilians and soldiers.

The Speidel Proposal

Evolving NATO doctrine and plans gave rise to an optional Canadian assignment in 1959. Even though it was still based on massive retaliation, MC 14/2 had recognized the possibility of war by accident or miscalculation and had stated that localized conventional attacks should be met initially by conventional forces. In December 1957 a new directive, MC 70, had ordered the Supreme Allied Commander Europe (SACEUR), General Lauris Norstad, to prepare a response to any type of incursion, possibly without the use of nuclear weapons. Land forces were called upon to defend NATO as far to the east as possible using balanced conventional and nuclear forces. NATO staff based their plans on the concept of a flexible division that could be tailored to meet the exigencies of terrain and the threat. Nuclear weapons, reconnaissance troops, additional armour, and helicopters could be added to the force at the divisional level.[77]

General Norstad steered the alliance towards graduated deterrence. He wished to be able to force a pause in military activity that would give the enemy time to consider the consequences of continued aggression. His commander of Allied Land Forces Central Europe (LANDCENT), General Hans Speidel, agreed that the mission of the shield forces was to impose the pause. He understood the dire consequences if this could not be done. In HOSTAGE BLEU, a 1958 LANDCENT war game, SACEUR had been forced to use nuclear weapons within hours and strategic nuclear war had quickly followed.[78]

Norstad and Speidel began working on creating a strategic reserve that could respond to any incursions. Speidel felt that the Canadian brigade group would be an ideal component of this force. He believed that, other than the US Army, the brigade group was the only really ready force in LANDCENT. At the time, it appeared that a British decision to leave seven brigades in Europe rather than reduce the British Army in Europe to five brigades would permit Canadian troops to be removed without seriously weakening 1 (British) Corps. Speidel and his chief of staff, Lieutenant-General Albert Crahay, proposed that Canada permit the use of its brigade as a SACEUR or LANDCENT reserve, equipped as an air-transportable or light armoured force, or a combination of both. Crahay added that the Canadian Army was most suited to the role of a border fire brigade because it was the only force that would not be viewed with suspicion by the Warsaw Pact countries and that also had the full confidence of the smaller NATO nations. Speidel and Crahay presented their views through Major-General George Kitching, the Canadian military representative to NATO. Speidel also wrote directly to Lieutenant-General Clark, the CGS, suggesting that with a slight improvement in manpower, mobility, and atomic firepower, the Canadian brigade group could be part of a hard-hitting counterattack force. This could be done without disturbing existing basing arrangements. He welcomed Clark's views on the matter.[79]

The army saw advantages to becoming the LANDCENT reserve, as no expensive base changes would be required, the role was consistent with its own equipment plans, and there was some dislike of the role they had within the British corps. Becoming the SACEUR reserve was a different matter, however. To be able to move anywhere in Europe, expensive logistic support would be required, as well as training and equipment for all climate zones; it was doubtful that SACEUR would permit the brigade to continue being based so close to the frontier; and a light armoured role would require the abandonment of the Centurion tank, which was relatively new and would be expensive to replace.

A response along these lines was sent from Foulkes to Speidel, who discussed the matter with General Norstad. Norstad invited Canada to move its brigade south, onto the American lines of communication and closer to the Air Division, suggesting that this would make the Canadian contribution more prominent and might result in some savings. Not surprisingly, Foulkes thought the idea had considerable merit (he had proposed the same thing himself in 1951). Norstad subsequently asked his staff to work out the details.

SHAPE staff did not think much of the plan, believing that NORTHAG would be seriously weakened if the Canadian brigade group were withdrawn. Moreover, the British became directly involved, with Minister of Defence Harold Watkinson telling Pearkes that the more he thought about the move of the Canadian brigade, the less he liked it. Moving the Canadian brigade would stall British plans to withdraw some of their own troops from the Continent. The British offered a none too subtle bribe, telling Canada that they were examining the possibility of appointing a Canadian divisional commander to 1 (British) Corps from time to time. There was also considerable lobbying at SHAPE, which effectively killed the proposal, although it was discussed on and off until Canadian Defence Minister Paul Hellyer revived it during the development of the 1964 *White Paper on Defence.*

The significance of the Speidel proposal lay in its demonstration of how inflexible Canada's NATO deployment had become. Whereas taking on the role of the SHAPE reserve would have meant costly re-equipping and rebasing, becoming the LANDCENT reserve would not. However, Canada's being a big fish in NORTHAG's small pond meant that change would encounter serious resistance. During the next decade, the immutability of the NATO contribution would become a significant factor in pushing civilians and soldiers apart on policy issues.

Modernizing the Reserves

In terms of size, the Militia was the equal of the Regular army. During the 1950s, it had an authorized strength of about 45,000, compared with 49,000 Regulars. Actual strength grew from about 35,000 before the Korean War to just over 43,000 after.[80] The Militia was organized on the concept of the need for mass mobilization of Canadian society to fight a war, and was organized as two corps, each consisting of one armoured division and two infantry divisions. This immense force co-existed with a full-time army that struggled to sustain four *brigades.*[81] While Canada had maintained a full army in the field during the Second World War, plus troops for the defence of Canada at home, outside the army itself the need for such a large force was no longer apparent.

Historically, the Militia had been the senior partner in the army family. Indeed, prior to the Second World War the regular Permanent Force had existed mainly to train the Militia. Since its inception, it had been a vehicle for patronage. During the 1870s, Colonel George Denison had commented that Militia drill pay "was the only form of public spending that penetrated down to every dusty concession road in the country."[82]

Despite its size, the Militia had not been able to provide formations or subformations to meet either Korean War or European NATO requirements. By 1949, Militia training was confined to the platoon level and was inefficient, "plodding" and dull. Recruiting faltered and after 1948 targets were continuously reduced. The army clung to the belief that it had community support when facts showed the opposite. Army Week in Victoria in 1949 produced only five inquiries about the Regular army, enrollment of several cadets, and no militia recruits. Those who attended displays were "mostly elderly people past military age or young children [while] the young men of suitable military age were most conspicuous by their absence at each evening."[83]

Militia turnout for the Korean War had been light, possibly as few as 2,600 volunteers. The government had not wanted to "disrupt" the Militia, experienced veterans had been preferred for the Special Force, and recruiters were unsure whether they were allowed to recruit Militia soldiers. As already noted, Simonds turned to the Militia to provide the base for the NATO Integrated Force after the fiasco of the Special Force recruitment. Numerical targets were indeed met, but only by raising age limits for lieutenants and captains by three years and accepting tradesmen up to forty-five years of age. There is no record of how many individuals recruited through Militia units for 27 Canadian Infantry Brigade had prior Militia experience, but it appears that a large proportion were recruited directly from the streets.[84]

By September 1952, Simonds, the CGS, was dissatisfied with the Militia's performance. He believed that its organization was uneconomical and had failed to accomplish its primary purpose – the provision of a trained nucleus for immediate expansion in war. He noted that the number and types of units composing the Militia did not correspond to mobilization requirements and that the low strength of most units hindered the progress of training; resulted in rapid turnover, improper selection of recruits, and high wastage of clothing; and would, in war, result in the likely release of large numbers of unsuitable personnel. He thought that the solution might be to classify Reserve units as either "A" units, which would be mobilized in the first year of a war, or "B" units, which might be mobilized later. The "B" units would eventually cease to exist and they could be disbanded or reduced to zero strength "without the inherent problems arising from an arbitrary decision at this point" – the "inherent problems" being, of course, the political backlash from those units that might be disbanded.[85]

Simonds's low opinion of the Militia was shared by most, if not all, of the senior army officers. Simonds wrote the General Officers Commanding (GOC) the regional commands, noting the problems of the Reserves and asking for thoughts on reorganization. He concluded that "the development of this proposal would call for a considerable reorganization of the Reserve Force, and the dropping of some units and the amalgamation of others with all the heartburning that a process of this kind inevitably engenders, but I am impressed with the necessity of increasing the real readiness of the Reserve Force."[86] The responses were highly uniform. Major-General Chris Vokes, GOC Western Command, agreed that "nothing short of something very drastic will do." He found unit training in the Reserves "pathetic" and suggested that the time had come to abandon historical but unworkable units and instead establish provincial regiments that could draw on larger manpower pools. He also recognized the political problem: "Of course, the great snag with certain armoured and infantry units is that we run smack into the regimental system fostered on an ethnic group – mainly Scotch and lesser Irish – and the locally named unit, all of which have built up traditions in peace and war."[87]

Brigadier John A.W. Bennett, the commanding general in Saskatchewan, went even further. He found the mobilization role to be "a dangerous self-delusion" as the training requirement for Reserve non-commissioned officers was so great that effective soldiers could never be trained within the Reserves. Moreover, he did not believe that the Militia in Saskatchewan was attracting very many with the potential to be NCOs: "The vast majority of the people we are getting ... are drifters off the bottom of the social and economic barrel." Faced with a lack of adequate training, the army was turning a "Nelson's Eye" to the problem. He cited the example of one of his reservists, who, with six months' service and no camps or courses, was given a junior NCO qualification by a corps school after a weeklong course, despite records showing that he had less than a hundred hours of training. Asked Bennett: "What sort of Corporal will he make on mobilization?"[88]

The army was of the opinion that it had no source of trained reservists in an emergency and obtained Cabinet approval for a Regular Reserve of soldiers who had served three years with the Regular Force and who would agree to train three weeks a year and be available for immediate call-up in an emergency. This could not be more than a partial solution, however.[89]

Simonds delegated the study of the Militia to a three-member board made up of two retired Militia officers – Major-General Howard Kennedy and Major-General E.J. Renaud – and one active Militia officer, Major-General H.F.G. Letson. The Kennedy Board of Officers report resulted in organizational reform, a de-layering of Reserve headquarters, a reduction in overhead, and a general realignment of units to meet army needs more closely. For example, several anti-aircraft artillery units were disbanded and coastal artillery units disappeared. Four new armoured regiments were formed from anti-tank and infantry units.[90] Nevertheless, Kennedy did not manage to resolve the fundamental structural issues that the GOCs had identified.

The two major problems were the diffuse and overly large organization of the Militia (which was partially addressed) and the problem of achieving training standards on a part-time basis. This was evident from the fact that reservists volunteering for both Korea and Europe had not required less time to reach a ready state than untrained volunteers. The NATO brigade – drawn mainly from the Militia – had taken about the same amount of time to complete training as raw recruits off the street. Kennedy tried to square the circle of maintaining standards but only training part-time by recommending increased training time and greater specialization. This was almost immediately deemed impractical by senior army officials. According to one analysis, it would still take a recruit four years to complete his initial training. Since Militia soldiers often left in less than two years (because they were frustrated with training), the Kennedy proposals appeared to be self-defeating.[91] There was little enthusiasm for more drastic measures, however. Simonds told the Cabinet Defence Committee that "personally, [I] would like to have seen more drastic recommendations but [I] realized that it was essential to retain the goodwill of the Reserve Force." Minister Brooke Claxton's first reaction to Kennedy's recommendations was that their premature release could result in "unpleasant and unwarranted repercussions."[92]

The question of what to do about the Reserves came up again in 1956 when the government was struggling with the question of how to maintain war reserves in case of a nuclear war in Europe. Foulkes, the chairman of the Chiefs of Staff Committee, disputed CGS Graham's argument that the Militia should be fully equipped since their efficiency was expected to improve. He thought that Graham was trying to expand the army establishment by the back door, contrary to ministerial direction that priority be given to deterrent forces and forces needed to meet Canada's commitments during the first thirty days of a war. He told Frank Miller, the deputy minister of national defence and a former chief of the Air Staff, that "the role of the Militia is still very nebulous and as time goes on it is going to be increasingly difficult to justify the expenditure of $30 million on a force for which we cannot clearly demonstrate any need that appears to be realistic, except the task of supporting survival."[93]

Faced with these pressures, Graham commissioned Brigadier W.A.B. Anderson as "a committee of one" to undertake a confidential study of the organization, equipment, and training of the Militia. One of the GOCs whose advice had not been taken by the Kennedy Board of Officers, Anderson was instructed that he "should try to work out on a purely military – as opposed to politico-military – basis, the most efficient organization for the Canadian Militia."[94]

Anderson found that the army knew very little about the condition of the Militia. "It is," he said, "extremely difficult to arrive at a clear appraisal of the adequacy of the Militia, consisting as it does of such a variety of units which are serving under such varying conditions." Statistics regarding the number of non-effective personnel were unavailable, but extrapolation from a survey taken by Central Command yielded a proportion of about 30 percent. There was no detailed information at Army Headquarters regarding the suitability of Militia quarters for training or administrative purposes. Furthermore, although the Militia had generally been able to fill officer and NCO positions, this had depended on a supply from the Canadian Officer Training Corps (COTC) and wartime experience. Both pools were aging, especially the NCOs, who were on average too old for field duties, and it was increasingly difficult to get young

COTC graduates to stay in the Militia. The rank and file were the principal weakness, however. The turnover of other ranks was so rapid that no training plan could be followed, leading to a vicious circle as the more ambitious recruits left because their training was in disarray. It was clear that relatively few Militia soldiers stayed long enough to qualify as tradesmen, yet the fighting efficiency of units depended on those highly qualified soldiers.

Anderson concluded that the Militia operated as a school for training officers and NCOs and was not well designed to fulfill its mission of providing a pool of trained manpower. The Militia might be able to mobilize two divisions, but if those troops were needed in less than twelve months, Militia turnover would have to be reduced. He noted that the Militia organization was still based on a mobilization plan calling for twice the number of fighting formations required and more corps and army support troops. This created a large surplus of units.[95]

Having received Anderson's unvarnished opinion, Graham then asked for options that would have a chance of being accepted by the government and the public. Anderson came up with four options:

- *Plan A.* Use existing Militia units to create a ready reserve of full-time, short-service soldiers recruited from sixteen- to twenty-four-year-olds serving for one year.
- *Plan B.* Make the strongest Militia units into the "Regular Army Reserve" as auxiliary battalions linked to Regular Force units. The remaining units would become the "Militia" and would be given basic training to provide a partly trained nucleus for home and civil defence operations.
- *Plan C.* Link Militia units in pairs, one to be deployable and the other to be a depot and training unit. Units would not know which had been designated as the deployable unit.
- *Plan D.* Some Militia units would become part of the Regular Army to provide troops to supplement the field force.[96]

Both Anderson and Graham favoured Plan B, but a federal election took place, and the Conservatives led by John Diefenbaker came to power. The new minister of national defence, George Pearkes, had been a strong supporter of a civil defence role for the Militia and, as we have already seen, did not believe that mass mobilization served a purpose in the nuclear age. The drift towards a "national survival" role for the Militia had begun several years earlier, however, and by 1954 Cabinet and the Chiefs of Staff Committee were aware of the devastation a nuclear war would cause and of the weakness of Canada's civil government to deal with it. The other services saw the Militia as a key component of the federal response, but Simonds had resisted this tasking. Nevertheless, in

1956 the GOCs were instructed to use all units within their commands – Regular and Militia – to provide aid to the civil power in case of attack. The instruction came too late in the year to affect Militia training for 1956, but momentum was building.[97]

When he retired, Graham was asked to prepare a report to Cabinet on civil defence. In early December 1958, his successor, Lieutenant-General S.F. Clark, was allowed to read the report, and at once initiated Army Headquarters planning for national survival. The resulting plan underlined the horrific consequences of nuclear war: mass casualties in all thirteen Canadian target areas would be followed by starvation, epidemics, fear, confusion, panic, and even anarchy. The proposed army response consisted of sixty-six Mobile Survival Columns, forty-four of them from the Militia. Following a meeting of the minister with the Conference of Defence Associations, Clark advised the GOCs on 29 January 1959 that the Militia would be trained for survival operations rather than field operations. This policy would be embedded in the White Paper that the government published in April that year. The White Paper included the announcement that military equipment not needed for survival operations would be withdrawn from the Militia.[98]

Although given a new role, the Militia had not been reformed. A study by Brigadier M.S. Dunn completed in October 1959 found that the Militia had continued its downward spiral. Dunn estimated that of the 41,000 Militia soldiers, 2,000 to 3,000 were non-effectives, but as there was "great scope for irregularities" in the way attendance was kept, the actual number was difficult to determine. Training was ineffective. Dunn reported that the cost of the Militia might be justified if candidates completed training, but they did not. The great bulk of training was never completed, resulting only in expenses for the department and frustration for the instructors. Because technical training had been encouraged, "a staggering amount of expensive equipment" had been issued to units, where it was "lost, abused or misused by personnel who do not have the time and skills to handle it." Dunn pointed to petty abuses in Militia pay. There was no effective method of determining who had been present on drill nights for training, and pay sheets were frequently revised. Moreover, with commanding officers allowed to hire and fire their own orderly room and quartermaster staff, staff had become bloated, consuming 21 percent of Militia pay and allowances, and most of the incumbents were unqualified.

Dunn observed that it had been logical at the end of the Second World War to think that with forty-five days of training a year (it had actually been sixty days then) satisfactory skill levels could be maintained, but this population was no longer active. He concluded that it would be better to set realistic standards than to stubbornly pursue a policy of training that is "platitudinous, frustrating, inordinately expensive and incapable of attainment." He recommended that the Militia be integrated into the Regular Force to carry out the national survival role, but was under no illusions that this would be popular: "I have no doubt that the above would be unpalatable to the Canadian Army (Militia), who are always 'ready to lick their weight in wildcats.'"[99]

The standard view is that assignment of the national survival role to the Militia shattered the institution. According to Granatstein, recruiting dried up except for those enlisted off the streets for special national survival courses, and "the Militia never truly recovered."[100] A second element of the standard view of Militia history is that the Militia's political influence on the government prevented the army from applying "professional" standards, ending the mobilization role, and turning it into a useful ready reserve.[101] Neither conclusion appears to be fully borne out by the evidence, however.

According to Urquhart, the overall strength of the Militia did not decline during the 1955-63 period; in fact, it reached its peak in 1962. This peak was attained through the Special Militia Training Program of that year, which was designed to train ten thousand soldiers for three to seven months in a variety of trades with civilian application. This was changed to fundamental military skills and rescue operations.[102] Civil defence missions had been popular with Reserve units, and involvement in operations such as flood relief had spurred re-enlistment.[103] It is likely that the initiative fell into disrepute because it was poorly implemented, and not simply as a result of rejection of a "non-military" national survival role. Units were not up to strength and could not conduct realistic collective training. In addition, combat service support units to provide Militia combat arms units with transport, medical, decontamination, and military police services had not been designated as late as 1962. One lieutenant-colonel writing in the *Canadian Army Journal* complained that "those in the Militia and Regular forces have almost reached the saturation point in knot-tying, lashing, bandages and somewhat dry lectures." The Canadian Infantry Association complained that a training program, including national survival skills, calculated to maintain the interest of Militia soldiers was needed. Poor implementation, rather than rejection of the role itself, appears to have been the central problem.

The claim that professionalism was stymied by politics also merits close examination. While there was a long history of patronage and a Militia lobby in Parliament, one has to question how strong their influence really was. Certainly, George Pearkes saw Militia interests as no impediment to assigning them a completely new role and stripping them of heavy equipment. It would seem that the army had considerable freedom to institute change. The Conference of Defence Associations, the principal umbrella group for branch and service organizations representing former officers, did complain in 1961 that there were "acute" problems with combat arms units not having military roles, and suggested that if the government did not see the need for an army reserve, the Militia should be abolished and funds given to a civilian national survival organization. The issue of a national survival role was not resolved by domestic politics but by changes to NATO strategy that created a need for more conventional forces.[104]

What is clear is that, although the army had recognized that the key problem with the Militia was the incompatibility of part-time training with the skills required, it failed to design a workable solution. Once the Second World War reservoir of military skill had been depleted, the Militia went into a death spiral. Anderson's option of enrolling sixteen- to twenty-four-year-olds for one year's service was the only option ever advanced that might have addressed this, and it was never seriously considered. Thus, the decline of the Militia was due not so much to its being assigned a civil defence role, or to political impediments to reform, as to the army's inability to develop solutions to a management problem.

The Officer Corps and Professional Education

What qualities a junior officer should have and how he should be trained became the first battleground over officer professionalism between the modernizers and the traditionalists. Each faction was represented by an officer who exemplified its values: Lieutenant-General (later General) Charles Foulkes, the modernizer, and Lieutenant-General Guy Simonds, the traditionalist.

The war in Europe had barely ended when Foulkes began planning for peacetime officer production. He approved a study recommending that all officers be produced through civilian universities and that the Royal Military College (RMC) be used for postgraduate officer training. In memos to the minister, Foulkes laid out his vision for officer training in great detail. His principal concern was the integration of the officer corps with society and its ability to work at the strategic level:

> A serious study of the science of warfare requires a good knowledge of economics and political science. For many officers a detailed knowledge of economics, political science, commerce and business administration, will be required to enable them to deal with the problems of administration and logistics of the services in modern war.
>
> Positions of responsibility in the services bring officers in close touch socially and professionally with some of the best minds and best educated members of

modern society. A good general education is, therefore, an essential requirement in the training of an officer.

The RMC old boys resisted Foulkes's plan, which would have decreased the prominence of the college. Neither the navy nor the Royal Canadian Air Force would agree to a degreed officer corps, except for technical support officers.[105]

The changing of the guard and the replacement of Foulkes by Guy Simonds in 1951 put the traditionalists in charge. Simonds wrote to Foulkes, now chairman of the Chiefs of Staff Committee, in April 1951, predicting a shortfall of two thousand officers and recommending that standards of education be lowered to meet the requirement. Candidates would be accepted after completing only "junior matriculation," or Grade 10.[106]

When his proposal was discussed at the Chiefs of Staff Committee, Simonds argued further that the service colleges needed "adjustment" because they put too much weight on science and academic qualifications. According to him, "this resulted in too many otherwise suitable students being unable to attain the required academic qualifications."[107] Simonds never elaborated on what he meant by "otherwise suitable," but its meaning can be deduced from the work of others. Lieutenant-Colonel H.F. Wood, in charge of army training, believed that before the Industrial Revolution the landed gentry produced natural leaders, but now "the lack of roots and stable home life, and the smaller family unit and the sum has produced a less well adjusted youth." The school system no longer produced leaders, but taught only "pragmatic skills." The army's solution was to recruit "quite young men" who "had not yet rounded off their characters" and mould them to the desired model.[108] Similarly, Colonel G.M.C. Sprung, the author of the only Canadian book on military professionalism published between 1950 and 1970, saw command as "a personal quality," "something which belongs to the whole man and is not a specialist skill which can be learned." Like Wood, he was nostalgic for the British class system, in which officers did not have to explain or justify their positions of authority. Men were "accustomed to have their decisions taken by the kind of person they saw their officers to be."[109] The traditionalist model centred on character and personal qualities, not academic or technical achievement.

Foulkes placed the problem in the hands of a committee chaired by Dr. O.M. Solandt, the chairman of the Defence Research Board and a civilian member of the Chiefs of Staff Committee. Solandt recognized that the basic dilemma faced by the services was that expansion had created many junior positions where "men who had a limited ability to absorb advanced education" could be successful provided they had leadership qualities, but that the services also required very high standards of education and "the very highest intellectual capabilities" for senior staff jobs.

In the end, Foulkes was able to get agreement on a deal that preserved the entry standard as high school graduation, with a two-year service college program for general service officers. Only technical support officers (and RCAF officers) would study for four years. To increase recruitment, it was proposed that cadets be subsidized, with an obligation to serve for five years. In addition, a preparatory school for francophones would be established to bring their math and science to the same standard as school leavers from other provinces, and to provide English-language training.[110]

With the end of the Korean War in 1953, the demand for junior officers fell. The army decided to send all service college graduates to university to complete a degree. According to the RMC commandant, however, the services were failing to attract the very best, and he told the minister: "We appeal to the mediocre man, not to the good man." That year, only 84 percent of RMC applicants were admitted to first-year engineering at Queen's University and only 38 percent to the University of Toronto. The commandant attributed this to the policy of applying provincial quotas to entry into the RMC as well as to the disparity in provincial educational standards. Simonds saw this as another reason to recruit below high school graduation.[111]

By the end of the 1950s, the dilemma identified by Dr. Solandt in 1951 had arrived. From 1957 to 1959, only 19 percent of applicants to the Canadian Army Staff College, where mid-level officers were trained, passed the entrance exam. Another 19 percent were granted a "Supplemental" pass, which required additional work. The highest rate of failure was in Tactics. Tellingly, 68 percent of those who passed had university degrees, proportionately almost three times as many as non-degreed applicants.[112] The army solved the problem by discontinuing the entrance exams on the grounds that staff college candidates had already been selected for promotion to major by examination.

John English has argued that during the 1950s officers had to pass a "battery of stiff formal qualifications at the lieutenant and captain rank" and that these exams were "meticulously administered" and "comprehensive." He attributes the decline in officer standards to the post-unification termination of army exams more than to any other single factor. To those responsible for professional development in the late 1950s, however, it appeared that a decline had already begun. In 1958 Brigadier Roger Rowley, the commandant at the Canadian Army Staff College, complained to the director general of military training about "the fact that the average Canadian student attending the [staff college] course does NOT have sufficient military experience background and basic knowledge on arrival at the college." In his opinion, officers lacked knowledge of combined arms operations at the battalion group or armoured regiment group levels. Students at staff college had lacked this knowledge for the past two or three courses despite passing the entrance exams. According to Rowley, about 60 percent of those arriving at the staff college lacked adequate unit experience and had not completed the captain-to-major qualifications or attended a squadron, battery, or company commander's course. His opinion was supported by that of the chief of the general staff, Lieutenant-General Geoffrey Walsh, who told army general officers in 1962:

> This summer I noticed some alarming deficiencies and vacuums in training. I will start with junior tactics, and cite you some examples which I noticed in my very quick visits to your exercises. Troops digging in daylight in exposed and skyline positions – company parading in soft-skinned vehicles within anti-tank range of the enemy – tanks with troops on the rear decks moving into enemy positions – poor handling of support weapons with no effort made to make the best use of their characteristics – lack of adequate reconnaissance especially with the armour, and finally one instance where a company was launched across country before first light to seize and hold a position without entrenching tools or even their haversack rations.
>
> To my mind all of this is inexcusable and point up to the lack of proper training by the company commander or squadron commander concerned, not only of his company but of his officers and NCO's and, perhaps, even by the commanding officers of the company commanders.

It is clear that the officer corps was having difficulties before the disruption of unification, although the latter would add an additional dimension to the problem.[113]

Were the 1950s a Success?

From the army traditionalists' point of view, the 1950s appeared to be a success. The Canadian Army had retained its British Army organizational ties during the Korean War as well as in its NATO assignment. It had also preserved its British Army culture and ways of doing business. The 27 Canadian Infantry Brigade was well regarded – even considered indispensible – within NATO, thus preserving the army's claim to being a "big army" with modern heavy equipment. The suggestion that it become a more lightly equipped force more closely linked to the Americans had been fended off. The army had not only developed new doctrine to fight a nuclear war but had by the end of the decade created new institutional capacity to deal with future technological and doctrinal challenges. It had halted the creation of ad hoc forces to meet contingencies and integrated its brigades into a single army.

Success was to prove fleeting, however. The army had not convinced the political level that there could be a prolonged ground war in Europe, which meant that support and resources for a large army were vulnerable. And although the army had published doctrine on how it would fight a nuclear war, the solution it proposed did not appear convincing. The fact that other allies were also unable to develop viable nuclear doctrine did not make things any easier for the Canadian Army. In fact, it tended to make the problem look irresolvable.

The Militia languished in benign neglect. The army was content to leave it maladministered and poorly equipped for whatever role was assigned – whether war or national survival. The army's own assessments of the Militia in the first half of the decade should put paid to the allegation that the Militia was wrecked by being tasked with the national survival role. It was already in an advanced state of disrepair. The usual explanation that the Militia could not be changed because of political influence should also be treated with caution; for example, George Pearkes changed its role almost completely. A more likely explanation is that the army really did not want to change the Militia very much. Making it more effective and better administered would draw resources away from the Regular Force, which was now the primary ground force. Making the Militia smaller and more efficient would detract from the army's goal of becoming a big army. It needed to have a manpower pool it could point to that could potentially fill the ranks, even if there were known weaknesses.

The army also missed an opportunity to bond with the new Canada that was emerging after the Second World War. Even as educational levels in society steadily increased, the army clung to the belief that "officer-like qualities" were what mattered most, and it actually decreased educational qualifications for entry into officership for the combat arms. Missing the opportunity that Foulkes pointed out to become one of the education-based rising elites in the country would haunt the army until the end of the century.

CHAPTER TWO

Soldiers, Civilians, and Nuclear Warfare in the 1960s

DURING THE 1960S, NUCLEAR weapons played a prominent role in Canadian politics. In June 1957, John Diefenbaker and the Conservative Party came to power after almost twenty years of unbroken Liberal rule. Diefenbaker did not like the military and did not trust the Department of External Affairs, which he thought was filled with too many "Pearsonalities" and links to the Liberal Party. He combined anglophilism and anti-Americanism in an uneasy mix that led to strained foreign relations all around. His opposition to Britain's bid to enter the European Common Market led D.I. Macpherson, the political cartoonist of the *Toronto Star,* to portray him as a mad scientist concocting a brew of anti-British trade and anti-American defence, drinking it, and transforming into ... Charles de Gaulle.

Diefenbaker began his term by acceding to the North American Air Defence Agreement with the United States, accepting that it was vital that Canada assist in protecting American nuclear deterrent forces. After that, however, nuclear policy became increasingly vexed. Diefenbaker was forced to cancel the over-budget and out-of-control Avro Arrow inceptor project, but the abrupt manner in which the cancellation was handled, throwing thousands of engineering and production staff out of work, became a nationalist *cause célèbre.* The government decided to replace interceptor aircraft with the US-manufactured Bomarc missiles, but these required nuclear warheads to be effective. The government deadlocked over whether to accept nuclear warheads for the Bomarcs and other systems and fell into a state of prolonged dithering. Diefenbaker caused already-strained relations with the Americans to break down completely by his delay in bringing Canadian air defences to the highest alert state during the Cuban Missile Crisis. Nuclear weapons became a critical issue during the 1963 election, which the Conservatives lost to the Liberal Party led by Lester Pearson.

The Pearson government accepted nuclear armament, but only reluctantly. Relations with the United States improved somewhat, but the level of American investment in Canada alarmed nationalists and led to a crisis when the United

States considered restrictions to solve its own economic problems. Intensification of the war in Vietnam, which the Pearson government viewed as a mistake, also caused tensions between the two North American countries. After Canadian peace initiatives failed, public opinion turned against the war. There was limited enthusiasm in Canada for either hot or cold war.

Nuclear weapons were not only a political issue; the introduction of nuclear weapons to the defence of Europe also created two sets of problems for the Canadian Army and for armies in general. First, the destructive power of tactical nuclear weapons meant that new tactics were required. The Canadian Army's first attempts had not resulted in solutions but had created the institutional framework required to develop more viable doctrine and plans. During the 1960s, the army would use its new combat development processes in attempting to resolve the tactical problems of nuclear warfare. Second, while soldiers became increasingly engaged in figuring out how to fight a nuclear war, the civilian policy community became increasingly doubtful of the contribution of armies to NATO security and, at the same time, more fearful of the possibility of a nuclear holocaust resulting from the confrontation between NATO and the Warsaw Pact. Nuclear weapons, which had previously been regarded as an unremarkable evolution in firepower, became a politically toxic and divisive issue. As these trends developed, it appeared that the army and the political leadership were travelling on parallel tracks, with minimal exchange between the two parties. The army became totally committed to the NATO role, whereas the political leadership fragmented into segments that totally supported NATO and its nuclear strategy, those that supported the alliance but not the nuclear role, and those that doubted the utility of the alliance itself. For the army, the 1960s was about the search for solutions to the tactical and strategic problems of nuclear arms.

Strategic Thinking, 1960-63

NATO's nuclear strategy was plagued from the beginning with political and military contradictions. Both the 1956 version – MC 48 – and its subsequent refinement in 1957 in MC 14/2 were based on massive retaliation. These policies conceptualized a war in Europe in two phases, with widespread use of nuclear weapons in the first phase followed by conventional warfare in the second phase. As noted earlier in connection with George Pearkes's reaction, the possibility of a second, conventional phase lacked credibility. Exercises indicated that NATO commanders would be forced to use nuclear weapons early to deal with Soviet forces that outnumbered theirs, and the resulting nuclear exchange would be devastating. Nevertheless, the NATO nations could not afford enough ground troops to provide an effective forward defence, and therefore had to rely on nuclear weapons.

NATO policies became increasingly dependent on the use of nuclear weapons, although ground forces were intended to be able to fight both nuclear and conventional war. Beyond the question of affordability of sufficient conventional forces to meet a Soviet attack, politics also played a role in NATO strategy. Germany did not believe that anything short of massive retaliation could dissuade the Soviet Union. There was also concern that a decoupling of the US strategic deterrent from NATO defence would be the first step in American abandonment of Europe.

The final step in the nuclearization of NATO forces occurred after the December 1957 adoption of a plan known as MC 70, which entailed the integration of nuclear delivery systems – including artillery, surface-to-surface missiles, and anti-aircraft missiles – into the shield forces. These weapons were intended to be tactical and for use only in defending the NATO area. As noted in Chapter 1, MC 70 tasked the Supreme Allied Commander Europe (SACEUR) with being prepared to defend against any type of incursion, with or without using nuclear weapons.[1]

The Canadian Army's doctrine and combat development staffs published definitive policy documents in 1960 and 1961. The first document was doctrinal: *The Infantry Brigade Group in Battle – Tactics* (CAMT1-8),[2] which was all about how to fight a nuclear war. It considered nuclear weapons "dominant," even when present but not employed. Infantry was merely the facilitator for a nuclear strike: "In nuclear war the main roles of formations and units will be to create the conditions for the effective use of nuclear weapons and the exploitation of their effects." Combat units were to compel the enemy to concentrate and become nuclear targets while remaining dispersed and concealed themselves. Mobility and digging in were both recognized as protective measures. *The Infantry Brigade Group in Battle* stated that protective measures, "although essential to survival on the nuclear battlefield, are passive and will not win battles. To win battles the initiative must be seized and tactical domination established through the use of nuclear weapons in mobile operations, based on the principles of attack and evasion. Offensive operations by hard hitting mobile battle groups of all arms exploiting the use of nuclear weapons, will then complete the destruction of the enemy."

Soviet parity in nuclear weapons was expected, and Soviet superiority in armoured fighting vehicles, artillery, personnel, and close air support was assumed. Soviet tactics were defined as deep strike, surprise, mobility, and shock action by armour supported by air and artillery. NATO tactical nuclear weapons were assumed to be a primary target, but the overall Soviet goal would be penetration followed by a complete breakthrough. To counter this, the army called for anti-armour in great depth, ground- and air-delivered nuclear and conventional weapons to break mass attacks, intelligence to enable the destruction of the enemy's headquarters and nuclear delivery systems, adequate air defence, reliable communications, and a strong, mobile reserve, heavy in armour.

NATO doctrine did not allow much room for thinking about air support to a brigade group. Tactical aviation was controlled at a much higher level and would initially be committed to theatre air strikes and reconnaissance. The brigade group would therefore operate under the threat of enemy air strikes in the opening phase of a war. Once the initial phase was over, "the amount of air support available will depend on the success achieved by our air forces in winning the air battle." Within the brigade group, air defence was limited to small arms and passive measures. There was no discussion of close air support per se.

The doctrine recognized that morale was going to be a problem. Wider dispersion and isolation, lack of information, and fear of the unknown would be coupled with "chaotic conditions following a nuclear burst, mass casualties and panic of civilian populations." Leadership at the unit and subunit level would therefore be a key to success. *The Infantry Brigade Group in Battle* counselled that "the dogged determination to hang on in the face of catastrophe and the indomitable will to win must be engendered down to the last man in the smallest fighting sub-unit."

Finally, it was admitted that the lack of cross-country mobility and small-arms protection provided by the wheeled vehicles in use would limit the ability of the brigade group to manoeuvre and would limit speed and shock in the attack. Nevertheless, the doctrine called for "maximum momentum" in carrying out deep penetrations following NATO nuclear strikes.

The second volume of the manual, *Administration,* was reproduced directly from the British Army manual of the same name.[3] Faced with nuclear attack, it put on a brave face: "It is easy, when considering the effect of nuclear weapons, to conclude that the destruction of ports, theatre stocks, centres of communication and methods of movement will be such that maintenance will virtually cease." Nevertheless, the Soviets did not have an unlimited number of nuclear weapons and had many targets. Moreover, NATO would likely take out a portion of the Soviet nuclear arsenal. The manual reasoned that "the administrative system clearly cannot be based on the assumption that it will be reduced to impotence by nuclear attacks but it would be folly to disregard the threat." Exactly how support was to be conducted was not clearly explained.

The *Administration* manual dealt with the morale issue somewhat differently from *Tactics.* Mere regimental pride was not enough. Soldiers had to look smart: "A smart soldier believes in the merit of looking smart because he gets a mental kick out of it or because he feels that by not looking smart he is letting down his friends, his unit or his girl."

The Infantry Brigade Group in Battle was more of a problem statement than a solution. Nuclear fires were the NATO solution to Soviet qualitative equivalence and quantitative superiority. Dispersion and manoeuvre were obviously going to be required, but whether this could be achieved effectively was unclear. Whether units could be controlled on the nuclear battlefield was problematic, existing transport was inadequate to support tactics, and air support was not to be counted on.

The combat developers, looking at a future at least five years distant rather than the present, were not much more optimistic. The first major product of the combat development process was *The Canadian Army 1966-70 Tactical and Logistic Concept*, completed in August 1961. Based on the *ABC [America – Britain – Canada] Armies Operational Concept 1966-70*, the *1966-70 Concept* was a comprehensive and detailed plan for the Canadian Army. It was deeply pessimistic in that it assumed that NATO forces would be facing Soviet armies just as well armed and much more numerous than the NATO defenders. Canadian society was dedicated to the dignity and preservation of the individual, and the combat developers believed that "this type of society does not usually produce hard, rugged soldiers." However, without any other advantage, tactical leadership was the "only real resource" remaining. The concept called for careful leadership selection, strenuous training, and ruthless elimination methods.

On the material side of the battle, the concept envisaged waves of Soviet forces driving forward, attempting to overwhelm the defenders. Anticipating the US Army's AirLand Battle by twenty years, the combat developers identified the need to strike deep into the enemy support zone to stop, divert, or damage reinforcements and to blind the enemy's target acquisition systems. Unfortunately, the provision of air support was still unresolved. Modern aircraft were regarded as too fast to allow pilots to provide close air support and the ground battle too confused to permit adequate control. The concept therefore limited close air support to "general support tasks" and shuffled it off for further study.[4]

The concept called for reconnaissance forces to be equipped with an amphibious light tank, an amphibious armoured personnel carrier (APC), and a scout vehicle with effective communications. In particular, it called for helicopter reconnaissance:

> Never before have we had the ability to move quickly over the nap of the ground as is now provided by the helicopter. With it the general search of large areas can be conducted rapidly. The air has never really been properly integrated into our reconnaissance activities. Air forces have used aircraft which were not particularly suited for gathering the type of information required by lower commanders ...

> Never have we had an air element truly integrated with our reconnaissance forces. In the recce unit proposed, helicopters have been closely integrated with the ground recce detachments.

The concept was similar to existing doctrine in that attack was to be carried out by small combat groups. These groups would be integrated tank/infantry companies of about two hundred men. They would be organized around a small headquarters, three APC-borne infantry platoons, two tank troops of four tanks each, a heavy mortar section, an anti-tank section, and a logistics section. The heavy mortar section would have sub-kiloton nuclear mortar rounds or, failing that, the US Davy Crockett nuclear weapon. The anti-tank section would have a rapid-fire gun, possibly 20 millimetres, and up to eighteen anti-tank missiles. These would be mounted on a tracked, armoured carrier.

It went further by describing attacks as not "tip and run" but full-shock action followed by disengagement to prevent unacceptable retaliation. The aim was to paralyze the enemy by imposing confusion and attacking his control systems. The combat developers believed that numerically inferior forces had no better choice, and that they could not afford to stand toe-to-toe and slug it out with Soviet forces. They commented: "In the face of the enemy's quantitative, and in some cases qualitative, superiority we must exploit our chief resource – our ability to react faster. This can best be done in a fast-moving, seemingly untidy situation where we keep control but force the enemy to lose his."

The 1966-70 Concept represented an advance in process over its 1950s predecessors. It was comprehensive and more disciplined in its approach and was less prone to being victimized by the pet ideas of senior officers. It also contained flashes of real insight regarding the importance of deep battle at the theatre level and the need for, and advantage of, real-time information regarding the disposition of one's own troops. It advocated a "tidy battlefield," made so by electronic position reporting of all vehicles.[5] However, the army remained chained to Canada's commitment to fight a nuclear war in Europe, no matter how unfeasible that was. The problem was solved by taking it off the table. Other problems, such as close air support, could not be solved by the army because NATO air forces (including Canada's) were not interested in maintaining suitable aircraft, and a single nation could not unilaterally alter NATO's air power doctrine – especially if its own air force saw no need to change it. Supreme Headquarters Allied Powers Europe (SHAPE) had so little interest in close air support that it had no doctrine. When Canadian officers questioned this, they were invited to undertake their own study.[6] Ultimately, the army accepted a concept that pinned its hopes on superior leadership.

Unfortunately, it did not have much of an idea of how to develop the superior leadership skills that both the concept and existing doctrine relied upon. The concept was based on small, company-sized groups fighting autonomously on a dispersed battlefield. This increased the need for improvisation at the company level, and for officers who would display greater degrees of opportunism, subtlety, and deception in engaging the enemy. At the brigade level, commanders experienced information overload from having to coordinate more units at a faster pace of decision making. Neither current training nor personnel selection appeared geared towards producing the required type of combat leader. The army's social scientists asked: "Can the rigid authority structure of the army, designed to produce groups tailored to meet predictable situations in more or less standard ways, function flexibly enough in peacetime to develop and maintain the kind of cohesive, autonomous groups and the delegated leadership needed to ensure quick action and group survival in battle crises when the objectives may be clear, but the means confused, or clear only to the leader?" Although the status quo was no longer acceptable, the social scientists believed that it was "unrealistic" to expect the army to make any radical change.[7]

It was only when the staff was released from the constraints of reality that the picture improved substantially. Simultaneous with the publication of the *1966-70 Concept*, the army released its *Post-1970 Operational Study.*[8] The study's objective was "to stimulate thought among present day soldiers," and its authors in the Directorate of Combat Development hastened to add that it did not have the status of a "concept." In it, the navy's prime role became the transport and support of a strategic (i.e., land) force, while the air force would shift resources from defence against manned aircraft to large, fast strategic transport aircraft. According to the study's authors, "the new strategic environment enhances the role of the land forces. They are now [post-1970] the prime means of applying force." The authors claimed that because the land forces were more flexible, better able to support a flexible foreign policy, and less expensive, they should be the basic element of any non-nuclear or United Nations force.

Internally, the authors foresaw an army that was fully mechanized and as air-mobile as possible. The combat arms would disappear as distinct entities and merge into an "integrated elite force with which to achieve decision on the battlefield." Once an integrated land force had been achieved, "integration of the Services [was] the logical follow-up." An army of 75,000 to 100,000 was envisaged, with a field force of two or more identical components, each of which could be airlifted to any part of the globe and conduct mobile operations "utilizing surprise, speed and firepower."

The study does not appear to have engendered much debate within the army. Non-NATO operations were not high on the army's priority list since "the meeting of these commitments inevitably detract[ed] from the Army's ability to fulfill its [NATO] wartime tasks." Because it was not considered feasible to accurately forecast non-NATO requirements, there was little incentive to do more than hold a contingency force at a higher state of readiness than would otherwise be required.[9] The study, however, was a first attempt to articulate a role for the army outside of the NATO Central Front. The army would be global and mobile, and somehow in support of an undefined Canadian foreign policy. Furthermore, it would stand at the pinnacle of a unified armed service, with the navy and air force reduced to supporting roles. The study did not comment on the NATO role one way or another, or attempt to define how mechanized a force could actually be before it ceased to be air-mobile, or how heavy an air-mobile force needed to be in order to operate against a sophisticated enemy. What is important is that the search had begun for a more appealing role than engaging in nuclear warfare on the Central Front.

MC 70 did eventually require the government to increase Canadian troop strength in Europe and re-equip the brigade group. The 11,571-personnel increase in the authorized strength of the army enabled it to bring 4 Canadian Infantry Brigade Group (4CIBG) in Europe and field force units in Canada up to their war establishments, and to form a Divisional Headquarters and Signals Unit.[10] Lieutenant-General Geoffrey Walsh, the chief of the general staff, ordered the 1 Canadian Infantry Divisional Headquarters stood up on 1 September 1962, along with the Army Tactics and Organization Board (ATOB). He made the Divisional Headquarters responsible not only for command of the division in war but also for the planning and analysis of divisional organization, including the study of all arms and services in light of new concepts, doctrine, and new equipment. The Divisional Headquarters was authorized to conduct studies to define tactical doctrine and to determine the method of command and control within the division. The ATOB would consist of the same staff as the Divisional Headquarters, and its work would occupy them during periods when the headquarters was not active. The ATOB would report to the CGS through a new Combat Development and Tactical Doctrine Committee (CDTDC) and would be responsible for conducting studies to determine tactics, doctrine, and equipment requirements. It would also provide input to war games and operations research studies and supervise field trials, experiments, and troop tests. Brigadier Roger Rowley was appointed to command both the Divisional Headquarters and the ATOB and was promoted to major-general. He would prove to be one of the most dynamic and forward-thinking senior army officers over the entire decade.[11]

The creation of the Divisional Headquarters and its organizational merger with the ATOB meant that the army was now totally focused on its NATO role and that "big army" and heavy forces were to be central. In October 1962, Walsh convened an Army Tactical Symposium of general officers to plot the way forward. After several days of discussion, he concluded that the anti-tank capability of the army must be improved. This might be done in a number of ways: by increasing the ratio of tanks to infantry, by making the infantry more capable of defending positions without the aid of armour, or by creating special anti-tank units at the brigade or division level. Walsh ordered the design of a division of three balanced brigades. The division needed adequate anti-tank capability and had to be able to fight at night. Although an increase in armour appeared inevitable, he wanted to make the best use of anti-tank guided missiles and surveillance equipment. He ordered the consolidation of all logistic elements into service battalions within each brigade, the consolidation of all aviation into a single unit at the division level, and the capping of the overall strength of the division at nineteen thousand personnel. This would prevent formations from becoming too cumbersome, and also enable the army to stay within budget. Walsh warned his commanders and staff that "organizations arrived at and recommended must be realistic and compatible with limitations of manpower, equipments and funds. The forces in being are those that are required to meet our requirement. We must get the optimum organizations within this framework." He also warned them to keep disputes within bounds: "There will be one party line. There are dangers inherent with ifs and buts which lead to negative result. We must go firm with the best solutions we can find even though they may not have the 100 percent solution."[12] The CDTDC subsequently tasked the ATOB with conducting studies on how the division (and hence the entire army) should be organized.[13]

Major-General Rowley led the design of "Division 1965" and completed the entire project in less than a year, including carrying out the field trials that Walsh and Vice Chief of the General Staff Major-General J.P.E. Bernatchez had ordered, as well as a series of supporting war games and operations research studies. He structured the studies by branch, but recognized that integrating the results of separate arms studies would be difficult. He therefore also commissioned a series of "function studies" of fire support, anti-tank defence, reconnaissance and surveillance, the infantry/armour relationship, air defence, aviation, and logistics. He brought these together through formal conferences at key points. The pragmatism of Walsh, the professionalism of Rowley, and the speed at which they worked stand in sharp contrast to later attempts by the army to develop forces and doctrine.[14]

Many of the major decisions regarding the composition of Division 1965 were made at the coordinating conferences, which Rowley chaired and took an active part in. The minutes show that there was lively give-and-take among the staff. Nowhere was this more apparent than in the debate over the infantry/armour relationship. Most of the ATOB staff and external branch representatives were not in favour of integrating armour and infantry into a single tactical unit. The main objection was that it would not make efficient use of armour resources and would be inflexible. Rowley simply did not think that the infantry could move without armour support, and that it was unlikely that the infantry would ever be in a position where tanks could not be usefully employed. Left to himself, he would have created a single land combat branch with soldiers cross-trained in infantry and armour tactics. Not only would this create a more flexible fighting force but it would also reduce overhead costs in schools, the command structure, and elsewhere. In the end, Rowley was forced to admit that the amalgamation of the armour and infantry branches could not be achieved by 1965 and that the changes required were "too vast" to accomplish in the short term. He decided that this would be presented only as an option in the final study.[15]

The coordinating conferences also recognized the need to build a force with significant conventional power. The Canadian Army Operations Research Establishment (CAORE) staff and some of the arms representatives argued that insufficient attention was being paid to the doctrine that nuclear weapons were supposed to be the main striking force. The ops researchers maintained that almost 90 percent of enemy casualties in war games had been inflicted by nuclear weapons, and that the proposed divisional structure should take this into account. Rowley simply disagreed, telling the staff that if they structured for nuclear war and were forced to fight a conventional battle the army "would have no hope." He insisted not only on conventional combat capability but also on the organizational integration of tanks and infantry. If the infantry could not survive without tanks, there was no justification for not giving them to the infantry on a permanent basis. There was no consensus, however, on how the infantry and tanks should be mixed together.[16]

The final Division 1965 report was far-reaching in its conclusions. Rowley's team concluded that neither current doctrine, as expressed in CAMT1-8, nor the *1966-70 Concept* was sound. CAMT1-8 stated that "the initiative must be seized and tactical domination established through the use of nuclear weapons in mobile operations based on the principles of attack and evasion ... any form of static defence ... must be avoided." The concept decreed: "There will be no static deployments: all actions will be mobile ... the enemy's tremendous fire-power makes it no longer possible for us to employ static or even semi-static deployments." Yet,

Rowley pointed out, both documents and the British doctrinal manual, *The Land Battle,* referred to the need to "stabilize, contain and delineate" the enemy. The Canadian documents referred to the increased importance of digging, prepared rifle positions, covering obstacles by fire, and the need to occupy ground. According to Rowley, "our tactical manuals, in describing the methods which will be adopted to fight the mobile battle, explain what are essentially static deployments when translated into action. This is confirmed by the way in which we conduct operations on exercises, where most of the time units are part of a static deployment." He concluded that "mobility is a relative concept."

Rowley reduced "stabilize, contain and delineate" to "stop" the enemy. To do this, he based Division 1965 on the need to conduct a more static style of warfare with greater dependence on conventional weapons. He rejected the concept that "we have then a picture of relatively small self-contained combat units embodying elements of all the arms and services rapidly moving about the battlefield; blocking, feinting, manoeuvring, backing off, dashing through gaps – at all times engaging in a pitched fire fight only when absolutely necessary." Rather, he saw "a vastly more determined and more concentrated application of fire." He also did not have much faith that tactical nuclear weapons would be decisive. While there appeared to be a consensus among military planners that nuclear weapons were dominant, there was other thinking about employing a graduated response, and even of ninety days of conventional war. Nuclear weapons were largely under the control of the US president and it was uncertain their use would be authorized or, if authorized, would be decisive. There was therefore an unquestioned need for conventional artillery and "substantial elements" of the other conventional arms. The ATOB did not accept that the idea that dispersion motivated by the need for nuclear safety was tactically sound.

Based on the operations research studies conducted, Rowley concluded that there was an "urgent requirement" to increase the tank strength in Canadian formations by 70 percent, the minimum acceptable ratio being ten tanks per infantry company. Even this was dependent on maintaining high anti-tank capability throughout the division. The CAORE studies and field trials indicated that anti-tank guided missiles (ATGMs) were not as accurate as their manufacturers claimed and had a first-round hit probability about the same as a tank gun, but without the mobility and protection of a tank. Although compatible with tanks, ATGMs mounted on vehicles would have to seek different fire positions, would not be as well protected, and would have a lower volume of fire. Improvements in tank guns also meant that the range of NATO tanks was at least equal to that of Soviet tanks. CAORE concluded that the tank was the most cost-effective anti-tank weapon.

The ATOB took a strong stand on increasing the proportion of armour but poured considerable water in its wine elsewhere, finding the Honest John tactical nuclear rocket (an unguided, truck-mounted missile with a range of about fifteen miles and an explosive yield of two to thirty kilotons) deficient for supporting divisional operations because of slow response time and poor accuracy. The CGS ruled out nuclear cannon for the Canadian Army, however. A large heavy artillery component would not fit within the nineteen-thousand-personnel cap, so Rowley consigned nuclear artillery to British and American corps support and to further study.

The ATOB also concluded that the division required an aviation wing of 104 aircraft, including reconnaissance helicopters, utility and medium-transport helicopters, light helicopters for artillery direction, and fixed wing Mohawk aircraft for surveillance. No air defence organization was included in the division because it also would cause the division to exceed its personnel ceiling; in addition, the candidate air defence missile – the Mauler – was considered to be a corps-level resource and, in any case, would not be available by 1965.

Finally, the ATOB commented on the nuclear/chemical/biological warfare (NCBW) decontamination requirements of the division. The Canadian Army had no capacity above the unit level, and the study recommended the creation of bath and decontamination platoons in the division. There was also a need to institute realistic training as there was no collective training in NCBW at the unit level or higher: "Collective training should be incorporated into tactical exercises, for the benefit of all units and specialist personnel. The Russians do this, apparently to good effect. If it does not get done, the problem gets pushed into the background, the equipment remains in stores, fresh needs are unknown, and early training is forgotten." Rowley recommended exercises simulating chemical attack on a battle group, a battle group that had passed through a radioactive area, and a brigade under threat of chemical attack.

Division 1965 was an extremely well done study that included all the planning staffs and senior command elements of the army. Yet it raised some troubling issues. It called into question the basic premises of both current doctrine and the concept for the future that had been agreed upon. It strongly suggested that the hallowed regimental system was not the optimum basis for organizing the army and that the infantry and armour branches should eventually be merged. It called for a budget-straining number of tanks, and for artillery, air defence, and aviation components that were unaffordable. While the army's staff system had never worked better, the results called into question the army's organization and its capability to perform its prime mission. Rowley had clearly failed to meet Walsh's directive that staff plans be realistic from a budgetary perspective. Either the budget or the staff assessment of the requirement was wrong. Division 1965 made the "commitment/capability gap" of the 1960s all too apparent.

Within a year the ATOB was instructed to prepare a divisional doctrine manual compatible with allied armies, but for a Canadian organization. VCGS Bernatchez directed that the manual deal primarily with "modern" or "conventional" war – that is, under nuclear threat rather than exclusively on the assumption that use of nuclear weapons was inevitable. He believed that although the United States and Britain thought it highly probable that a war in Europe would be nuclear, this looked less likely in other theatres. Apparently out of touch with American doctrinal development, Bernatchez speculated that the US Army was already working on non-nuclear doctrine and directed the director general of military training to find out what was going on.[17] Rowley expressed some skepticism regarding this, but Bernatchez was correct. After several years of preliminary work, the US Army had authorized the study of a "Reorganization Objectives Army Division" (ROAD). President John F. Kennedy informed Congress that the army needed divisions with greater conventional firepower, greater mobility, and the flexibility to fight in any environment, and that he had authorized reorganization in May 1961.[18] There were many similarities between the US ROAD and the Canadian Army *1966-70 Concept:* both were heavily mechanized, both focused on destruction of enemy forces rather than occupation of ground, both envisaged nuclear weapons at the manoeuvre unit level, and both incorporated helicopters. There were differences, however. ROAD was based on the battalion as the manoeuvre unit, whereas the *1966-70 Concept* was based on a two-hundred-man combat team. Equally important was the difference in the use of helicopters. Whereas the US Army placed great emphasis on using the helicopter for mobility and vertical envelopment, the Canadian Army saw it only as a reconnaissance vehicle. Bernatchez and his colleagues on the CDTDC would continue to have grave doubts about the survivability of helicopters in air-mobile operations in enemy territory and would attempt to persuade the Americans to reduce their emphasis on air-mobile operations.[19]

While the army worked on organizing itself for nuclear warfare in Central Europe, or at least for fighting under the threat of nuclear war, Canadian and NATO war games called the basic premises of the army's plans into question. Even when military targets and the battlefield were restricted to Central Europe, NATO war games would go nuclear in the first couple of days and result in 3-7 million NATO civilian casualties immediately, and 18-19 million NATO civilian fatalities if fallout was included. Throughout the 1960s, NATO leaders assumed that they would have to rely on nuclear weapons.[20] In Canada, CAORE completed a comprehensive study of corps- and brigade-level war games carried out from 1958 to 1961.[21] Canadian doctrine based defence on a natural obstacle, such as a river, which would cause Soviet forces to bunch up and present a nuclear target. In war games, this would result in a "massive nuclear exchange" with very heavy casualties on both sides. The operations researchers concluded: "The battles in these games, with their rapidly accumulating nuclear casualties indicate that a coherent doctrine – in which the enemy is forced to react to our manoeuvres and is finally 'contained' and destroyed by nuclear fire, while the defence suffers relatively light casualties – is not consistently feasible." Both sides would usually suffer one-third casualties and become ineffective within twenty-four to forty-eight hours. Combat became a roll of the dice, with a narrow margin between victory and defeat. Attempts to avoid being struck by moving units frequently did not work because troops then gave up cover. Trying to reduce vulnerability by spreading out troops on the ground led to loss of control. Researchers concluded that the outcome of nuclear battle was predetermined to a greater degree than conventional war, and was, in fact, decided solely by the number of nuclear weapons available. They considered that 4CIBG had only half the number of Honest John nuclear rocket launchers required, and called for increasing the brigade's capability so that it could fire twenty-five nuclear rounds. Other units within the brigade could be decreased to accomplish this. They estimated that infantry – even mounted in APCs – would be less effective than in the Second World War, and only half as effective as armoured troops on a man-to-man basis. The value of engineers had increased, but planners could count on losses triple those suffered in the Second World War. Overall, a brigade group with two to three Honest John batteries versus the one actually deployed, fighting with similarly armed NATO allies, could prevent the initial wave of Soviet forces from penetrating Western Europe, but could not keep the follow-on forces out.

As for non-nuclear combat, studies of the ABC (America-Britain-Canada) Armies' Operational Concept concluded that in order to crush the enemy at decisive points and then disengage, tanks and APC-borne infantry with effective anti-tank weapons were required. No such anti-tank weapon existed, and Canadian tanks could not swim obstacles without elaborate preparation. Combat Development staff informed the VCGS that "war games conducted by CAORE have shown that our NATO brigade is completely incapable at the present time and with current equipment of conducting protracted operations against typical USSR groupings that are currently in the USSR order of battle unless more tank support is added." They recommended eight tanks per infantry company. Moreover, the ratio of three infantry battalions to one tank regiment appeared inadequate to provide both infantry support and heavy manoeuvre forces. A 3:2 ratio was recommended – the same as a Soviet motor rifle regiment.[22]

As in the 1950s, the army mostly ignored the results of war games and worked on refining minor tactics and doctrine. In a way, it had few alternatives. The government had committed it to NATO's Central Front (albeit with its agreement) and at brigade group strength it was too minor a force from too small a country to influence NATO strategy overall. The army had become myopically fixated on the NATO role, however. Serving it required almost the entire energy of the doctrine and planning staffs and senior leadership. Not a lot of capacity remained for thinking about the problems that could not be solved except by changing the army's assignment. Nor did there appear to be much effort made in discussing these problems with ministers. The parting of ways continued, and the civil-military gap widened.

Civilians and Nuclear Weapons

Civilian decision makers in the Canadian government did not share the army's enthusiasm for its nuclear mission on NATO's Central Front. While they generally supported NATO, their concept of what that support should consist of differed significantly from the views of the army and the armed services in general. To begin with, civilian politicians and senior bureaucrats had to be concerned with military expenditure as an important call on resources for which there was not a great deal of public support. Following the Second World War, both social and defence program costs increased well beyond their prewar levels. Defence spending peaked in 1952-53 at $1.882 billion, 43.4 percent of the total federal budget. By 1960, this had declined to about $1.6 billion, or around 25 percent of the budget, where it stabilized. Unfortunately, the economy weakened beginning in 1957, with industrial production dropping 6 percent and unemployment rising to 7.5 percent, leading to six years of weak economic performance. Internally, the defence budget suffered from inflation, which eroded 40 percent of its purchasing power between 1952 and 1962. Personnel, operations, and maintenance costs increased from 45 percent of the budget to almost 78 percent. Between rising capital costs and increasing operating expenses, the ability to buy new equipment declined by 75 percent.[23] Externally, defence expenditure had to compete with both social programs and the rising cost of servicing the federal deficit. Social programs enacted before and during the war, including child benefits and family allowances, limited pensions, and unemployment insurance, were increasing in cost during the term of the Conservative government elected in 1957. Pressure for increased social spending grew because the defeated Liberals made social programs their main policy plank and a fundamental part of their plan to retake power. The mission on the Central Front in Europe required expensive heavy equipment, and cost alone raised questions in the minds of the political leadership of both parties.

The military's standing as a manager of money was not enhanced by the report of the Royal Commission on Government Organization, usually referred to as the Glassco Commission after its chair, J. Grant Glassco. The defence study team was led by retired Air Vice-Marshal Frank S. McGill, and included Brigadier Earle R. Suttie and Captain (N) Eugène F. Noël, both retired, plus a civil servant seconded from National Defence. Their 1963 report noted the unprecedented size and cost of the peacetime military, with 125,000 Regular military and 50,000 civilians. The report criticized the growth of administrative tail, which the commissioners believed had grown disproportionately. It also faulted the armed services for lack of coordination and integration of support services, and found that the two hundred standing committees used to manage the services "permit[ed] procrastination." Military personnel cost 10 to 18 percent more than civilian labour, but there was excessive resistance to civilianization of jobs. The report stated: "It is open to question whether it is in the national interest to employ such a large number of uniformed personnel in tasks that could be performed by civilians at less cost."[24] It said that procurement and materiel management were inefficient, and called the results of the study both "disturbing," because of the inefficiency found, and "encouraging," because of the possible savings. National Defence policy called for no more than three months' worth of stock to be held and no more than one year's worth to be purchased at one time. Yet the commissioners found that the army had an 83-year supply of flashlights and a 197-year supply of black coveralls, size 1. They estimated that annual inventory management savings of 10 percent could be achieved. Certainly the report did nothing to build sympathy for expensive military programs.

Expense alone was not at the root of civilian concern over Canada's NATO role, however. Canada had committed itself to nuclear defence policies by degrees and without systematic analysis. Pulled along by NATO policies such as MC 48, both the Cabinet Defence Committee and the Chiefs of Staff Committee considered the acquisition of nuclear arms in late 1956 and early 1957. Nuclear weapons themselves were not controversial, and the main concerns were over sovereignty issues raised by control of the warheads supplied by the United States. On 20 February 1959 Prime Minister John Diefenbaker formalized the decision to acquire nuclear weapons. Referring to the RCAF's Bomarc air defence missiles and the Honest John surface-to-surface missiles acquired by the army, he noted that "the full potential of these defensive weapons is achieved only when they are armed with nuclear warheads." Diefenbaker stated that the government was confident it could work out weapons control arrangements with the United States.[25]

The appointment of Howard Green – a man horrified by the prospect of nuclear war – as secretary of state for external affairs and Diefenbaker's own growing conviction that the majority of Canadians opposed nuclear weapons stopped the slide towards nuclear acquisition. By 1960 no final decision had been made and no timetable for implementation had been accepted by the government. National Defence began to develop a position supporting acquisition, but it took until 1961 for its strategy to be articulated by the joint staff, in a paper that dismissed concerns that Canadian acquisition would enlarge the nuclear club, that it would impair Canadian disarmament efforts, that it would sacrifice sovereignty, or that it would reduce Canadian diplomatic influence. National Defence argued that Canada's disarmament focus was inconsistent with her sales of uranium, purchase of nuclear delivery systems, and membership in NATO, a nuclear alliance. Moreover, it contended that Canada's interest lay not with non-aligned nations but with the West, and that refusal of nuclear arms would damage its reputation and influence with countries that shared its political and ideological heritage.[26]

The Department of External Affairs did not share the military's views on nuclear weapons. The under-secretary, Norman Robertson, believed that Canadian acquisition of nuclear weapons would bring the world that much closer to disaster, and therefore External Affairs needed to oppose the policy. The department agreed only reluctantly with negotiations to allow the Americans to store nuclear weapons in Canada, and convinced Cabinet to withdraw approval for a 1959 US Strategic Air Command (SAC) war game that would have temporarily shut down civil aviation in Canada to test electronic countermeasures. In December 1960 Robertson sent Green a memo that outlined his thoughts on the nuclear issue. It would be "inconsistent and hypocritical" for Canada to adopt policies that would "compound" the nuclear problem. He did not favour the ongoing discussions with the United States, as they implied an ultimate intention to acquire the weapons. He was also critical of an agreement allowing American storage of weapons in Canada, as it would appear to be a first step to actual acquisition. External Affairs began to emphasize Canada's position in disarmament negotiations and established its own disarmament division in 1961. By 1960 it had become convinced that nuclear weapons created instability and represented a grave peril because their eventual use was a virtual certainty. In December that year, Canada, over National Defence objections, supported an Irish resolution at the United Nations calling upon the nuclear powers to declare a moratorium on nuclear weapons, and upon non-nuclear states to declare, on a temporary and voluntary basis, that they would not acquire nuclear weapons.[27]

Within the Privy Council Office there was also opposition to the army's NATO role and, indeed, to the government's entire defence policy. In January 1960, D. Bevis Dewar,[28] then a junior Cabinet office official, wrote a paper called "The

Defence Problem," which Cabinet secretary R.B. Bryce passed on to the prime minister and later forwarded to General Foulkes, saying that it had some "useful and proactive ideas" and asking for comment. Dewar believed that the country was facing a defence policy crisis that was likely to become worse rather than better. The government was being pressured to go along with the easy acceptance of a US policy that was "sterile at best and provocative at worst." Critics urged the government to take an independent line and slash the defence budget, concentrate on foreign aid, and eventually disarm unilaterally. Behind this was the fear of nuclear annihilation and the knowledge that Canada was paying dues to a club whose policies it could not shape. Dewar concluded that disarmament must be a major goal for the government, and that "proposed defence policies in the period ahead of us must therefore be examined not only to determine whether they are the best for the purposes of defence; they must also be appropriate for a period when we are trying to achieve disarmament."[29]

Dewar dismissed Canada's NATO forces in Europe as merely proof of honouring treaty commitments rather than effective military forces. NATO's shield forces could be a "fire-brigade and a warning function," but Soviet attack would bring strategic nuclear forces into play. The real danger was that a Canadian withdrawal from Europe would put pressure on the United States to bring its troops home. He thought it unclear whether European rearmament could fill the gap of a North American withdrawal, and thought that the policy of weak conventional forces armed with nuclear weapons only reduced warning time and stability. To the extent that NATO was reliant on nuclear weapons, it was incapable of dealing with probing attacks or border incidents without escalation. He did not believe that there was any effective defence against Soviet strategic nuclear weapons, and therefore doubted that Canada should acquire either nuclear anti-aircraft or anti-submarine weapons. He proposed that the navy be given the duties of a coast guard rather than an anti-submarine warfare (ASW) role, and suggested that the CF-100 interceptor not be replaced. More useful were radar lines to give strategic US forces greater warning, and the granting of landing and refuelling rights to SAC to enable its bombers to disperse.

Dewar proposed the replacement of NATO shield forces with an international force for control and inspection, but with the capability of dealing with incidents. This force would have US and Soviet components, but no nuclear weapons. He acknowledged it would be difficult to achieve. In the meantime, he advocated pressing the United States to maintain shield forces to prevent the development of an independent European nuclear force. He suggested that there should be a moratorium on the introduction of nuclear weapons into shield forces (which would bring Canadian nuclear force development to an end) and that negotiation of mutual phased nuclear reductions should begin. He also suggested that the Canadian government consider an alternative role for the armed forces. Conflicts were likely to occur in the Middle and Far East, and it was likely that Canada would be asked to contribute peacekeeping forces if such wars were to break out. According to Dewar, "the provision of suitable standby forces in Canada for such wars should be one of the objectives of Canadian policy." Canadian forces could make the greatest contribution to the defence of the West if they concentrated on preparation for limited war. These forces should be mainly land forces and should be air-transportable.[30]

Foulkes sent the paper to the National Defence disarmament group for study. The group questioned whether there was any crisis in defence policy at all, and viewed NATO policies as a success. As Europe developed the ability to defend itself, the United States could be expected to withdraw from Europe. This would present Canada with the opportunity to realize savings or to display initiative. Defence thought it premature to dismiss anti-missile defence as impossible; at any rate, bombers should not be allowed a free ride. As for Dewar's fears of nuclear proliferation, the group pointed out that Britain already had its own nuclear weapons and it was likely that France would soon be at least a nominal nuclear power. An international force would be problematic and, without its own nuclear weapons, could not defend Western Europe against Soviet forces. The alternative was a phased withdrawal of Soviet and North American forces from Europe and the phased withdrawal of other forces to within their national borders. This would be coupled with nuclear disarmament of Germany and the Soviet satellites but the continuation of nuclear forces in Britain, France, and the Soviet Union. The group did not comment on the proposed new role for the Canadian army.[31] Foulkes never replied to Bryce, retiring as chairman of the Chiefs of Staff Committee in May 1960.[32]

Dewar may not have impressed National Defence officials but he had the substantial agreement of his boss, Cabinet secretary Bryce. Bryce made his own attempt to sort out defence policy dilemmas arising from the Great Power nuclear stalemate. In a paper that appears to have gone no further than his immediate staff, he described the problem as an alliance structure that put the honour and prestige of the United States (and especially that of the Pentagon and the State Department) behind a threat to use nuclear weapons even if the other side made only a conventional attack. Moreover, since both the United States and Soviet Union could destroy each other with their strategic forces, the military necessity for the defence of Europe no longer seemed valid. To recognize this would be "unfriendly, disturbing and impolitic," however. In Bryce's opinion, it was possible and desirable for both Canada and the United States to withdraw from NATO in the next five to eight years. Canada, he thought, could work out some useful role with other middle powers based on conventional weapons and collective security. Although Bryce's paper does not seem to have left his office, it nevertheless indicates that skepticism of NATO was a strong force outside National Defence.[33]

The Privy Council Office was not alone in its belief that the army should be given another role. The *Calgary Herald,* in a series of editorials from 29 August to 3 September 1960, concluded that "perhaps the most useful contribution Canada could make to the security of the West and the maintenance of peace would be a tightly-knit, highly-trained ground force, capable of being airlifted *in its entirety* at short notice to any spot in the world where a 'brushfire' war has broken out or is threatening to break out." This would mean not only intensifying the training of the army but also equipping the RCAF with fast long-range transport aircraft. While expensive, it would cost less than bombers. The *Herald* also advocated re-equipping fighter squadrons with "a new type of fast, fighter aircraft ... so that at least part of our home-based air force might accompany the Canadian army on these 'brushfire' missions."[34]

The government's perspective on the usefulness of the brigade in Europe can be judged by Cabinet's reaction to the Berlin Crisis during the summer of 1961. In June, Nikita Khrushchev announced that the Soviet Union intended to conclude a peace treaty with the German Democratic Republic that would undermine the right of the Western powers to occupy Berlin. Khrushchev's move resulted in East Germans flocking to West Berlin to seek asylum. The infamous Berlin Wall was the response. In August, the Soviets began an extensive series of atmospheric nuclear tests culminating in a gigantic fifty-megaton blast. Cabinet's response to the crisis was low-key. The chiefs of staff advised that the Soviets were unlikely to intentionally start a war, but one might result nevertheless. The minister, Douglas Harkness, told Cabinet that Canada had met its force goals but might consider completing agreements for the procurement of nuclear weapons and taking steps to increase defence preparedness, raise manpower ceilings, improve weapons and equipment, and evacuate dependents from Europe. Cabinet agreed to initiate civil defence measures, but to give only further consideration to bringing the brigade in Europe up to full strength. During further discussions at the height of Soviet bomb testing in August, Cabinet agreed to bring the brigade up to full strength and add not more than 15,000 more men to the Regular Force, but looked upon expansion of the army largely as a winter jobs program. The major concern with a program to employ 120,000 individuals in the Militia receiving disaster response training intended "to alleviate the unemployment situation" was that it would become known as a relief project. Ministers were cautioned that the Berlin Crisis "would be a sufficient and satisfactory explanation" for the program.[35]

The views of key civilians in the Department of External Affairs and the Privy Council Office regarding the most appropriate employment of the army were therefore quite different from those of the army itself. Some civilians were averse to nuclear weapons in any form and had become aware that membership in NATO had committed them to a nuclear warfighting strategy. Opposed to the alliance-based, heavy, nuclear-armed army that was under construction, civilians imagined an air-transportable global intervention force. The conflict between these two visions played out over the decade, with each encounter taking its toll on the army.

The arguments made by National Defence failed to convince the government of the desirability of nuclear weapons, and the breakdown in relations with the Kennedy administration during the 1962 Cuban Missile Crisis did not help. Rather than give the Americans unqualified support, Diefenbaker (with Pearson's support) called for UN inspection of Soviet activities in Cuba. He then delayed bringing Canadian elements of the North American Air Defense Command (NORAD) up to full alert, even though Defence Minister Douglas Harkness had told the chiefs of staff to do so as unobtrusively as possible. The trip to the brink lent credence to the fears of those who opposed nuclear weapons, and also damaged the credibility of the government and of the prime minister personally. The ensuing debate regarding acceptance of nuclear weapons witnessed an unsuccessful Cabinet revolt and Harkness's resignation. The Liberal Leader of the Opposition, Lester Pearson, introduced a no-confidence motion in the House of Commons and the government fell on 6 February 1963.[36]

The Liberal Party was scarcely more enthusiastic than the Conservatives about nuclear arms. Since 1961 its policy had been to oppose nuclear weapons for Canada's NORAD forces and to accept them in NATO only if they were under collective NATO control. John Gellner, the defence correspondent of the Toronto *Globe and Mail* and an adviser to Pearson and Paul Hellyer on defence matters, called the situation created by the Diefenbaker government's dilatory policy a "vexing difficulty" for the Liberals. The Liberals had rejected the government's policy, but for the sake of relations with Canada's allies would be forced to continue with nuclear weapons until policy could be changed by negotiation. Seeing the government's continued drift and sensing the mood of the country, Pearson stated in a speech on 12 January 1963 that he "was ashamed if we accept commitments and then refuse to discharge them" – he was in favour of discharging commitments but also renegotiating a way out of the nuclear role over the long run.[37] The Liberals thus used the government's ambivalence and confusion as the election issue instead of defending the utility of nuclear weapons for Canada.

The Liberals won the 1963 election, but not with a majority. Nevertheless, the Pearson government undertook a fundamental review of defence policy that resulted in dramatic changes to the army. A significant portion of the political leadership was skeptical of the utility of armies to the defence of Europe, and even less convinced of the value of tactical nuclear weapons. They were ready to try something different but had no concept of a possible alternative. Defence Minister Paul Hellyer's 1964 *White Paper on Defence* would be the first attempt to describe one.

CHAPTER THREE

The Army and the Unified Force, 1963-67

THE LIBERAL PARTY'S ACCESSION to power on 22 April 1963 resulted in the formation of a cabinet of twenty-six members. No less than eight were former public servants, including Bud Drury, a former deputy minister of national defence who became the industry minister, and Jack Pickersgill, the secretary of state. Unlike Diefenbaker, who had ruled as "the Chief," Pearson's consensus style reflected his career as a diplomat. Pearson tended to discourage Cabinet consideration of defence and foreign affairs. Instead, strategic policy was concentrated in the hands of a few individuals: Pearson himself; Paul Martin, a lawyer from Windsor, Ontario, who was secretary of state for external affairs; and Walter Gordon, the minister of finance. Martin was a strong NATO supporter and believed in the value of maintaining troops in Europe. Gordon, on the other hand, did not share his colleagues' faith in military programs. He summed up his views in his memoirs: "The whole idea of spending a great deal more money on defence was nonsensical, both because I failed to see what Canada could gain by having a larger or better-equipped military establishment and because I felt that the money could be spent in better ways."[1]

The appointment of Paul Hellyer brought a *rara avis* into Cabinet – a minister of national defence with an actual policy agenda. The defence establishment appeared structurally broken. The Diefenbaker government had lurched from one military controversy to another – NORAD membership, SAC exercises, and confusion over command during the Cuban Missile Crisis and over nuclear weapons. Civilian ministers did not appear to have firm control. According to J. Grant Glassco, chair of the Royal Commission on Government Organization, the existing system was convoluted and inefficient. Structural change was therefore in order. Moreover, the substance of defence policy appeared to also require reform to ensure that Canadian interests were being served by military programs. Reform would affect the army in two principal ways: it would remake the army into a mobile force capable of deploying globally and fighting anywhere along the spectrum of combat intensity; and it would integrate and then unify the armed services, thereby replacing the army's command and staff structure with that of a single, unified armed service.

The newly elected government had promised a defence review, not surprising given the prominence of defence policy in the defeat of its predecessor. The first step was the establishment of a Special Committee on Defence in the House of Commons. The committee's hearings began in June 1963 and were wide-ranging. Each service presented its own overview, as did the Department of External Affairs. The army's was a fairly straightforward description of the status quo. Focusing on the Canadian commitment to field a division on the NATO Central Front, it ignored the concern expressed in Hellyer's own brief that Europe could not be reinforced. The committee also heard from individuals, including former Chief of the General Staff Guy Simonds, who stated:

> I believe that a role which is suited to a country of our size and having regard to the financial burdens possible to be borne out over a lengthy term, would be a tri-service force whose main objective was peace-keeping. I believe its organization would be very much like that of the United States Marine Corps, which is a mobile force complete with all its ancillaries and able to meet what are commonly called brushfire situations.

Simonds favoured moving away from nuclear commitments on the NATO Central Front, but did not spell out the details of the force he envisaged. The US Marine Corps was mechanized and had its own integral close air support, but was lighter than conventional US Army formations.[2] Simonds did say that the mobile force he envisaged would be the size of a division and have strategic air support.[3]

Charles Foulkes, the former chairman of the Chiefs of Staff Committee and Simonds's predecessor as CGS, also testified on the possibility of a mobile force for peacekeeping. He had previously suggested that the brigade group in NATO be re-equipped as an air-transportable formation capable of nuclear and conventional operations. He did not provide any additional specifics, choosing instead to talk about command arrangements for troops tasked for UN duty and the necessity of maintaining national command over them.

The committee attempted to resolve the matter by recalling Lieutenant-General Geoffrey Walsh, the CGS, who explained the force structure of the army in some detail. He informed the committee that while there were two brigades in Canada earmarked as a strategic reserve for NATO, there was insufficient shipping to move them and their equipment to Europe in an emergency. The government became aware of this following the 1961 Berlin Crisis, but had not corrected the deficiency.[4]

Hellyer did not depend on the Special Committee on Defence as the main source of policy ideas. During the summer and fall of 1963, he had numerous unrecorded informal meetings with the chiefs of staff: Air Chief Marshal Frank Miller, the chairman of the Chiefs of Staff Committee (and previously the vice chief of air staff and the deputy minister of national defence), Vice-Admiral Herbert Rayner of the navy, Lieutenant-General Walsh of the army, and Air Marshal C.R. Dunlop of the Royal Canadian Air Force. The roles, force structure, organization, and weaponry of their forces were discussed. They went through a "framing" exercise with the object of topping off or reducing a number of lower-priority projects. As a result, Hellyer began to make and implement decisions to freeze major procurement programs, including cancelling the naval frigate program, not ordering additional CF-104 Starfighters and CF-101B Voodoo aircraft, and dropping the Bobcat armoured personnel carrier in favour of the proven and cheaper US M113.[5] Hellyer had no intention of allowing the inertia of the status quo to prevent him from reforming the armed services.

Neither did the new minister allow himself to be chained to existing staff processes. His style was reminiscent of that of Simonds and Graham: he was his own source of "big ideas," and staff were there merely to work out the details. Nor was his style extremely collegial. Advice went to him; decisions emerged. He did not rely on the normal staff structure. In reconceptualizing the army, he established two task forces: the Ad Hoc Committee on Defence Policy, chaired by R.J. Sutherland, the chief of operational research of the Defence Research Board, and the Ad Hoc Committee on the Study of a Mobile Force, under Brigadier H.Q. Love, with two other one-star members from the other services.

The Sutherland committee on defence policy was tasked with studying the entire field of Canadian defence policy and examining all major alternatives. It was specifically instructed, however, not to make recommendations. The members of the committee were A.C. Grant from the deputy minister's office, Captain (N) V.J. Wilgress, Brigadier D.A.G. Waldock, Group Captain J.K.F. Macdonald, and Group Captain C.H. Mussells. Sutherland was the only star among them and was the Defence Department's leading strategic thinker.[6]

Sutherland quickly set out the central issue of Canadian defence policy: Canada was under no direct threat and had no extraterritorial ambitions. He noted that "from the point of view of the Department of National Defence, it would be advantageous to discover a strategic rationale which would impart to Canada's defence program a wholly Canadian character. Unfortunately, such a rationale does not exist and one cannot invent it." Canadian plans were those of supranational headquarters, namely NORAD, the Supreme Allied Commander Atlantic (SACLANT), and the Supreme Allied Commander Europe (SACEUR).

Unlike other small countries, Canada had no national plans to fall back on, instead basing Canadian defence on an alliance strategy. Unfortunately, Sutherland pointed out, "this rationale has upon occasion been considerably less than rational." For example, SACEUR planned for a thirty-day war whereas SACLANT planned for convoys to support a long war. NATO planning was "absurd" and "a perusal of the War Plans prepared by the three supra-national headquarters to which Canada contributes forces shows that all too frequently these owe more to Alice-in-Wonderland than to Clausewitz." Canada needed to participate in alliance politics with less innocence, and needed to have a single chief of defence staff responsible for planning rather than allowing each service to deal with and become "excessively involved" with the interests of an international headquarters.[7]

Program management was also weak. The department was under severe financial pressure, with appropriations having fallen 13 percent in absolute dollars and 38 percent in purchasing power since 1952. Operating costs had increased 50 percent. Since the principal component of operating costs was wages, and since the armed services were already understaffed, further reductions would require reductions in commitments. The army and navy had been attempting to deal with financial shortfalls by deferring equipment programs, but if the present trend was allowed to continue the equipment budget would soon hit zero. "The trend would be for Canada to acquire a South American-style military establishment: a substantial number of uniformed personnel, no modern equipment and no significant capability." It was fair to say that the defence budget was no longer based on any clear rationale.[8]

The capability that Sutherland thought necessary for Canada to maintain was modest. For the defence of Canada itself there was a need to maintain surveillance, deal with small lodgements or incidents, and participate in air defence sufficiently "to give these forces a Canadian complexion." Defence of Canada was the highest-priority demand on resources, and Sutherland believed that economies could be achieved if other operational roles were compatible with it. He did not believe that anti-submarine warfare (ASW) was important as Soviet submarine-launched missiles were redundant with other Soviet forces, and it was not obvious to him that other Soviet submarine operations would be damaging to Canada. The defence-of-Canada force suggested was therefore a "moderate number" of destroyer-type ships; one air-transportable brigade group, including a parachute element but without heavy support; and air transport, long-range patrol aircraft, an air defence ground environment, surface-to-air missiles, and a limited number of close air support aircraft. The only real threat to North America was from the air, but he expected air defence to decline in importance. The navy needed a coast guard–type force, but the rationale for any further capability could be found only in alliances. The role of sea power in NATO strategy was "far from clear," although Sutherland admitted that dropping ASW would be a dramatic change because of prior investment in it. If Canada continued in the ASW role, ASW carriers could be used to transport a brigade group at almost no additional cost. Building a "minor league" amphibious force capable of disembarking a brigade group over a beach against light resistance was within Canada's means, but it was difficult to envisage a NATO or UN scenario that would require more than administrative landings at dockside. Outside of NATO, such a force would be very useful in a "wide range of plausible circumstances," but Canada had no commitments that required maintaining amphibious forces.[9] The committee trenchantly dismissed the idea of an "independent" Canadian defence policy as "Gaullism without *grandeur*."[10]

Sutherland's report went on to discuss Canada's role in the defence of Europe. The existing commitment of one brigade group stationed in Europe and the Air Division in a strike/reconnaissance role was an "inheritance of difficulties." While defending the Central Front was the most important job in NATO and was where the fate of Europe would be decided, it was costly, required nuclear weapons, and separated the roles of the army and the air force. The divergent roles of the army and air force "impose[d] very great demands on public understanding" (although it is unclear exactly what Sutherland meant by this). It also created diplomatic inflexibility in that withdrawal from such a key role would raise questions regarding Canada's continued participation in NATO; it would also raise commitment issues for the United States and make relations with that country more difficult.

Accordingly, Sutherland did not recommend abandoning the Central Front, suggesting instead that the RCAF strike/reconnaissance role be replaced. Strike airfields were increasingly vulnerable to surface-to-surface missiles and Soviet air defences were improving. Manning ballistic missiles was a possibility, as was the acquisition of a vertical/short takeoff and landing (V/STOL) strike aircraft to replace the Starfighter, but these were dismissed. The United States wanted to limit the spread of medium-range ballistic missiles, a position that Canada had supported. STOL aircraft were of low performance, and dispersion would result in weapons control problems. The most practical role for the RCAF was general tactical support. This would mean that the same aircraft could be used in both Canada and Europe, that a substantial part of the Air Division could be based in Canada, and that the operational roles of the army and air force would be compatible. Moreover, it appeared that NATO tactics would require additional tactical air support in the future.[11]

As for the army, the Centurion tank required replacement, but "to the extent that Canadian policy objectives are served by keeping a certain number of uniformed personnel in Europe, the Army is the best buy." Contradicting the statement earlier in the report that SACEUR was planning for a thirty-day war, the committee claimed that the short-war/no-strategic-warning scenario had been a Canadian invention to support the policy of not equipping to war scales troops committed to NATO. It claimed that it was plausible to maintain reinforcements in Canada and thought that stockpiling in Europe should be reconsidered. What was "truly indefensible" was the 1959 decision to equip the two brigades in Canada only to training scales.[12]

The committee examined Canada's major options for providing forces to NATO, including complete withdrawal. It did not regard this as "unthinkable" and noted that when forces were originally dispatched to Europe in 1951, it had seemed a response to an immediate threat. Withdrawal and disbandment of forces would result in a huge cost saving, estimated at almost $1.2 billion, or a reduction of about 75 percent. The Canadian military contribution was not of "crucial importance" to the alliance and the case for continued basing in Europe was "not compelling." There would be very significant diplomatic costs, however. Canada would not be able to convince the Europeans that it was paying its way in NATO through either NORAD, which the Europeans regarded as a massive misdirection of resources, or the UN, to which the Europeans contributed proportionately more. Similarly, a greater naval contribution would not be persuasive, as NATO's naval policies were unclear and the Europeans regarded naval forces as an "inexplicable" Anglo-Saxon preoccupation and "somehow typifying the essential unreliability of the Anglo-Saxons." The British would be particularly annoyed with a Canadian withdrawal because it would make the German component of the Northern Army Group larger than the British and would raise the question of whether Britain should continue in command. The United States would be displeased and any further problems in NATO would be charged to Canada's account.[13]

If Canada were to base its forces in Canada, the most ambitious force structure would be a "triphibious" force or Canadian Marine Corps (anticipating Simonds's suggestion at the Special Committee on Defence a month later). This would consist of an army element capable of landing operations, a tactical aviation element that could follow the force ashore, and a naval element capable of sealift and its own defence. If the force was only a light one, it would have limited offensive capability and would be unsuitable against an enemy with medium armour (i.e., main battle tanks). The Sutherland committee therefore proposed a Canadian Marine Corps of one brigade group with main battle tanks and self-propelled artillery supported by a tactical aviation wing of thirty V/STOL aircraft operated from two light carriers. The naval force would provide anti-submarine warfare and air and surface defence. The force would be self-supporting for sixty days. Such a force would be able to carry out landings against minor opposition, but would be inadequate to deal with a major threat from shore-based aircraft or to land against organized beach defences. The estimated cost was in the order of $2 billion, a substantial amount given that the annual defence budget was about $1.6 billion.[14] What this force could be used for was questionable, however. If it was a heavy force, it could be used on the Central Front, but a normal brigade group could be moved to Europe at less cost. Canada had no obvious interests in the Mediterranean and the military weakness of northern Norway was caused by the Norwegian government's unwillingness to accept the stationing of foreign forces in times of peace as well as the low strategic value of the area. It was not Canada's job to remediate a problem caused by Norway's policy, which would require Canada "to carry out a major and potentially hazardous operation in a remote corner of the NATO area which is of no great strategic importance." A brigade group, at any rate, was insufficient for the job and the prospects of stopping a Soviet invasion of Norway were "distinctly unpromising," resulting in a high probability that any Canadian force would be destroyed. In addition, it appeared unlikely that the UN would be prepared to sponsor a small war requiring such a force or to use Canada as its agent, or that Canada would be prepared to commit forces to the UN.[15]

Alternatively, Canada could choose to reinforce the European theatre with heavy forces. If emergency sealift were to be employed, little would be gained from NATO's point of view, since troops would become available only between two and four months after mobilization. However, if $130 million were spent on standby sealift, a brigade could be placed in Europe between twenty and thirty days after mobilizaton, and an entire division between seventy-five and ninety days. Another $250 million spent on stockpiling and airlift could produce a division in Europe by one month after mobilization. Reinforcement of Europe with light forces was not so attractive even though they could be moved quickly. Once in Europe, they would lack heavy weapons, logistic support, and tactical mobility. There was no immediate need for such forces and their value to Canadian diplomacy within NATO was questionable.[16]

Finally, the Sutherland committee turned to the option of Canada's contributing to SACEUR's mobile forces as Speidel had suggested in 1959. The forces required were in general compatible with those required for the defence of Canada, and the committee believed that a strong prima facie case could be made that it was more appropriate for Canada to contribute by providing mobile forces than by assigning troops to the Central Front. There would be two advantages: there would be no need to replace the Centurion, and there would be other savings in army equipment and heavy logistics. The RCAF could get out of the strike/reconnaissance role and be re-equipped with aircraft that could also be used in continental defence. The roles of the army and air force would be compatible and interdependent. The army could rotate units without dependents, and nuclear weapons would no longer be required. NATO would benefit by having its mobile force requirements met by a force with its own permanent headquarters staff and its own air transport.

On the other hand, there were numerous disadvantages. The diplomatic costs to Canada were imponderable and it was not clear that Canadian national interests would be served by deploying troops to "an ambiguous incident in Northern Norway or in some obscure corner of the Mediterranean." The committee concluded that "mobile forces as presently constituted are a rather unsatisfactory vehicle with which to carry out the delicate operation of disengaging Canadian forces, and especially the Canadian Army, from the Central Front." NATO plans had kept the nuclear option for the mobile force open, pending political solution of weapons control. Inserting the mobile force to halt aggression was largely a bluff. If the bluff were called, Canadians would have to decide whether to escalate. The problem with small tactical nuclear weapons was that they were less destructive and accordingly "possess[ed] the characteristic that they might actually be used."[17]

The Sutherland committee was not supposed to make recommendations, but it came exceedingly close to making one about mobile forces:

> The proposition that Canada can best contribute to the defence of the NATO area by participation in a strategically mobile force is an extremely attractive one. This is the role which is most compatible with Canada's position as a North American nation and with Canada's other military responsibilities for the Defence of Canada the support of the United Nations. There is every reason to suppose that this should be Canada's basic long term objective and that no opportunity should be lost to move in this direction.[18]

At the moment, however, the mobile force was not a viable alternative to the commitment of Canadian troops to the Central Front. Canada could stake a preliminary claim in the course of the current NATO review of strategy and could also earmark a battalion for NATO's proposed Mobile Land Force as a notice of intent. Equipment could be stockpiled on Canadian bases and the Starfighter and Voodoo replaced with a single general-purpose aircraft. In addition, Sutherland suggested that it would be possible to form a "Headquarters Mobile Command," including the Army Tactics and Organization Board (which was double-hatted as a divisional headquarters), an RCAF component, and possibly a small RCN element, and make it responsible for developing doctrine and operational procedures for strategically mobile operations. Taking this step would not be premature, although doctrinal development would take several years. Doctrine for mobile operations would be an important contribution to both NATO and the United States because of the "state of doctrinal discontinuity" that existed between the US Army and US Air Force. Canada would be able to establish military links with the US Army Strike Command and the British Strategic Reserve. It would also provide a platform for developing a fully integrated Canadian joint staff.[19]

The Sutherland committee was probably hurt by its inability to make recommendations. It had provided the minister with a comprehensive and frank account of the issues facing the defence establishment. Its central tendency was to put more weight on the army and less on the navy and air force as an instrument of policy. While it did not endorse NATO strategy, it acknowledged that allies had interests and expectations that Canada would upset by attempting to change the status quo. Rather than an abrupt ringing down of the curtain on the Central Front, a slow, quiet tiptoe exit was recommended. Taking this advice would not have been easy for any of the armed services. The navy and air force would lose, or face reductions in, their most glamorous roles. The army would become central to Canadian policy but might have to give up its aspirations to be a heavily equipped "big army" in a prestigious international role. Overall, the armed services would become affordable within the appropriation allocated by the government, but once again at the cost of aspirations. The elimination of nuclear weapons was equally unpalatable, as neither NORAD nor NATO forces were designed to work with conventional weapons only. The committee's inability to make recommendations therefore left many important issues up in the air. It appeared that a mobile force, introduced at an opportune moment, would be able to square the circle of providing affordable forces, built on Canadian requirements and interests but also meeting the expectations of allies. At a technical level, this masked the fact that forces heavy enough to fight in Europe would not be very mobile, and if mobile would not be effective either in Europe or in various other scenarios. The effectiveness of a non-nuclear mobile force was questioned but the issue was not resolved, and the consistency of likely uses of a mobile force with Canadian foreign policy was also left on the table. The Sutherland committee had accomplished much, but failed to realize its full potential.

A second task force was at work at the same time as the Sutherland committee: the Ad Hoc Committee on the Study of a Mobile Force. Unlike the broad terms of reference given the Sutherland committee, Hellyer's directions regarding the study of a mobile force were exceedingly specific. Referring to earlier discussions with the chiefs of staff, he stated:

> The type of mobile force I have in mind is basically an air transportable fighting unit which could be airlifted with its equipment for quick deployment anywhere in the world. The force should be mechanized and have a high fire power and great flexibility which would make it adjustable to varying circumstances. It should be flexible enough that it could form the mobile reserve of the Supreme Allied Commander Europe or serve in a United Nations operation or other circumstances as required, to meet national policy. It may be desirable that some units be air-droppable, but the principal criterion is airportability of the entire force.
>
> The unit of study should be one mobile division with its own air support. By air support, I mean all necessary tactical air support for the force in the field. The unit chosen is merely for convenience and for the purposes of the study the level of equipment support and supplies could be taken to be that which would meet SACEUR's standards for his mobile force.

Hellyer went on to direct that the study include the composition of the force, its table of organization and equipment, the cost of equipment, and the annual cost of operation. He also requested supplemental studies for the air- and sealift of one-third of the division.[20]

As Hellyer would discover in a few weeks when he received the report of the Sutherland committee, his proposal contained some contradictory elements. Air transportability appeared to contradict the requirement for mechanization and high firepower. He provided no direction on nuclear weapons. Although he met with the Ad Hoc Committee (now the Joint Service Study Group) shortly after receiving Sutherland's report, he merely instructed them to leave the question of nuclear weapons for military consideration for the purpose of their study.[21] There is no record of whether the CGS and the other service chiefs attempted to explain to the minister the obvious difficulties with what he proposed. For his part, Hellyer can now recall no expression of concern from senior military or civil staff.[22] Thus a serious breakdown occurred, and failure to confront the issues inherent in the mobile force concept would come back to haunt the army.

The army analyzed the minister's concept by applying a bottom-up approach rather than working top down as Sutherland had. The combat development process, so painfully developed over many years, could not be used due to the minister's wish to have the study completed by mid-November. Instead, the army staffed the project by asking each individual branch to develop its requirements in parallel. The results were integrated by stapling them together. Not surprisingly, the report was a monster. Colonel E.W. Henselwood, the head of the Army Planning Group reporting to Brigadier Love, the committee chairman, reported that 20,000 troops would be required, which "obviously [did] not meet the need to economize." An armoured regiment equipped with Sheridan light tanks was proposed, but APCs and anti-aircraft missiles were considered supplemental and were not provided. Artillery was reduced by one-third to one light battery and one medium battery instead of a full artillery regiment. Henselwood concluded:

> To sum the division up, it is light in armour and medium artillery and the infantry have very little battlefield mobility. It does have good anti tank support and probably could withstand a determined attack from a modern army but only long enough to carry out an orderly withdrawal. It has no real offensive capability nor could it carry out protracted defence against strong attack. Is this what is wanted, is it too much or not enough?"[23]

The planning group completed a table of organization and equipment of 20,000 men and 35,000 tons in weight. It recognized that it had not created a light force.[24]

Love did not address Henselwood's question directly, but supplied additional assumptions for the air transportation study. He told the planning group that the total force was to remain a division of which one brigade group was to be deployed in Europe, but that planners should assume that allied forces would provide most of the combat support. According to Love, this was militarily unsatisfactory but not outside the bounds of current NATO practices. He recognized that the brigade group in Europe would be a token force and would have little fighting capability, but would not be less effective than the mobile force that SACEUR was planning. The planning group was instructed to reduce the need for air transport by relying on other means, and was informed that although a division was being planned, the maximum overseas deployment would be one brigade group.[25] The Army Council considered the options presented by Love on 31 October, and told him that a mobile force with light armour, only medium artillery, and unmounted infantry was unviable; that a force that depended on allies for armour and artillery support was unbalanced; and that basing all three brigade groups in Canada would be a last resort. The Army Council pressed for the inclusion of main battle tanks and heavy sealift.[26]

Love briefed the Army Council again on 1 November 1963. Although the proposed force was of doubtful air-transportability, the army brass reiterated their request that the planning group add main battle tanks in place of the Sheridans in order to have a "balanced Army force." Love was able to persuade the Army Council to wait for the full planning group recommendations before insisting on heavier tanks.

As directed, the Joint Service Study Group tendered its report on 15 November. It admitted in the preface that it had diverged from the original concept after seeking additional guidance from the chiefs of staff and the minister. It believed that its proposal was affordable, but only if Canadian commitments to NATO were substantially altered. The study group did not believe that the force being proposed could accomplish the existing NATO assignments and that the mobile force would therefore replace the army and air force in Europe. The mobile force was to be "nuclear adaptable" but not nuclear-equipped. One-third would be stationed in Europe and would depend on allies for logistic and operational support. Mobility had been given precedence in the selection of equipment, so main battle tanks might have to be dropped. The study group had not been able to reconcile mobility with firepower and told the minister that if such a force were deployed in the face of a serious and sustained enemy invasion of NATO territory, it would be very rapidly overrun. Love's group staked the viability of the force on a theory that the fact that North American troops were involved would increase the probability of a nuclear counterattack, and "it may be thus argued that such a force would form a credible contribution to the current and future NATO deterrent strategy."[27]

The study group believed that the mobile force could support Canadian policy by responding to the complete spectrum of military operations that might arise in the future, would integrate all three services in pursuit of a common goal, and would possess the capability of deploying the force to an area before it was actually committed. The roles envisaged were: (1) augmentation of SACEUR's mobile forces; (2) contribution of forces to the UN; (3) provision of forces to ad hoc bilateral or multilateral alliances; and (4) the defence of Canada. Love's group recognized that the lightly armed mobile force could not take a front-line position in Central Europe and would therefore have to be assigned to SACEUR mobile forces that would be employed in fringe areas such as Norway, Western Thrace, or Turkey. Because an incident could escalate beyond the capabilities of a light force to handle, nuclear capability was required, as well as strong anti-tank elements and close air support trained in anti-tank operations. The study group noted (as Sutherland had) that Supreme Headquarters Allied Powers Europe (SHAPE) had been unable to work out nuclear weapons custody questions with the United States for its mobile force. It also noted that there was no doctrine for this type of force and that it might require additional support and additional wheeled or even tracked vehicles.

The mobile force would not come cheap. Three brigades, one of them stationed in Europe, would cost $144 million annually, plus $50 million in capital equipment. The aviation component would require three squadrons of interceptor aircraft and six squadrons of attack and reconnaissance planes. This would add 2,000 to 4,400 personnel, and $211 million to $457 million to the operating costs. The required naval forces required would centre on a light carrier, which would add 2,500 to 3,500 sailors, operating costs of $37.8 million, and capital costs of $174 million. Airlift would require fifty C-130s in addition to the fourteen already in the budget; they would cost $214 million. Although the report pronounced the proposed force affordable, the total costs were estimated to be $456 million annually if the entire force was based in Canada and $540 million if one-third were deployed to Europe, assuming that there would be no net change to the naval budget. Only $349 million had been appropriated that year for NATO and UN operations and capital equipment.[28]

Taken together, the Sutherland and Love committee reports ought to have given Hellyer pause. Sutherland supported the creation of a mobile force, but only as an evolutionary process that would require Canada to abandon NATO's Central Front by degrees. He also raised warning flags regarding the viability of a light force even on NATO's flanks. Love had come to the conclusion that a mobile force would be large, costly, and militarily ineffective. Employed in NATO, its putative utility was based on the wishful thinking that the Soviets would perceive attacking a Canadian force as more likely to escalate to nuclear warfare than attacking local forces, and it was going to cost over one and a half times the amount available in the budget. The army presented the facts of its study clearly enough, but fudged the conclusions.

Hellyer quickly decided, however, that he could have his cake and eat it too. Within weeks of receiving Love's report, he informed Walsh, the CGS, that the army could plan on the premise that NATO and continued contributions to the UN would be the cornerstones of Canadian defence policy. The Canadian brigade group would continue to be based in Germany. In general, the army could expect the status quo to continue in its organization and a new tank would be considered for the 1966-69 time frame.[29] Apparently adopting the strategy suggested by Sutherland, Hellyer reaffirmed the centrality of NATO to Canada's defence. His first draft of a White Paper was far more critical of the viability of UN peacekeeping than the final version, in which External Affairs replaced a section questioning the validity of UN standby forces with a list of UN operations in which Canada had participated. The discussion of UN requirements focused on the need for highly mobile forces. In addition, the final *White Paper on Defence* forecast increased UN peacekeeping operations due to continued communist subversion and expansion through measures short of all-out war. "Wars of liberation" were expected to multiply where intervention by Great Powers or alliances would be difficult. This strategic appreciation pointed out a requirement for independent intervention forces to be maintained by smaller powers.[30]

Hellyer dealt with the question of nuclear weapons by stating that Canada was a member of a nuclear alliance that would use nuclear weapons only if necessary. Nuclear arms for the Canadian armed forces was a "subordinate issue," dependent on how Canada could contribute most effectively to the alliance.[31] The question of the NATO brigade group and the Air Division was discussed in detail. The White Paper stated that after the most careful consideration, the option of an air-transportable force based in Europe and available for employment on the NATO flanks had been rejected. Withdrawal of the brigade group from the Central Front might be "misinterpreted." Moreover, the requirements for a mobile force could be met more economically by increasing air transport and basing troops in North America. The White Paper announced that the two brigades in reserve for NATO based in Canada would therefore be re-equipped and retrained as a mobile force as well as for rotational service with the NATO brigade. The fourth brigade would be converted to a special service force with air-transportable and air-droppable equipment. In addition, one battalion of the reserve brigades would be committed to SHAPE to be part of its mobile force. The RCAF would lose its nuclear strike/reconnaissance role and be re-equipped with a "high performance aircraft ... to provide sufficient flexibility for any task we might undertake from ground attack to air surveillance." The new aircraft would be able to self-deploy from Canada to overseas bases. Ultimately, the squadrons in Europe would be associated more directly with the brigade group, but it was recognized that this would require negotiations with NATO. Strategic air transport would be substantial, although civilian air carriers might be relied upon for troop transport. Tactical air transport would also be augmented. Three out of four of the government's priority defence expenditures centred on the creation of the mobile force: re-equipping the army for the mobile force role, acquiring adequate air- and sealift for its immediate deployment, and acquiring tactical aircraft. The remaining priority item was to maintain "relatively constant improvement" of anti-submarine warfare capability.[32]

The creation of a mobile force lent additional substance to the most controversial part of the White Paper, the integration of the armed services into a single service under a chief of defence staff. This was justified as a response to the criticisms of the Glassco Commission that the existing management structure of separate services coordinated by a Chiefs of Staff Committee was inefficient, and also as a means of improving civilian control of the military. An integrated mobile force would provide a tri-service task that the new integrated service could work on together, rather than remaining in their alliance-based stovepipes. But while the concept looked tidy from the high-level perspective of a White Paper, a tangle of loose ends lay just below the surface. The mobile force concept had originally been proposed to make the army organizationally uniform. The White Paper required three types of troops: heavy mechanized infantry in Europe, some undefined lighter force capable of being mobile as well as filling rotational requirements for Europe, and a pure light infantry/ parachute formation. The cost issues were left unaddressed. Service integration also raised questions of who would be in charge of what, and how an integrated staff system would function. Sutherland had suggested that a mobile force headquarters could be formed from existing army staffs, but this was the sum total of the planning that had taken place. Although the Army Council had been reassured that the status quo would remain, the White Paper made it clear that the long-term intent was to make the army into something quite different.

According to Tom Axworthy, a Liberal Party strategist who would become Pierre Trudeau's principal secretary in the Prime Minister's Office, Hellyer would have made a heavily equipped mobile force the centrepiece of the White Paper. Lester Pearson, however, had formed a Cabinet committee consisting of himself, Walter Gordon, Paul Martin, and Mitchell Sharp to review the drafting. Tom Kent, Pearson's policy assistant, also helped. Gordon's desire to reduce the NATO commitment was rejected, but Pearson deleted a section on Northern sovereignty. Gordon's main achievement was to cap the defence budget at about $1.5 billion. Unification of the services gradually became more and more prominent as force structure issues disappeared. If a camel is a horse designed by committee, the 1964 *White Paper on Defence* was designed by several of them.[33]

Implementing the Mobile Force

When the White Paper went to the Cabinet Committee on External Affairs and National Defence, Hellyer promised savings of $100 million a year, support for the principle of collective defence, and the creation of forces that could be put to multiple uses. He invited the chiefs of staff to provide their opinions to the committee. The chairman of the Chiefs of Staff Committee, Air Chief Marshal Miller, noted that the savings would be contingent on personnel policy and that it would take effort to convince service personnel of the concept. Vice-Admiral Rayner, the chief of naval staff, forecast a decline in naval competence and professionalism because of integration, and he was joined by Air Marshal C.R. Dunlop, the chief of air staff. Only the vice chief of the general staff, Major-General Bernatchez, supported the minister, commenting that he and the CGS found the proposed structure "workable." After asking his military officials to withdraw, Pearson pronounced the draft White Paper to be "satisfactory." The ministers concluded that there was sufficient support at the senior level in the military that in a short period of time the "universalists" would move into positions of power and criticism would become muted.[34]

Legislation implementing the changes to the structure of the armed services proposed in the White Paper was enacted by Parliament and came into effect on 1 August 1964. After that date, the Canadian Army still had legal existence, but the position of chief of the general staff and the General Staff itself were abolished. In their place there was one chief of the defence staff (CDS) and an integrated, three-service staff in a single Canadian Forces Headquarters (CFHQ). CFHQ was organized around "functional" rather than service lines. The top-level staff officers were the vice chief of the defence staff; the assistant chief of the defence staff; the chief of operational readiness, who was responsible for collective training, operational doctrine, and tactical development; the chief of personnel, who was responsible for recruiting, manning, individual training, personnel administration, and services such as medical, dental, and chaplain services; the chief of logistics and engineering; and the comptroller general. A functional orientation for the headquarters was chosen because it was assumed that future operations would be joint, or involving more than one service, and because the minister and senior military staff supporting him were determined not to let the services in by the back door. In the case of doctrine and force development, this resulted in the devolution of much of the function to the new Mobile Command, but with CFHQ retaining control of major force structure decisions.[35]

The creation of a Mobile Command for the new mobile force had been proposed by both the Sutherland and Love committees. As mentioned earlier, Sutherland proposed a headquarters combining the Army Tactics and Organization Board with RCAF and RCN staffs in order to develop doctrine and procedures for mobile operations.[36] The army's own study said that the creation of a chief of the defence staff was a prerequisite for the formation of a mobile force and assumed that the force would be created as one of a number of unified commands, reporting to the CDS. It was assumed that the commander of the mobile force would have an integrated staff and land, sea, and air commanders reporting to him.[37] In June 1965 Hellyer selected Lieutenant-General Jean Victor Allard to command this new organization. Allard had fought in the Second World War, had been the Canadian brigade commander in Korea, had commanded a British mechanized infantry division in Europe in the early 1960s, and had served as vice chief of the general staff and most recently as the chief of operational readiness in the new CFHQ. In his memoirs, he claimed that he had threatened to resign to oppose the throwing of his regiment (the Van Doos) "into the melting pot" of a Canadian Marine Corps, but had been talked out of it by the CDS, Air Chief Marshal Miller, with a promise to re-examine the place of francophones in the army. Given that the Sutherland committee had rejected the concept of a "Canadian Marine Corps" and the army's mobile force study was not based on it – which Allard as a member of the Army Council would have known – the perceived threat to the regimental system seems exaggerated.[38] Nevertheless, when Hellyer visited Allard while he was hospitalized with severe back pain and offered him Mobile Command, Allard accepted. There is no doubt that Allard wished to improve the status of francophones, and many of his subsequent decisions regarding the structure of Mobile Command were aimed at achieving this end.

Allard's first task was to give substance to the White Paper concept of Mobile Command. In his memoirs, he wrote: "I was immediately confronted by several questions. What was meant by Mobile Command? A force to intervene in unknown theatres of operations? A force for internal stabilization? A force for the defence of the northern territories?" Miller suggested that he convene a think tank outside Ottawa to consider the matter. Allard convened a small study group consisting of Major Ramsay Withers, a future CDS; Major-General W.A.B. Anderson, the deputy chief of reserves and next commander of Mobile Command; and Major-General F.J. Fleury, the comptroller general. The study group recommended that Mobile Command be capable of northern operations, nuclear warfare, and airborne intervention in limited conflicts, and that aviation be included to support these missions. Perhaps its most important decision, however, was to endorse Sutherland's recommendation to include the Army Tactics and Organization Board as part of the Command headquarters.[39] Acquisition of the ATOB meant that Allard was able to add Major-General Roger Rowley to his staff. The ubiquitous Rowley took over the design not only of the headquarters but also of the field force – in other words, remaking of the army from top to bottom.

In March 1965, while Allard was still the chief of operational readiness in CFHQ, he had asked Rowley and the ATOB to study the commitments, roles, and missions assigned to the army in the *White Paper on Defence*. The objective was to determine the most suitable field force and unit structures required to meet the White Paper commitments. The ATOB reached several major conclusions. First, the army was being given more commitments for formed units than forces to meet them. If all commitments had to be met at once, a division of three brigades, two independent brigades, and a separate battalion group would be required, whereas the army had only four brigade groups. Rowley concluded that the army required two basic types of troops: (1) light airborne or air-transportable forces for defence-of-Canada operations, peacekeeping, the Allied Command Europe (ACE) Mobile Force, and small, limited wars; and (2) heavier armoured and mechanized forces for the NATO Central Front. Modifying the two brigades in Canada to be more air-transportable would require a change in their role because they would be too light to be useful on the Central Front. Moreover, as all previous analyses had stressed, there was insufficient airlift capacity, and if the entire planned airlift was committed to moving one battalion group, such as the ACE Mobile Force, the rest of the army would be "rendered strategically immobile for approximately seven days." There was insufficient manpower to staff both the required field force and the balance of the support elements for a division. This would require putting Canadian forces in NATO on the supply lines of an ally who could provide support on a cash reimbursement basis. Only the United States was capable of this and, as all Canadian equipment was North American, it would be uneconomical and inefficient to remain on British lines of communication. Unlike the Love committee, which assumed the availability of naval sealift, the ATOB considered the sealift capability of the RCN to be "negligible" and "of limited value." There was a conflict between using the navy for ASW and using it for transport, and the Provider-class auxiliaries would not arrive until after 1970. Rowley suggested that the force structure of both the navy and the air force be re-examined in order to ensure enough transport for the army.[40]

The ATOB considered four options. The first closely resembled the status quo: a NATO force of one mechanized brigade group, a rotational force of one mechanized brigade troop, and a Mobile Striking Force of one light infantry division consisting of a headquarters and two air-transportable brigades. This did not meet the existing commitment of a division to NATO and could result in a reduction of Canadian influence within that organization. Alternatively, Canada could form a NATO reserve force of one airborne or air-transportable division and form a Mobile Striking Force of one light infantry division. Not only would this require a major renegotiation of the NATO role but it would also likely harm relations with allies. The requirement for massive airlift was beyond Canada's military budget and would unbalance the air force's structure. The entire field force would be unsuitable for large-scale conventional or limited nuclear war, and the army's newly acquired APCs and self-propelled artillery, as well as its tanks, would be rendered surplus. A third option would be to use troops available for duty in Europe to form the skeleton of a light mechanized division (keeping air-mobile elements with training-scale equipment in Canada) and also maintain a Mobile Striking Force of one light infantry division. This option was much more palatable. It would meet NATO commitments, although some renegotiation of Canada's role would be required. It would use all the new equipment that had been purchased, and there would be sufficient personnel if salary dollars were transferred from the air force as the CF-104 Starfighter was withdrawn from Europe. The light mechanized division would be less capable than a standard mechanized division. The final option was the same as the third – a skeleton division in Europe, plus the Mobile Striking Force – but based on a standard mechanized division instead of a light mechanized division. This option would maximize political and military advantages but would be the most expensive.[41]

Rowley's four options, put forward in April 1965, were the last attempt to structure a force that could meet the White Paper model of a heavy brigade group in Europe and two brigades in Canada that could both meet the NATO commitment and have a degree of air-transportability. The concept of a skeletal light mechanized division in Europe was inspired, but depended on the air force and to a certain extent the navy, diverting resources to pay for its implementation. This alone probably doomed the idea, no matter how important the concept of a mobile force had been to the minister. Hellyer had already watered down his original mobile force concept. He was preoccupied with a myriad of issues relating to integration and the complete reorganization of the armed services. The organization of the army was fading into the background.

The matter of Mobile Command force structure was still unresolved at the end of November 1965 when Lieutenant-General R.W. Moncel, the VCDS and the highest-ranking army officer at CFHQ, brought it to the CDS's staff meeting. A few weeks earlier, Moncel had received a paper from Sutherland recapping the work of his committee two years earlier and outlining his current views. While Sutherland believed that the diplomatic climate had become somewhat more favourable to a Canadian withdrawal from the Central Front, he thought that to actually negotiate such a change "would involve demands upon Canadian diplomacy which are excessive." Although moving into the role of SACEUR's reserve was very appealing, he believed that the existing mobile forces represented an "unsatisfactory instrument" with which to carry out the delicate operation of disengagement from the Central Front. It would be easier to simply change the RCAF role from general tactical support to one of air transport.[42]

Moncel had his own ideas. When he met with the CDS and senior staff, he explained that the organization of Mobile Command was the last high-level decision remaining in order to implement the White Paper structures. He noted that it would be especially difficult for the support arms to play both heavy and light roles, and suggested that Mobile Command be told that the brigade group in Europe would have first claim on resources. Taking a cut-the-suit-to-fit-the-cloth approach, he suggested that Mobile Command maintain one mechanized brigade group in eastern Canada as a rotational backup for 4 Canadian Infantry Brigade Group (4CIBG) in Europe, and that support troops be organized on a divisional basis to provide support to both heavy and light formations. A single light force of battalion size should be organized as an airborne special service force, and the rest of the forces in Canada should be organized as light forces. In the ensuing discussion, concerns were raised regarding the difficulties such a structure would create for troop rotation, its impact on the regimental system, and whether it could cope with a UN requirement for a heavy force. Air Chief Marshal Miller, the CDS, took the position that it might be possible to negotiate with SACEUR a change of role for the brigade in Europe. He deferred consideration of the land force structure pending completion of a study of an alternative to the heavy, mechanized role in NATO. The discussion had now come full circle. In the beginning, the search for an alternative to providing heavy forces on the NATO front had been civilian-driven. Now the military would take over, seeking a role that was doable and affordable and that would not upset the balance between the three services.[43]

The core of Moncel's proposal was included in the ten-year defence plan that Miller sent to Hellyer on 25 February 1966. Miller reported that a force planning review directed by the NATO Council for the purpose of adjusting national contributions based on a more realistic assessment of future NATO requirements was not yet complete, but was at a stage where some conclusions could be drawn. The principal one was that deliberate major aggression against NATO was unlikely, provided that deterrent strength and balance were maintained. The second major conclusion was that the greatest practical danger to NATO was unpremeditated limited aggression arising from a political crisis. This could be over Berlin, pressure on NATO's flanks, or spillover from troubles in Eastern Europe. According to Miller: "From this conclusion has come general acceptance that there is a growing NATO requirement for ground forces capable of quick effective response to such aggression: strategic reserves held at a high state of readiness, airportable, primarily non-nuclear and with their own tactical air support. The ACE Mobile Force is the first step in developing such strategic reserves." Furthermore, NATO thinking was that if there should ever be a major war in Europe, it would end within a few days, "one way or another." This challenged the rationale for war reserves, resupply of Europe, and convoy operations, and made existing Canadian plans more and more questionable. On the aviation side, opinions had been expressed at NATO ministerial meetings that ACE nuclear strike aircraft were of marginal value and should be replaced by medium-range ballistic missiles, freeing the aircraft for non-nuclear operations.[44]

Thus NATO's developing position was converging with that expressed in the White Paper. Miller thought that "at an appropriate time" the NATO mission could be "updated." In the interim, he proposed to maintain 4CIBG in Europe as a mechanized brigade group and provide an infantry battalion group to the ACE Mobile Force. The balance of the army in Canada would be vaguely defined mobile forces that would provide rotational backup to the NATO brigade group. The strike/reconnaissance role for the air force would be retained for the life of the Starfighter.[45]

Here, the matter rested for the balance of Hellyer's term as minister. NATO's force structure plans had not been as definitive as Miller had suggested, asking only for fewer forces permanently committed to forward defence, a higher proportion of mobile reserves, and less emphasis on strike/reconnaissance but more on close air support to ground troops. The SHAPE document on Force Proposals 1968-72 warned that "current trends toward a concept of strategic mobility must not be allowed to so weaken the conventional force posture that this aspect of the deterrent loses its credibility." Air Marshal F.R. Sharp, the VCDS, counselled General Allard (who had been promoted to CDS) that "the opportunity, if indeed not the necessity, to change the Canadian role for the post-1972 period appears possible from the current SHAPE studies on defence postures." Going further than previous mobility advocates, Sharp argued that the force should be air-mobile, that is, transported by helicopter. He regarded this as the next major evolutionary cycle in land force development. Major powers were increasing their air mobility; population densities in Europe were making vehicle movement more difficult and, once canalized, vulnerable to nuclear fire.[46] Land staff in CFHQ did not think much of Sharp's proposal and raised the familiar objections of lack of tactical mobility, lack of firepower, lack of transport, and cost. They added that there was no airfield or hangar space in Europe for additional close support aircraft, and that the ACE Mobile Force already had enough. Finally, they did not share Sharp's enthusiasm for air-mobile forces and were of the opinion that no one had ever suggested that air-mobile forces could cope with a concerted Soviet mechanized ground attack. They dismissed the concept of a uniformly structured Canadian army as neither feasible nor desirable, concluding that "history has proven the folly of this expedient."[47] Allard took the whole matter under advisement and deferred it for further study.[48]

Upon being appointed commander of Mobile Command in 1965, Allard had asked what was meant by Mobile Command. Two years later, after watching the VCDS and the land staff debate the issue, he answered his own question. Allard's "Rationale for Canadian Defence Forces" will be outlined in the next chapter.

Mobile Command as "Army Headquarters"

Not only did the 1964 *White Paper on Defence* call for a new type of army but, by integrating the three services under a single chief of defence staff and doing away with the former structure of field commands, it also required a rethinking of how the army was to manage itself. Although the Canadian Army would have legal existence until the unification of the armed services in 1967, integration effectively spelled its end as an organization. Mobile Command was responsible for the three Canada-based brigade groups, but not the NATO brigade group or the Militia. As the first commander of Mobile Command, Lieutenant-General Allard struggled to define the limits of his authority.

Major-General Rowley prepared the first Mobile Command Organization Book in August 1965. The commander was responsible for preparation of plans and operational requirements in support of assigned commitments, objects, and contingencies in Canada or overseas. The commander was also responsible for the formulation, testing, and documentation of *current* tactical doctrine, operational procedures, and techniques; the organization, equipment, and training of assigned land and air forces; the conduct of trials of field organizations and establishments; and the conduct of troop trials of equipment. Mobile Command was therefore more than just a troop generator or field command, but less than "army headquarters." It had no direct responsibility for doctrine above the tactical level and none for combat development. The long-range future of the army was to be the province of the integrated staff at CFHQ. In his foreword to the Organization Book, Rowley noted that the air headquarters was yet to be designed and that the aviation brigade would not be formed until after 1970. He also noted that there were problems "of a fundamental nature" involving Mobile Command's relationship with CFHQ and the other commands.[49]

In November, Allard wrote Air Chief Marshal Miller complaining that after three months' experience with the new organization, he wished to have certain problems corrected. While he had had few difficulties with the other commands, there had been "misunderstandings" with CFHQ staff. In his opinion, CFHQ was meant to be a "policy headquarters" that would issue only statements of principle and guidance for action to the commands. Mobile Command was not merely a "field headquarters" according to the army's use of the term, as it was not mobile. Mobile Command could itself form and deploy field headquarters. Allard challenged the opinion of CFHQ staff who believed that Mobile Command forces deployed overseas would pass to their command upon leaving Canada. He could not understand why this would be so, and compared it to ships and aircraft coming under CFHQ if they left the country. In his opinion, deployed units should be under the command of a task force commander while Mobile Command would be "the father of troops in the field" and responsible for seeing that those troops got what they needed to do their job.[50]

With regard to training, this should continue to belong to the command at the appropriate unit, formation, or headquarters level. Operational staff training conducted by the Canadian Army Staff College should be supervised by Mobile Command. In this he had the agreement of the commander training command, to whom the staff college reported. He also believed that Mobile Command should be responsible for equipment planning, as this went hand-in-hand with organization. Equipment proposals would be based on long-range forecasts as well as current operational experience, intelligence, operational analysis, and materiel management reports. Allard proposed that Mobile Command be responsible for the management of all personnel likely to remain in the army combat arms for their entire career. Combat support and combat service support troops could be co-managed with other commands. As for logistics, he proposed to establish bases to provide field units with logistic support so that the field force commander could concentrate on operations. He regarded operational support forward of port facilities a Mobile Command responsibility.[51] Allard's concept would have all but recreated Army Headquarters.

Miller was not entirely receptive to Allard's views of what Mobile Command should be. He thought it correct that CFHQ should not get involved in the day-to-day conduct of specific operations, but made it plain that the Long Range Plan, the Integrated Defence Plan, and the Estimates (that is, all long-range planning and major budget decisions) were the responsibility of CFHQ. Inherent in this were the determination of force development objectives and equipment objectives and requirements. While CFHQ would of course seek the advice of Mobile Command, he could not agree that the national headquarters should confine itself to statements of principle: "Such a limitation would certainly usher in the millennium. But it is not at hand, and I am afraid it will not come to pass in our lifetime." Regarding deployed elements, Miller did not think it was inconceivable that the government would insist on direct and instant communication with the commander overseas, but conceded that Mobile Command was bound to have some responsibility for administration and logistic support. He preferred to develop more experience before defining these in detail. He had "some reservations" about Mobile Command's being made responsible for operational staff training, and informed Allard that this was under study at CFHQ. He flatly denied Allard authority over organization as it involved establishments and budgets, telling him: "You must be aware that I have relatively little authority myself in these matters, and obviously I cannot delegate to you authority I do not have. Moreover I see little reason to expect the minister will consider any such delegation; in fact, the current trend is in the opposite direction." Moreover, Command determination of equipment requirements would "not be acceptable." Personnel authorities were a difficult problem as there were many practical difficulties in delegating this to the commands, and it appeared that a single, unified personnel system would be more economical. Nevertheless, he was intrigued by Allard's suggestion of a personnel command and his ideas regarding delegation. For the time being, however, he told Allard that "we shall have to make do."[52]

Mobile Command was therefore left in a muddle. It was more than a field headquarters but much less than the national headquarters of an army. Long-range planning, budgetary control, and personnel administration were all going to be controlled by the integrated staff at CFHQ. Over the long run, this would foster resentment, which would break out into the open.

The most obvious advance made by Mobile Command Headquarters in shaping the post–White Paper army was the publication of CFP 165, *The Conduct of Land Operations.* Written under the direction of Major-General Rowley (when he was not organizing Mobile Command Headquarters or the land forces as a whole!), CFP 165 was largely a pedestrian, branch-by-branch exposition of each combat and support arm in the army, with a heavy emphasis on nuclear warfare throughout. Unlike the 1960 *Infantry Brigade Group in Battle,* it was not an integrated concept for how to wage war. It did, however, contain a number of innovative concepts and clarified army thinking on several others. Most interesting was the inclusion of "cold war" as the lowest level in scales of conflict, below general war and limited war:

> Near the lower end of the scale of conflict, limited war passes into the area sometimes referred to as cold war. Other terms in common use for this are: situations short of war; peace-keeping; and internal security. The dividing line between limited and cold war is neither distinct nor absolute. The basic characteristic of cold war is the absence of overt armed conflict, but military forces may be required and should be prepared to conduct cold war operations which are to all intents and purposes combat operations. In some cold war situations political, economic and psychological measures may play a role equal to or more important than military strength.[53]

The manual contained a chapter on situations short of war that recognized "classic" peacekeeping, involving a neutral force separating parties in conflict and operating within a demilitarized zone, but went beyond this by including internal security and counter-guerrilla operations.[54] Thus it translated the counter-subversion strategy of the White Paper into doctrine. There was a clear recognition that situations short of war were fundamentally political in nature. The tactics of relying on police, small-unit patrols, ambushes, and "spreading ink-blot" operations to protect the populace would have been familiar to contemporaries who had studied the British defeat of communist insurgents in

Malaya.[55] It is interesting to note that these principles have been recently rediscovered.

Two short chapters covered airborne/air-mobile and amphibious operations. Whereas airborne operations were considered to be potentially large-scale, of considerable duration, and strategic, air-mobile operations were considered to be of only tactical significance. This was not surprising, as the army had never viewed helicopter operations in enemy territory as survivable and had tried to persuade the Americans to reduce their emphasis on air-mobile tactics.[56] Interestingly, tactical aviation was considered to include only reconnaissance and surveillance, observation of fire, tactical transport, and liaison – the traditional roles for aircraft operated by the army. Close air support, which was to be organizationally part of Mobile Command as a key plank in the White Paper defence policy, was curiously absent from the discussion.[57]

The Mobile Force and Aviation

The White Paper increased air transport for the Mobile Force (the two brigades in Canada) and also authorized new tactical aircraft. Even though the provision of air- and sealift for the Mobile Force was listed as a priority in the White Paper, it was never treated as such. The thirty-five C-119 Flying Boxcars and twenty-nine North Star transports of Air Transport Command were aging, and the air force showed no desire to replace them. At one point the entire Flying Boxcar fleet was grounded and Hellyer decided to personally investigate Air Chief Marshal Miller's claim that nothing was seriously amiss. The condition of the aircraft so shocked him that he increased the order for C-130 Hercules aircraft from four to twenty.[58] Sixty-four transport aircraft were replaced with twenty-three C-130s between 1964 and 1966, but this actually decreased the tonnage capacity and sortie rate. Tactical transport capacity was increased, however, by the addition of five CV-7 Buffalo and sixteen DHC-4 Caribou aircraft. The Caribous were not retained for very long and were sold to Tanzania in the 1970s. The twelve Yukon strategic transports were replaced with five Boeing 707s.[59] In January 1966 Allard wrote to Miller outlining the lack of airlift capability. According to him, even if the existing UN and NATO commitments requiring routine airlift were cancelled, the existing fleet would not have sufficient capacity to move a brigade group to a likely trouble spot in less than two and a half months. This was probably an overstatement of capacity. A year later, a study found that ten Yukons, twenty-two C-130s, and a naval supply ship would take thirty-three days to transport a battalion group – one-third of a brigade – to Mozambique.[60] Allard suggested that doubling the C-130 fleet would go "part way" to meeting his requirement, but an air fleet this size would create excessive personnel requirements. Instead, he suggested acquiring ten C-141 Starlifters, which would require fewer than half the staff to operate. The C-141 could also be used as a tanker for the CF-5 tactical fighters that the air force would eventually require, as well as a VIP aircraft if outfitted with a passenger module.[61] After being appointed chief of the defence staff a few months later, Allard received a report on the ability of the Forces to deploy a battalion group to either Norway or Turkey. It concluded that neither deployment could be accomplished in the time allowed, even without a CF-5 deployment. Staff recommended the purchase of eight C-141s and four giant C-5A transports. The Defence Council (the senior management committee revived by Hellyer as his "Cabinet of DND" and consisting of the minister, the chief of the defence staff, the deputy minister, and the chairman of the Defence Research Board) approved the purchase of four C-141s on 27 June 1967, but no money for these large aircraft was ever allocated.[62]

Although the army had not embraced air-mobile tactics, it did see a need for helicopter transport on the battlefield. In November 1966, the Defence Council approved a helicopter battalion of 85 light, 110 utility, and 18 heavy helicopters. An analysis of the requirements of a Canadian task force deployed to a non-NATO theatre concluded that 112 aircraft would be required, 84 of them helicopters. In addition to the CF-5s and Buffalos, the study recommended the acquisition of Mohawk fixed-wing reconnaissance aircraft. Funding could be found for only half the helicopter requirement – spread out over a ten-year timeframe – and none for the Mohawks. Accordingly, beginning in 1968 a fleet of 70 utility helicopters (UTTH) and 15 large cargo helicopters was acquired.[63]

More tangled, but with no better outcome, was the acquisition of a tactical aircraft. The White Paper had promised:

> During the decade, we propose to give increasing emphasis to the provision of aircraft for direct support of our ground forces. We anticipate that a high performance aircraft will be available to provide sufficient flexibility for any task we might undertake from ground attack to air surveillance. These versatile tactical aircraft will possess adequate radius of action to allow rapid deployment from Canada to bases overseas. This will permit squadrons to be stationed in Canada or Europe as required.[64]

The initial study of the cost and composition of the Mobile Force had called for an aircraft capable of short takeoff and landing (STOL), aircraft carrier compatibility, high speed, and long ferry range. It noted that many countries had "semi-sophisticated" air defence systems and that subsonic aircraft would not be viable. The McDonnell Douglas F-4C Phantom almost met the stated requirements but was complex and costly. Other existing aircraft were less costly but also less capable.[65] The Department of Defence Production backed the F-4C because it could be built in Canada and because the British government was willing to permit F-4 fighters with British Spey engines to be produced in Canada. Hellyer, however, involved himself in the process in what would be the first of many interventions aimed at "situating the appreciation" until the only possible answer was the Northrop F-5.[66] Reversing the position taken in the White Paper, he claimed that the contention that an all-purpose aircraft could best serve Canada's needs "has not been proven." He questioned whether the CF-104 Starfighter should be replaced for a number of years, if at all, and also thought it "premature" to replace the CF-101 Voodoo for air defence. He therefore directed Air Chief Marshal Miller to undertake a "new close look" at requirements, specifically at the best means of providing close air support to ground forces.[67] Miller and the air requirements staff at CFHQ were slow to take the hint, and came back with a recommendation of 60 to 72 F-4Cs rather than the 108 originally requested. The estimated cost of $700 million for 72 aircraft was astronomical and would have required Hellyer to forgo the acquisition of Caribou transports to move the Mobile Force in the field. Hellyer was both determined to fund the army equipment program overall and hemmed in by the finance minister's cap on his budget. The F-4 began to appear as a threat to his wider goals.[68]

Hellyer pushed the staff for several additional rounds of analysis, which concluded in the end that several light attack aircraft were viable but that the F-5 was "not a suitable aircraft." Miller and CFHQ produced an assessment that underlined many of the F-5's limitations but nevertheless left it on the table as an option. Hellyer recommended purchase of the F-5 to Cabinet on 9 July 1965.[69] With that, the Mobile Force was saddled with an aircraft of astonishing limitations. It was a clear-air fighter only, lacking radar. It had a lower combat ceiling and greater turn radius than the MiG-19. It lacked the required range to ferry itself, and could not carry a high enough weapons load to be an effective ground attack aircraft.

As commander of Mobile Command, Allard would defend the selection of the F-5 several times before parliamentary committees. His testimony consisted of carefully crafted irrelevancies, distortions, and gross exaggerations. His claims of the ease of field maintenance had been irrelevant to the selection process, as was the fact that the aircraft met the US Air Force requirements for an export aircraft it did not intend to acquire itself. His testimony that the aircraft "offered the best characteristics" was true only if one took Hellyer's final edit of the requirement into account. Allard's first assessment had been that the plane was unsuitable. Finally, the F-5 had severely limited reconnaissance capabilities.

It lacked the structural strength to carry a detachable reconnaissance pod, so the engineering staff decided that cameras for clear-air and night photography would have to go into the nose. Although five camera stations could be designed, there was enough space for only three cameras at a time.[70] Even this design was reduced in capability, and the night illumination pod was dropped completely due to shortage of funds.[71] Allard's claims during testimony of a secret technology reconnaissance system would appear to be a fantasy.

Speaking to an internal audience, Hellyer owned up to what he had done. At the Defence Council, he acknowledged the limitations of the CF-5 and promised that in a few years it would be possible to acquire an aircraft that could meet the requirement.[72] The air force took Hellyer's statement of intent to heart (and possibly also took note of the government's partiality to Northrop). Staff recommended to Allard that the Forces approve a requirement for a Canadian Advanced Multi-Role Aircraft (CAMRA). This airplane would be capable of replacing the CF-104, CF-101, and CF-5 in the 1973-83 time frame and perform all the roles assigned to these aircraft. The planners noted that Northrop Project 530 came close to meeting all their requirements, and recommended that Northrop be engaged to undertake further studies. No funding was immediately available for this project, but in the end it led to the acquisition of 138 CF-18 aircraft in 1980.[73]

The air element of the Mobile Force was central to its raison d'être. Not only was it supposed to provide strategic and tactical mobility but it also was to be a demonstration of service integration. The integrated organization was achieved, with Mobile Command having control of its air assets. The assets themselves left much to be desired, however. The force Hellyer sketched out in the White Paper was simply unaffordable. Strategic lift remained inadequate and close air support had more of a training than a warfighting capability. Tactical helicopters were introduced to the army in significant numbers, but at a much slower rate than was desirable. The Command was, in the end, immobile.

The Reserves and the Mobile Force

Just as thermonuclear war called into question the viability of the brigade group in NATO, so it affected the viability of the Militia. The military consensus was that any war in Europe would be a short one. Either it would "go nuclear" or there would be a quickly negotiated end. Flexible-response doctrine was intended to strengthen deterrence and, if deterrence failed, provide some time to negotiate before nuclear arms were used. It created a need for more and better conventional forces – but forces in being, not a mobilization base. NATO doctrine therefore did nothing to provide a role for the Militia.

The option, or course, was the national survival role that the Conservative government had assigned to the Militia. The Militia had grown in size but, as noted earlier, the army had not been able to develop a credible national survival program. As both the size of the Soviet nuclear arsenal and the size of its weapons increased, the prospects for survival of a full-scale nuclear war diminished.

Belief that a mobilization force was no longer required had penetrated civilian thinking fairly deeply. The Diefenbaker government's Special Committee on Defence Expenditures, chaired by G.E. Halpenny in the spring and summer of 1960, had heard George Pearkes's views that any war would be fought by forces in being and that there was little likelihood of a large-scale reserve call-up. Forces in being were endorsed again in 1963 by the Glassco Commission, which concluded there was "no need to plan directing establishments for hypothetical forces and to maintain nominal elements of those establishments at a level which makes any peacetime employment impossible."[74]

By mid-1963 the army budget was under severe pressure and Lieutenant-General Walsh, the CGS, was prepared to make drastic cuts. His five-year program would reduce the division commitment to NATO to two from three brigades. Equipment demands would be reduced, and the army would shed responsibility for the Northwest Highway System and close Fort Churchill. National survival activities, other than the warning system, would be suspended and the Militia would be reduced by two-thirds of effective strength by amalgamating or disbanding units, making some units dormant, and closing units in rented or unsuitable accommodations.[75] The army's mobilization plan consisted largely of redistributing its Regular manpower and providing replacements and reinforcements to the brigade group in Europe. If a war lasted longer than three to six months, Militia officers would be called upon, but staff lumped the bulk of the reserves with new enrollees, who would require extensive training.[76]

Along with the other ad hoc committees established by Hellyer was an Ad Hoc Committee of the Chiefs of Staff Committee to study "the continuing requirement for the Reserve Forces." The minister asked the committee to consider whether or not the Reserves should continue to provide a mobilization base or to participate in national survival operations. The committee found it unlikely that a mobilization base would be required, since there would be no time to deploy the Reserves and no transportation plans or equipment stocks. Reserves might be used as individual replacements for Regular Force soldiers withdrawn from logistic and training units to reinforce combat units. As for national survival, the Reserves would be required to meet the need for vulnerable point guards and to staff internment camps, but little else. The committee estimated that, given their requirements, the Militia could be decreased from

51,000 to 30,000. Hellyer announced the cut on 5 December 1963.[77] In the White Paper that followed three months later, Hellyer promised a Militia reorganization under a ministerial commission under the chairmanship of Brigadier E.R. Suttie. The White Paper said that the primary role of the Militia was to support the Regular army and that the plan was that they would replace Regular soldiers withdrawn from support units to fill out the field force. The Militia might also form logistic and special units not required in peacetime, perform internal security duties, and assist the Regular army in its national survival responsibilities. Suttie's commission was merely to advise on the best organization of these roles, not rethink the Militia.[78]

The commission made twenty-six recommendations on a wide range of topics, including badges, uniforms, expenses, and disposal of surplus assets, but the key recommendations were the designation of "major" and "minor" Militia units and reduction in the number of Militia Group Headquarters, from twenty-five to fifteen. The commissioners estimated that $5.7 million could be saved if all their recommendations were accepted. Hellyer, who had a low opinion of the effectiveness of the Militia, not only cut units, removing thirteen regiments from the order of battle and closing 114 armouries, but also eliminated all the Militia Group Headquarters and assigned Militia administration to 12 Regular Army District Headquarters. This effectively ended the Militia's career as a parallel force to the Regular army and placed it under Regular control.[79]

When Mobile Command was established in 1965, it was not given control of the Militia. This left the organization adrift until September 1965, when Major-General W.A.B. Anderson was appointed the deputy chief reserves at CFHQ, responsible for the reserve forces of all three services. His successor, Major-General Mike Dare, was tasked with establishing realistic tasks for the Militia within the concept of forces in being, and incorporating the Militia into Mobile Command. Dare created a Militia organization reporting to him in Ottawa, based on five regions commanded by Regular Force officers and seven districts commanded by reservists. The Militia was divided into a Ready Reserve, which would fill vacancies within the Regular Force; the Canadian Regional Reserve, which would have responsibilities for internal security and the defence of Canada; and the Mobile Command Reserve, which would consist of subunits that would be trained to a sufficient level that they could augment Regular Force units directly.[80]

The problem with both Suttie and Dare was that their reforms were only structural. Twenty thousand of the 30,000 Militia soldiers were assigned to the Mobile Command Reserve, which was supposed to be able to deploy at the subunit or company level. This meant that Reserve soldiers would not only have to master their individual trade skills but also be trained together to work in groups of forty to one hundred troops.[81] The recruiting, training, and turnover problems identified by Major-General Howard Kennedy and Brigadier W.A.B. Anderson a few years earlier (see Chapter 1) were ignored, but they made the idea of effective Militia subunits optimistic to say the least. Worse, Dare's structure was found to be "a terrible system – unwieldy, duplicative, confused and disliked." The problem was that the Reserve regions did not control the resources they needed in order to do their jobs; everything had to be referred to Ottawa, where the deputy chief reserves would have to coordinate support with a functional command. In addition, the Militia was cut off from a direct relationship with Mobile Command, resulting in significant administrative problems. The organization was changed again in 1968.[82]

The Denouement of Unification

Most of the substantive changes required to implement the White Paper were achieved through the integration of the armed services and the replacement of individual chiefs of staff with a single chief of the defence staff. This created an integrated Canadian Forces Headquarters, with Mobile Command as an integrated command under it. The White Paper had called integration "the first step towards a single unified defence force for Canada."[83] Paul Hellyer did not regard this merely as a long-term vision but rather as the end state he wished to achieve during his term as minister. Accordingly, he introduced Bill C-243 in the House of Commons on 6 November 1966 to unify the armed services by placing all members of the forces on a uniform personnel list and to formally abolish the three services, which, by this time, had "a more conceptual than actual existence."[84] The decision to go beyond integration to complete unification would lead to a costly and emotional process, with months of parliamentary hearings, attempts by the Conservative opposition to filibuster Bill C-243 and block a vote of supply, and the "revolt of the admirals" and firing of Rear-Admiral William Landymore.

The ins and outs of the unification battle are beyond the scope of this book, but unification had both short-term and long-term effects on the army. The most obvious short-term effect was in senior personnel – who was promoted and who left the service. Lieutenant-General Robert Moncel was the vice chief of the defence staff and the obvious successor to Air Chief Marshal Miller as the CDS. He had made it plain to Hellyer, however, that he did not support unification. He told Hellyer it was a matter of "if, when and how ... we should not rush into unification with a few notes on the back of a cigarette package ... we must know where we are going. We will get down immediately to practicalities – issues of badges, caps, ranks, careers, etc." Moncel believed that it was one thing to have "a single designation which would encompass multiple families that do certain things ... It was possible to perpetuate the single bits that have no civilian counterpart and retain the great names that go with them. The Corps names were meaningful to personnel and should be retained."[85] Two years later, he still felt rushed and believed that the armed services were "moving on an uncharted course at a very, very high speed towards a very, very dim destination."[86] What was clear was that Hellyer had no intention of promoting to CDS an officer who was not an enthusiastic supporter of unification. Rather than Moncel, he selected Lieutenant-General J.V. Allard, the commander of Mobile Command. Allard's selection was not a popular one at CFHQ. Moncel resigned, as did Lieutenant-General Frank Fleury, the comptroller general, and Vice Admiral Ken Dyer, the personnel chief. It is unclear whether the resignations were due to philosophical differences over unification, dislike of Allard as a superior, or the fact that the careers of these men had been affected. There is no doubt that senior military officials did not like the manner in which Hellyer had announced the decision to proceed to complete unification, which had come across as an unanticipated ultimatum to implement the policy or resign.[87]

What is interesting is that Moncel and Fleury had had little or no trouble accepting the massive changes to the army brought about by integration without – as Allard had found – even a complete concept, much less a plan, but balked at unification, which would involve cap badges and personnel administration. In this, as in other matters, Allard took a different view. In his memoirs he wrote: "Narrowly defined esprit de corps and outmoded traditions, red uniforms and parades modelled on the British forces were no longer essential for Canada in view of the importance of the forthcoming law [Bill C-243]. Moreover, twenty years after the end of the Second World War, the new generation of servicemen might be expected to have a different attitude from ours."[88] Allard was possibly more representative of most soldiers than those who wanted to preserve the Britishness of the army. According to Major-General F.F. Worthington, there was no rejection of the new green uniform and response to early trials was favourable.[89]

On the other hand, creation of the Mobile Force had not precluded the "big army" model of the brigade group in Europe. In fact, by recommending the acquisition of APCs, self-propelled artillery, and nuclear surface-to-surface missiles, the White Paper had seemed to perpetuate it. Unification was seen as more of a direct threat to the army as a society or culture. One of the least-accepted elements of unification was the application of the air force's policy towards the rank of corporal to the other former services. To the air force, the rank meant a pay promotion based on skill or knowledge in a trade. To the army, it was a designation of field leadership. Acceptance of the air force policy throughout the unified force created a great number of new "Hellyer corporals" who had rank but no leadership responsibility. Numerous other differences in personnel policy arising largely from integration of personnel management functions would become matters of concern to a significant number of army officers.

As Canada marked its centennial year in 1967, the army appeared to be keeping pace with the country. Its change of uniforms and adoption of Canadian heraldry in its flags and badges matched the new flag the country had adopted in 1965, and the army appeared to be moving ahead with integrating and advancing francophones along with the rest of the federal government. By and large this perception was correct, but the battle for the soul of the army was far from over and would have to be fought again during the 1980s. Moreover, unification had not resulted in a consolidation of civil and military views regarding the role of the army. The government had reaffirmed the NATO role, but neither the Canadian army nor its allied counterparts had a convincing concept of how a nuclear war in Europe could be fought. The army had been reorganized as a "mobile force," but the problems of how to create a force that was both transportable and survivable were unresolved. The resources for strategic lift had not been found, and close air support capability had been botched. The army's progress in developing an effective staff structure was disrupted as Mobile Command and CFHQ began fighting for control of the army. Unification had turned out to be a mixed blessing, at best.

CHAPTER FOUR

Trudeau and the Crisis in Civil-Military Relations

THE LATE 1960S AND 1970S saw the tension between the civil and military views of the role and structure of the army develop into the most serious crisis in civil-military relations since the Second World War. Civilians became increasingly skeptical about the utility of a heavily equipped army on NATO's Central Front, whereas the army sought to retain this role. It did this first by guile and working with its allies at the political level and then by foot-dragging and non-cooperation with its minister. The minister, Donald Macdonald, responded by restructuring National Defence Headquarters (NDHQ) to permanently reduce the independence of the military and to create civilian alternatives to military advice. This central conflict was complicated by growing budgetary pressures, a flawed post-unification staff structure that created rivalry between Mobile Command and NDHQ, and the continuing evolution of Canadian society away from the ideal preferred by the army.

The Legacy of the Early 1960s

Paul Hellyer had expected sufficient savings from the unification of the armed services to allow about 25 percent of the defence budget to be devoted to capital spending. The minister of finance had imposed a ceiling of $1.55 billion for defence starting in 1965-66, with an annual increase of no more than 2 percent a year for the five-year period ending in 1969-70. Just how Hellyer had arrived at his estimate was never clear. Although the Glassco Commission report had been cited extensively in the 1964 *White Paper on Defence* to demonstrate the inefficiency of the three separate services, the commission had never presented an estimate of the amount of savings that could be achieved.[1] During the analysis preceding the White Paper, R.J. Sutherland had informed the minister that although his committee had attempted to cost alternatives, they "could not produce estimates which could be taken at all seriously" and had abandoned the attempt, preferring to work on proposals for a new program budgeting system instead. Sutherland predicted (correctly) that a full costing of the mobile force would come in at over $1.8 billion.[2] Hellyer had cut support services by 10,000 personnel, or 20 percent of strength, and Canadian Forces Headquarters (CFHQ) by 30 percent. Army strength was reduced from 49,760 in 1963 to 40,192 in 1968. Inflation, however, jumped to 6 percent rather than the 2 percent allowed for by the minister of finance. Worse, the entire government budget had made no provision for higher inflation, leaving National Defence in a bind with no place to turn. Personnel and operating costs continued to rise even as strength dwindled.[3]

In June 1967 Air Marshal Sharp, the vice chief of the defence staff, informed General Allard that the annual program exceeded resources by $65 million a year. In addition, the five-year Integrated Defence Plan allowed only $270 million for capital, whereas staff estimated that $350 million was required. The department was also short of development funding, with the $20 million allocated being less than one-third of the requirement.[4] A month later Major-General N.G. Wilson-Smith, the deputy chief operations, reported that Mobile Command was now 4,900 personnel short of the number required by the force structure. Funds were clearly lacking to equip both one of the air-transportable brigades and the mechanized brigade stationed in Canada. Allard was reduced to complaining that, whereas the mobile force was supposed to be a force capable of meeting all possible commitments, budgetary limitations had reduced it to "a policing type of force." Elgin Armstrong, the deputy minister, counselled that equipping of the mechanized brigade in Canada to only a training level "appeared inevitable."[5]

In response to the looming budgetary crisis, and anticipating an accompanying political crisis, Allard assembled his senior military officials in Kingston in August 1967 to discuss the foundations of the military profession in Canada. In his opening address, he stated that the purpose of the meeting was to "confirm, deny or develop theories and principles on which our profession must stand." Allard was sensitive to the fact that many Canadians did not see the requirement for a military force at all. However, he did not think that the advocates of a "purely Canadian strategy" had addressed the practicalities of Canada's being a small country or thought their way around the realities of nuclear deterrence or the need to participate in NORAD to preserve Canadian sovereignty from American "help." Allard saw the Canadian military as primarily a political tool for the government. In the face of nuclear weapons and the American-Soviet confrontation, no Canadian military force could ever truly defend the country. Nor could Canada's brigade and six air squadrons in Europe be considered a significant weight in the strategic balance. Even peacekeeping operations did not look particularly effective; for example, in the Middle East, rather than ensuring peace, the UN Emergency Force had allowed the antagonists to rebuild their forces and fight another war. "The consequences of all this," said Allard, "are that it is really difficult to know how much Canada should spend on national defence and what type of military posture would be best for her to adopt." He encouraged his senior staff to exercise some boldness in their efforts to address these problems, and not to shelter sacred cows. He stated that "the economic situation is more serious than you think" and that inflation was consuming the operations budget.[6]

Allard's accompanying "Rationale for Canadian Defence Forces," drafted by a joint Defence/External Affairs team, assessed defence objectives against its budgetary share. Air defence of North America was considered indispensible at $125 million per year to avoid giving Soviet bombers a free ride and to keep the United States out of Canada. Anti-submarine warfare (ASW) was not considered to be so cost-effective. At $200 million a year it was the largest single item in the budget, making Canadian ASW forces one-third as large as those maintained by the United States. It was thought that savings could be made where maritime forces were concerned. Canada's contribution to NATO in Europe was equally vulnerable. The Canadian forces in Europe were obviously not essential to the maintenance of European confidence, and Europe could, if it wished, offset any Canadian withdrawal. Moreover, specific evidence of Canadian influence gained by stationing troops in Europe was hard to come by. The paper concluded that "because the importance of Canadian forces in Europe is to some extent symbolic, it is difficult to predict when their withdrawal might become feasible." It noted that the brigade group cost $114 million a year and the Air Division another $80 million; together they accounted for one-quarter of the budget for operations. According to the drafters of the document, it was "probably not too early" to begin studying the organizational and financial implications of withdrawal from Europe. As to peacekeeping forces, it was difficult to estimate the incremental cost and, at any rate, maintenance of forces for this purpose was "a voluntary act."[7]

It is not known exactly how the senior military officials received either Allard's introduction or the paper he presented, but it would take almost a year for a consensus document to emerge. We will return to its fate later.

Léo Cadieux, who had been elevated from associate defence minister to minister when Hellyer departed in September 1967, decided that it would be necessary to take the issue of budget and military roles to Cabinet. He directed the headquarters staff to study whether the Supreme Headquarters Allied Powers Europe (SHAPE) study "Defence Planning – 1972 Onwards" would provide Canada with an opportunity to change roles from heavy forces on the Central Front to one in the regional reserve based on mobile forces, and whether the strike role of the Air Division could be replaced by an "integrated air-ground contribution."

He asked that he be in a position to advise on whether forces provided to NATO could be reduced, and also for a military assessment of withdrawing either the brigade or the Air Division. He told staff that he expected them to address the basic goals and strategic concept behind forces recommended, optional capabilities that these forces should have should the government be prepared to assign additional roles to them, and the strategic lift required.[8]

Wilson-Smith was given a negotiating position from Allard to take to the Supreme Allied Commander Europe (SACEUR). He was to stress that "this new and serious study is not a rehash of previous requests for a change in role. Financial constraints require that [Canada] now wring every dollar if we are to improve and modernize our forces." SACEUR was to be told that Canada could no longer afford two armies and two air forces and must bring her assigned roles into closer correlation. In Canada's view, SACEUR's post-1972 study provided for this by recognizing the need for reserve forces and the future of air-mobile concepts. Canada was integrating its land and air elements into a single force and developing new doctrines and procedures. It was Canada's plan to have a single force under a single administrative command in some general location. This force would be equipped with helicopters and Buffalos to provide mobility as well as integral tactical aviation. Backup strategic transport and tankers could be provided if it was committed beyond Central Europe. There would be an overall reduction in numbers but an increase in general utility. If this was not possible, Canada would be prepared to look at alternatives such as a new role in corps or regional reserve with the same equipment, or a new role as regional reserve with light vehicles and helicopters.[9]

To Allard, the SHAPE study appeared to support such a move. It had called for a regional reserve of highly mobile forces of brigade or divisional strength. Three to four divisions were to reinforce forward deployed forces on the Central Front and the flank area of the Centre, especially the Baltic, using airlift capability. The SHAPE study envisaged mobile forces equipped with armoured vehicles with amphibious and night fighting capability, but not main battle tanks. Air-mobile units were thought to be particularly flexible and could, in SACEUR's opinion, be effectively used in Europe.[10] By taking this position, Allard was advocating not only a mobile force without heavy armour but also an air-mobile force based on helicopters. To date, neither of these had been accepted by the army. The advocacy of air-mobile forces was especially radical given that the army had spent a decade trying to get the US Army to de-emphasize the concept in combined American-British-Canadian standardization discussions.

SHAPE's reaction was unenthusiastic. Any change was equated with a reduction, and despite the "high-sounding tactical clichés" in its "72 Onwards" study,

SHAPE did not really accept that reserves must come from existing forces. It lacked enough forces to meet its forward defence needs, let alone provide a reserve. The Canadian request was therefore regarded as a reduction in strength. This was complicated by the disparity between NATO's Northern Army Group (NORTHAG) and Central Army Group (CENTAG). If the Canadian brigade went into regional reserve with CENTAG, it would diminish the already weak NORTHAG. SACEUR informed Canada that while a full study had not been possible in time allowed, "certain fundamental considerations" were already clear. The basic requirement at that time was for mechanized forces of the type currently provided by 4 Canadian Infantry Brigade Group (4CIBG). The reduction plans of other nations had emphasized the importance of retaining direct defensive (as opposed to reserve) forces as well as having the maximum number of nations represented in direct defence. SACEUR grudgingly allowed that it would be militarily feasible for 4CIBG to go into corps reserve if it remained organized as a mechanized force, but it would not be feasible to move it out of the British Corps area because of "administrative difficulties." Careful examination over a period of time would be required to assess the Canadian proposal.[11]

While the SHAPE option played out, senior military staff responded to Allard's "Rationale" paper. It was a case of the mountain having laboured only to bring forth a mouse. Musings about cutting ASW and NATO were terminated, as the final paper firmly endorsed the status quo. It concluded that any reduction in defence expenditures would isolate Canada from like-minded states, lead to the abandonment of efforts to promote a multinational approach to peace and security, limit Canada's ability to develop relations with Third World countries, and decrease Canada's ability to respond to contingencies calling for the use of armed force. It endorsed a continued Canadian presence in Europe and added a section comparing Canadian defence expenditures unfavourably with those of allies, commenting that since Canada also spent a lower percentage of its GNP on foreign aid, it was questionable whether a Canadian diversion of funds from defence to aid would impress the NATO allies.[12]

Defence staff suggested to Cadieux that the "Rationale" paper be sent to Pierre Trudeau, the prime minister–designate. Not everyone was so enthusiastic. R.L. Raymont, the executive staff officer to the chief of the defence staff and a long-time presence at senior levels, cautioned against this, telling Allard:

> It is obvious from some of his statements and discussions, that Mr. Trudeau has already gone into some depth regarding Canadian foreign and defence policy since World War II. As a member of the previous Cabinet he certainly will know

> Externals [sic] present view and our policy. I am wondering therefore how convinced he will be after, reading our rationale, which is based on the traditional view since World War II, of our approach to Europe.
>
> I would have thought that what Mr. Trudeau is now looking for is some real original thinking as to present and future trends in Europe and what our resulting approach should be. In this connection I have underlined portions of the rationale speech you gave at Kingston. [The section on NATO was underlined.]
>
> While the consensus of views of our ambassadors to the Nato countries is to look with disfavour at a Canadian unilateral withdrawal of troops *based* in Europe with an opinion that it might start a break-up of Nato there is the other side of the coin that in order to keep France as a partner in a wider political [context?] within Europe, after 1969 Nato should take on a different form with a lessening of influence from North America.
>
> Apart from this Mr. Trudeau will probably want to know what specific examples are there of particular influence and advantage Canada has received during e.g., the last 5 years, both political and economic because of Canadian troops *based* in Europe.[13]

In spite of this counsel, Cadieux did send a summary to Trudeau, making the analysis appear even more pedestrian than it was. There is no record of Trudeau's response, if any, but Cadieux blocked Allard from printing the "Rationale" paper and distributing it to senior defence and central agency officials. This ended Allard's efforts to head off the financial and political pressures he had foreseen a year earlier. No sacred cows had been harmed in the process.[14]

Cadieux finally sent a memorandum to Cabinet on 30 April 1968, recapping the department's situation and stating that it was no longer possible to operate under the spending cap without a complete re-examination of defence commitments. Based on the analyses he had received from the department and CFHQ, he presented three options: (1) proceed with the present defence program and increase the budget by $250 million in 1969-70 with subsequent adjustments for inflation; (2) reduce the Force's strength to 98,000, thus undermanning units by 18 percent and closing bases but preserving all commitments while requiring a budget increase of $125 million, inflation adjustments, and additional increases in capital; or (3) meet the Cabinet budget guidelines. Staying within budget would require reducing military strength by 10,000 and the civilian workforce by 3,500. Some forces would be retained in Europe, but the Air Division would be dispensed with. Additional reductions would be made in air and naval forces in Canada, as no other savings could be extracted from the army as long as a brigade group was in Europe. To meet the budget line, it would probably be necessary to withdraw and disband all the forces stationed in Europe.

Cadieux pointed out that Canada had committed itself to maintain current force levels in Europe until 31 December 1968 and that NATO plans indicated the alliance's intention to maintain the present force levels for the next five years. A Canadian withdrawal would necessitate adjustment to these plans and consultations would have to be undertaken very quickly. Cadieux made it plain that he favoured increasing the defence budget, since a rapid withdrawal from Europe "would be serious and could have unfortunate effects from which it would be difficult to recover for many years." Given Canada's already relatively low defence expenditures, it would be difficult to convince NATO allies that reductions were required because of economic necessity, and reductions would be "tantamount to Canada taking a unilateral decision in favour of significantly reduced defence efforts regardless of the consensus of its partners as to the defence needs of the Alliance." Such a move might destabilize NATO's security system and would adversely affect diplomatic and economic links with Europe and the United States.[15]

Cabinet was now set for a replay of the debates that had raged through the Diefenbaker Cabinet and continued in a lower key during the preparation of the 1964 *White Paper on Defence*. This time the question was not nuclear versus non-nuclear forces or heavy versus light forces, but whether Canada should have any forces in Europe at all. Moreover, Cadieux's memorandum to Cabinet arrived at the same moment that Prime Minister Trudeau himself was preparing to pick up the defence file.

Pierre Trudeau and Defence Policy

Pierre Trudeau had become prime minister following the general election of 25 June 1968, after only three years in Parliament. He had been brought into Cabinet at the insistence of Jean Marchand, to whom Lester Pearson had turned in an effort to find a Quebec lieutenant who could deal with the increasingly independent and antagonistic province. Marchand had made Gérard Pelletier, the editor of *La Presse*, and Trudeau, a law professor and leftish activist, part of the deal. Trudeau was not initially regarded as a welcome component of the transaction, but Pearson found his counsel on Quebec to be useful. By 1967 Trudeau was minister of justice, a position in which he proved himself both as a reformer and as a verbal duelist. As the confrontation with Quebec intensified, he further distinguished himself as a forceful and no-holds-barred advocate of federalism. When Pearson decided to step down as leader of the Liberal Party, Trudeau was not the only candidate to replace him; members of the old guard, such as Robert Winters and Paul Martin, also sought the job. However, the party judged that Trudeau best fit the needs and tenor of the country. He won the party leadership on the fourth ballot on 4 April 1968, and won a majority in Parliament on 25 June. The changing of the guard would affect not only the social and constitutional files but also foreign and defence policy.

Trudeau's lack of enthusiasm for the military, his desire to construct an independent foreign (and defence) policy for Canada, and his Cartesian approach to policy analysis and political dialogue are all well known.[16] He would gather around him in Cabinet and the senior bureaucracy individuals who did not accept the unthinking rhetoric of the Cold War and for whom NATO was not the anchor of foreign and defence policy. In fact, to Trudeau and many of his colleagues, Canada had allowed NATO to displace other Canadian interests, such as English/French harmony at home and healing the North/South split at the global level. And, like predecessor governments, Trudeau was of the opinion that NATO and Canadian forces were not very important as long as American strategic nuclear forces were the fundamental guarantor of world peace. In addition, he did not regard National Defence as a strongly managed or led department. To him, it seemed that the department worked in an unstructured, incrementalist way, piling expensive programs and commitments on top of each other. This did not suit his management style at all. He did not think much more highly of the Department of External Affairs.[17]

Trudeau announced his intention to conduct a "comprehensive review ... [of] Canada's armed forces policy, including alternative forces' structure and costing," on 15 May 1968. The review was to be completed by July. It was headed by National Defence but included the Department of Defence Production, the Treasury Board, the Privy Council Office, and the Department of External Affairs.

The Defence Policy Review essentially repackaged and updated Cadieux's earlier memorandum to Cabinet, wrapping it in a lengthy strategic appreciation. In terms of the army's structure, the policy review noted that the two brigades in Canada in reserve to NATO could not be transported to Europe in a useful period of time and had been, since 1959, equipped with only a training scale of equipment. The 1964 *White Paper on Defence* had left the brigade group in Europe because of the concern of the Germans and SACEUR regarding a withdrawal and the fact that the brigade group did not need any major new equipment; it was considered useful to maintain expertise in mechanized warfare. If Canada were to continue providing forces to Europe, a decision would be necessary in the near future as to what role they should assume and whether they should be equipped similarly to other Canadian troops. A wider range of options was presented than had been contained in the earlier Cabinet memo. The status quo was not the favoured option even if it was the most acceptable to the allies. Instead, the policy review tilted towards acquiring a new role and fielding an air-mobile brigade and a tactical air group operating under a single

Canadian headquarters. Cadieux reported that SACEUR would prefer the existing force, but told his colleagues that a Canadian contribution of a mobile force "would clearly be a substantial one with military value and there is no reason to believe it would not constitute a contribution that would serve adequately Canada's political aims on collective defence." The requirement for additional spending was recognized but, unlike in the Cabinet memo, not quantified.[18]

While an air-mobile light force in Europe might pass for radicalism in Canadian Forces Headquarters, the Cabinet Committee on External Affairs and National Defence was unimpressed and dismissed it as merely defending the status quo. It also emerged that some ministers, led by thirty-six-year-old Donald Macdonald, newly appointed as president of the Privy Council, had strong pacifist tendencies. Macdonald expressed outrage that the drafters had not considered neutrality for Canada (although, in fact, they had) and urged withdrawal of all Canadian forces from Europe. Canada's role in NATO, he thought, should be the same as Iceland's.[19] When the committee reported back to the full Cabinet, Cabinet directed that Canada continue its NORAD, NATO, and UN commitments until March 1970. National Defence was ordered to maintain its establishment at the lowest financial level consistent with its obligations. A final recommendation on defence policy was to be made by November 1968. Trudeau added that Cabinet members should make no public statements that could be interpreted as supporting a continuing commitment to NATO.[20]

If this did not fill senior officials at CFHQ with dread, then a 9 December meeting between Trudeau, Secretary of State for External Affairs Mitchell Sharp, Cadieux, and their senior officials surely should have. Trudeau posed dozens of basic questions regarding the utility of Canadian participation in NATO:

> If we fight [the Warsaw Pact] with conventional troops, eventually the Russians will win with a few conventional troops left over. What happens then? Does the USA then take over with nuclear weapons? In terms of world strategy, NATO is only a tactical weapon of the USA. Will the US sacrifice Europe and NATO before blowing up the world? Where does Canada fit in?
>
> NATO would only need to form a peacekeeping force to look after local incidents. What is the point of having large conventional forces if they are going to lose the conventional battle anyway? The alternatives seem to be not to use atomic weapons and write-off Europe to the Russians, or to use atomic weapons and write-off the world.
>
> Though many reasons are given for keeping Canadian troops in Europe, such as the smaller European countries will stay in NATO if we stay; Canadians are professional troops, etc., what if we decided we are not vital to the defence of

> Europe? Could we not use our withdrawal as a bargaining weapon? For example, Canada would withdraw from Europe if the USSR would withdraw from Czechoslovakia ... Would this not be a method of de-escalating the confrontation? Surely the USSR are as afraid of us as we are of them.
>
> We keep saying we must stay in NATO for various reasons. We do not seem to look at the problem from the point of view of whether we now need NATO at all. Is NATO the best way to secure peace at the moment?
>
> If we assume that if Canada bows out, NATO will continue to exist. In what way is NATO of value to Canada?
>
> The questions I am asking must be considered in the Review of Defence and Foreign Policy.[21]

While often presented as evidence of Trudeau's radicalism, nearly all of these questions had been raised before by Charles Foulkes, by successive ministers of defence such as George Pearkes, and by the ad hoc committees Hellyer had assembled to assemble background material for his White Paper. What is remarkable is that the defence establishment had no answers that satisfied the political leadership of the country. Lieutenant-General F.R. Sharp, the vice chief of the defence staff, had to go off and draft a paper to sort out his own thoughts.[22]

Cadieux is sometimes portrayed as a sort of second-rate figure who had been appointed to the National Defence portfolio because no one else wanted it. He has been termed an "honest and upright footsoldier" who "no one expected to innovate or surprise" and a "footnote to history."[23] In the debate about the army's role in NATO, he was up against not only the formidable Trudeau himself but also his *wunderkinder*, Donald Macdonald, the Privy Council president, and Ivan Head, the prime minister's foreign policy adviser. There were also other Cabinet members, such as Eric Kierans, who were anti-NATO. However, although Cadieux did not get his way entirely, he succeeded in keeping the army on NATO's Central Front.

When Cabinet assembled on 28 March to consider the department's Cabinet paper on defence, ministers found another paper in their briefing binders called "Canadian Defence Policy: A Study." Penned by a group of senior bureaucrats led by Ivan Head, the short, twenty-page paper went to the heart of the issue. It began: "Not since Confederation has there existed a viable threat to the territorial integrity of Canada. Nor does one exist now." The physical security of Canada was at risk, however, due to the threat of nuclear war. From this, the paper deduced four goals: (1) protection of the credibility of the US deterrent second-strike forces; (2) cooperation in deterring wars that might escalate to nuclear war; (3) contribution to international peace forces; and (4) dedication of an increasing percentage of the GNP to relieve or remove such traditional causes of war as economic insecurity. The paper argued that none of the stated goals required primarily or essentially a military output. The United States was capable of defending its deterrent forces, and Canadian assistance could consist of bases and ground environment support. NATO Europe had a population of 300 million and a GNP of $500 billion and could look after itself without Canada's marginal contribution. Peacekeeping activities had been military to date, but in the future it was more likely that conflict resolution and diplomacy would dominate. This left Canada free to make major defence policy decisions based on political considerations. Canada needed forces for aid of the civil power, coastal surveillance, disaster relief, search and rescue, and as a technical training establishment. The current force had created "narrow specialists" and could do none of these essential roles adequately. In fact, the paper argued that the current force structure undercut defence goals by inadequately supporting protection of the US strategic deterrent; by maintaining ASW forces to harass Soviet second-strike forces, thus weakening stability; and by maintaining nuclear strike forces in Europe that were themselves a soft target and thus useful only as a first-strike force. Finally, the paper accused the European allies of a "degree of hypocrisy" in their opposition to Canadian withdrawal of forces from Europe. Basing in Europe was costing Canada $100 million a year in net foreign exchange costs and "the hard-currency profit-motive stimulates the desire of our NATO allies to retain full Canadian membership including, as is so often repeated, the stationing in Europe of Canadian forces (with dependents)."

Head's paper proposed that the mechanized brigade group be withdrawn and replaced with a light mobile combat group assigned to the ACE Mobile Force (Land). One battalion group would be stationed in Europe on a four-month rotation, with no dependents overseas. The army would be reduced to four combat groups plus support, maritime forces would be cut by 50 percent, and the Air Division would be withdrawn and replaced with three squadrons of CF-5 fighter jets to support the combat group, also on a four-month rotation. Interceptor aircraft would be replaced and negotiations undertaken with the United States on anti-bomber defences. Head estimated that the defence budget could be reduced from $1.946 billion to $1.427 billion.[24]

In contrast to this remarkably concise tour de force, National Defence and External Affairs had once again endorsed the maintenance of NATO commitments, possibly replacing the brigade group with a "somewhat lighter, tactically mobile and air transportable force," in an elephantine 137-page paper.[25] The reaction to Head's paper was instantaneous. Cadieux threatened resignation and was backed by Mitchell Sharp, a Cabinet heavyweight and key Trudeau supporter. Trudeau thereupon withdrew Head's paper.

In the two days of Cabinet discussions that followed, Trudeau managed to keep policy development moving in the direction he favoured (a dramatic reduction in Canada's contribution to NATO), while keeping anyone from resigning. Cadieux provided the words for Trudeau's policy statement that kept him on board: "a planned and phased reduction," not a withdrawal.[26] Trudeau issued his defence policy statement on 3 April 1969. It rejected a non-aligned or neutral role for Canada and stated that Canada required armed forces within the country to supplement the civil authorities and to contribute to national development, maritime security, and the defence of North American air space. The Canadian Forces were capable of playing important roles in collective security and peacekeeping operations, but the precise military role in alliances was a matter for discussion. Canada was committed to NATO until the end of 1969, but the future would be discussed at the NATO Planning Committee meeting at the end of May. Trudeau promised that "our eventual forces will be highly mobile and will be the best-equipped and best-trained forces of their kind in the world."

On 20 April, Cadieux presented Cabinet with a plan for achieving this. It had been developed by a task force chaired by the deputy minister, Elgin Armstrong, but the main concepts came from the CDS, General Allard. Cadieux proposed an overall reduction of the Canadian Forces to a strength of 81,000, from 98,000. Forces based in Europe would be reduced from 10,100 to approximately 3,500, and forces would be structured to meet Canadian requirements, with the land force being air-transportable. Whereas the air element of the NATO force would remain in Central Europe, the land element would be assigned, as Head had suggested, to the ACE Mobile Force (Land) on the northern flank.[27] Mechanized forces would be dropped completely. Armoured, self-propelled artillery, and mechanized infantry units would be disbanded, even though reacquiring these capabilities later would be expensive and take a long time. On 15 and 20 May, Cabinet agreed to this plan and gave Cadieux authority to negotiate with NATO on the basis that the army element would be reduced to 3,500 and moved from the Central Front to the flank, with the proviso that "if after consultation with NATO, modifications to the planned posture as agreed are strongly desired by NATO, then the suggested modification or modifications will be referred to Cabinet for further discussion and decision." How well this direction to return to Cabinet was followed would become a matter of great debate a few years later.

The force structure to which Cadieux agreed flew in the face of Canadian military thinking up to and including the 1964 *White Paper on Defence*. Faced with constant financial pressure and the obvious advantages of having one uniform type of formation in a small army, new thinking had developed. Allard backed the concept of air-mobile forces and had personally introduced the concept into the planning discussions leading to Cadieux's proposal to Cabinet. He told the planning group that intent was to remain in Europe in the short term but to leave around 1974. He made uniformity and air-transportability the driving criteria in force structure, with heavy equipment being sacrificed as required. The proposed force was Allard's creation. It does not appear to have been based on force development studies or detailed staff work of any type. The details of a viable mobile force were to be worked out in the future, even as the department was committed to negotiating with NATO only a few weeks hence.[28]

Cadieux presented the Canadian proposal to his fellow NATO ministers at a luncheon at the Canadian ambassador's residence in Brussels on 25 May 1969. The reaction was even worse than he anticipated. The Belgians and Dutch were shaken, and the Belgian ambassador actually burst into tears. The Americans and British were brutally frank in their reactions, Denis Healey, the British Secretary of State for Defence, telling Cadieux that he was passing the buck to others who would have to fill the gap.[29]

Parallel military talks with SHAPE provoked even stronger reaction. The Canadian team was led by Rear-Admiral R.W. Timbrell, the deputy chief of plans. His presentation did not clearly distinguish between what was being proposed as an interim force and the government's ultimate intent to move the Canadian Forces to a flank role. He proposed a ground force of about 1,500 troops organized in three "commandos" with the Carl Gustav light anti-armour weapon.[30] The force would also have one reconnaissance squadron; one artillery battery equipped with pack howitzers; engineering and medical elements; and a headquarters. It would be air-transportable and have armoured personnel carriers and light observation helicopters. One squadron of utility helicopters, eight Buffalos, and national airlift would be provided to move the proposed combat group. Under questioning from SHAPE, it emerged that the force would not be equipped with helicopter gunships, which had apparently been discussed with SHAPE previously. The senior SHAPE representative, Deputy SACEUR General Sir Robert Bray, and Brigadier-General W. Caldwell, SHAPE Plans, could not understand the Canadian concept. It lacked sufficient airlift capacity integral to the force to move more than one-third of the force at a time; it was organized in three "commandos" that appeared designed to operate independently but had only one artillery battery to support them all; and it had no tanks. Bray and Caldwell assumed that the Canadian force was meant for the Central Front, whereas Timbrell stated that "the CDS wishes for the land element would be [sic] the role in Central Europe in the EDP [Emergency Defence Plan], secondly in the same geographical area in the reserve role and thirdly other commitments such as AMF (L) North." Timbrell's further explanation reduced Bray to near-apoplexy. In the verbatim transcript, he can practically be heard spluttering:

> I mean it's nothing like as valuable to us on the ground or in the air as what you have got now. I mean it's no good ... and that is why the timing ... you said six months but when you think of all the waffle that is going to go on before ... it takes a lot of time ... I mean our initial reaction is one of dismay naturally. To have taken out of the Central front, which is the one place where I think armour is really required or useful, to have such a chunk taken out which is naturally one ... our counter proposals ... and obviously we'll try to get them done as soon as possible.[31]

What is significant in Timbrell's proposal is the evidence it contains that Allard had no real idea how to create a viable light unit when he proposed it as an element of national policy. In addition, his instructions to Timbrell apparently contradicted Cabinet's direction to end Canada's role on the Central Front and to move the Canadian commitment to the flanks, where a light force would be more suitable. Future discussions would concentrate on structuring forces for the Central Front.

In July the land operational research staff was tasked by Allard to game scenarios based on the missions of the SACEUR reserve, namely, "to reinforce forward deployed main forces in the Central Region in the event of a large scale attack." A hypothetical version of "4 Canadian Combat Group" was pitted against a reinforced Soviet motor rifle regiment, a force of equivalent size. The 4 Canadian Combat Group consisted of two 712-man battalion combat teams plus 1,424 additional engineering, aviation, support, and headquarters groups. Each battalion group had an anti-tank company of two SS.11 and two ENTAC anti-tank guided missiles, two 106 mm recoilless rifles, and a mortar section with two 81 mm mortars. The battalion also included a reconnaissance company with six Lynx transport vehicles and five Direct Fire Support Vehicles (DFSV), a lightly armoured vehicle with a gun sufficient to defeat a tank.[32] Each battalion also had a battery of six 105 mm pack howitzers. The combat group had a strong aviation squadron, with ten liaison helicopters, a reconnaissance flight of eight light observation helicopters and six utility helicopters armed with TOW missiles, a fire support flight of twelve attack helicopters based on the HueyCobra, and a transportation flight of six utility and three medium helicopters. The combat group differed from the standard Canadian table of organization and equipment in that it had only two manoeuvre units rather than three, it was heavy in anti-tank weapons and helicopters, and it had the DFSV rather than tanks for fire support. Although light and air-transportable, it remained a fairly muscular organization.

Knowing that helicopters were very vulnerable to Soviet anti-aircraft fire, the staff made aircraft visibility models very detailed. The Soviet motor rifle regiment had its normally attached tank battalion, plus an additional tank battalion and an additional motor rifle battalion in its attack. All Soviet artillery up to the divisional level was considered to be available to the motor rifle regiment.

In the first simulation, Soviet forces were able to advance twelve kilometres in three hours of play and reach the general area of their final objective, but only with losses so high that it was questionable that an attack would have gone forward. Overall losses were 480 Soviet and 442 Canadian. The motor rifle regiment lost 51 of its 68 tanks and a total of 112 armoured vehicles of all types. The combat group lost 15 of its 18 attack helicopters and 9 of its 12 DFSVs. The second game ended in a similar manner, with high losses on both sides. The operational research staff concluded that the combat group lacked adequate artillery, and that attack helicopters, although accounting for 40 percent of Soviet losses, also suffered high casualties and might have incurred more if the motor rifle regiment had been equipped with man-portable anti-aircraft weapons. Staff playing the Canadian side found that having only two manoeuvre units was a serious limitation and that the headquarters organization was too small to effectively coordinate fire.[33]

The simulation showed that although a light force was viable, the large aviation component and new type of fire support vehicle would make it expensive. The aircraft were also extremely vulnerable on a high-intensity battlefield, and would become even more so as Soviet forces improved their already impressive anti-aircraft capability. The size and equipment of a light force nominally equal in capability to an equivalent Soviet force stood in marked contrast to what had been proposed to SACEUR in May.

On 3 August, General Andrew Goodpaster, the Supreme Allied Commander in Europe, responded to Canada with SHAPE's proposal. In his transmittal cable he laid it on with a trowel:

> On 1 August, I visited your forces in Germany to inform myself at first hand of the current Canadian role and contribution to ACE. I was impressed with the professional calibre and the efficiency with which your country's resources have been converted into a qualitatively unsurpassed military contribution. My visit re-emphasized to me the demanding operational task with which our defence

> forces in the Central Region are confronted, and the degree to which the present Canadian force contribution suits their current role. The prospect of a change involving reduction in this Canadian capability is of deep concern to me and my force commanders, as well as to each of the other countries directly involved in the defence of the Central Region since it is obviously going to be extremely difficult to find comparable replacement forces from other resources.[34]

Goodpaster obviously preferred the status quo. He stressed that Canada should continue to play a "meaningful role" in implementing NATO's flexible-response doctrine, and quoted Trudeau's pledge in his 3 April 1969 defence policy statement that Canadian forces would be "highly mobile and will be the best-equipped and best-trained forces of their kind in the world." The force proposed to SHAPE staff by Timbrell obviously fell far short of that standard. Goodpaster suggested that Canada could take on one of three roles: (1) in the Central Region, the occupation of blocking positions, reconnaissance and flank surveillance, limited action as part of the main battle, and rear-area security, including defence against airborne assault; (2) rapid reinforcement of the ACE Mobile Force (Land) in the Northern and Southern Region; and (3) dual-capable (i.e., nuclear and conventional) strike attack air forces. Goodpaster suggested that the force personnel ceiling proposed by Canada would not provide a "fruitful basis for renewed consultations" and indicated that SHAPE thought that 6,500 troops were the minimum that could be useful. The basic manoeuvre element should not be the lightly armed "commando" proposed by Timbrell but a battalion-sized armoured cavalry squadron based on the US Army pattern. This would have tanks organic to each reconnaissance platoon, as well as helicopter gunships – in other words, much more similar to the force that CFHQ operations researchers had gamed for Allard. Goodpaster proposed that Canada provide three manoeuvre units – a conclusion that the war gamers had also reached – which would require 8,300 troops. More integral helicopter lift would also be required. In the end, Goodpaster suggested a force structured much as CFHQ staff had gamed, except that it included a light tank rather than the hypothetical DFSV. He also wanted almost three times more troops than the Canadians were willing to provide.[35]

Allard instructed Major-General M.R. Dare, chairman of the Force Structure Working Group, to come up with a force that used existing equipment to move towards a future air-transportable force. Dare recommended a 2,800-soldier force consisting of an armoured regiment with tanks, two mechanized infantry battalions, and an artillery regiment with two batteries of self-propelled guns. With three CF-104 squadrons, this would bring the total strength of Canadian Forces Europe to about 5,000.[36]

On 13 August 1969, Cadieux took Allard's force structure proposal to Cabinet and received a blessing for a land force half the size of the brigade group; the force would continue to use existing equipment until new light equipment became available in two to three years. The interim land force was to be in place by 30 June 1970, and Canadian Forces Europe would total approximately 5,000 by that date. Three CF-104 squadrons would be maintained, but the nuclear strike role would be ended by 1972 and the reconnaissance role would be re-examined.[37] Cabinet gave no direction as to where the army was to be stationed in Europe or what role it was to play. Trudeau was concerned by the lack of specifics in Cadieux's plan and "wanted to be sure there was no surprise in store for the government at the end of the three year period." He stressed that the government was not changing its intentions as expressed in the defence policy statement, and accepted that the interim plan appeared to be the only one open to the government. Nevertheless, he wanted it made clear to SACEUR that Canada was going to proceed with its plan.[38]

It seems clear that Cadieux and Allard had never seriously considered a role on the flanks and had committed Canada from the start to remaining on the Central Front. The apparent plan was to bring the mobile force into being, if on a smaller scale than considered in the 1964 *White Paper on Defence*. Both CFHQ war-gaming and SHAPE staff concluded that a well-equipped light force could be viable on the Central Front. It is much less clear that Cabinet was fully aware that the army would remain there. The supposedly second-rate Cadieux had faced down the prime minister, his brain trust, and half the Cabinet by keeping the Canadian army on NATO's Central Front. Although the force was much reduced in size, he had also obtained Cabinet's approval to modernize it.

Cadieux and Allard were able to secure NATO agreement on the proposed force. What had emerged was certainly an improvement on Canada's first proposal, and the two men had made it clear that Canada was now making a take-it-or-leave-it proposition. At the NATO ministerial meeting on 3 December 1969, Cadieux told his colleagues that Canada had made significant concessions in increasing the size of its land force in Europe by almost 50 percent over the original plan and deferring reorganization by six months. He made an additional promise of force modernization, informing them that after 1972 the land forces in Europe would have "a high degree of mobility, together with the maximum firepower compatible with that mobility." In addition, forces based in Canada were committed to the protection of the northern flank. Cadieux claimed that this new Canadian posture was inspired by the SHAPE special study "1972 Onwards." He also reminded his colleagues that most Canadians thought that European countries, now strong and prosperous, were in a better position to assume a larger share of their own defence.[39]

Cadieux and Allard were not under any illusions that the force in Europe was anything but a stopgap. CFHQ's 1970 "Defence Planning Guidance" noted that the pre-cuts NATO brigade group had insufficient artillery to support its manoeuvre units and was weak in anti-armour capability; in addition, its tactical air support had only limited capability. Nevertheless it was going to be reduced by about 50 percent to become a "battle group." As such it would lack its own nuclear firepower after withdrawal of the Honest John battery, have only enough artillery to support two of its three manoeuvre units, and lack air self-defence weapons because no effective weapon was available at a "realistic cost." A good case could be made that in the long term Canada's contribution to flexible response should consist of air-transportable land forces, but there was no certainty that these would continue to be based in Europe. The question was how to provide fire support while remaining air-mobile. According to the Defence Planning Guidance, the jury was still out as to whether armed helicopters could be the solution. There was also no clear answer to the question of how either strategic airlift or air support should be provided. The purchase of aircraft for these roles would be expensive. The Defence Planning Guidance speculated that perhaps pre-positioning of equipment could obviate the need for strategic airlift and that allies might be able to provide close air support.[40]

The day after the Defence Planning Guidance was issued, Cadieux resigned as minister of national defence to become ambassador to France. He was succeeded on 24 September 1970 by Donald Macdonald, the Cabinet member who had been perhaps his strongest opponent regarding the NATO commitment.

Donald Macdonald and the 1971 White Paper

Donald Macdonald had been the chief NATO skeptic in Cabinet and had argued that Iceland was a suitable model for Canada's military policy. Nevertheless, when Cadieux resigned the ambitious thirty-eight-year-old minister requested the defence portfolio and got it – with certain conditions. Prime Minister Trudeau told Macdonald that he had to consider the 3 April 1969 defence policy statement's support of NATO as final, and that he could ask for neither more money nor troop cuts; what Trudeau wanted was improved military morale and a new defence policy statement.[41] Macdonald accepted on this basis, no doubt expecting to complete the conversion of the army to a light, mobile force, part of which would be committed to NATO's northern flank.

He was to find that the concept Cabinet had agreed upon was not accepted by CFHQ. In early September the vice chief of the defence staff, Lieutenant-General Michael Dare, had recommended that "adoption of the Air Mobile European-Based Commando Force be postponed to the later 70s and the continuation of the mechanized role in Europe. Our rationale for this is the development of the philosophy that it is probably too early for the time frame envisaged." While the United States, Britain, and Germany were developing air-mobile forces, they considered them to be ancillary. Following considerable discussion of the matter at the Chief of the Defence Staff Advisory Committee, CDS General F.R. Sharp suspended further consideration of the item. He subsequently approved a 1971-72 program forecast that included new tanks. This program forecast was never considered by new minister Macdonald.[42] Because of the October Crisis, during which the Front de libération du Québec kidnapped and killed a Quebec cabinet minister and kidnapped a British diplomat, Macdonald did not get a full briefing on force planning until December. He was then informed that a number of light, air-mobile force structures had been designed and war-gamed but were not viable. The force most closely examined was almost identical to the BRONZE NIMBUS organizational model that had appeared to be a match for a Soviet motorized rifle regiment, but with considerably more transport helicopters, the more modern TOW anti-tank missile, and the Scorpion light armoured vehicle with a small 76 mm gun, as opposed to the hypothetical BRONZE NIMBUS vehicle that mounted a gun large enough to defeat a tank. Macdonald was not told about the earlier, more favourable appraisal of the light force. Instead, he was informed that it lacked organic tactical balance, that it was unable to create and hold an engagement to create a nuclear target, that it could not exploit a nuclear strike, and that it was unable to achieve a clean break during withdrawal or redeployment operations. These limitations were no doubt real, but one wonders whether any 2,800-man force with only two ground manoeuvre units would have been exempt from them. Combat development staff recommended that the Canadian Forces extend the mechanized role beyond 1 September 1974 and that it continue to analyze the air-mobility concept. Combat development staff believed that the Forces should allow at least four years between the decision to adopt the new role and the fielding of an operationally ready force.[43]

When Macdonald suggested that any change would require Cabinet approval, Elgin Armstrong, the deputy minister, noted that since the force in Europe was supposed to be an extension of the force in Canada, re-equipping the whole army for an air-mobile role would be vastly more costly than simply replacing the tanks. The VCDS piled on by noting that SACEUR preferred Canada to remain in its present mechanized role as he believed it was too early to make major decisions on the air-mobile concept. Because the Centurion would reach the end of its life in September 1974, an early decision was necessary. Macdonald responded by directing that discussions be opened with the Americans concerning the acquisition of a replacement tank, and that data be assembled both on the cost of remaining in the armoured role and on the effective use of helicopters in an air-mobile role.[44]

Macdonald did not like being put off by staff. A few weeks later he wrote both the deputy minister and the CDS that he had reviewed the documents surrounding the 1969 Cabinet decisions regarding the form of the Canadian contribution to NATO, and told them:

> I note in particular the interdepartmental working group memorandum of April 30, 1969 on Phase II of the Defence Policy Review recommended "... that the land force element be assigned for employment with the Allied Command Europe Mobile Force (Land) on the northern flank of NATO." According to the Cabinet Decisions, Cabinet accepted this recommendation, but deleted the reference to the northern flank and apparently it was reconfirmed by Cabinet on May 20th, 1969.
>
> I do not recall and cannot find any further Cabinet discussion of this question, but it seems to me that on the face of that decision, there is no necessity for us to become involved in a heavy role in Central Europe at all. In fact, the Cabinet Decision is quite to the contrary, namely, that we should get out of this role in such a way that they can be of assistance to the Mobile Force, presumably for the use of the flanks of the Alliance and presumably, in particular, on the northern flank. Since that was a clear decision of the Government, how did we get into the situation where we are committed to CENTAG rather than to the AMF?[45]

The other shoe had now dropped. Macdonald realized that staying on the Central Front would be a major impediment to transforming the army into a light force.

General Sharp's reply included a closely typed, seven-page account on legal-size paper summarizing every Cabinet decision taken and policy statement made since March 1967. Sharp reminded Macdonald that Cabinet had given his predecessor leave to negotiate the Canadian contribution with NATO, and said that the revision of plans was reflected in Cabinet Records of Decision in July and August 1969. Moreover, Cadieux's public statements at the conclusion of negotiations with NATO had been cleared with the Prime Minister's Office. A review of Sharp's summary shows that the Cabinet decisions had been silent on where the army was to be or what role it was to have. Sharp argued that Cadieux's statements made it clear that the Forces fully intended to implement the air-mobile force, and that the placement of the NATO force on the Central Front would become an issue only if it was not feasible to meet the basic policy of having the army overseas equipped and trained in the same manner as the army in Canada.[46] Macdonald was therefore correct – Cabinet had never agreed to keeping the army on the Central Front, and Cadieux had made the commitment to SHAPE on his own, albeit after having his text reviewed by the Prime Minister's Office. No one had taken the time to explain the consequences of remaining on the Central Front in terms of equipment, and for Sharp to argue that the Forces had always intended to implement the air-mobile force while at the same time staff were telling the minister it could not be done must have seemed to Macdonald to lack sincerity. Macdonald did not contest Sharp's response directly, but the matter was far from resolved and would reappear during the finalization of the White Paper the minister had been asked to produce.

Macdonald had hired Gordon Smith, a recent Massachusetts Institute of Technology PhD graduate who had worked with the Defence Research Board and the Department of External Affairs, to draft the White Paper. Smith set to work from first principles, using the prime minister's April 1969 defence policy statement as the starting point. Working from a realpolitik viewpoint, he concluded that there was no direct military threat to Canada, but that the remote possibility of Soviet-American nuclear war required Canada to maintain its role in NORAD and its anti-submarine warfare capabilities. Because Europe was the most likely arena for an East/West confrontation, Canada also had a role to play in NATO. Macdonald was no friend of NATO but found himself convinced by arguments based on Canadian interests, as were Ivan Head and the prime minister. The armed forces were another question.[47]

Macdonald had asked the deputy minister and the CDS to consider a number of questions related to the White Paper. The CDS Advisory Committee met on 17 February 1971 to consider them, including the question of the land force in Europe. The senior staff did not consider any option other than continuing the role of a mechanized force on the Central Front. In fact, they suggested that if the government wanted to adopt a policy of having forces in Europe be compatible with forces in Canada, the same policy should be applied to the navy as well! Existing heavy equipment could be extended to 1975 or Leopard tanks could be leased from Germany; in either case the government could delay making a decision on conversion to a mobile force to sometime in the future. The minutes stated that "as a result of this discussion it was agreed that the White Paper should recommend that the mechanized role be continued until 1975." The committee also disagreed with the allocation of more resources to the sovereignty role, with using CF-104 Starfighters in an interceptor role, and with not asking the United States to assume the air defence role played by the CF-101 Voodoos. It was clear that the senior military staff and the deputy minister were taking issue with many of the policy views of the minister, and indeed of the government itself. According to Major-General Charles Gauthier, head of the headquarters secretariat, Macdonald was "infuriated." Macdonald's sounding of the Liberal caucus led him to understand that others shared his frustration and that Liberal MPs simply did not believe they were getting an honest assessment of how Canada's forces in Europe could be made compatible with forces in Canada.[48] When Gordon Smith met with the CDS Advisory Committee on 24 and 25 March to conduct a final review of the White Paper, he was presented with a shopping list of equipment that would have resulted in defence spending exceeding the budget by a significant amount. The VCDS merely noted that no attempt had been made to discipline the inputs to the force structure. Smith informed Macdonald that the department had ignored the policy priorities of the government and had made proposals focused almost exclusively on additions to the defence program. He expressed concern over the "almost total lack of analysis" behind departmental proposals.[49]

Macdonald informed Trudeau that "at some point the decision of the Government that the Canadian Land Forces in Europe, after the 1972-73 period, should be set up as lightly armed mobile force to operate with the ACE Mobile Force (Land) has become completely lost in subsequent discussions in Defence Headquarters and with NATO staffs." The government now faced the "unpleasant choice" of either committing to a heavy role in Central Europe or being faced with the accusation that it was backing down on its NATO commitment. According to an investigation by the minister's staff, after the Timbrell briefing to SACEUR, Canadian officials had never indicated that it was the government's intent to commit forces to the AMF(L) rather than to CENTAG or CINCENT (Commander-in-Chief Allied Forces Central Europe). Trudeau asked Macdonald to undertake a complete investigation and report to Cabinet. In particular, he wanted to know why the CDS and the deputy minister had not ensured that Cabinet direction had been implemented. He also hoped that Macdonald could devise a way of returning to the original force structure plan.[50]

Macdonald conducted a personal investigation that included a lengthy telephone conversation with Cadieux in Paris. He discovered that Allard had originated the concept of a light force but had lost his enthusiasm as equipment costs and the inability of existing equipment to meet the requirements of such a force became clear. According to Cadieux, the Cabinet decision had made no provision for what the land forces were to do in the interim period, and he could not recall whether he had ever again discussed the matter with Trudeau or in Cabinet. NATO staffs were "evasive" in discussions about a new role for Canadian land forces, and Cadieux said that he regarded the whole matter as something that Cabinet would have to focus on when the military came up with a proposal that could meet Cabinet's objectives of a NATO force compatible with forces in Canada while being stationed on the Central Front. In the end, Macdonald put most of the blame on Allard, who had proposed and promoted an "unsound idea ... developed on the spur of the moment." Cabinet had been left in the dark.[51]

Trudeau thanked Macdonald for his work and expressed his hope that the minister had made it very clear to the senior military and civil officials of the department that "whatever excuses they may have, failure to conform to Cabinet decisions cannot be accepted." Cabinet as a whole, however, concluded that most of the responsibility was Cadieux's, and the subject was laid to rest.[52]

It should be noted that throughout this debate about the type and placement of Canadian Forces in Europe, the sides were not simply civilian against military. Rather they were NATO advocates versus NATO skeptics. Advocates had included Léo Cadieux and Elgin Armstrong, while General Allard must be placed in the NATO-skeptic column. Nevertheless, this case and a parallel case of senior management insubordination over the design and construction of the navy's new warship, the DDH 280 destroyer, drove Macdonald to the conclusion that he needed to reform the headquarters structure so that it was accountable to the minister and the government.

The White Paper, *Defence in the 70s,* did not reflect the core views of the NATO advocates regarding the army and its role. Macdonald is said to have refused to allow the draft to be edited without personal reference to him.[53] Quickly approved by the prime minister and Cabinet, *Defence in the 70s* retained the goal of a light, air-mobile force. The Centurion tank was to be replaced by "a light, tracked, direct-fire-support vehicle" that could be airlifted. Macdonald, however, was forced to accept that the army would remain on the Central Front. Trudeau used the occasion of the discussion of the White Paper in Cabinet to have Macdonald report Cadieux's failure to follow direction, and openly wondered whether senior officials had fulfilled their responsibilities. He reluctantly agreed that little could be done to correct the situation, but said that he would look at new suggestions from the department with a "particularly critical eye."[54]

The White Paper said that the land force would be reconfigured to have the "high degree of mobility needed for tactical reconnaissance missions in a Central Region reserve role." The goal of an army with a uniform domestic and overseas structure was also retained, with the White Paper envisaging the result to be "enhanced compatibility of Canadian and European based forces, and a lighter, more mobile land force capable of a wide range of missions." The commitment to NATO's northern flank was explicitly retained through the allocation of a battalion group to the ACE Mobile Force (Land) to defend Denmark or Norway, as was the further commitment to send the balance of an air/sea-transportable combat group to the northern flank in an emergency. In addition, *Defence in the 70s* claimed that "extensive trials" of the CF-5 in Europe had confirmed its suitability for that theatre, and the government was therefore prepared to commit two squadrons of the aircraft to reconnaissance and ground support on the northern flank.[55]

The White Paper also addressed the freeze of the defence budget and consequent cuts to deployed forces. NATO forces had been reduced because the government believed that twenty-five years after the Second World War, the European economy had revived and Europe was now able to support a greater share of the conventional forces necessary to defend itself. Moreover, times were tough at home and the government needed to "adjust" the forces to make foreign and domestic roles compatible. *Defence in the 70s* rejected the notion of some set of defence requirements that placed an absolute call on resources, stating that "there [was] no obvious level for defence expenditures in Canada."[56]

Macdonald also announced in the White Paper that he had appointed a Management Review Group (MRG) to examine the organization and management of the department. He explained that this was an extension of the study of the DDH 280 naval procurement project to acquire new destroyers for the navy that had been announced in February that year. The review group was to make recommendations "to ensure there exists effective planning and control" and would report directly to the minister. Drafts had said "effective *civilian* planning and control." Although it appeared innocuous enough, the MRG would bring about fundamental changes in how the headquarters was organized and would have effects on civil-military relations that would last for decades. These will be discussed more fully in the next chapter.

Outside the Department of National Defence, the White Paper was largely a non-event. Some believed that the emphasis on sovereignty was misplaced, but most commentators and the public appeared to agree with the government's priorities. There was certainly no backlash demanding increased defence budgets. The most incisive commentary came from one of the few foreign defence analysts interested in Canada, Colin Gray, a British academic. Gray called the White Paper a "landmark in Canada's slow retreat from the consequences of the collective security impulse that have formed the central pillars in the structure of Canadian external relations for more than twenty years." In his opinion, NATO was a purely optional role for Canada – "the benefit of NATO and NORAD memberships are marginal, while the costs are really not at all excessive." Although he believed that, on balance, Canada should remain in NATO, he thought "a perfectly respectable argument" could be made that Canada had neither capabilities nor ideas to contribute to the stability of the superpower arms race or to European stability and should just drop out. Not having been privy to the manoeuvre and counter-manoeuvre of NATO advocates and skeptics inside the government, he was puzzled by the decision to maintain Canadian troops in Europe while capping the army component at 2,800, which he noted "is in itself an insult," and to emphasize the commitment to the northern flank. He speculated that Macdonald had accepted the role to maintain diplomatic access within the alliance, or maybe even because he believed that Soviet military action against the northern flank was possible. He recommended that the northern flank role be shed "as soon as decently possible." Gray also noted that the government's policy of a domestically oriented military was being resisted by officers who enjoyed the "big league" culture of alliances, especially NATO.[57]

Inside the department it was a different matter. Despite the appointment of a new deputy minister, Sylvain Cloutier, who came from the Treasury Board with the strong support of Macdonald, and changes to the structure of the headquarters that were intended to make the deputy minister equal to the CDS and impose Cabinet's agenda on the department, only slow progress was made in implementing the White Paper. According to the head of the NDHQ secretariat, the CDS, General Sharp, had told the Management Review Group that the White Paper "did not provide meaningful policy declarations from a military viewpoint." Most senior military staff appeared to agree. The opinion was even expressed at the Defence Management Committee that the White Paper was not really binding on the department. After Macdonald's departure as minister in January 1972, interest in the White Paper declined even further.[58]

As Gray suggested, the White Paper was a milestone in the battle between the "big army" NATO advocates and NATO skeptics who wanted a lighter, more mobile force. It was a particularly painful and destructive one. Under the Conservative Diefenbaker government, the army had been allowed to maintain itself along the lines of a great power force but with no real prospect of augmentation or expansion. The Liberals, while Paul Hellyer was minister, had broken the old vessel and replaced it with the concept of an integrated, mobile force. Unfortunately, there were insufficient resources to equip such a force and too little work for it to command the required political support. Considerable resources had been squandered by Hellyer on the CF-5 and more diverted by the navy to turn the DDH 280 into the all-singing, all-dancing warship it desired. The Macdonald iteration kept the corpse of the mobile force animated, but it was effectively dead. NATO advocates had been successful in keeping the army on NATO's Central Front, but the skeptics had cut it to half strength and planned to equip it so that it would be of marginal utility in that role. No one had really won the debate.

Towards a New Land Force Policy

The post–1971 White Paper army faced an array of challenges: how to integrate tactical aviation into its operations, how to mount effective anti-tank and anti-aircraft defences, and most of all how to cope with a fixed budget under ruinous inflation. The army was poorly equipped to deal with issues pertaining to its own future. Fortunately, Macdonald's reforms had improved National Defence's ability to deal with its budgetary problems.

Doctrine and force development had not evolved as distinct organizational components until the 1960s, and then had been disrupted by Hellyer's integration of the services. The struggle between Mobile Command and National Defence Headquarters for control over the future shape of the army would last for several decades. In the early 1970s, doctrine was organized at the senior staff officer level (lieutenant-colonel) in Mobile Command Headquarters and dealt with low-level topics such as duties of the artillery battery commander and observers, grenades and pyrotechnics, and map reading training for soldiers.[59] Only in 1979 was agreement reached that NDHQ would be responsible for combat development (i.e., the future shape of the army) and Mobile Command for doctrine. An Army Doctrine and Tactics Board (ADTB) Secretariat was created at the same time and included the staff colleges, the Combat Training Centre in Gagetown, the Brigade Group in Europe, the director of land plans at NDHQ, and Mobile Command Headquarters.[60]

In the interim, the situation was, if not chaotic, at the very least unfocused. Although Mobile Command and NDHQ chief of land operations staff met once a year, doctrine was not a standard agenda item. The commander of Mobile Command and that of the brigade group in Germany discussed the need to coordinate doctrine, but an offshoot of the conversation forbade Mobile Command to censor the brigade group's comment on doctrine. The staff colleges were not part of doctrine development and the overall staff system had been ignored and "fogged" by Macdonald's changes at NDHQ.[61]

A review of land doctrine a year later revealed that while there was no shortage of doctrinal publications within the army, they had been cobbled together from locally produced documents and foreign publications. There was no framework for doctrine overall, save the now-venerable CFP 165, *The Conduct of Land Operations,* which had been drafted by Roger Rowley in 1967 and simply reissued in 1973. While it was a basic guide to the fundamentals of each branch of the service, its focus on nuclear warfare was increasingly out of touch with NATO's stress on "flexible response" and conventional operations, and its emphasis on counter-guerrilla operations was out of sync with the army's lack of capability for conducting such operations now that the mobile force had been cast aside.[62]

The army was not even able to compile a list of doctrinal publications until September 1975, and then it was only in "rough form." The Canadian Land Force Command and Staff College informed Headquarters that it would continue to use British manuals until credible Canadian replacements could be developed. The director of land plans wrung his hands, complaining that "all earlier attempts to produce a unified staff system have floundered on varied rocks or shoals and the land forces seem to be drifting without a definite concept or philosophy." The army was divided into two factions: one headed by the Land Force staff college that favoured the two-branch British staff system, and the other led by the Canadian Forces Command and Staff College that promoted the "J" system used by US and NATO forces.[63] NDHQ staff "solved" this problem by directing that all organizations at or below the divisional level would use the British system while all higher formations and NATO would use the "J" system.[64] None of this addressed the fundamental problem that both doctrine and combat development required a common concept of what the army should be. Nor could force development models be assessed and refined solely through thought experiments at a national headquarters. Real-world field trials and experiments were needed. While Mobile Command and NDHQ engaged in bureaucratic debate, no institutional home existed to develop the future army.

The army faced four pressing problems: (1) what sort of Direct Fire Support Vehicle it should acquire; (2) where helicopters fit in its anti-tank capability; (3) what sort of anti-tank defence it required; and (4) how fixed-wing tactical aircraft would be incorporated into the overall structure to provide air support to ground troops. These issues could not be considered separately, for they were all interconnected. Nor could doctrine be neatly divorced from force structure issues. For example, if the problem was (as it indeed was on the Central Front) how to defend against a large armoured and mechanized infantry force, then what should one use to kill tanks and armoured vehicles? Tanks? Anti-tank guided missiles? A tank destroyer? Attack helicopters? Fixed-wing aircraft? Or some combination of all the above? One could not simply select a force structure component (for example, attack helicopters) and then assign staff to work out employment doctrine. In resolving the details of the best use of the platform, staff would inevitably find new issues and faulty preconceptions that would affect how the force should be structured. Moreover, doctrine and force structure issues cannot be easily determined unless one knows what the force is to be used for. The army's problem was complicated by the fact that in using the back door to win the argument over the role of the force, it had not secured a commitment from the government to pay for it, or even a long-term commitment to the role.

Given the state of disarray of policy and staff processes, it should come as no surprise that each of these issues was addressed in a random way by separate, disconnected processes. The fate of the Direct Fire Support Vehicle was decided quickly. The BRONZE NIMBUS war game had assumed a tracked light armoured vehicle with a large-calibre gun capable of defeating tank armour – the classic tank destroyer. No such vehicle was currently available, however. The only available candidate was the British Scorpion, which mounted only a 76 mm gun, incapable of engaging a tank. Although National Defence obtained Treasury Board approval to purchase the Scorpion, the manufacturer and the British government knew that they were the only option under consideration and the Department of Supply and Services therefore had no confidence in their delivery promises. National Defence was less than enthusiastic about the Scorpion and pursued it only because it was consistent with policy. In March 1973 the CDS asked to meet with Trudeau to discuss a draft memorandum to Cabinet that recommended retaining the Centurion tank until 1976 and informing the British that Canada would not buy the Scorpion. Ivan Head and other members of the Prime Minister's Office detected another ploy to tie the government to heavy forces indefinitely. Head advised Trudeau not to allow an extension in the life of the Centurion to become "the thin edge of the wedge," and told the prime minister that to accept the department's recommendation would be to stand "our resources, our priorities, indeed our principles, upside down."

Trudeau consequently responded to Minister James Richardson by stating that he had no objection to prolonging the life of Centurion and not purchasing the Scorpion if the intent was only to save money and would not jeopardize the long-term rational realignment of the land force through undue delays in planning or training, or through missed opportunities to re-equip the force. He asked for Richardson's assurances on these points and said that he was disturbed by the suggestions in the draft memo to Cabinet that continuation of the Centurion would open the door to a reassessment of policy. He told Richardson in a most unambiguous manner that if that was what the department had in mind, he would oppose it.[65]

On 31 May 1973 Cabinet agreed to terminate negotiations for the Scorpion and to retain the old Centurion tank until 1976, but reaffirmed its earlier decision that the eventual force would have no tanks and would be air-transportable and compatible with Canada-based forces. The fact that each of these vehicles had vastly different characteristics (the air-transportable/tank killer DFSV, the air-transportable/no anti-tank capability Scorpion, the not air-transportable/tank killer Centurion tank) shows clearly that there was little or no tactical thinking behind the decisions being made.[66]

The army was also working on the problem of incorporating attack helicopters into its force structure. The BRONZE NIMBUS war games had shown that, in theory at least, attack helicopters were effective anti-tank and anti-armour platforms. Such a major decision demanded field trials, so Canada joined with Germany and the United States to undertake trials of the American HueyCobra attack helicopter in 1972 and 1973 at Ansbach, Germany. Fully instrumented teams of Cobras and Kiowa light observation helicopters were pitted against tanks supported by tracked air defence artillery vehicles. The trials were free play on unfamiliar terrain. The helicopters worked in pairs, with the scout aircraft flying nap-of-the-earth or landing and sending observers forward. The attack helicopter would then ambush the attacking armour from behind terrain. The trials proved that attack helicopters were extremely effective in destroying attacking enemy armour, with the helicopter killing more than ten armoured vehicles for every aircraft lost. The helicopter could fire from positions not available to ground vehicles and, while tanks generally could not see targets over a thousand metres away, helicopters with TOW missiles could engage targets at twice that distance. Helicopters could avoid becoming decisively engaged in a slug-out with the enemy and could retreat quickly. Although vulnerable to ground fire, they were hard to engage if they used cover effectively. Similarly, they were vulnerable to artillery but could move quickly unless hit by the first round. An attack helicopter did cost more than a tank (about $400,000 versus $240,000), but given the exchange ratio forecast, it was still the most cost-effective choice.

The main problem with the attack helicopter was that the current generation – the Cobra – had only limited capability to operate in conditions of low visibility and had virtually no armour. Given Soviet emphasis on night operations and the number of poor-weather days in Central Europe, these were important deficiencies. A main battle tank was still required, but if NATO was prepared to conduct a retreating defence, the attack helicopter would be the preferred platform. Large armies could afford a mix, but smaller forces were faced with a difficult choice. In the end, the limitations of the existing aircraft and the fact that there was no army branch to argue for the helicopter tipped the balance back to the tank. The army was prepared to accept attack helicopters – so long as the tank remained part of the mix. Together with the disappearance of the Scorpion light armoured vehicle as an option, these trials effectively foreclosed acceptance of the light mobile force.[67]

The Land Force Policy Review undertaken in the summer of 1973 by a team from National Defence, External Affairs, and the Treasury Board Secretariat was placed in the position of trying to square the circle. The prime minister and Cabinet wanted a force in Europe, but a light force for which suitable equipment did not exist. The review therefore essentially abandoned the Cabinet direction to design such a force and recommended a return to the big army. The study team found that the army was so understrength that the "prudent limits of multiple tasking have passed" and the ability to maintain operational readiness and combat skills had been "seriously prejudiced." The overall structure was seen as unbalanced and lacking a rationale. The three combat groups that formed the core of the structure did not have the personnel or equipment to conduct independent combat operations, and resources would have to be withdrawn from at least two of the groups to meet the Canadian Air-Sea Transportable Brigade Group (CAST) commitment to the northern flank or form a brigade group for the defence of North America. The review reported that while land forces in Canada and Europe were mostly compatible, it was the "considered judgement" of the chief of the defence staff that forces in Europe should be heavy, incorporating armour, anti-armour weapons, effective artillery, and air defence.

The review reported that the Militia was at a low level of operational readiness and effectiveness, was well below its peacetime establishment, and could likely generate only 2,000 personnel without more than thirty days of training. While recent improvements to pay and equipment had slowed the decline of the Militia, more needed to be done. The review thought that a peacetime ceiling of 18,000 for the Militia supported by 1,000 Regular Force troops could produce 6,000 Militia soldiers in less than thirty days. It went on to note that there were no current policy provisions for mobilization, and suggested that for National Defence's concept of mobilization to work, legislation would be needed to provide protection of civilian employment for former Regular Force members returning to duty as well as for members of the Militia. The review recommended meeting personnel requirements by revitalizing the Militia.

As for the army in Europe, the review did not believe it could be useful without replacement of the Centurion and a major reconfiguration to a force highly specialized in anti-tank and anti-aircraft defence that could be integrated at the division, corps, or army level with allies. Re-equipping the army in this manner would cost about $300 million, however, and would have to be paid for at the same time that funds were needed to replace the CF-104 and purchase a new long-range patrol aircraft. The CDS and the review study group therefore recommended that the status quo be preserved in Canada's air and land contributions to NATO, but that the armoured capability be replaced either by modernizing the Centurion (as the Israelis had done at a cost of $10 million to $12 million) or by purchasing a new tank for $24 million.[68]

Just how replacement of the tank alone would remedy the problems of the army's force in Europe was unclear. Within a month of the review's completion, the Yom Kippur War between Israel and Egypt and Syria underlined the points that it made regarding the danger posed by forces equipped with modern Soviet anti-tank and anti-aircraft capabilities. The Egyptians decimated Israeli armour and ground attack aircraft early in the war by advancing with infantry heavily equipped with anti-tank guided missiles (ATGMs) and protected by a layered air defence system. The Americans and Soviets were greatly impressed with the vulnerability of armour and the new potential of infantry, and the Canadian army began to rethink its position. Prior to the Yom Kippur War, some had insisted that the tank was the ultimate anti-tank platform, regarding it as "relatively immune" to air and infantry anti-tank weapons[69] and even believing that for the next fifteen years no system other than the tank itself would emerge as a tank killer.[70] After the war, however, there was a growing realization that while tanks in defence could still defeat tanks, the ATGM meant that infantry could do so too, and could be decisive in some circumstances. There was also recognition that air defence could no longer be ignored. Analysts noted that the weapons employed by the Egyptian army had been issued to the Group of Soviet Forces in Germany five years earlier. The Canadian army had had no anti-aircraft capability since 1960, and it would be 1975 before even the rather puny, man-portable Blowpipe surface-to-air missile would be issued to Canadian troops.[71]

The Land Force Policy Review nailed the army's colours to the mast: it was now abandoning any pretence of building a light force and was headed towards a heavily equipped big army.

The Defence Structure Review

The review of the army's structure was interrupted by the need to address the budget crisis of 1974. The defence budget had been in crisis since the early 1960s. Hellyer's unification of the services had not produced sufficient savings, and even cutting the European commitment in half had been insufficient to stabilize the budget as double-digit inflation and escalating energy costs overwhelmed the annual 7 percent increase that Sylvain Cloutier had won for the department from the Treasury Board in 1973. The CDS, General Jacques Dextraze, had spent the first eighteen months of his term watching the strength of the Forces decrease to 78,000. In April 1974, he "poured his heart out" to the Defence Management Committee, telling his colleagues that the "situation had now reached a degree of gravity where he had a genuine and deep rooted fear of the consequences, both in terms of what it meant for the Forces per se and what it meant to the country in terms of risks." The 1971 White Paper's force required 83,970 personnel and now the Forces were overemployed to the point of compromising their safety. He complained that "the Forces cannot be viable on a diet of expedients in terms of policy and manpower" and stated his belief that the government had not heard the true facts expressed "as a professional military assessment unmodified by political considerations." By making these points he was implicitly criticizing Cloutier, who had refused to press the government for additional resources.[72]

The dam burst at the 29 September 1974 meeting of the Defence Council, where the VCDS informed Defence Minister James Richardson that "your Department is now on a Procrustean couch, scaled to an invalid funding formula of seven percent. With current rates of inflation running well beyond this, we have begun to hack off arms and legs." An "intense discussion" followed between the CDS and the minister, during which Dextraze did not hesitate to share his professional military assessment unmodified by political considerations. The government, he explained, must decide what it could afford and then pay whatever bill is involved. Richardson did not agree. National Defence received 10 percent of the federal budget and about 2.5 percent of the GNP to fund its programs. It was the department's responsibility to design the kind of forces needed within that envelope. Moreover, the department should have anticipated the budgetary crisis and acted earlier. Dextraze insisted simply that if the government would not pay for 83,000 troops, his only responsibility was to point out the consequences. Richardson responded that he thought, from a personal point of view, that it would be better to have a smaller force that was well trained and equipped than a larger one that was constantly out of money, but that if National Defence could "clearly and specifically" demonstrate the need for additional funds, he would carry their case forward. National Defence subsequently asked Cabinet to commission a study to reconcile the budget with policy direction. The Defence Structure Review (DSR) was the result.[73]

The DSR was carried out by a committee of senior officials chaired by Michael Pitfield, the secretary to Cabinet. The first step was to get Cabinet approval for the tasks assigned to the armed forces. The memo to Cabinet was forthright in setting out the problem of designing a land force for operations in Central Europe, where Soviet forces were more heavily armed and more concentrated than anywhere else in the world, that would also be compatible with light, mobile defence-of-Canada forces. The memo argued that even though Canada could be defended by paramilitary forces, the foreign policy goal of preventing escalation of local conflicts and major military involvement by the Great Powers could not. If Canada wished to make good on the 1971 White Paper's stated intention of contributing to the protection of US retaliatory forces and to collective defence in Western Europe, it would require heavier forces than those required "for the protection of sovereignty in the limited sense." The DSR acknowledged that ministers had reservations about heavy forces, but argued that they were "the heart of combat effectiveness." Concerning the army, the DSR repeated the options developed in the Land Force Policy Review of either a mechanized brigade group with tanks or a specialized anti-tank and anti-aircraft unit. The specialized force was dismissed as requiring sophisticated weapons of little or no utility in either peacekeeping or domestic operations, diminishing Canadian identity because it would be merged into allied units, being dispersed and difficult to support, being expensive and incompatible with the army in Canada, and requiring Canadian training facilities. The mechanized option would lack strategic mobility and its heavy equipment would also be of little use in peacekeeping or domestic operations, but the DSR argued most of the equipment and the basic organization would be similar to those maintained in Canada and could be employed in any role without the heavy equipment.

The tank was regarded as essential. "Analysis of recent combat," said the memo to Cabinet, "confirms that the tank properly used is, and will continue to be for the foreseeable future, the most potent component of the overall system required to meet the tank threat in Europe, or elsewhere in the world where there are sophisticated forces." Initial successes by the Egyptians in the Yom Kippur War were ascribed to Israeli tactical error that, when corrected, had confirmed established doctrine. Tanks were essential to a defensive battle and also to the maintenance of "the full range of skills essential to professionalism." Finally, in contrast to the sophisticated weapons and mobility requirements of the specialized anti-tank/anti-aircraft force (which were never described), the lower cost of equipping and training a mechanized force made it "an attractive option." A "balanced, general purpose force" that reflected Canadian society socially and technologically was recommended. This included a mechanized army, including tanks.[74]

The position that went to Cabinet was therefore a one-sided advocacy document. It assumed that the army's NATO role would be on the Central Front. It reduced the mobile force option to an undefined specialized anti-tank/anti-aircraft capability that would not function as a Canadian formation. Finally, it made claims (as had the Land Force Policy Review) that mechanized forces would be much cheaper than the specialized force. Although Cabinet was not presented with any financial data at this point in the process, it is worth noting that when Canada eventually replaced its tanks a few years later, the cost was $183 million, compared with the $24 million estimated in the Land Force Policy Review. The army also eventually purchased better anti-tank missiles and a low-level air defence system that were required whether the force was light or mechanized.

Cloutier supported the initiative and suggested that the wording be changed to make sure that ministers knew that the decisions they made would determine whether or not the Canadian Forces would continue to be a military force. He also suggested adding material underlining that Canada needed to be seen as making a "fair and reasonable" contribution to collective defence if it was to continue having diplomatic influence. Finally, he suggested extensive additions making clear the gravity of the Soviet threat, the fact that general hostilities resulting from a local crisis could not be ruled out, and that it would be in Canada's interest for NATO to have options other than surrender or general nuclear war. Canada also needed to consider the possibility of a long war that would require deployment of the CAST and the reinforcement of European forces.[75]

Michael Pitfield, the clerk of the Privy Council, appeared highly taken with the department's submission. In a briefing note to Prime Minister Trudeau, he stressed that ministerial decision and guidance were absolutely essential, otherwise "the Armed Forces can only resort to their own appraisal which led to the impasse which has existed for so many years between Ministers collectively and DND as to what the forces should be doing and how they should be equipped." He thought that National Defence had done an excellent job in developing tasks on the basis of national aims, but acknowledged that the department had, not surprisingly, done so from the context of NATO and NORAD thinking, which were assumed to be supported by the 1971 White Paper. Pitfield recommended that Trudeau read the entire paper, which he found to be one of the most cohesive the government had ever received from DND. He noted that some of the contingencies put forward by DND were "arguable" and might not be credible to ministers, but suggested that the prime minister seek the advice of the Intelligence Advisory Committee so as not to be captive to DND's assessment of the threat. Nevertheless, it appears that Ivan Head, Trudeau's foreign policy adviser, thought that the DND paper was consistent with his own views.[76]

The overall concept was apparently approved by Cabinet on 17 April 1975, and the Defence Structure Review moved into its second phase: the development of detailed force structure options. Because Cabinet had not made up its mind about the army and NATO, the second phase (DSR II) was to advise on how

> to contribute to the NATO deterrent and combat capabilities in Central Europe by stationing there in peacetime, or providing through fly-over capability, a mixture of land and air forces as at present, or an all-air force, or an all-land force, with any land element being made up of either several anti-tank/anti-air units or a single mechanized formation with heavy tanks as at present.

The Cabinet decision emphasized that none of the force structure options had been approved and that Cabinet would consider all options again.[77]

Cabinet papers prepared by NDHQ in May and June 1975 did not contain any new ideas. Rather, they recycled the status report contained in the Land

Force Policy Review and previous memoranda to Cabinet outlining the parlous state of the disorganized and overtasked army and the seriousness of the Soviet threat it faced in Europe. Various force structure options were offered for fulfilling the NATO commitment. Maintaining the existing CAST commitment was not recommended. The force was regarded as effective in Norway but not in flat Denmark, where the lack of tanks and anti-tank weapons would be serious deficiencies. Attempting to strengthen the CAST force would compound the strategic lift problem and would seriously deplete army units in Canada. The paper leaned towards either continuing or reinforcing the ACE Mobile Force (Land) commitment to the northern flank while dropping CAST. This would free up resources for 4 Canadian Mechanized Brigade Group (4CMBG) on the Central Front. The option of maintaining 4CMBG in Canada with flyover to Central Europe was considered impossible due to the air transport required. It would also be expensive in other ways. Units would have to be maintained at almost full strength and at high readiness, and would have to be flown over to Europe regularly to maintain credibility. As for the brigade group itself, the favoured options would increase its war establishment to 6,000 troops and its peacetime strength to 4,550. Tanks would be replaced or refurbished.[78]

The tipping point came in July 1975 when Prime Minister Trudeau met with West German Chancellor Helmut Schmidt at the Helsinki Final Act Conference on Security and Co-operation in Europe. Schmidt made a strong case for West Germany's security problem and the necessity for NATO to maintain a strong conventional deterrent force. Trudeau was impressed by the case made by a fellow social democrat and was at the same time seeking to broaden Canadian trade ties with Europe. He therefore took the final step in concluding that re-equipping the forces and replacing the army's tank was necessary. The final results of the Defence Structure Review were announced in Parliament on 27 November 1975 by Minister Richardson. It committed the government to increasing the capital expenditure portion of the defence budget by 12 percent a year for five years in real terms. A rational plan for re-equipping the army (as well as the other services) could now be undertaken.[79]

An extremely important footnote to the 1974-75 budget crisis was the re-creation of the air force. A major component of the mobile force had been air support. This had been problematic from the beginning, when Paul Hellyer pushed the CF-5 on the Forces, an aircraft with a range that was too short, ordnance capacity that was too small, and avionics that were too primitive to provide effective close air support. It had taken until 1970 for tactical aviation doctrine to be issued. Even then, doctrine was based on the RCAF concept that air power should be centralized at the highest level of command possible – the tactical air force – but did allow that tactical transport and tactical helicopters could be decentralized either to the control of national formations or to the task force commander if a Canadian formation was working independently.[80]

Mobile Command had retained control of 10 Tactical Air Group (10 TAG), which consisted of the CF-5 squadrons and all the land force helicopters. Former RCAF officers believed that whereas the army and navy had each found a post-unification institutional home in Mobile Command and Maritime Command, respectively, the air force had been fragmented and left without a voice. Neither Allard nor Sharp as CDS was prepared to make organizational changes, but the game changed when Jacques Dextraze was appointed CDS in September 1972. Dextraze had reorganized NDHQ so that it had chiefs of Maritime, Land, and Air Operations, and, according to some, had a desire to see "armies, navies and air forces" again. In this he was opposed by Major-General S.C. Waters, the deputy chief of the defence staff, who was promoted to commander of Mobile Command in 1973. The budgetary crisis of 1974 provided an occasion for Dextraze and Richardson to propose to Cabinet that Air Defence Command and Air Transport Command be combined into a single Air Command to save about a hundred staff positions. Senior air officers were not satisfied with this, as air defence was seen as a dwindling role and major air assets were still outside the reach of Air Command in the Maritime Air Group and 10 TAG. They were able to obtain Maritime Command's support for their proposal to place all air assets under a single Air Command, and Richardson announced his intention to do this in January 1975, at the annual Conference of Defence Associations meeting. The change was made despite the objections of Waters, who retired soon after. His successor, Major-General J.J. Paradis, supported the change as it "relieved" Mobile Command of purely air matters. Although the army would retain operational control of aviation assets providing tactical support to land operations, the vision of an integrated mobile force was completely dead.[81]

The Resurrection of Combat Development

In parallel with efforts to restore funding to the army through the Defence Structure Review, Mobile Command launched an initiative to revive the combat development process – the army's ability to plan and develop itself for the future. Although the Defence Structure Review proclaimed that the Yom Kippur War had changed nothing, a good portion of the officer corps was not so sure. Capacity to address development and doctrinal issues had diminished, however, and the army's keystone manual, CFP 165, *The Conduct of Land Operations*, which Rowley had produced in 1967, was regarded as out of date. In Rowley's day about two hundred personnel had been engaged in solving doctrinal problems; in 1976 there were only seven. Clearly, something had to be done to provide the army with a blueprint for its future.[82]

Efforts began with small-scale staff meetings between Mobile Command and NDHQ in 1974 and progressed steadily even though the same staff at NDHQ was also working on the DSR. By the summer of 1976, a process for combat development and doctrine had been agreed upon and a proposed plan of action prepared. The commander of Mobile Command, Lieutenant-General Jacques Chouinard, reinstituted the Land Forces Combat Development Committee and called the first conference for senior army staff officers in July 1976. Although Chouinard was chair of the Combat Development Committee, the principal staff officer managing the process was the new chief of combat development and land operations at NDHQ, Brigadier-General H.C. Pitts. Under Chouinard and Pitts, staff designed processes intended to link the combat development process with DND's overall Defence Program Management System (DPMS). This was intended to ensure that army plans were consistent with defence policy and would support budgetary submissions. The resulting *Combat Development Guide* (1976) regarded tactical developments as having been evolutionary rather than revolutionary even though the battlefield had become increasingly lethal and a twenty-four-hour operation. Efforts centred on high-intensity operations in Northwest Europe. Adopting a realistic position, the *Guide* concentrated on the brigade as the key organizational level for the Canadian army.[83] The program of studies proposed by staff was therefore both significant and doable, consisting of an examination of the brigade group, including the possibility of adopting a divisional structure in peacetime, an air defence study, an anti-tank study, an infantry combat vehicle study, service support, tactical aviation, and communications.[84]

Political and budgetary realism did not go unopposed, however. Brigadier-General P.V. Grieve, the commandant of the Canadian Land Forces Staff College, argued that combat development could not be adequately done under existing manpower constraints. He also objected to the choice of the brigade as the fundamental building block for the army, and suggested that "the organization chosen could not be an organization compromised by current political restraints but had to be representative of the professional military assessment necessary for high intensity operations." Chouinard stood his ground, and explained that the *Combat Development Guide* had to strike a balance between the ideal and practicable and had to be considered in terms of reality. He and other senior staff believed that the army could make its budgetary case by presenting its requirements in the form of a brigade combat "system," rather than attempting to justify each individual piece of equipment separately. As the senior officer present, Chouinard won the debate, but the position of development guided by realism would be abandoned by his successor in less than two years.[85]

The Combat Development Committee also heard from Dr. J.J. Conn, the director of land operational research. Conn's directorate was staffed by twelve military and eighteen civilian personnel, and was carrying out simulation studies of air defence, tactical air support, communications and intelligence, internal security operations, and the development of simulation models. In his opinion, the research war games were the directorate's most important project. He described this as a "scientifically designed simulation of battle with which to contrast the effects of various firepower and manoeuvre capabilities and to study the effectiveness of current and proposed force structures." The directorate had developed models of land combat at the brigade level with detail down to platoon-sized subunits. Both the CAST commitment to northern Norway and the NATO Central Front had been studied. Conn suggested that research war games could be used to give "reasonable indications" of what organizations were best suited to deal with given problems, which weapons were best for given tasks, and what doctrine offered the most reasonable prospect for success. The minutes give little indication of how Conn's offer of assistance was received, but perhaps the note that there was a lengthy discussion of how to interpret war-game results indicated less than wholehearted support for a scientific approach. The committee made no firm commitment to any future program, merely suggesting that the operations research program should be based on priorities contained in the *Combat Development Guide.*[86]

The most important research war game under development was BRONZE RAMPART, a study of a proposed mechanized brigade in mobile defence against a reinforced Soviet tank division. The operations researchers presented their results at a symposium six months after the Combat Development Committee met in January 1977. The Canadian brigade was based on how a brigade group in Europe was likely to be equipped in 1984. It still had Centurion tanks, but with laser rangefinders and a ballistic computer, four batteries of M109A1 self-propelled guns, Blowpipe surface-to-air missiles for air defence, and four mechanized companies per battalion equipped with M113 armoured personnel carriers and TOW and Dragon anti-tank missiles. In addition, the brigade was supported by fourteen utility helicopters, seven with unguided rockets and seven with TOW missiles. The brigade was opposed by a Soviet tank division followed by a motor rifle division, both equipped according to NATO intelligence estimates. Enemy air support included seventy-six fighter ground attack and twenty reconnaissance sorties every twenty-four hours. The Soviet forces were equipped with the existing T-62 tanks and BMP infantry fighting vehicles. They had strong artillery, air defence, and helicopter support.

The war game identified several shortcomings of the Canadian brigade group structure. The TOW missile was effective at long range, but once Soviet tanks closed within 1,500 metres, the tanks were able to equalize their losses. The Canadian brigade did not have an effective short-range anti-tank weapon. The study suggested that tanks were needed as part of the main anti-armour defence. Helicopters fitted with rockets were deemed to be worthless as attack vehicles, due to the strong anti-aircraft defences of Soviet forces and the limited range of the rockets, and they were used only for transport. The TOW-armed helicopters were effective, but few remained at the end of the engagement. Soviet air defences were much stronger than those of the Canadian brigade group, and the study recommended acquiring an equivalent to the Soviet ZSU-23-4 self-propelled air defence gun.

Most significantly, the officer who played the BLUE force commander (i.e., the Canadian brigade commander) was compelled to ask: "*What* role does the infantry play on the armoured battlefield?" He found that at no time had infantry been a decisive factor in or influence on the battle, and concluded that "organized and equipped as they were, the infantry companies were a nuisance if not a liability." This was because the M113 armoured personnel carrier did not provide enough protection or firepower to make them truly mobile. Soldiers had to dismount and dig in to obtain protection. The M113's firepower was insufficient to defeat Soviet infantry fighting vehicles or to protect itself from air attack. These deficiencies rendered the infantry immobile and turned them from assets into liabilities. The Soviet tactic was to have some of its BMPs sit back in overwatch while the remaining BMPs and tanks assaulted the defenders. The Canadian forward company commander could either use his long-range anti-tank resources – Centurions and TOWs – to engage the overwatching BMPs in the fire base and risk being overrun, or engage the assault and then be picked off by the overwatching BMPs and their anti-tank missiles. In addition, because of its limitations, the Canadian infantry could not be used for local counterattacks. The conclusion was that infantry, to play a role in the mobile battle, should be mounted in a vehicle with almost the same protection as a tank and carrying weapons effective against BMPs and attack helicopters up to 2,000 metres away. This problem of how to equip the infantry and what level of mobility they should have on the Central Front battlefield was to become the key issue facing combat development for the next twenty years.

Overall, BRONZE RAMPART concluded that the Canadian army had "little appreciation" of the speed and intensity of armoured and mechanized operations, and that the lack of appreciation was reflected in the organization and equipment in use. This was only a "product-improved" version of the pre-1970 NATO brigade group. While TOW missiles and self-propelled artillery had been added, it was apparent that the overall situation had not been addressed. The main problems were the relative lack of offensive firepower, the inadequacy of organic air defence, the failure to allocate sufficient long-range anti-armour resources to the brigade group commander, and an excessive reliance on infantry in a battle that would be aimed at destroying equipment. The paucity of occasions in which infantry was the decisive arm was not unique to this war game; it had been a consistent finding of operations research studies and training games.[87]

If the army had continued on the path apparently established by the first meeting of its revived Combat Development Committee and the findings of BRONZE RAMPART, it might have developed into a force that was both affordable and well equipped. Unfortunately, it would shortly abandon both political and financial realism as well as science, and strike out in a direction that it found more emotionally fulfilling but that would ultimately lead to a dead end.

Civil-Military Relations in Disrepair

By the end of 1975 the army had successfully resisted two alternative concepts of what Canada's army should be: Paul Hellyer's mobile force, which would be capable of spanning the world and fighting brush-fire wars, and Donald Macdonald's light force, which would also be capable, to a certain extent, of providing forces to NATO and the United Nations. While neither concept was totally infeasible (although the cost of Hellyer's mobile force would have made the full concept unrealizable), political support for both was shallow. There was a strong pro-NATO faction both in Cabinet and in the civilian bureaucracy, and it did not hesitate to bend decisions in the direction desired by SHAPE. The charge, levelled by some, that the Trudeau government had "established defence objectives from which they could not escape but which they did not wish to honour"[88] is misdirected criticism. Cadieux and the National Defence bureaucracy had conspired to ignore Cabinet direction and to commit Canada to a role that cost more than Cabinet was prepared to pay. There had been a breakdown in civil-military relations, but neither Trudeau nor Cabinet was to blame.

Those who wished to reorient the army were also hampered by its lack of staff processes to plan and develop forces. The combat development function had barely come into existence in the early 1960s when integration and unification disrupted it. Throughout the 1970s there had been little capacity to develop and test prototype light forces on paper, much less attempt field trials. Doctrine was in such disarray that the army had had difficulty even cataloguing what was in use, much less developing anything new. What studies were done seemed disconnected from decision processes. The BRONZE NIMBUS war game indicated that light forces could fight Soviet formations to a standstill – but a light armoured vehicle with a big gun was required. However, when the army proposed to actually equip itself as a light force, the Scorpion with its 76 mm gun – ineffective against tanks – was selected because it was all that was available. Only the failure of contract negotiations and the expense of the purchase saved the army from a terrestrial version of the CF-5. On the other hand, the successful trials of the Cobra attack helicopter at Ansbach, Germany, were discounted and ignored. The discussion of attack helicopters had turned into a debate over a helicopter versus a tank, not a discussion of how to incorporate a powerful new technology into the force. Since the army had an armoured branch prepared to defend the tank, the outcome was perhaps inevitable. The formation of Air Command and the transfer of aviation to it meant that helicopters would not have a voice or funding within the army. The BRONZE RAMPART war game indicated that the Canadian army had fallen, both materially and conceptually, far behind the requirements of high-intensity mechanized warfare. It should have provided either a sobering blueprint for the future or justification for finding a new role. It did neither.

Civilians contributed to this analytical deficit by trying to do the entire job themselves. Trudeau brought in Ivan Head to draft a defence policy for him, while Donald Macdonald brought in Gordon Smith. Although this could be seen as a reaction to the DND's inability and unwillingness to develop policy based on political direction, it did not develop any responsive policy capacity within the department until the Management Review Group recommendations resulted in the creation of a Policy Group at NDHQ. As we shall see, however, this did not integrate policy into the Forces but rather heightened civil-military contention.

Finally, the central role of finances needs to be considered. In the analytical vacuum of National Defence, ministers seemed free to hypothesize forces and establish policy without reference to costs. The military, on the other hand, had a tendency to make pronouncements regarding the unaffordability of unwanted options without much supporting evidence. They felt free to give lowball estimates of options they preferred (like the tank) or ignore the Financial Administration Act when it suited them (as in the case of overspending on the DDH 280 destroyer). This led to the Richardson/Dextraze contretemps at the Defence Council, with the minister taking the position that the military had been given 10 percent of the federal budget and should be able to figure out how to achieve the government's policy goals with it, and the chief of the defence staff arguing that the government had selected a policy and should pay whatever bill the military placed in front of it. Dextraze would have been in a stronger position if ministers had trusted the Forces to spend money wisely and follow direction faithfully. Sylvain Cloutier and the Defence Structure Review did much to repair the breach in civil-military relations but did not close it completely.

For the balance of the decade, the army would return to trying to rebuild itself as the "big army" it had always wanted to be.

CHAPTER FIVE

Reform, Regimentalism, and Reaction

THE UNIFICATION PROJECT and the Trudeau government's efforts to reorient Canadian defence policy disrupted the current orthodoxy sufficiently to enable initiatives to reform the Canadian Forces (and thereby the army) to take root. The first of these was internal – the Officer Development Board – and was an attempt to modernize the officer corps and to make it both more "Canadian" and better able to tackle national strategy issues. The second was the Management Review Group established by Donald Macdonald in reaction to the failure by the army, the Canadian Forces, and the Department of National Defence to implement Cabinet direction.

The report of the Officer Development Board would be accepted but not implemented. That of the Management Review Group would be largely put into effect and would result in massive disaffection in the army officer corps with the governance of the Defence establishment and with society itself. In the end, reform and modernization had too few supporters on the inside, and the tide of reaction was too strong. Even though the unified headquarters was not overthrown, the new structure failed to capture the hearts and minds of the majority of the officer corps.

Professionalism in the 1970s

Integration produced significant changes in how the army was run. As part of a general economy drive, army strength was reduced from 49,760 in 1963 to 46,264 in 1965 and 40,192 in 1968. The army received new armoured personnel carriers and self-propelled artillery, and the air force more transport aircraft to move the army. Support functions of all three services were integrated into a single comptroller's branch, a unified personnel branch, a single logistics branch, and a single technical services branch. The Canadian Army ceased to exist organizationally as it was transformed into a Mobile Command combining both ground troops stationed in Canada and tactical air squadrons, while the brigade in Europe became part of a separate Canadian Forces Europe. These major structural and role changes were relatively uncontroversial compared with the final stage of Paul Hellyer's reforms: complete unification of the armed services. This involved a makeover of the rank structure, a new single-service uniform, and new badges and names for branches. Many senior army (and naval) officers had strong objection to these changes and there was considerable resistance and several high-profile resignations. Hellyer prevailed, however, and while the army preserved its regimental structures and identities, it lost much of its outwardly British appearance in the new green uniform, which was accompanied by the disappearance of the word "Royal" from the names of the branches and the merger of the branches themselves into Canadian Forces–wide organizations.[1]

Unification also saw changes to the army's regimental system. Previously, the army was organized on a regimental system modelled on Britain's, but with some significant differences. Militia regiments had been weak, single-battalion units based on the local population. During the Second World War, their historic names had been used, but few retained their regional character. The Special Force recruited for Korea had made no use of the Militia structure. However, the need for a permanent regular army force stationed in Europe led Chief of the General Staff Guy Simonds to organize the army on a Cardwell-like regimental system, with multiple-battalion regiments whose formations could be rotated from Canada to Europe.[2] Regimental depots for training recruits and small regimental staffs developed. At Army Headquarters, directorates had been based on regimental lines for doctrine, equipment, training, manning, and operational standards of units. To make changes on an army-wide basis, the director of armour and the director of infantry first had to achieve consensus among the regimental groups. Regimental senates typically controlled promotions and the selection of regimental personnel for key positions.

Unification installed a new "green," tri-service personnel system to manage promotions and staffing based on military occupations, each with its own merit board, career managers, and a branch adviser who was a senior officer responsible for the well-being of the occupation. The army, however, maintained a parallel and only partly authorized structure to manage "regimental affairs." Regiments had an Executive Committee, chaired by the colonel of the regiment, and a Senate, chaired by their senior serving officer and consisting of all regimental officers of general officer rank. This was backed up by an Advisory Council of former colonels and incumbent and former honorary colonels of their associated Militia battalions. The Senate provided advice on officer promotions, appointments, and postings. There was almost universal commitment by each regiment "to get our guy into a key command or staff position." One colonel would later define his role as

> to act on behalf of the regiment to manage the postings, career development, major corps selections and grooming of our officers and NCOs and soldiers in order to maintain the health and vitality of the regiment as a whole, the battalions in particular. And more importantly [to manage] individuals in their development so that in the longer term the regiment would not suffer any declines through mismanagement of the personnel assets.[3]

The existence of these regimental "mafias" outside the formal management and accountability structure of the Forces would have dire consequences in the 1990s.[4]

Three years after unification, a staff college student polled his colleagues on "problems of morale, motivation and attitude within the [Canadian] officer corps." Based on a questionnaire sent out to students at the Canadian Forces Command and Staff College (tri-service), the Canadian Army Staff College, and the Canadian Forces Staff School (mainly RCAF), he concluded that the majority did not consider the roles, aims, and tasks of the Canadian Forces to have been "spelt out" to them in a realistic and meaningful way. Fewer than one-quarter of them were "content and happy" and intended to serve their full career, fewer than one-quarter said they were challenged and motivated, and 28 percent were troubled and were considering resignation. A further 11 percent had considered resigning but were "pension trapped," while 12 percent were troubled but considered it their duty to continue to serve. Almost none were enthusiastic about unification as a project and detected an uncertain drift in Canadian foreign policy coupled with a rapid and continuing decline in the defence budget.

The dissatisfaction of mid-level officers was especially serious as it undermined the already weak program for developing senior officers who could operate at the strategic level and deal easily with government and business leadership. Attrition of university-stream officers reached 50 percent and there was increasingly heavy reliance on short-service officers. Educational levels were far below those of the political and public service hierarchies. In the federal public service, about 80 percent of officer-equivalent levels had degrees and over 40 percent had postgraduate degrees. Education was spread out over law, social sciences, engineering, and science. Twenty percent of the public service executive had entered directly from the "higher professorial ranks" of the universities. By comparison, the Forces had only 35 percent degreed officers, with the proportion of engineering and science versus the arts the reverse of that of their civilian counterparts. Dr. Frederic Thompson of the Royal Military College (RMC) believed that the officer corps had lost prestige and influence in decision making and was in a downward spiral, with every slip in influence resulting in further declines in the attractiveness of the military as a career.[5]

The army was also unable to solve the problem of needing a large number of junior officers with no career path above major for most of them. The American practice of forced retirement of officers who were twice passed over for promotion was considered but not seriously entertained.[6] More serious attention was given to the possibility of dividing the officer corps into two: those with a full career with a path to the top ranks, and "limited-career officers," who would be trained and developed only within their occupation and who could be recruited from inside or outside the service. Limited-career officers would not be able to rise above the rank of lieutenant-colonel, and most would stop at major. This proposition went nowhere. Hellyer did not like the idea of "second class citizens" and, as one senior military official commented, the scheme "lead[s] one to ask – what does the limited career officer have to attract him to a life of service with all the penalties on page 13 of the report? The only honest answer is nothing ... One might also ask – does a young man who deliberately enters such a limited career display the good sense and judgement required of a service officer?"[7]

The massive changes and the obvious dissatisfaction and unease at junior and middle levels triggered action by the senior leadership of the armed services. In March 1969 a comprehensive study of officership by Major-General Roger Rowley was commissioned under the direction of General Jean V. Allard, the chief of the defence staff. Neither Allard nor Rowley was a likely iconoclast, although Allard had benefited personally from unification, first by being appointed the first commander of Mobile Command and then by being promoted over more senior generals to chief of the defence staff. Allard had held a postwar appointment as the commander of a British Army division, and his British Army appearance belied his focus on making the army fully bilingual and giving francophones an equal place in it. Rowley was an even less likely radical. From a privileged family with ties to the British aristocracy, he had a London tailor, shirtmaker, hatter, and bootmaker. Prior to the Second World War, he had been an Ottawa bond trader and militia officer. As we have seen, Rowley had been an intellectual support to Allard for years. It was therefore not surprising that Allard would rely on him to lead the assignment.

According to Allard, a review of officer development was needed because of the lack of a coordinated education, training, and career management system in the now-unified Forces; the loss of too many educated and highly trained young officers before their normal retirement age; and the implications of unification for future officer training and education.[8] Allard's initiative set in motion the first fundamental study of officership undertaken by the Canadian Forces or any of its predecessor services.

The Officer Development Board (ODB) led by Rowley was not confined to solving problems of either recruiting or career management as had been done previously, but was mandated to address the entire question of officership and its place in the Canadian security establishment. Rowley defined a "professional" as someone who worked in a "social context" and performed a service that was essential to the functioning of society. A professional required expert knowledge acquired by study and from practical experience, and professional knowledge was "intellectual in nature" and recorded. A professional was aware of the history of his profession and how it had formed part of the cultural tradition of society. This, according to Rowley, distinguished a profession from a trade or skill. Moreover, the professional was motivated by the desire to serve, not profit. A profession had customs and laws codified into a professional ethic, and had control and direction of its members.

The military clearly met these criteria. Furthermore, the Officer Development Board rejected Huntington's restriction of officership to the combat arms. "When the skills required by the officer corps were fewer," the ODB said, "it was plausible to define the nature of the competence peculiar to the military function as the control of violence. The enormous nature of the modern military function makes a simple definition of this nature irrelevant and renders comparison on a function basis with other professions artificial and limiting." Putting itself squarely in the tradition of Charles Foulkes, the ODB concluded that officership required a broad general education on which to build specialist expertise, and, equally important, that the primary function of the officer was to maintain national security.[9]

Unlike the traditionalists who gloried in the British military association of the Canadian army and Forces, the ODB was severely critical of what it regarded as the officer corps' colonial heritage and orientation. It noted the many ties with the British Army prior to the First World War: officer appointments in British units for RMC graduates; the many similarities between the RMC and a British public school; links between British and Canadian regiments; and the exchange of British and Canadian officers for regimental and staff duties. "The Canadian officer," it said, "tended to adopt the outlook and attitudes of his British contemporary; his pride of class, his expectations of respect and his professionalism were all recognizably British in character. This attitude served to isolate him from the society in which he lived." According to the ODB, during the First World War, the role of Canadian officers had been restricted to the implementation of British plans and the resulting high price in blood had not enhanced the image of the military profession in the eyes of Canadian society.

During the interwar period, the Canadian military had continued to follow a policy of Imperial centralization while their political masters opposed it. The ODB commented that "gradually we find the professional Canadian officer isolating himself from his own society and viewing his military role in terms of Imperial defence and strategy, with little or no concern for the study of the strategic problems likely to face his own country." The Second World War saw a repeat of this pattern of colonial subordination as Canada failed to develop the organizational machinery necessary to develop its own national strategy, and once again supplied troops and materiel for war machines to be planned, organized, and commanded from elsewhere.[10]

Looking into the future, the ODB saw the armed forces as increasingly army-centric, joint (that is, involving more than one service), and technology-based. In line with the current rationale for the Canadian Forces, the board forecast the need for well-balanced, strategically mobile land, sea, and air forces to keep peace, suppress insurgencies, and engage in non-nuclear conflict if necessary. It anticipated a greater emphasis on balance and a close integration of the Canadian armed services, which, since the Second World War, had developed in an increasingly divergent manner, with highly specialized and individual alliance roles. To achieve this, naval officers would need to add expertise in providing naval support to land operations, including shore bombardment, landing operations, and vertical replenishment; and air force officers would need to develop knowledge of all forms of tactical aviation, including close support of land operations and strategic lift. The integrated force would require officers to have broader knowledge outside their own branches and specializations, and high command would require the "broad understanding of the humanistic aspects of warfare," including the social sciences and the liberal arts. The problem of the force structure's requiring too many junior officers to enable a reasonable proportion to progress to senior rank was solved by anticipating the delegation of junior command functions such as platoon commander and aircraft commander to non-commissioned officers, thus "permitting the more highly trained and educated officers to spend only a minimum period in such relatively unchallenging tasks."[11]

The board was also concerned with the reintegration of the officer corps into Canadian society. To claim that war was the natural state of world affairs "completely lack[ed] plausibility to even the uncommitted majority of ... Canadian youth." The board recommended that a call to arms must be a call to defend the country directly or to bring peace to a troubled world. With world peace as "our prime concern," the Forces could honestly call on youth to be ready for the "role of interposition."[12]

The ODB report also came down strongly in favour of a degreed officer corps. To maintain quality, the Forces had to recruit from the top 15 percent of school leavers, who, by 1970, were almost all university-bound. The board rejected past attempts by the armed services to assess the number of officer positions that "needed" a degree. Rather, it simply accepted that the baccalaureate was the educational standard required for commissioning and must eventually be achieved by all officers. In the short term, provision would have to be made for those with less than a BA to improve their formal education. The board rejected the concept of a two-tier officer corps and advocated equal opportunity for all members. Rowley saw the need for not only the existing staff college system but also additional development of the top end. The board recommended an advanced military studies course at the lieutenant-colonel level to broaden what it called "list" or occupational competence and to study high-level operations. In addition, it saw the need for a national security studies college to develop awareness of the national and international environment and to develop military executive capability. Integrated with this would be a postgraduate program and a Master of Military Science degree that could be achieved by those accepted into the program and willing to do extra work. Finally, the national security studies college would include a strategic studies research group rather than having only an administrative staff. The report concluded:

> Nowhere in Canada do we properly meet the requirement, by means of content, for the broader kind of military expertise required by senior officers above the rank of lieutenant colonel. We do not study concepts of operations, theatre operations, air power or sea power. This is a weakness, for as professional military advisors to government or members of international staffs, very senior officers must have a deep understanding of the military capabilities of our allies and potential enemies, even if Canada by itself does not have the larger capability which this kind of knowledge might imply. We cannot depend upon the war experience of our present senior officers to continue to fill this need, for these officers are rapidly leaving the force through retirement.[13]

The balance of the multi-volume report was a detailed implementation plan for the education and development of the officer corps.

The Officer Development Board represented the highest point that the modernizers would reach before the end of the twentieth century, putting together a comprehensive and coherent vision of the officer corps that addressed its internal needs, its link to the political structure, and its links to the Canadian people. Unfortunately, the plan proposed by Rowley was never implemented. Allard retired in 1969 and reform lost its most powerful patron. Reform of the officer corps went into study mode, where it stayed until the twenty-first century. All the subsequent reports agreed with the essentials laid down by Rowley:

the need for a degreed and bilingual officer corps, the requirement for advanced study for senior officers, and the establishment of a centre for national security studies were all recommended again – sometimes more than once.[14] There seemed to be neither the will nor the resources to strengthen the officer corps.

The Threat of "Civilianization"

The last major reform initiative undertaken by the Department of National Defence was as least as disturbing to traditionalists as unification itself. This was the work of the Management Review Group (MRG), also known as the Pennefather Committee. The structural changes to National Defence Headquarters, along with increased awareness of the orientation and values of members of the Forces, created concern that the armed services had become "civilianized."

The MRG was created ostensibly to help deal with the budgetary crisis faced by National Defence. In 1974 operations and training were cut back 30 percent and further force reductions to 79,000 were announced.[15] There were, however, other concerns pressing upon Donald Macdonald, the minister. Macdonald had been greatly distressed by the dogged refusal of the army and the department to follow Cabinet direction and arrange for the withdrawal of land forces from NATO's Central Front. He and his chief policy adviser, Gordon Smith, had experienced considerable non-cooperation in the drafting of the 1971 White Paper. The straw that broke the camel's back was the navy's pursuit of a major new class of warship, the DDH 280, contrary to government direction and Treasury Board expenditure authorization.

Paul Hellyer's 1964 *White Paper on Defence* had committed the government to continue the anti-submarine warfare role as part of Canada's NATO contribution, but had deferred the question of fleet composition to further study. No commitments were made beyond the statement that Canada would maintain "a modern and well-equipped fleet of appropriate size."[16] Hellyer rejected the navy's own plan for a balanced but expensive fleet centred on eight of the large surface warships known as General Purpose Frigates (GPFs), largely on the basis of cost. An additional factor was the lack of consensus within the navy regarding fleet composition, with nuclear submarine and naval aviation advocates vying with the surface warfare community for primacy.[17] What Hellyer finally authorized was a program based on the acquisition of four new helicopter-carrying destroyers (DDHs), two operational support ships, a major refit of the aircraft carrier *Bonaventure,* and the modernization of the *Restigouche*-class escorts and Tracker aircraft.[18] The original plan for the new ships was modest: an updated version of the *Nipigon*-class ships fitted to carry one helicopter. The new design would lengthen the *Nipigon* hull, equip the ship with updated sonar, radar, communications, and electronic warfare gear and arm it with a 5-inch gun and a point defence missile. The DND submission to the Treasury Board estimated the cost of four ships to be $142 million, plus $2 million for the missile system.[19] In July 1965 the Defence Council approved the substitution of gas turbines for steam turbines in the ship, which was estimated to increase the total cost modestly to $147 million.[20] As detailed engineering design proceeded, however, the cost ballooned to at least $225 million, leaving the minister, Léo Cadieux, begging the Treasury Board for more funds and arguing that failure to increase the budget would cause a loss of goodwill in the shipbuilding industry – a political and public relations disaster should the government have to admit that its largest naval project was out of financial control.[21] The Treasury Board approved Cadieux's request only "because there appeared to be little practical alternative at this stage" and because Cadieux committed to holding the cost to $225 million.[22]

Nevertheless, costs continued to escalate to over $250 million, leaving Donald Macdonald with an ongoing source of embarrassment when he took over from Cadieux as minister. Taken to task by the Committee on External Affairs and National Defence in February 1971, Macdonald suggested:

> There should be in effect a management review board to try in so far as possible to improve procedures within the Department responsible for this to have as early as possible a better reporting on troubles of this kind when they occur ... I have the feeling that what we are involved with here is a structural problem with the Department, the relationships on the one hand between those who are concerned with providing the most effective warship and on the other hand those concerned about living with a fixed budget.[23]

In an effort to deal with his noncompliant headquarters, Macdonald commissioned John B. Pennefather, a prominent businessman, to head a committee to examine the organization and management of the entire Department of National Defence. In particular, the MRG was tasked with examining the relationship between the military and the civil and research branches of the department, the relationship between the headquarters and the commands, logistics and acquisition policy, and the proportion of resources devoted to support activities. Although senior officials angled to have the study staffed by "carefully chosen Government representatives," Macdonald ignored their advice and went outside for advisers. Pennefather's committee consisted largely of senior businessmen and was supported by a departmental staff of thirty-one, twelve of them officers ranging in rank from lieutenant-colonel to brigadier-general.[24]

The MRG's report took the high road. It did not censure individuals, or even organizational units below the departmental level. It tended to stay away from specifics and used a broad brush to describe the problems of National Defence as the review group saw them. The message was unmistakable, however. The department and Canadian Forces Headquarters had refused to follow government policy direction and had "gamed" the financial system to gain approval for projects by providing misleading and incomplete information.

According to the MRG, National Defence had not adapted to the "changing environment." In essence, this meant that the department had resisted implementing Trudeau's April 1969 defence policy statement and Macdonald's 1971 White Paper. The department had not made protection of Canada or the creation of armed forces capable of operating outside alliance structures its priority. Moreover, it had ignored the government's budgetary ceiling for defence. "Erroneous, though it may be," the MRG said, "there still exists a belief that the assigned roles actually require much more in the way of operational and capital expenditures than is being made available and that the cutbacks are temporary. In the minds of some Departmental officials, the attitude towards the military roles remains cast in the larger scale, traditional perspective."[25] The review group also informed the department that the domestic political landscape had changed. Parliament was becoming more critical of defence expenditures and less willing to accept requests for funding, while the public had grown indifferent to security matters and preferred economic, social, and cultural programs. This meant that the government could no longer assume that defence spending would have political support.[26]

The review group criticized what it called the department's lack of contribution to policy development, although what it seemed to mean was the department's resistance to government direction. In one of the few specific references in the report, it said that "one senior officer remarked to us that the White Paper did not provide meaningful policy declarations from a military viewpoint."[27] As already noted, according to Major-General Charles Gauthier, this was none other than the chief of the defence staff, General Sharp.[28] Furthermore, the department had failed to translate government policy into meaningful and explicit operational and management goals. In short, the department and the Canadian Forces were foot-dragging in implementing what they had been told to do.

In the same oblique manner, the review group condemned the department for having misled central agencies and Cabinet about its spending plans. It reported that the jurisdiction of central agencies was "not understood." Instead:

> There is a prevailing attitude that initial submissions to the Treasury Board Secretariat have to be "sold." Once this is achieved and approval received, Departmental officials seem to feel that they have no further responsibility for the accruing total of incremental costs that might be approved in the course of additional related submissions. The implicit assumption is that the Treasury Board has responsibility for this role. We believe that this is an abdication of responsibility on the part of the Department, based on an incorrect concept of the Treasury Board's role as a central agency.[29]

Central agencies needed "adequate, frank and factual information," and ministers relied on officials to present "an unbiased and factually complete case." In this, they had been "disappointed."[30]

Finally, the review group viewed the military profession as incompetent to manage technical support functions at the national level. The report condemned what it called questionable operating norms that had had "disastrous consequences." Specifically, this referred to "the firmly held belief" that military officers without technical training could manage specialist functions. This was compounded by what the review group considered to be lack of individual accountability of senior military officials who signed off on behalf of the minister or the chief of the defence staff. This, coupled with a professional brotherhood, had led to a "closing of ranks" and a "tolerant attitude" towards poor performance. The report stated that no instances of serious corrective action with respect to senior people, other than that related to unification, had occurred since 1945.[31]

While the report was written in a way to cause the least possible offence, there should be little doubt about the MRG's central message regarding its diagnosis of the problems of National Defence. The headquarters was collectively insubordinate and could not be relied upon to tell ministers and central agencies the truth. The MRG's recommendations were meant to restore "the widely accepted philosophy of firm, visible, efficient management and control of the Forces by the Civil power."[32]

The MRG concluded that there was a greater need to rely on civilians to manage defence issues, and that modern management techniques could significantly improve outputs and outcomes, even in the face of declining budgets. In addition, it recommended unburdening the minister by giving greater decision-making authority to public servants and military officials. The MRG found many problems with the organization of the department. It had little policy analysis capacity and had played only a small role in the development of the 1971 White Paper. Responsibility at the top of the department was not clear and military officers without specialist backgrounds were appointed to senior administrative positions for which they lacked the necessary skills and experience.[33]

The MRG recommended that the military be stripped of much of its administrative role and be confined to the conduct of military operations. It proposed a new structure for National Defence Headquarters that placed the deputy minister above the chief of the defence staff. Civilian assistant deputy ministers would head the major divisions for policy, personnel, finance, and procurement. Finally, the senior management committee of the department, the Defence Management Committee, would be an advisory body to the deputy minister and be dominated by the civilian assistant deputy ministers, leaving the chief of the defence staff with only his own vote and that of his chief of staff.

This structure was adopted for the most part. By the time the review group tabled its report, however, Macdonald had moved from National Defence to become the minister of finance. Sylvain Cloutier, the deputy minister selected to fix the headquarters, had ideas of his own. Although he had initially supported the promotion of Vice Admiral H.A. Porter, the commander of Maritime Command, to CDS to succeed Sharp, Cloutier eventually became a strong supporter of Lieutenant-General Jacques Dextraze, who he thought was likely to become an able CDS, and quickly formed an alliance with him. According to Cloutier, their agreement was that the deputy minister and the CDS would be equals, although Dextraze would later say that Cloutier had agreed that the deputy minister would be subordinate to the CDS. It made no difference: legally, the CDS was not subordinate to the deputy minister and a management "diarchy" emerged. As long as Cloutier and Dextraze held office, this appeared to work effectively. Over time, however, problems emerged.[34]

The dominance of civilians at headquarters was resented by many in the military, especially because of the attitude of some of the most prominent senior civilians, who acted as if they were imperial proconsuls sent to administer occupied areas. To take one example from the author's experience, one civilian assistant deputy minister had a pair of olive drab high-top runners hanging from the ceiling tiles over the seating area in his office. When visitors inevitably glanced up, he would deliver a standard rant on how the shoes cost thousands of dollars each because the military had managed the acquisition and had "milspec'd" it. He would conclude by saying that procurement was a task that could not be entrusted to military officials.

Not only was the army beset by internal changes in the balance of power but demographic change in Canada also created problems for the military. Young people became progressively better educated so that the proportion leaving school after Grade 10 dropped dramatically. Expectations changed, and young people no longer tolerated employer interference in their private life. There was greater expectation of upward mobility and less acceptance of traditional authority patterns and status arrangements. What Desmond Morton called the "liberation generation" had come into being:

> Personal liberation had become a watchword, cherished as fiercely by separatist terrorists as by drop-outs in the drug culture. Liberation ranged from long hair and blue jeans to unblushing acceptance of premarital sex and unmarried cohabitation. Members of religious orders demanded freedom from their vows. Censorship became intolerable. So did the burdens of marriage, child-rearing, and family. Homosexuals emerged to defy the "straight" majority for the sake of "gay rights." A dependable and seemingly safe birth-control pill ended the baby boom in the early 1960s. Maternity, once defended by feminists as the highest role of womanhood, became an interlude that could be avoided at will.[35]

The army, already falling behind educationally, was almost completely left behind by this social revolution. It was also being left behind by other changing demographics. In 1967 the Pearson government had introduced a point system for selecting immigrants that ignored national origins and preferred countries. Immigration was based on labour force needs, and the sources of immigrants shifted to Asia, Africa, the Caribbean, and Central and South America. These immigrants did not join the military. The Defence Department did not find any evidence of systematic racism in itself; rather, it attributed the problem to the immigrants themselves, whom the department regarded as self-segregated and whose community organizations "blocked access" to military careers. By the 1960s and 1970s the military was failing to attract the more desirable applicants and failing to retain enough of those it did attract. In the opinion of one analyst, "it was becoming a last-resort employment option and earning a reputation as a social daycare for misfits and reprobates." By 1975 the Forces' personnel research unit argued that "the majority of recruits are persons who are pushed towards application after marginal employment experiences."[36]

This dynamic also affected the Forces internally. Once inside the armed services, better-educated recruits gravitated towards the administrative-technical sectors of the military rather than the combat arms, there being "an apparent intolerance among high-quality – notably more educated – recruits for the conditions of service in operational sectors." The combat arms themselves shrank to the point where they made up only about 20 percent of the armed services, as increasingly complex military technology and computer-based administrative support systems required a larger "tail."[37]

The declining prestige of the combat arms within the armed forces, and particularly within the army, created serious morale problems. A landmark study by the Canadian Forces Applied Research Unit, based on a survey of military personnel in Mobile Command (i.e., the army), concluded that "the majority [of other ranks] are reluctant soldiers who, if given the chance would opt for the greener pastures of static settings where they can 'work' at their 'trade' in predictable daily routine." A significant minority (14 percent overall and 27.8 percent of junior support troops) said they would avoid combat. Combat soldiers had a negative self-image, referring to themselves as "Kill Techs" or "Death Techs," and had a "collective sense that they [were] a necessary evil in a military bureaucracy." Over 57 percent of the junior combat troops surveyed identified with a nine-to-five "employee" occupational model.[38]

The study also pointed to wide gaps between the combat arms and their associated support elements. Support troops were less military in their attitudes in almost every case, being more likely to identify with civilian employee occupational models, less supportive of regimental traditions, and preferring a static, unified headquarters or depot posting to a land operations base. The interview data were telling. One logistics officer told researchers that "most of my problems would go away if we could only get rid of the Combat Arms." Logistics personnel saw the combat arms as denying the legitimacy of their role, and support technicians reciprocated by rejecting the combat arms, referring to their activities as "juvenile games" and "combat crap."[39]

Overall, the army – and especially the traditionalist elements – was under intense pressure by the end of the 1970s. They had lost power at National Defence Headquarters, their recruiting base was vanishing, and their core values had been eroded. The modernist vision of a degreed officer corps, which placed additional emphasis on policy and its relationship to the political level, not only did not appear to address these concerns but appeared to even accelerate negative trends. By the end of the decade, the reaction began to consolidate.

Regimentalism and Reaction

Whereas the modernizers were concerned with increasing the capacity of the officer corps to absorb technology and further integrate with civilian government and society in general, the traditionalists wished to halt these initiatives and reverse the trends. Brigadier-General D.G. Loomis, then the chief of staff, operations, at Mobile Command Headquarters, wrote in the Command newsletter in July 1975 that action was urgently needed to restore the regimental system. He believed that there needed to be a clear separation between the military and the "industrial" ethos that was based on "manipulation and group consensus" and "a wide range of egalitarian innovations designed towards narrowing the differences between military ranks and status." You cannot fight battles based on consensus, he explained, and those who failed to grasp this "sow[ed] the seeds of destruction of their society" either by external conquest, revolution, or both.

Loomis disparaged the US "Continental" system, which he saw as "eminently suited for inducing hoards [sic] of conscript soldiers to go over the top in the face of withering machine gun fire or to mount 1000 plane daylight air raids which press on to their target regardless of loss," but which were unsuited for low-intensity war requiring a high degree of individual initiative and what he called "military entrepreneurship."[40] He advocated instead a return to the regimental system, which he saw as based on family groups organized on the basis of artificial kinship. He rejected the concept of consolidation of the army onto a few large bases, considering this the equivalent of collectivizing a family neighbourhood around communal kitchens. The consolidation of messes was a type of socialism being carried out by experts in budgeting, cost control, and management who wanted to destroy military entrepreneurship. To him, messes were "the linchpin of the Canadian System" and an "essential tool" for commanding officers to ensure that units were both militarily effective and reliable under all conditions of political and social stress. The "Canadian System" was flexible, unlike the US, French, Russian, and Chinese "revolutionary industrial armies." At the staff level, according to Loomis, this flexibility precluded "dogmatic adherence" to one organization or set of techniques, thus dispensing with the idea that armies needed any sort of doctrinal basis or central General Staff.[41]

Other officers joined in the condemnation of civilian management. According to two colonels, the civil service was characterized chiefly by "respectability" and business management by singleness of purpose, whereas military administration required sensitivity and flexibility. For this reason, they complained about the number of specialist officers and what they regarded as the centralization of decision making at National Defence Headquarters. This increased the bureaucracy and the influence of outside civilian professional associations such as the Society of Professional Engineers. To them, "staff officers are true bureaucrats; they usurp or are given the authority of the commander and generally escape his responsibility." Worse than staff officers were civil servants, who had scant knowledge of military affairs but who, in the new system, wielded significant influence. Staff and civilians flourished because senior commanders lacked confidence in their subordinates and the means to measure performance, and because of the self-interest of staff officers.[42]

The traditionalists, however, did not have an opportunity to press their attack on modernization and civilianization until the election of a Conservative government in the summer of 1979. The priority of the new minister of national defence, Allan McKinnon, was to reverse unification. He had no particular plan for doing this, and received no support from the incumbent chief of the defence staff, Admiral Robert Falls, or the deputy minister, C.R. "Buzz" Nixon. In order to advance his initiative, he therefore set up a Task Force on the Review of Unification of the Canadian Forces under G.M. Fyffe, a former naval officer. The minister allowed all members of the Forces to come forward as individuals to give testimony to the task force, a direct challenge to Falls and Nixon, who had not been consulted about the commission, its members, or its terms of reference. McKinnon asked the task force to examine the merits and disadvantages of unification, apparently in the belief that he would receive a report listing many disadvantages and few advantages, presenting him with the easy decision to kill unification.[43]

No one made a stronger argument for undoing modernization than Lieutenant-General J.J. Paradis, the commander of Mobile Command. Paradis pulled together the regimental philosophy championed by Loomis with the personnel attitude studies done by the Applied Research Unit to contrast what was claimed to have been a solid military social structure of "cohesive sub-units and units, well-socialized men, self-discipline and pride, positive paternal leadership and good administration" with the civilianized attitudes of the support trades. Civilianization had resulted in pay comparability with the civil service, but also in the abolition of canteens, adequate quarters, and "paternalistic leadership." Paradis's solution was the "creation of a new military society" that would re-institute military traditions, vocabulary, and trappings. He wanted nothing less than the complete reversal of unification and the "restoration" of the authority and responsibility of army commanding officers.[44]

Submissions to the task force by senior army staff officers extolled the regimental culture of the past with its unit messes to develop morale and cohesion, rewards that were not dependent on the motivation of money, and paternalistic care for soldiers. Instead, civilian values such as universality, uniformity, and human rights had been installed along with promotion for technical skill instead of for leadership. Commanding officers, once "paramount authorities," had been stripped of their power to reward, punish, and administer their men.[45]

What the army establishment seemed to want was a military based on battalion-sized units ruled by lordly commanding officers who would take care of "their people." This military village society would somehow exist outside the grubby, individualistic, materialistic civilian society that supported it. Where the other ranks recruits would come from to populate the village was never considered – but the army was already scraping the bottom of the barrel in recruiting and the combat arms had the least appeal to civilians. It was equally unclear how an army of individualistic battalions could manage complex weapon systems without the assistance of the despised staff specialists in higher headquarters.

It is also unclear that the traditionalist model presented to the task force by the army had a basis in fact. While the survey conducted by the Personnel Applied Research Unit showed that there were real reasons to be concerned about the orientation, motivation, and morale of the late 1970s army, it would be a mistake to conclude that things had been substantially better before that time. The study, after all, represented a snapshot in time and did not purport to establish trends. The most recent scholarship on the Korean War shows that the so-called "soldiers of fortune" Special Force recruited off the street from Second World War combat veterans performed better than the regimental soldiers of the Regular army who took plenty of spit, polish, and regimental silver to Korea but lacked the aggressiveness and combat skills of the Special Force. The Regular Force also had its fair share of combat avoiders, who transferred out of their units before they were sent overseas.[46] Much of the regimental tradition senior officers were so fond of often had little appeal to the other ranks. A 1951 Defence Research Board study found that the postwar army was haphazard in the socialization of recruits. Studies in the 1970s concluded that many soldiers were indifferent to badges and regiments, and some even challenged the researcher by asking what difference identifying with a home unit in Canada would make. Combat motivation studies in Britain and Germany indicated that cohesion and loyalty were founded on company-sized, or even much smaller, units.[47]

The National Defence Headquarters staff that had to respond to the army's critique also raised questions regarding its factual basis. One staff colonel who had recently been a deputy commanding officer of a regiment reported that some commanding officers had been less than enlightened despots and had used their "totalitarian powers" to wreck careers. He thought the central personnel system with greater corporate management provided some checks and balances to the arbitrariness of commanding officers. He also believed that many people who were complaining about the "lost powers" of commanding officers didn't know what they were talking about.[48] His opinion was borne out by a separate staff group's study, which showed that the power to promote soldiers from private to lance corporal and corporal was the only power possessed by commanding officers prior to unification that had been taken away. The real problems were resource shortages and the high level of rotation of officers, which, to other ranks, made the officer corps look like a group of self-serving careerists.[49]

The conclusions of the task force were constrained by its methodology, which was based on interviews rather than fundamental analysis. The task force therefore reported the army's concern about the unified staff system and the "presumed prevailing influence of civilian management philosophy and techniques." It commented on the "perceived civilianization" of National Defence Headquarters and allegations and claims that civilians had undue influence over matters that were more properly military and that the co-chairmanship of the Defence Management Committee by the deputy minister and the CDS and the long tenure of civilians in their jobs added to this improper level of civilian control. It was "the opinion of many" that military personnel had become civilians in uniform with a nine-to-five attitude towards work and that pay parity with the public service had "downgraded the military ethic."[50]

The task force also reported the perceived erosion of the authority and control of unit commanding officers, for which it blamed the centralized personnel system and the base concept. These detracted from the ability of commanding officers to be seen as the source of advice and guidance to their troops and the source of redress of grievances. The task force concluded that the CO had been supplanted by the career manager.[51]

The task force made a number of recommendations, most significantly that the environmental Command commanders (Maritime, Mobile, and Air) be included on the Defence Council and Defence Management Committee. If that proved insufficient to provide them with adequate influence, the task force recommended they be moved to Ottawa and formally established as service chiefs of staff. With regard to issues affecting the military profession, the task force merely recommended that greater reliance be placed on formal lines of authority by the central personnel system and that separation of rank and trade skill and the base system be given further study.[52]

The sudden fall of the Conservative government in early 1980 meant that those who favoured the status quo once again had the upper hand. The new minister, Gilles Lamontagne, had no desire to dramatically reverse the policies of a former Liberal government, and his senior advisers were happy to oblige him. The task force had proposed no detailed implementation plan for its recommendations, so Lamontagne directed that an "appreciation" of its recommendations be prepared so that appropriate action could be taken. The job was assigned to Major-General Jack Vance, a widely respected army officer. Vance was given free rein to make recommendations – except to bring the commanders to Ottawa and to separate NDHQ into its military and civilian components. The fact that the task force had largely reported on the basis of opinion and perception made his job easy.[53]

Vance's review group did not find much substance in the allegations of excessive civilian control and passed it off as a "misunderstanding" that created "an educational task" to correct the "misperception." The review group did agree, however, that there had been a gradual imposition of civilian standards and values in managing the armed services: "The dilemma facing the Forces as a profession is that civilian standards and values are displacing proven military counterparts and, in the process, are eroding the basic fiber of Canadian military society. At the risk of overstating the situation, the Forces are facing a crisis of the military ethos."[54]

The problem, according to Vance, was that the military had not defined its own ethos and had rarely spoken of it. As a result of the lack of clearly defined and defensible military values, the Forces had turned to civilian values. Vance did not attempt to define what these "military values" were, but he referred to the "valiant rearguard actions" to preserve regimental messes and the "difficulty" in reconciling operational effectiveness with human rights and access to information legislation. Vance recommended that a carefully selected officer be tasked with researching and writing down the military ethos and that it be approved by the chief of the defence staff and used as a policy touchstone.[55]

A statement of ethos finally appeared in May 1983 in a document titled – perhaps tellingly, from the traditionalist point of view – "Personnel Concept." It was pretty thin stuff and recognized as such by the assistant deputy minister (personnel), who issued it with an apology, in his cover letter, for the "motherhood" nature of the document. The document did not spell out what was unique about the profession of arms, not even that it involved the application of deadly force or that its members accepted unlimited liability when undertaking their tasks. If anything, it confirmed that the armed services were subject to civilian personnel policies such as bilingualism and the employment of women. Even central personnel management was blessed.[56]

The strongest reaction to the work of the task force came from the deputy minister, Buzz Nixon. Nixon surprised officers at what they assumed would be a routine "this is my job" briefing at the Canadian Forces Command and Staff College in Toronto by instead delivering a harangue. He told his audience that the role of civilians had been misunderstood, and proceeded to outline the extensive powers and responsibilities given to him in law by the Financial Administration Act, the Public Service Employment Act, the Public Service Staff Relations Act, the National Defence Act, and the Interpretation Act, and which he delegated to military officials. This would have been bad enough, but Nixon went on to impugn the ability of the senior military to manage an organization as sophisticated and complex as National Defence. He told the staff college that while it would be unthinkable to make a neophyte the commander of a military unit,

> we have done precisely this in some critical areas of the Department. We have placed military officers who are tops in their field and who have excellent reputations as military specialists in areas which required the [civilian] abilities and competencies which I mentioned earlier. As an example, we still have military officers in charge of important and significant parts of the *Department.* With all due respect to the current and past incumbents of these positions, they do not have the knowledge, the expertise, the awareness, the contacts within government, the historical perspective, with which to make the judgements which are required in managing this multi-billion dollar and strategic organization ...
>
> We are making unreasonable and increasing demands on military operational personnel by putting them into positions for which they are not trained, they have not the experience; they are unaware of precedent and cannot possibly understand the magnitude of their jobs.
>
> I wish to make it very clear that I have the utmost regard for these individuals as military officers and I believe that they have distinguished themselves by their military accomplishments. However, I believe we are engaging in incremental but planned suicide by hoping that people with inadequate backgrounds and experience will make the right type of decisions in areas far removed from their military operational experience.[57]

At least some army officers agreed with Nixon's analysis, if not with his solution of civilian rule. Richard Evraire, a civil engineer and infantry officer who in 1978 was the commander of Canadian contingents of the United Nations in the Middle East, recalled that he had had no training to prepare him for his position as director general management services at National Defence Headquarters, which made him responsible for information technology throughout the department. His solution was to go into Ismailia, Egypt, and buy the best book on data processing he could find. His experience convinced him that the preparation of senior officers for senior staff jobs was severely deficient, especially for jobs requiring the formulation of national policy and defence strategy.[58]

By the 1980s, the army (and the rest of the Canadian Forces) had no clear view of its own profession. The investment in officer education championed by Rowley had not taken place, and the officer corps was no better placed to advise the government than it had been when Foulkes first raised the issue in 1947. Modernization had seized the structure of the organization and implanted management forms and systems, but it had not won the hearts of the officer corps. A reaction had set in that rejected modern management as "civilian" and civilian society as self-seeking and indulgent while hoping to re-create a folkloric regimental past based on a neo-aristocratic officer corps whose orders would not be questioned by the other ranks and who would not be given many instructions by senior headquarters. The traditionalists could not control the national headquarters and therefore had to live with its management systems. They could push back, however, and refuse to participate in areas such as operational readiness management and go underground in others, such as promotions and postings. Lieutenant-General Paradis had told the Task Force on Review of Unification that the army had lacked "*legitimate* influence" for personnel management, but he did not mean to imply that it had no influence at all.[59] These two factors would combine to create the most serious breakdown in professionalism the army had experienced since the Second World War – the Somalia debacle.

CHAPTER SIX

The Plan for a "Big Army"

THE LATE 1970S AND EARLY 1980S saw a sharp rise in international tension. The Soviet Union reacted to perceived threats to its sphere of influence in both Afghanistan and Poland. In Afghanistan, the Soviets first increased military assistance at the request of the government and then launched an invasion when it appeared that the Afghan government was not only becoming increasingly oppressive but also coming under Pakistani and Chinese influence. In Poland the rise of the Solidarity trade union, which with the support of the Catholic Church sought popular reform, resulted in a propaganda campaign against "Western interference" and the placing of Soviet forces on high alert. Second-echelon forces were mobilized, and the readiness of elements of the Soviet nuclear forces was increased.

These international crises unfolded on an already-tense field. The Warsaw Pact maintained its huge quantitative advantage versus NATO and pressed ahead qualitatively. New T-72 and T-64 main battle tanks were deployed, along with BMP-2 infantry fighting vehicles and new self-propelled guns. The density of artillery increased. Soviet forces became more air-mobile, with large numbers being deployed by helicopters of all kinds. Western analysts became aware of the Operational Manoeuvre Group concept, which aimed at putting large combined arms formations into NATO rear areas, destroying command and control and logistics. The situation was bad enough that a Belgian general, Robert Close, published a widely read book that argued that NATO could be overrun by Warsaw Pact forces and defeated within forty-eight hours.[1]

NATO opposed the Warsaw Pact with improved forces of its own. Under General Bernard Rogers, Supreme Allied Commander Europe, NATO adopted the doctrine of Follow-on Forces Attack (FOFA), which was intended not only to blunt the first wave of Warsaw Pact forces but also to strike their second echelon and rear areas as well. NATO fielded sophisticated reconnaissance and battlefield management systems to extend their commanders' reach back to the

Soviet Union and enable the identification of force concentrations, command-and-control and logistic nodes, and communications and storage sites. NATO forces were strengthened with new generations of tanks, infantry fighting vehicles, attack helicopters, and smart munitions.

In short, the strategic balance had not improved, although it was unclear whether NATO was very much worse off overall. It was still faced by a numerically superior Warsaw Pact that was also well equipped and practising a new and threatening offensive doctrine. What did change radically, however, was the political posture of Britain and the United States. Under the "Iron Lady," Margaret Thatcher, in Britain and President Ronald Reagan in the United States, politics took a sharp turn to the right, and the contest with the Soviet Union became overtly ideological. Reagan famously referred to the Soviet Union as an "evil empire."

Pierre Trudeau was the odd man out in this move to the right. He was genuinely concerned that the worsening of tensions after the Soviet invasion of Afghanistan would lead to wider war. He had little faith in Reagan's "Star Wars" Strategic Defense Initiative to counter nuclear missiles or in Washington's belief that a nuclear war was winnable. He used the occasion of the 1983 G7 summit of industrialized nations to push Reagan and Thatcher for accommodation with the Soviet Union. He deplored the militant American reaction to the shooting down of an off-course Korean airliner by the Soviets. In October 1983 he launched his own peace initiative, proposing a nuclear test ban, a ban on high-altitude weapons testing, a five-power conference on nuclear arms control, and the implementation of a NATO/Warsaw Pact consultative process. Trudeau's initiative was a complete failure. The Reaganites dismissed him as a lefty high on pot. The Soviets ignored him.

The Canadian army thus found itself on political terrain where, more than ever, the concepts it favoured were more in tune with allies than with its own government. The army's aim was to become a "big army."

Mobilization and Control of Defence Policy

The army's key to bigness was gaining acceptance of the need to mobilize a far larger force than the government was prepared to fund during peacetime. Underlying this perceived requirement was the army's vision of future war. As envisaged at the 1980 Canadian Land Forces Staff Course, the next war would be fought for the survival of entrenched ideologies:

> It will certainly involve mass armies, in fact nations-in-arms, impressed to defend those ideologies. It will not necessarily be short, and it may encompass the world. It will be fought under the threat of nuclear annihilation. It can and will be fought

> by forces of widely varying quality but these forces will include, at the upper end, elements of great mobility and fire-power, including tactical nuclear weapons which are able, if properly concentrated, to penetrate any fixed defence and aim at deep objectives ... It might look something like the German campaigns in Russia, fought in Western Europe.[2]

Although armoured forces had the potential to achieve breakthrough, disrupt and paralyze command and control, and strike at exposed population and civil infrastructure to end the war quickly, this was not regarded as inevitable. With firm national morale, "and, if necessary, ruthless leadership and a military that does not disintegrate in adversity, deep penetrations cannot only be worn down but eliminated." The staff college assumed that mobilization would be required, and students were told that the current Canadian concept called for augmentation of existing units, possibly followed by expansion of the army.[3] The chief of land doctrine and operations, among others, considered that "to organize and prepare for the next war as a 'come as you are' war is folly and that our structure, equipment policy, training and plans must all be capable of being adaptable to protracted war. Thus a proper mobilization plan must be developed and doctrine must cater to its needs."[4]

However, the central policies that governed the development of mobilization plans did not enthusiastically endorse this vision of nation-in-arms conflict modelled on four years of German-Russian warfare during the Second World War. Instead, the three key documents – NDHQ Policy Directive P16, Department of National Defence Procurement Policy; NDHQ Policy Directive P26, The Development and Employment of the Primary Reserve and the Supplementary List; and the Chief of the Defence Staff's Guidance for the Development of Mobilization and Readiness Plans – were all carefully hedged and severely constrained financially. P16, the Procurement Policy, was issued by the former CDS, General Jacques Dextraze, and former deputy minister Buzz Nixon in February 1976 to ensure that monies obtained through the Defence Structure Review were carefully husbanded. For the most part, the policy was unexceptional. However, it said that the "quantitative requirement for major equipment procurements will be decided by a fundamental review of the tasks to be performed and not on previously determined scales of issue or equipment tables." This meant that the army could not automatically obtain funding based on its war establishment but only for Cabinet-authorized tasks.[5]

P26, the Reserve Policy, was a model of the bureaucratic ploy of appearing to be more than it was. Intended to define how the Primary Reserves (in the case of the army, the Militia) would be developed in the future, it held out the promise of augmenting the Regular Force with formed units of Reserves.

Moreover, the Reserves were to be provided with "contemporary equipment" purchased on a total force basis, with the difference between peace establishment and war establishment requirements going to the Reserves. There was the provision, however, that application of the policy would be on a case-by-case basis managed by the Program Control Board, and that commands were expected "so far as is practicable" to make up the current shortfall by reallocating existing resources. Likewise, Reserve training equipment was to be increased "commensurate with the availability of such equipment," and implementation of the entire policy was, again, to be undertaken "commensurate with the availability of resources."[6]

The CDS's Guidance for the Development of Mobilization and Readiness Plans, dated 22 August 1978, set out seven objectives for augmentation of the Forces in an emergency, based on the "real limits" of present resources. In general, only NATO and NORAD commitments and a basic defence-of-North America force were included in what could be actively planned for. Everything else was retained by the CDS under his personal control. Although the guidance recognized that the seven objectives did not even include all augmentation requirements, much less the full requirements of expansion, and assumed that a war in Europe would last "a minimum" of several months, it did not allow for planning beyond the barest minimum required to meet treaty commitments.[7]

Taken together, these three policies recognized the possibility of a long war in Europe but made it plain that there was no intention of actively planning for this contingency, and that no resources were available to support any such plan should one be developed.

The army noted these constraints almost immediately. Tasked with redrafting the mobilization plan, Brigadier-General N.G. Trower, the director general military plans and operations informed the deputy chief of the defence staff (DCDS) in April 1976 that the project was "doomed to frustration and failure." Trower correctly saw that P16, by limiting equipment purchases to tasks, did not support mobilization and that there had been no government recognition of a need for forces beyond the total of the current Regular and Reserve Forces. In his opinion it was "becoming increasingly difficult to postulate any type of reasonable scenario to justify mobilization planning." He had therefore directed his staff to cease working on the project.[8]

Mobile Command was also dissatisfied with plans to use the centralized personnel system during war. Although the system met peacetime requirements of providing a lifetime career and family stability, Mobile Command did not believe that it could accommodate the surge in manpower it anticipated in war, and did not believe that a career management system was necessary under wartime conditions. Its preferred approach was to delegate the authority to recruit, call out, post, and promote to the lowest workable level. In the case of the army, a wartime system based on Militia units was the preferred option.[9]

Staff also recognized the problems with the Militia. According to the director general reserves and cadets, the paid ceiling (that is, the personnel budget), the establishment, and the equipment holdings of the Militia had been the result of horse trading between the Conference of Defence Associations, the minister, and senior military staff, and were in no way based on the needs of the army. Moreover, this was still the case and the rank structure and numbers of the Militia did not fit with any known requirement. Job protection legislation and the definition of civilian manpower that would be protected from military mobilization had been requested through the assistant deputy minister (policy), but had been held in abeyance for three years and had yet to go to Cabinet.[10]

Nevertheless, NDHQ pressed on with an emergency manning plan based on existing policies and the centralized personnel management system. Army staff at NDHQ continued to find these plans unrealistic in their expectations of large numbers of trained personnel to come from the Militia, even though no additional funding had been provided to implement P26. WINTEX exercises had also demonstrated (at least to the army) that the central personnel system could not meet army needs during mobilization.[11] The matter continued to be debated among staff without resolution until it came to a head in the spring of 1979.

Several initiatives converged to make it urgent to clarify the army's mission. First, the implications of reassigning the Canadian Air-Sea Transportable (CAST) Brigade Group task (reinforcement of Norway) from the 5[e] Groupe brigade du Canada to the Special Service Force had become clear. The task would require almost all the resources of the Special Service Force, along with an infantry battalion and artillery from 1 Combat Brigade Group. Upon deployment of these troops, there would be no personnel left to provide a basis for expansion in central Canada, other than the Militia. There would be no airborne troops left for the defence of Canada, and no base on which to mobilize the brigade group and full airborne regiment called for in the second phase of the Defence Structural Review (DSR II).[12] This now fatal flaw in the army's ability to implement mobilization as it saw it was bad enough, but the plan for improving the Reserves had arrived at the Program Control Board with an impressive price tag. The director general reserves and cadets estimated that existing deficiencies of the Militia would cost almost $274 million to remediate and that post-1983 costs to modernize the Militia would cost another $734 million, which he regarded as "totally beyond achievement" and not supported by current mobilization planning. Figures submitted to the Program Control Board varied, but were, if anything, higher: $356 million in non-recurring costs plus an additional $43,250,000 a year.[13]

Additional fuel was thrown on the fire by the commander of Mobile Command, Lieutenant-General J.J. Paradis, who sent the deputy chief of the defence staff a comprehensive plan for what he called "a limited expansion of the army." Paradis's plan recapped the difficulties in reconciling the various policies and plans, which collectively reduced the entire authorized portion of mobilization to "readiness." Achieving even that much, which would amount to "Canada [having] simply honoured its defence commitments, retained the minimum acceptable operational level within Canada, and established the rudiments of a permanent reinforcement chain and training flow," would require 14,000 to 16,000 fully trained Militia combat arms soldiers. Moreover, Paradis proposed extending planning beyond thirty days of combat to include maintaining and expanding the field force, preparing for expansion of the war effort, and preparing for general mobilization of the country. This would require not only additional resources but also restructuring of Mobile Command to include a completely autonomous training organization, because "it is evident that the whole army training function would rapidly become the total responsibility of Mobile Command as the mobilization process extends beyond the augmentation phase." For good measure, the army would retain responsibility for territorial defence as the Militia was "already tuned to the demography of the nation."[14] Paradis did not include a cost estimate and the additional manpower figures are not entirely clear. However, the DCDS staff estimated that, to satisfy the plan, the army as a whole would have to expand to 85,000 troops (larger than the peacetime Canadian Forces as a whole) within 120 days of the declaration of the emergency.[15]

Paradis capped off his set of initiatives by writing to the vice chief of the defence staff in July 1979 and proposing that the equipment policy question be settled by "clarifying" P16 so that it would be clear that Reserve requirements were not going to be met by redistributing Regular Force equipment holdings to the Reserves. This could be done if the words saying that requirements rested on a "fundamental review of the tasks to be performed" included both the Regular Force and the Reserves. This legerdemain would have effectively erased any existing surplus held by Regular units.[16]

Paradis's initiatives were lightly rebuffed by NDHQ. Lieutenant-General C.G.E. Thériault, the DCDS, replied that his readiness and mobilization plan would be "an excellent basis for future planning," but that the matter of mobilization was already under study within NDHQ and that it was unlikely that senior staff could meet to discuss the issue until September; approval of his paper would therefore be delayed. Lieutenant-General Ramsey Withers, the vice chief, agreed that there was indeed some confusion around procurement policy and that the equipping of the Reserves was the central issue. However, there was a need to clarify whether the Reserves as constituted met the needs of the war establishment and how well the war establishments matched the *assigned* wartime missions of operational formations. Until these issues were resolved, both the Reserve plan and the procurement policy would be placed on hold. Withers ended by stating that he knew he could rely on the "strong support" of Paradis.[17]

A major senior staff meeting was planned for 8 August 1979. The army staff was consumed with frustration over what appeared to be its impending defeat. Colonel D.K. Dangerfield told his boss, the acting chief of land doctrine and operations, Brigadier-General J.B. Riffou, that his "gut feel" was that the DCDS intended to chair the meeting himself and was likely to take positions uniformly contrary to those of the army. Thériault did not favour a mandate for expansion planning or for an independent army training system, nor did he believe in buying equipment to scales or general-purpose war establishments. According to Dangerfield:

> He feels that the Army is out of control and is pushing, rather than being pulled by, policy. I feel quite strongly that we must indicate that we *are* following the stated policy in accordance with the DPMS [Defence Program Management System] and that we have acted in a responsible manner. In fact, without being too disloyal, I believe that the present senior management has not read or does not support what was stated in Dept [departmental] policy ... otherwise we wouldn't be having as many difficulties as we are having today.
>
> The Army is viewed as the culprit primarily because we are doing what we were told to do in policy papers and no one else is; ergo, we are rocking the boat.[18]

Riffou and Paradis met to plan their strategy about a week before the meeting. Two themes dominated their discussion: the need to convince senior management that they must plan for a long war, and the related need to tell the government that this was the requirement. They agreed that "we are mobilizing for war (not deterrence)." They recognized that they had to somehow overcome the argument that a plan to produce people would be of no use if the equipment was not available. They expected that 4 Canadian Mechanized Brigade Group (4CMBG) would have to be replaced entirely, not merely reinforced. Finally, they wanted to convince senior management that the mobilization plans would not be used to blackmail the department for equipment.[19]

The 8 August meeting went much as Dangerfield had feared, however. Chaired by Thériault and attended by over twenty senior staff, the meeting agreed that the 1978 CDS's Guidance, which limited mobilization to augmenting existing formations assigned to alliance treaty commitment tasks, would remain the basis for mobilization planning. A Mobilization Planning Task Force was set up to examine the expansion phase.[20] This effectively ended the first phase of the army's attempt both to change defence policy and to become "big." It was, however, far from the end of the issue that changed its focus to the Militia and to the House of Commons. Throughout the process, the army had clearly recognized that its views were opposed, yet it stubbornly insisted that it was correct. Ignoring blatantly obvious and extremely significant qualifications or limitations to policies, it doggedly parsed them until they yielded the answer the army wanted. There seemed to be a persistent belief that the department could simply will a change of policy on Cabinet. There is no evidence that the army consulted with anyone outside itself, although it seemed obvious that explicit acceptance of a long-war policy, significant changes to the army budget, major changes to the personnel management processes, and legislation to provide job protection for the Militia were issues that involved nearly all the NDHQ groups, the minister, and Cabinet. Nor had the army considered the practical difficulties of either equipping or paying for the expanded force it proposed. Its only response to these questions had been to deny their existence. It had waged anything but a skillful bureaucratic offensive.

In spite of its failure to obtain agreement to its model of mobilization, Mobile Command continued to carry out detailed planning until at least February 1980, when it presented NDHQ with a massive document containing an entire plan for mobilization down to tables of organization and equipment for each new or re-roled unit. The document was prepared without any apparent consultation with NDHQ.[21]

Through its staff college course, the army explained to its junior officers what had happened. This presentation was more a jeremiad than a lecture, and at times crossed the line into direct criticism of civilian authority. It claimed that the Canadian Forces "simply could not meet current commitments or expand" due to "paralysis in the planning process." There had been a "marked erosion in the required capabilities of the Canadian Forces" because of "the adjustment of national priorities in the 1960s," which de-emphasized the military in favour of other national programs. Forces-in-being were deemed viable if there were enough properly equipped troops, but in the case of Canada, "in light of the ongoing fiscal crises and limited resources, the concept provided exactly the right vehicle to substantiate the emasculation of the Canadian Forces." Part of the criticism was that little consideration had been given to requirements beyond those actually stated by the government! The presentation stated that there had been a complete collapse of contingency plans and capability for any tasks beyond those authorized, mobilization plans had been discarded, war establishments had been eliminated, training plans had not been developed, and physical items needed for logistic support had ceased to exist. Some slight hope was found in the total force policy, although it was noted that a reserve designed to support general-purpose forces was a new departure, being neither a force-in-being nor "classical mobilization." It stated that "Canada is unique in the post war world military community in having unified its Armed Forces. Unfortunately, the difficulties encountered in unifying Canada's three military services are nowhere more readily apparent than in the field of land force training." The pre-unification Canadian Army was described in glowing terms, while the current Canadian Forces training system was depicted as unresponsive and incapable of generating the large numbers required by the army's version of mobilization. The presentation concluded by citing a 1977 resolution of the Conference of Defence Associations that advocated increasing the war establishment of the Canadian Forces to 250,000 personnel, designing a land force capable of "sustained operations," providing equipment to these levels, and developing an outline plan for industrial, manpower, and resource mobilization on a national level.[22]

The presentation substantiated Thériault's concern that the army was "out of control." While some might argue that it is the business of military staffs to plan for all contingencies, even those not approved by the political level, planning for unapproved objectives is at best a waste of resources and at worst insubordination. The army is the agent of the civil government, not the other way around. It was apparent that the army had not totally accepted the premise that its civilian masters "had the right to be wrong."

NDHQ, in the meantime, had launched a study of its own by creating a Mobilization Planning Task Force headed by Brigadier-General J.J.A. Doucet. The task force began work in October 1979 and reported in May 1981, although most of its findings were in its interim report a year earlier. Established to develop a realistic conceptual basis for mobilization planning and to develop appropriate supporting plans, it found that "as far as can be determined, there is no Force Development Plan or statement of force level objective in existence for the CF and there is no evidence of a direct correlation between the demands of force objectives or commitments and the resources available." The detailed findings were even more unpalatable. Based on the attrition rates experienced in the BRONZE TALON 1 war game, the planners estimated that 4CMBG would require the replacement of seven infantry battalions, one armoured regiment, and one brigade group within thirty days of combat. The CAST Brigade Group would require the replacement of three infantry battalions, one armoured regiment, and one brigade group within the same period. Based on these estimates, the army required an additional 78,700 personnel with supporting equipment. Assuming that all 15,500 Militia soldiers were effective, the army would still be 63,270 personnel short. As Mobile Command had pointed out, augmenting overseas combat units would drain the combined resources of the units in Canada. The task force also forecast that the brigade group in Europe would have no tanks after ten days and no reconnaissance vehicles after sixteen days, that anti-tank missiles and armoured personnel carriers would be depleted after twenty-two days, and that guns and mortars would be down to 20 percent of holdings in a month. Overall, the Canadian Forces would require 55,000 personnel in the Primary Reserves for a total force level of 179,000. This would require non-recurring costs of $1.8 billion over five years and an annual budget increase of $280 million.[23]

Other than acknowledging the need for mobilization and informing the Conference of Defence Associations that the work of the Mobilization Planning Task Force would require political decisions, the minister and NDHQ took little immediate action on the report.

In Parliament, the government's position was clear: the international situation had deteriorated, but the government was already making the maximum effort to direct additional funds to National Defence. Gilles Lamontagne, the minister, told the Standing Committee on External Affairs and Defence during hearings on the estimates that the government acknowledged that its earlier expectations that economic and social development would moderate the Soviet Union's behaviour had been disappointed. Instead, there had been an "unrelenting and continuing" military buildup by the Soviet Union, creating a "grave potential threat to NATO." Lamontagne reported that the 1980-81 estimates represented an increase to the defence budget of $611,700,000, or 13.8 percent. After 9.3 percent inflation was deducted, this represented 4.1 percent real growth to fund major acquisitions such as the Leopard tank, the CF-18 Hornet aircraft, and the Canadian Patrol Frigate.[24] Nine months later, speaking of the 1981-82 estimates, Lamontagne took much the same position. Although the Soviet threat was described as dire, the government's response was to continue with its program of 3 percent real growth a year. Lamontagne noted that the size of the Canadian Forces would increase by four hundred personnel. He also informed the committee that the government recognized the need to revitalize the Reserves and had established a Mobilization Planning Task Force to deal with the mobilization issue. "This should give us a much better appreciation of what will be required to bring our forces up to war strength in crisis situations," he said. "I would look forward to the valuable contribution of a sub-committee of this committee in dealing with the important subject of Canada's Reserve forces, an area of priority for me." He cautioned, however, that although he would always like to see his portfolio more generously funded, he had to be "realistic." Creating domestic instability and dissatisfaction by diverting funding to defence would not put the country further ahead.[25]

The Standing Committee did indeed hold hearings on the Reserves and produced a report, *Action for the Reserves.* The report documented the poor state of the Militia but fell far short of adopting the army's point of view regarding mobilization. It did not accept the army's concept of what a "long war" would be. To the subcommittee that had been set up at Lamontagne's request, a long war would last two to four weeks or longer, different from the pattern of the two world wars. It endorsed the concept of forces-in-being as "crucial," but concluded that "there does seem to be some prospect of sending in reinforcements and Canada must have the trained troops ready for this eventuality." It was critical of the government for not preparing the Reserves to fill their *augmentation* role, but did not address the idea of using the Militia as a recruiting and training framework for expansion of the army. The subcommittee recommended a greater government commitment to the status, capability, and role of the Reserves, which it argued, should "be publically enunciated at the highest political level and supported by increased funding." It suggested more clearly defined roles for the Reserves, and more and better training and equipment of the type "they could learn to operate and maintain within the limits of the time they are able to devote to training and peace-time service." As for mobilization of the Reserves, the subcommittee favoured a tax exemption for Reserve pay, but not for compulsory release from employers for training. Such a policy, it said, "would be regarded as a serious infringement of both personal liberties and societal values." It would disrupt economic activity, especially for small businesses, and make it more difficult for reservists to find employment. In the subcommittee's opinion, "it is preferable in Canada to concentrate on improving the array of persuasive mechanisms," leaving the question of leave for Reserve training and job protection in the hands of employers.[26]

The subcommittee report showed that the government had more or less correctly gauged the level of public support for army expansion and mobilization. Allan McKinnon, the Conservative defence critic and a member of the Standing Committee, continued to badger the minister to do more for the Reserves, but the minister and the CDS, General Ramsey Withers, easily fended off criticism by pointing to increases in Reserve funding.[27] In March 1983, Lamontagne announced:

> The issue of mobilization has been given a good deal of attention this year, attention that benefited in no small measure from the valuable contributions of the Commons and Senate reports on Canada's defence forces. While the accent will

> continue to be placed on investment in capital equipment, the government has agreed that, in principle, the Canadian forces should be able to meet and fully sustain their commitments in an emergency, and, if directed to do so, further expand their capabilities.[28]

The "in principle" clause was a meaningful one, as Lamontagne had only $20 million earmarked for improving readiness and sustainability, although he hoped more would be available in the future. He clarified the government's position in his statement on the 1983-84 estimates, in which he recognized that the Regular Force could undertake only limited tasks for a short period of time without augmentation. The government plan did not envisage the type of mobilization that had occurred in the two world wars, but only one that would enable the Forces to immediately activate its full war establishment.[29]

Within the Department of National Defence, mobilization was reduced to the status of "a plan for a plan." The Land Forces Operational Effectiveness Study recommendations, which advocated mobilization planning of the nature recommended by Mobile Command, were triaged according to cost and politely shelved. Wartime tasking of the Reserves, definition of a concept of operations for the defence of Canada, pre-positioning of stocks in Europe, and an increase in allied support to deployed forces were all deferred until more analysis was done. The mobilization concept was announced to be complete, as was the sustainment policy. This was, as the minister had stated, a concept based on current commitments, on what could be achieved with available resources, and provided for only thirty days' sustainment. Longer-term sustainment and expansion of the Forces would be considered only in "outline and conceptual terms."[30]

When McKinnon later asked Lamontagne whether there was in fact a final mobilization plan because he could get no clear response from officials, Lamontagne replied: "Mobilization, I think, is a word we should maybe discard completely, because it is a term that was used in the previous wars and things like that. I think now we should use more adequately these two words, which are preparedness and system ability, because they go together." He went on to talk about the Reserves, the use of civil aviation and transport, the care of casualties in hospitals in Canada, and the place of civilian fire departments, and concluded: "So there it is." McKinnon responded: "Mr. Chairman, an answer like that tends to make one forget what the question was."[31]

Thus the problems of the Militia were left largely unaddressed, with the Reserves being used as a pawn in the debate (if one can call it that) over mobilization and the mission and size of the army. Improvements in equipment would be no more than incremental – not the comprehensive program that seemed to be promised in P26. Job protection legislation was definitely off the table. The inherent conflict between the demands of an increasingly complex, mechanized army and part-time service had been touched on by the subcommittee, in the hope that equipment could be found that part-timers could operate, but the issue was scarcely resolved. The essential problem was that military occupations had become so complex that individuals could not become proficient on a part-time basis. In addition, the Forces did not have a scheme to recruit skilled individuals into parallel military jobs and give them rank based on their civilian skills and knowledge. This made advancement extremely slow and was very discouraging to those who did join. Moreover, attempts to reduce Militia training to the time actually available made the Militia appear to be second-class citizens and further increased resentment. In consequence, Militia soldiers were almost 70 percent students and turnover was rapid: over 70 percent had less than a year of service, an additional 13 percent had one to two years of service, and only about 15 percent had over two years of service. As a result, most of the Militia never reached the basic level of their occupational qualifications.[32]

The situation was clearly recognized by the army, but no effective measures were put in place to remediate it. A good part of the problem was the army's insistence on the Militia's being its expansion base. Colonel D.A. Nicholson, the deputy chief of staff militia at Mobile Command Headquarters insisted that "the Militia is essentially a highly localized, regional force whose real reason for existence is to provide a recognized, accepted army presence in every community in Canada and thus a workable local basis for quick, voluntary expansion of the field force." According to him, the Militia was not to produce individual replacements but "formed, trained, mutually-confident groups of about battalion/regiment size. Hence the term 'Regimental System.'" This meant that a large number of units had to be maintained, spreading the available training cadre too thinly. Nicholson could see the defects of the system. It generated "a crowd of confused, inadequately trained under-aged strangers of doubtful operational effectiveness or survivability" as the reinforcement pool for the Regular Force. It left units quartered in buildings he described as "squalid." It resulted in an organization based on students with little attraction for the more mature, because "how does one promote the idea of being 'a man among men' in an organization filled with teenagers and led by school teachers?" The community "movers and shakers" and the solid "yeomen" stayed away. Excessive paperwork and the recruitment of women rounded out Nicholson's complaints. He did not propose any solutions.[33]

Matters were not simplified by the fact that the Militia still thought of itself as a sort of alternative army to the Regular Force that should be managed autonomously. Brigadier-General P.J. Mitchell told the Land Forces Staff College that the Militia was an "entity distinct" from the Regular army but unfortunately had not been recognized as such. The Militia was not so much "part-time" as it was "amateur." That is, it was a secondary, volunteer community activity with the management problems of most volunteer organizations: a slow and spasmodic pace, recruiting and leadership difficulties, lapses in continuity, and frustration with the failure of some members to meet their responsibilities. To be seen as a "good thing" in the community, sound military training was not enough. There was a need to keep the organization in the public eye and to advertise the service it performed. There was also the problem that "to ensure a regular intake of useful members, the organization must also accept some members who may be less than useful." It was inevitable that some members "will be only notable for their enthusiasm," but rejection would mean enthusiastic detractors and therefore "enthusiasm must be rewarded even when accompanied by inferior ability." This meant that seniority should always be a factor in Militia promotions and appointments, and that the Militia needed a different style of management than the Regular Force. Mitchell also pointed to the parochialism of the Militia. To him, the argument that the Militia should be organized as brigade groups just like the Regular Force was unacceptable because it would place Militia units in Newfoundland under the command of a headquarters in New Brunswick. Militia soldiers would vote with their feet and stay home under these circumstances.

The Conference of Defence Associations made a similar point in a submission to the subcommittee on the Reserves. It advocated considering the Reserves as a "complement" to and "associates" of the Regular Force, and not simply as replacements. It believed that Reserves should be given the same equipment, the same level of training, comparable facilities in all material aspects, and equal pay and fringe benefits – this despite the fact that a reservist would "never possess the same capabilities and skills" as a Regular Force soldier.[34]

Yet an alternative did exist, although it would have required the army to accept the government policy that it remain small. It would also require the Militia to focus on functionalism and effectiveness rather than parochialism and its history. Army Signal Corps Militia units had been transferred to Communication Command in April 1970. Once transferred, signallers had been required to complete their trades training to Regular Force standards and to serve a period of on-the-job training with a Regular Force unit. The purpose of the Communication Reserve was not to provide expansion but to augment Regular Force units to enable twenty-four-hour communication service in an emergency. Efficiency was monitored closely by Communication Command Headquarters. Giving soldiers viable and visible tasks, ensuring that they were well trained, and monitoring their progress produced units that were at or close to full strength, with 90 percent of soldiers meeting their occupational training standard, compared with the Militia, where trained strength amounted to only about 40 percent of the establishment.[35] Such a Militia would have been much smaller, incapable of becoming the mass army sought by Mobile Command or the community, clubby organization sought by the Militia itself.

On a more positive note, the army's push for a mobilization plan spurred efforts to align the defence budget and policy. D. Bev Dewar, the deputy minister, launched an initiative to define what he called "the normative Defence program." This was a double-barrelled strategy. Clothed in neutral language, Dewar's "normative" program attempted to define what the military believed its minimum requirements were in order to implement the government's policy, even though funds might not be immediately available. He then hoped to be able to negotiate the closing of gaps and shortfalls with ministers.[36]

Doctrine and the "Big Army"

The opening of the financial spigot (albeit slowly) and the acceptance by Prime Minister Trudeau in July 1975 of a small mechanized force with tanks on NATO's Central Front meant that the army could think not only about mobilizing a mass army but also about designing one. The doctrine development process, so slowly constructed during the 1950s, had been disrupted by unification of the armed services. Beginning in 1974, the process was substantially reorganized and revived through the establishment of the "combat development" process. As defined by the army, "combat development" was the process of determining the concepts, organizations, materiel, doctrine, and training for use by the land forces at some future date, and the orderly evolution of the land forces towards goals set by those concepts. The process was directed overall by the Combat Development Committee (CDC) chaired by the commander of Mobile Command. The committee consisted of twenty general officers representing all the headquarters, formations, teaching establishments, and NDHQ branches that collectively formed "the army." This massive committee was envisaged as a "senate" for the army.

Although the commander of Mobile Command chaired the governing committee, the actual staff work was done by the Directorate of Land Combat Development in the DCDS Group at NDHQ. Doctrine was considered to be a subsidiary component of combat development and had its own steering committee, the Army Doctrine and Tactics Board. The ADTB was based at Mobile Command Headquarters and was directed by the Mobile Command deputy chief of staff combat development.

The process through which forces were to be designed involved the issuance of a Combat Development Guide that provided staff with guidance on long-range army requirements; outlined the threat, scientific and technological developments, and NATO and ABCA (America, Britain, Canada, Australia) concepts; and provided guidance on the aim and scope of individual studies. The guide was conservative in tone. It stated: "It can be confidently predicted that present concepts of land warfare and the employment of land forces remain valid. Indeed, because of the long lead time from concept to operational capability much of the equipment in use by military forces fifteen years in the future will be based on scientific and technological knowledge which is known today." It acknowledged that there would be significant technological improvements, but denied that these would have a major impact on battlefield mobility because mobility improvements would be countered by improvements in fire and barrier weapons. The appearance of the Soviet infantry fighting vehicle in the 1973 Yom Kippur War, presaging deep battle doctrine aimed at striking hundreds of kilometres beyond the front lines in both the US and Soviet armies, went unremarked. The guide also specified that Canadian planners were to employ only off-the-shelf weapons, a direction that would be ignored as plans developed.[37]

Combat development was conceived as a bottom-up process, built on a series of individual branch studies and then pulled together by a "Land Force Combat System Study 1986-95," which would define the requirements of "the system" or formation. This combat system study, and indeed the entire project, became known as "Corps '86."[38] There were a number of difficulties with the combat development process. One of the most important was that it was not an integral part of the department's budgeting system, the Defence Program Management System (DPMS). NDHQ viewed the process suspiciously as a backdoor attempt to obtain a commitment to resources without going through departmental challenge and priority review. When the Combat Development Guide was presented to the Defence Management Committee by Major-General René Gutknecht in October 1978, the CDS, Admiral Robert Falls, questioned whether it should have been brought to the committee for endorsement at all. The DCDS, Lieutenant-General G.C.E. Thériault, withdrew the submission, but in the following discussion Buzz Nixon, the deputy minister, said that "great care must be taken to ensure that Combat Development Guides do not become momentum generators which create unrealistic expectations and much wasted effort by staffs." Admiral Falls agreed and cautioned that the army needed to balance requirements against available funds.[39]

The question of constraints to the process had already been raised at the Combat Development Committee meeting in June 1978. Opinion in the army had been divided as to whether real-world constraints, especially financial limitations, should be applied to combat development recommendations. The Combat Development Committee had decided that "the studies would continue as planned, i.e., to develop the required organizations for the high-intensity battlefield from a basis of professional analysis rather than from financial expediency." The rationale given for this decision was that only when all the individual studies had been completed could it be determined whether there was a budgetary problem. Mobile Command staff was directed to prepare a paper on constraints.[40]

The staff paper was tabled at the Combat Development Committee the following year by Colonel J.F.T.A. Liston, the deputy chief of staff combat development at Mobile Command Headquarters. Liston's thoughtful paper spelled out the problem for the army. It was an examination of how to structure the army rather than a technical paper on how to incorporate constraints into the combat development studies. What made the paper different from the army's major staff effort was that he based his appreciation on the tasks the government had actually given the army, rather than attempting to design an abstract, ideal formation.

Liston pointed out that in addition to the NATO role, the army could expect to be tasked for peacekeeping operations and, in an emergency, home defence. These roles needed to be given due consideration in the combat development process because a combat system organized for Europe alone would result in a unique structure that would perhaps be inappropriate for the other tasks. (This comment echoed the critique of those who had advocated light forces in order to make the NATO formation consistent with those maintained in Canada.) He estimated that existing commitments would require one "combat system" stationed in Central Europe; one combat system based in Canada allocated to the CAST group; one system for defence of Canada and North America equipped with "general purpose combat" (i.e., mechanized infantry) equipment, multitasked as a backup for all other missions; a battalion group plus a service support group for peacekeeping operations; and additional infrastructure in Canada to augment the training system and provide garrison support and four thousand troops for "home defence," which together added up to another "system." This came to a total of eight "systems" or about fifty thousand troops, with a further requirement for continued training of reserves and provision of additional home defence troops as needed. Four of these formations would require equipment for high-intensity operations and a fifth set of equipment would be required for training.[41]

Liston noted that although sustained war still appeared to be NATO policy, Canada had attempted without success to meet even the thirty-day support requirement. Canada was dependent on allies for the resupply of most items and had only a seven-day supply of TOW missiles and AVGP (Armoured Vehicle General Purpose), and Leopard tank ammunition on hand. In addition, the quality of troops would have to be high because the warning period would be minimal. This called for regulars or highly trained reserves, whereas the army was caught in a cost bind for personnel. Low military pay, low prestige, and competing civilian education and employment options made a military career unattractive, but solutions to improve conditions of service had increased costs and reduced the numbers that could be maintained. If there was a short warning period, the Militia would have to be structured around a system of one to two years of rigorous training followed by a short mobilization commitment to a Regular Force unit. If the requirement was to develop large units that would have time to organize and conduct individual and collective training, then emphasis should be placed on the development of a cadre of leaders, recruiters, and storesmen in autonomous Militia units who would go out and recruit their units up to strength upon mobilization, as well as train them.

The equipment requirements to be worked out by the combat system studies would have to address the difference between the desire of NATO to have specialized heavy armoured forces to win the first battle and Canada's need to have equipment compatible with as many other roles as possible at home or in other theatres. Liston asked whether all of the equipment purchased would be "general-purpose" or whether some would be "mission-oriented." If all Regular troops were to be equipped as general-purpose units, would second sets of equipment be purchased for other missions? Moreover, unlike the army's mobilization planners and his bosses, Liston thought it was unlikely that equipment could be made available quickly in an emergency. He thought it was "self-deluding" to maintain personnel for whom there was no equipment, and noted that in the Second World War the Canadian Army had initially been equipped by the British.

With regard to funding, Liston disagreed with those who "feel the role of the Soldier is to indicate his requirements and it is then up to the Government to meet it or to reduce the tasks." He found that there were few either/or solutions to force structuring. Costs could be influenced by the type and sophistication of equipment and establishments, the degree of readiness, the percentage of regulars, the intensity of training and amount of equipment and supplies, and "double-tasking." At the time, the department was programmed to support about 24,000 in the army (Regular and Reserve) at an annual cost of about $432.4 million. An additional 4,279 civilians supported the land force, making the total personnel cost $580.4 million. Operations and maintenance cost $192.5 million and capital $189.4 million, rising to $373.6 million by 1987. If all the troops for eight combat systems were Regular, 53,144 person-years would be required. A mixed system of Regulars and Reserves therefore looked more practical. A mixed force of two Regular and six mixed systems would require just 36,317 person-years; a force of two Regular, one mixed, and five Militia would require 24,024 person-years; and a force of three Regular, one mixed, and four Militia cadre systems would require 24,167 person-years. The last two options were within the constraints of the current personnel budget. No matter what option was selected, however, full equipment for eight combat systems would have to be acquired. Liston concluded:

> The government allots both the tasks and the budget. The army requires a mechanism such as the one outlined above to ensure that a rational force structure is developed to meet its tasks, as effectively as possible, within the financial constraints. The force structure for the Army could vary between something just short of eight regular systems down to two regular, one mixed and five militia systems.

Liston did not think that his paper constrained the system study, but he did believe that the study should devote thought to formations that required lesser degrees of sophistication. If the system study did not develop a structure within conceivable levels of procurement, could compromises be made between the required levels of capability and the required number of systems? Should an impasse be reached, either the tasking or the budget would have to be adjusted.[42]

The 1979 Combat Development Committee meeting for which Liston's study was prepared did not discuss the paper. Lieutenant-General Paradis noted that the Combat Development Guide had not yet been approved by the department and that there was a "need for a solid 'Army' front." Major-General D.G. Loomis, the chief of program, informed the committee that it was highly unlikely that funding would exceed current levels or that there would be changes to planned procurement before 1985. Nevertheless, "some members replied that it would be undesirable to allow the definition of 'need' to be determined by the current funding level; real need should be stated." A "purist" approach thus became the basis for Corps '86.[43]

Affordability was not the only problem with the Corps '86 study. Although the army called Corps '86 a "systems study," it had little in common with the methods used by formal systems analysis, which would have required all weapon systems to be considered in a comprehensive and integrated manner using quantitative analytical techniques to the largest extent possible. Corps '86 explicitly rejected this approach. The chief land doctrine and operations wrote:

> The supremacy of the scientific method and the successful application of it to so many aspects of day-to-day life have led to a tendency to demand that decisions be based on absolutes which can be measured in a scientific way. It is often forgotten that human affairs are far more intricate and perplexing than the more predictable structure of atoms and molecules. Organizational development, falling as it does, in the realm of social sciences has no universally held precepts and provides no precise basis against which to measure new military organizations. Therefore, although this study will stress application of the most generally accepted of organizational development techniques, when it comes to weighing alternatives and assessing options the final arbiter will have to remain, as ever, sound military judgement.[44]

Corps '86 was based on an extensive review of Canadian and allied studies and a series of field visits to the United States, Britain, Germany, and Switzerland. Discussions with the Americans were perhaps the most intensive. The study team observed a complete test phase of the new US infantry battalion developed by the US Army Divisional Restructure Group at Fort Hood, Texas. It was briefed by the principal American combat developers and General Donn A. Starry, the commander of the US Army Training and Doctrine Command. Other senior US Army officials attended presentations on Canadian concepts at the Canadian Land Forces Command and Staff College. However, only a single new operations research study and no field trials were used to develop the concept. Methodologically, Corps '86 was a step back from the Division 1965 project led by Roger Rowley (see Chapter 2).[45]

The wide-ranging research undertaken aside, there was a tone of self-satisfaction with the Canadian status quo in the deliberations of the force developers. After a briefing on reorganizations completed by the US, British, and Australian armies, the Infantry Study Team concluded that "no action is being taken by other nations that are of such significance that it requires conformity by Canadian Infantry." The Infantry Study Team agreed that the Canadian battalion defence concept of battle positions, alternative battle positions, and "hides" remained valid and was the "best concept for the foreseeable future." It was predicted that the US Army would soon adopt Canadian tactics once it tried to implement its own new concept published in FM100-5, the US Army operations field manual. No significant change was thought to be needed, only the addition of anti-armour capability.[46]

Unlike a genuine systems study – which would start with a problem such as "How can a Soviet armour assault be stopped?" – Corps '86 seemed to start with a solution. The Combat Development Committee decided that "as the basis of any land combat system can be assessed as being the capability to defeat any enemy's aggressive intention by our physical control of ground, the first study required was determined as being that of examining the Canadian Infantry."[47] Ignoring previous analyses that had cast doubts on the utility of infantry on the high-intensity battlefield, infantry primacy was defended on the basis that "although the most dangerous threat is and will be the Warsaw Pact tank masses, the ultimate requirement will be the destruction of enemy infantry who, once the tank threat is halted, will dismount and try to wrest physical control of the ground. The Warsaw Pact objectives are based on their seizure of terrain." This last statement belied the consistent position taken elsewhere in the infantry study that Soviet doctrine was based on manoeuvre and blitzkrieg tactics to attempt to disorient and paralyze their opponent while bypassing strong points.[48] The decision to conduct a series of branch studies founded on the infantry had two effects: (1) by focusing on the control of ground, it tied the army to a positional, attritionist doctrine; and (2) it meant that each branch study would be conducted individually and somehow combined at the very end into a "combat system." This would prove easier said than done.

Although the Infantry Study declared that there was "an apparent misconception" that a new anti-armour combat arm had evolved and insisted that there were "still only two close combat arms with anti-armour being part of the capabilities of each," it struggled to establish a unique role for the infantry. The infantry's traditional role was "to close with and destroy the enemy," but armour could also lay claim to the same mission. Something different was required, otherwise the obvious conclusion would be that there was really only one combat arm. Corps '86 therefore suggested that "only the infantry creates the actual battlefield framework to which all other arms and combat support can be regulated as regards such factors as amount of support, location, timings and type." It concluded that the role of the infantry was "to create the battlefield framework through its physical control of ground and its destruction of the enemy in close combat."[49] Exactly what this meant was unclear. It was another step away from Rowley's realization that the relationship between armour and infantry had changed and that the problem was how to manage the merger.

Corps '86 was similar to Division 1965 in rejecting manoeuvre as the fundamental approach to a defensive battle. Its concept was an attritional battle in which a Canadian combat team of company size would have to defend a one-kilometre front against an assault by thirty tanks, twenty BMP infantry fighting vehicles, and 180 dismounted infantry. In addition, Warsaw Pact forces could be expected to bring to bear one hundred artillery tubes per kilometre, mobile air defences, armoured reconnaissance vehicles, fixed- and rotary-wing tactical aircraft, and electronic warfare. The defenders would have to destroy 65 percent of the assaulting troops in order to be successful. The Infantry Study envisaged support from attack helicopters, artillery firing anti-tank munitions, air-mobile forces with anti-tank firepower, and tactical air support to back up the infantry combat team, but it did not say exactly how these forces were to be integrated or how much was to be expected from each type of platform. It did conclude, after a close examination of NATO combat exchange tables, that a mix of anti-tank weapons would be required. Ideally, the combat team would have six heavy anti-tank weapons (such as the TOW missile), four "rapid-firing, fire-and-forget" medium anti-tank weapons, and two crew-portable medium anti-tank weapons (such as the MILAN missile). The "rapid-firing, fire-and-forget" platforms were either tanks or a "tank-destroyer-type weapon system." The infantry study also concluded that Canadian infantry would have to be mechanized and mounted in "Canadian Infantry Fighting Vehicles" (CIFVs), which, like the tank destroyer, did not currently exist. The CIFV's purpose was to move a complete infantry section from one defensive position to another, help it dig in, and provide defensive fire out to one thousand metres against other infantry fighting vehicles and perhaps tanks. It was not conceived of as a manoeuvre or assault platform, and the study gave no thought as to how the gun on the CIFV would be integrated into the combat team or how command-and-control arrangements would be altered by the integration of so much firepower at the company level.[50]

Corps '86 identified six different types of infantry (armoured, mechanized, light, air-mobile, airborne, and marine), but recommended that all Canadian troops assigned to NATO be mechanized infantry and that light infantry also be maintained for defence-of-North America and UN roles. Consistent with earlier Canadian army thinking, the study recommended against the creation of Canadian air-mobile troops, arguing that air-mobile infantry could be provided by using mechanized infantry temporarily transported by helicopters.[51]

The infantry study was not only conceptually unimaginative but also socially conservative. Saying that "an examination of the infantryman as a human is essential," it assessed the social and organizational situation of the army and found that it was not only the Soviet army that created challenges. Canadian society had grown soft and recruits had "an increasingly lower resistance to physical privations." Moreover, "humanistic values, concerns for the safety of children, workers and the general public ... increasingly tend to isolate young Canadians from the realities of immediate sickness, pain, wounds and death." Even worse, Canadian schools were less structured than before, and there was resistance to "instant incorporation into a structured group." Recruits had a sense of individuality and personal dignity and were "ever more resistant to activities which appear to be pointless."[52] Faced with the extraordinarily destructive nuclear battlefield, only the strongest measures could overcome the perceived decline of Canadian society.

The proposed antidote was, not surprisingly, the regimental system. The infantry study's version was based on what it called "authoritative leadership."

> In any army, it is at platoon and company level that men relate to their fellow soldiers and to their leaders. On operations the only authorities available to give direction, provide for security and the physical necessities of life, and solve problems are the company officers and NCOs. Soldiers are completely dependent on their immediate superiors for every aspect of their existence ranging from their physical survival down to their most intimate personal administrative problem. The Canadian tradition has been to provide leadership at this level which merits the confidence of infantrymen. It is unabashedly paternalistic.

Leaders therefore needed complete legal authority over the led, must condition them to "an acceptable level of discipline" by drill, gain trust by success in looking after their needs, and be able to motivate them through both significant rewards and "meaningful punishment." Accordingly,

> Identification of the recruit with his regiment brings the recruit to accept and embrace, not only the unique dress of his regiment, but its whole sub-culture of leadership style, history and glorious traditions of proven performance. It is in this way that the regiment induces the most reluctant recruits into accepting the legitimacy of its demanding authoritative leadership, its costly battlefield role and its requirement to carry out every task given it effectively.

The infantry study recommended what was essentially a restoration of the pre-unification Army Headquarters and army control of its training and personnel systems, rather than dependence on Canadian Forces–wide systems managed by NDHQ.[53]

The armour study was roughly consistent with the foundational infantry study. It regarded infantry's role as that of holding ground while manoeuvre was accomplished by armour. It imagined the main defensive battle as anchored by positional anti-armour elements protected by the infantry. Armour would manoeuvre, supported by attack helicopters, artillery, and close air support. Rather than integrate tanks with the infantry, the Armour Branch concept was to use tanks in mass, "superimposed" on the primary anti-tank framework, which was largely the infantry's responsibility. The Armour Branch suggested that a tank destroyer would be more cost-effective than a tank in this role. The study concluded:

> The tank should not, however, be the sole or even primary anti-tank system. Recalling "the battle of manoeuvre," tanks should be relatively free to use their battlefield mobility and not be tied down in pill-box fashion as anti-tank emplacements. As noted in Chapter 9, in the defence the anti-tank defence could be based on a cheaper and simpler anti-tank destroyer (gun) and supplemented by a range of missiles and an indirect fire capability.[54]

The air support study had a completely different concept of a NATO/Warsaw Pact battle. Unlike the Infantry and Armour Branches, which envisaged a rather static role for the infantry, the air support study advocated air-mobile forces as the response to the Soviets' ability to concentrate superior forces at any point. Air-mobile forces could concentrate where ground forces would find it impractical. Air-mobile troops would be backed up by attack helicopters armed with anti-tank guided missiles. According to the air support study:

> The attack helicopter with its flexibility and freedom of movement coupled with its accurate firepower capability provides the land commander with the effective means of countering the enemy breakthrough until such time that he can commit land resources to effectively counter the threat. The attack helicopter can also commence the destruction of enemy armoured forces at ranges beyond those of land direct fire weapons.

Based on the 1972 US/Canadian/German study, the air support study estimated that attack helicopters could account for 65 percent of tank kills.

All-weather air-mobile forces could be used to reinforce ground troops or act independently. Moreover, they could help defeat enemy armour not only by direct fire but also by moving engineering troops who would rapidly erect barriers and create obstacles. The air support study forecast that by 1986 helicopters would have overcome their vulnerability problems and inability to conduct round-the-clock operations. Survivability would be achieved by nap-of-the-earth flying in all types of weather and by passive and active electronic countermeasures. To achieve this capability, the corps would include a helicopter wing of sixteen light observation helicopters, twenty-four attack helicopters, twenty-eight utility helicopters, and eight medium transport helicopters. One squadron of attack helicopters would be available on a 24/7 basis, and the wing would have the capability to lift a company in a single sortie.

The air support study did not ignore fixed-wing aircraft. It called for a high-performance multi-role fighter capable of air defence and offensive air operations. It was discreetly silent concerning the provision of close air support.[55]

It was up to the Combat Development Committee to integrate the various concepts developed by the individual branches. It appears to have done this, as in the case of earlier reports, by stapling the branch reports together, and both the armour and air support reports were approved with minor revisions. The main concerns were that the wording of the latter did not adequately establish the primacy of the land force over air support, and doubts were expressed regarding the cost-effectiveness of close air support compared with artillery, obviously with the air force's costly New Fighter Aircraft project in mind. Brigadier-General C.A. Lafrance, the chief of staff air and the commander of the 10 Tactical Air Group, laid this issue to rest with the comment that the only cost that could be attributed to close air support would be minor incremental costs specific to that role – the air force needed the aircraft for air superiority and interdiction anyway.

Operations research war games to assess the proposed organization were not completed until November 1981, by which time all the fundamental decisions had been made. The BRONZE TALON series of studies assessed both the existing brigade group and the proposed Corps '86 brigade group in defensive and counterattack battles. The Canadian mechanized brigade group was placed within a German division and the battle was fought on the German/Czech border. The very detailed and thorough studies concluded that the proposed brigade group organization would be "extremely effective" at holding ground. This should have not been a great surprise because the new organization was much larger, had almost double the number of guns supporting it, benefited from the addition of tank destroyers and multiple-launch rocket systems, and was backed up by attack helicopters and fixed-wing ground attack aircraft from higher headquarters. The results should have given army planners pause, however. Rather than the infantry-centric battle – or even infantry/armour-centric battle – that Corps '86 envisaged, the battle narrative of the BRONZE TALON 3 war game makes it clear that artillery was the critical combat arm. BLUE (i.e., NATO) artillery accounted for 41 percent of RED (Soviet) vehicle casualties and 72 percent of RED personnel casualties. RED artillery caused the greatest proportion of BLUE equipment casualties and 83 percent of BLUE personnel casualties. The study concluded that "this total should quite clearly indicate to BLUE that the dominating system on the battlefield is RED artillery. It is the major threat and therefore countering it must be a major concern to BLUE." To achieve this, BRONZE TALON recommended that commanders and staff locate and direct fire onto RED batteries, rather than targeting tank concentrations, "as is often the case."[56]

The CIFV was able to hold its own against Soviet armour, but fell victim to artillery fire. When losses to artillery were considered, its loss rate was almost 2:1. The CIFV created a dilemma for commanders: they wanted the support of its gun, but if it was sited with the infantry, the range at which fire could be opened would be restricted and fire would be drawn onto the infantry once the gun was engaged. If it was sited elsewhere, the commander would face command-and-control problems and possible loss of his vehicle to transport the section.[57]

The tank destroyers – indeed all the 105 mm guns, whether on tanks or tank destroyers – were very effective. RED forces manoeuvred to avoid obvious killing zones and chose ground to stay masked from long-range TOW missiles. They also used smoke to blind missile guidance systems. The study cautioned, however, that the performance of the tank destroyer had been modelled on the Leopard 1 tank; a real tank destroyer was expected to perform less well. One is left to conclude that the tank destroyer concept was the result of doing the Corps '86 study by branches. The Infantry recognized the need for a direct-fire support vehicle with its units, but the Armour Branch opposed dispersing tanks, preferring to keep them grouped together. The tank destroyer was therefore a tank that was not a tank, thus satisfying everyone. Except that the vehicle did not exist.[58]

The overall concept was for a corps-sized formation based on mechanized infantry divisions that would fight a defensive battle, using infantry-heavy forces to stop and hold the enemy on a major obstacle and an armour-heavy mobile force to mount counter-moves.[59] This concept was at variance with US Army doctrine, which had been evolving rapidly since 1976. General William E. DePuy, the first commander of the US Army Training and Doctrine Command, had become convinced that the huge numerical imbalance between Warsaw Pact and NATO forces meant that mobilization had lost any meaning. He advised US field commanders that they should utilize all their forces at the outset of battle and not rely on an attempt to absorb attacks until the superior US economy could dominate the enemy. His stated objective in the 1976 US Army operations field manual (FM100-5) was to "prepare to win the first battle of the next war." Adopting tactics similar to those used by Germany in the Second World War, he planned to attrite Soviet attacking forces by firepower, attacking flanks or narrow penetrations, destroying enemy support and command and control, and finally defeating their combat forces in detail. American forces would be based on combined arms, battalion-sized task forces with field and air defence artillery, engineers, attack helicopters, and close air support. DePuy was also convinced that the US Army needed a true infantry fighting vehicle – that is, an infantry carrier that was more heavily armoured than the M113 armoured personnel carrier, with a heavy gun to provide covering fire and defence against similar vehicles. The Soviet BMP, the first infantry fighting vehicle fielded by any army, had proven to be "a particularly nasty surprise" to the Israelis during the Yom Kippur War.[60]

DePuy's successor, General Donn Starry, substantially revamped FM100-5, making it manoeuvre-based rather than attrition-based. Starry's revision dealt with the threat of Soviet numerical superiority through the doctrine of "AirLand Battle," striking attacking forces throughout their depth to rear areas. Although the concept of the extended battlefield was accepted by Corps '86, it fit uneasily with the concept of conducting a defence based on a natural obstacle. Staff talks with the US Army found "considerable, sometimes irreconcilable, differences" with one of the major allies Canada expected to operate with in Europe: the Americans were planning on a "come-as-you-are war," whereas the Canadians were using "a more ideal approach"; the Americans also intended to use manoeuvre tactics, whereas Canada required "an essentially continuous linear obstacle."[61] There were also differences with Germany, the army's other main ally in Europe. Here the major difference appeared to be command-and-control doctrine. Whereas the Canadian army relied on detailed orders down to the lowest level, the Germans delegated the corps concept to the divisional commanders. The German plan was built bottom-up through delegation, whereas the Canadian one (as had been the case since the Second World War) was specified top-down. Discussions concluded that a Canadian division would probably not be deployed in the area where the corps counterattack was expected to be delivered because of command-and-control problems.[62]

The Corps '86 concept was staffed to completion, including a complete set of staff data tables necessary for logistic support to the imaginary corps. The table of organization and equipment required a turretless tank destroyer mounting a 120 mm gun and weighing six tonnes more than a main battle tank. After considerable debate, the corps model also included an "armoured personnel carrier" rather than infantry fighting vehicle – but an APC with a 30 mm chain gun and the capacity to carry a full ten-man infantry section. Neither of these vehicles existed anywhere, although the Soviet BMP-2 seemed close to the Canadian requirement. The corps equipment included an array of heavy weapons that Canada did not possess, including Lance surface-to-surface missiles, Patriot ground-to-air missiles, Multiple Launch Rocket Systems, and the Gepard self-propelled anti-aircraft gun.[63]

There was little capacity in the real world to implement the concept. When it reached the Army Doctrine and Tactics Board, the board found that the process had been "untidy" and the concepts "too progressive" and unimplementable due to technical, financial, and political constraints. Consequently, the report "suffer[ed] from a lack of credibility." The board believed the end document had swallowed US doctrine whole, placing too much emphasis on enemy rear areas 150 to 300 kilometres beyond the forward edge of the battle area.[64] The Canadian army had no ability to strike beyond 30 kilometres, even if the field army was a full corps in size. In spite of this, the report was eventually approved and the branches began implementation planning.[65]

The problem of squaring the corps concept with budget and policy was never resolved. When the system study was presented to the Defence Management Committee in December 1981, the committee acknowledged that it was logical and a defensible way of developing new requirements for the army, and that the idea of a blueprint for a larger force had some utility. It approved the results for study, training, adjustments to force structure, and guidance for future equipment purchases, but insisted that any proposed changes be submitted through the normal budgetary process. Moreover, the departmental executive insisted that any changes to the army be related to current commitments, tasks, and force structures, and take into account the fact that current army commitments called for only brigade groups or smaller units.[66]

The army pronounced Corps '86 a success, but one that it did not want to repeat in detail. In considering what should be done for the next iteration of combat development – Corps '96 – the Army Doctrine and Tactics Board suggested that "developmental" guidelines be separated from "implementation" guidelines. The former would be pure concepts, the latter based on government policy, manpower restrictions, and fiscal and other real-world constraints. "Without considering these implementation guidelines," said the ADTB, "we run the risk of producing yet another totally unattainable 'pie in the sky' corps model which may jeopardize the credibility of the entire CD [Combat Development] process. CLDO [Chief Land Doctrine and Operations] has agreed that this approach makes good sense and has tasked DLCD [Director Land Combat Development] to pursue it further."[67] Terry Liston, now a brigadier-general and doing graduate work at the École nationale d'administration publique, wrote in his thesis that Corps '86 "envisaged a force structure beyond what is currently perceived to be our commitments and which is indisputably unaffordable under present circumstances." He found the entire policy and programming system to be flawed and recommended that National Defence adopt a system similar to that used by the US Army, which began with an ideal concept but then developed a succession of ever more affordable force structures from it until both the civil and military leadership found an acceptable combination of forces, risk, and funding. Unfortunately, little of this advice would be taken.[68]

Not only did Corps '86 produce doctrine that was not compatible with the very allied forces for which Canada's army was supposed to be the reserve, that contained internal contradictions, and that required non-existent equipment to implement but it also diverted scarce staff resources away from the real-world problems of the army.[69] As will be seen in Chapter 7, the failure to develop adequate plans for real operations would result in both exercise and operational failures.

Corps '96 – Planning to Be Big Continues

In 1985 there was a brief flirtation with light forces when the CDS, General C.G.E. Thériault, saw an opening to change Canada's NATO land force commitment from the Central Front to Norway. Thériault's thinking had much in common with that of Ivan Head and Pierre Trudeau, who saw both cost reductions and diplomatic flexibility in making the army more uniform in structure and more available for non-NATO assignments. He was able to make considerable progress in selling his concept to NATO military staffs, but the initiative fell apart once Erik Nielsen, the minister, became involved. Nielsen took over the file personally but was rebuffed by both his British and German counterparts. He quickly buried the plan upon his return to Canada.[70]

The Corps project therefore moved ahead unhindered. The tenth meeting of the Combat Development Committee in April 1984 had considered the results of Corps '86 and pondered the lessons learned. Unlike the working-level Army Doctrine and Tactics Board, the general officer corps considered Corps '86 to have been a "resounding success." It had resulted in a common body of doctrine and provided a basis for army plans and budgetary submissions. Even its proponents, however, agreed that the organizations it had produced were too large and unwieldy, and well beyond the resource capabilities of the Canadian Forces to build. The generals now thought that the worst-case scenario that had guided Corps '86 should not be used to generate requirements for the next cycle, and that rather than continuing to construct model organizations unconstrained by size or function, the next cycle should be guided top-down, reflecting current policy. It was also admitted that the relationship between the army's combat development process and departmental planning and budgeting was "not very effective" and that guidelines for integrating the two processes were needed.

The CDC came to realize that "the key to the application of the CD process ... is common sense." What was needed were organizations to meet the army's current and projected assigned missions. The committee insisted that future force structure models be developed to meet political and executive direction, be economically feasible, reflect anticipated Canadian Forces and Canadian industrial capabilities in wartime, and present the level of risk associated with the resulting capabilities. These constraints should have resulted in the design of a radically different and much more realistic force structure. Two additional constraints were placed on planning staffs, however: plans had to reflect the "total force" concept, and a general-purpose capability had to be maintained. These two requirements worked against all the rest. Although "total force" had been government policy since the 1971 White Paper, the government saw the Reserve only as augmenting the Regular Force to the full war establishment for its existing commitments, not as a basis for expansion of the army. The general-purpose capability requirement was also rooted in policy, namely, the commitment to NATO's Central Front, but if applied to the entire army, it too would work against an affordable plan intended to implement government policy.

The CDC also gave the planners the reasonable direction that doctrine should be "based upon a battle in high level conflict in the NATO environment, but include differences in operations in lower levels of conflict and other levels of operations." The general officer community was not willing to give up control, with the CDC saying that "short of war, the primary method of validating a combat system is through military judgement." The committee, however, placed more emphasis on the use of operations research and exercises in producing data to aid the process. Operations research, which was the only method capable of producing quantifiable results, was to be used as often as possible.[71]

Although the direction given to the planning staffs appeared to address the excesses of Corps '86 and direct Corps '96 onto a path that would result in a reasonable plan for the army, the result, if anything, was worse. In May 1986, planning staff reported to the Army Doctrine and Tactics Board that Corps '96 would be similar to its predecessor but smaller, and would include designs for light, medium, and heavy divisions. Rather than start with a clean slate, Corps '96 would attempt to "resolve CD's relationship to CF assigned tasks and in doing so produce an improved capability in the army in peace and war."[72]

The army's appreciation of the international situation can be likened to Malthus and Hobbes in equal parts. Population growth in less developed countries would constrain democracy and lead to authoritarian regimes that might "impose drastic solutions causing destabilization of world order." Rapid urbanization was creating problems, causing hopes of prosperity for young urban masses to diminish. National identities were threatened by religious, social, and linguistic differences and charismatic leaders would exploit religion, nationalism, and messianic fervour. Stocks of energy and minerals of all types were diminishing, resulting in greater competition for supplies among developed nations. Food production was not keeping pace with population growth. The military-age population in the developed world was declining.[73]

The outlook for NATO was equally bleak. Both Soviet nuclear and conventional forces had continued to grow, providing the Warsaw Pact with greater potential to overrun larger portions of NATO territory more rapidly. Soviet power had continued to grow in almost every category, from sea denial capability to offshore power projection. NATO's qualitative force improvements had come at the expense of quantity, and if the trend continued it would have "a serious and debilitating effect" on NATO's conventional forces. NATO's Northern Region was short of resources and an adequate manpower base; the Central Region was challenged by a lack of readiness, availability, and sustainability; and the Southern Region was plagued by obsolescent equipment and questions about sustainability of materiel.[74]

The direction taken stemmed from a calculation that the political landscape was changing to favour a large Canadian army and a conviction that its analyses supporting Corps '86 had been right all along. The planning guidance therefore reinterpreted the objectives and constraints until Corps '86 would require no more than a light revision, rather than being discarded completely. To begin with, the objective of Corps '96 was to determine the organization and equipment required in order for the army to be combat-effective on the battlefield during the 1996-2005 time period. The Combat Development Committee, however, directed the study to develop, as its first priority, an effective army combat system at the corps level related primarily to a threat in Europe. Other high- and mid-level conflict tasks would be assigned to "separate studies," which, however, would never be conducted.[75]

The strategic goal of the army was "to prevent hostilities by deterring armed attack," but the implementation of the army structure necessary to achieve this was limited by peacetime constraints. Nevertheless, the committee regarded the mandate of the combat development process as being the development of a corps model as a framework for the required structure. The goal therefore became the ability to carry out sustained operations against a sophisticated enemy in high-intensity combat. For peacetime, this was modified to the execution of sustained combat against specific threats "until the level of commitment is altered."[76]

Other constraints were similarly minimized. The planning guidance acknowledged that the most recent department policy framework did not really support the direction being taken, but it was dismissed as an "interim document whose publication was necessary to meet the specific needs of the early 1980s and will likely require revision in line with the current initiative for a new White Paper on Defence." Since policy changes might occur, the planning guidance informed staff that "aspects of the CD studies related to the assigned tasks might best be deferred until the impact of the changes are clarified." The guidance also took comfort from the most recent Capabilities Planning Guide, which was the first major departmental document to recognize "the necessity for, and the rationality of unfettered CD studies that are beyond current affordability." The guide suggested that the army should orient itself to the collective defence of Europe and be based on balanced, general-purpose, mechanized forces that could also contribute to the defence of North America.[77]

The guide dealt with readiness and sustainment by backing off a notch from the large Corps '86 organization, which was designed to absorb a Warsaw Pact attack without immediate reinforcement, to an assumption that the support system would be able to provide a stream of casualty replacements. The question of materiel support and industrial mobilization was simply set aside because the department was in the midst of independent studies of those problems – despite the conclusions already reached by the mobilization planners that even if "supplemented generously by allies," Canadian manufacturing capability would require at least two years to prepare forces for expansion, and that broad expansion could not begin until the third year of a war. The first two years would see little change in the size of the Canadian Forces other than the existing forces being brought up to strength.[78] Linkage to the departmental budgeting system was reduced to bafflegab about the need to separate studies of high-intensity conflict from other tasks. Beyond stating that there had been no connection between army planning and departmental budgeting in the past, not much was clarified.[79]

Finally, the planning guidance endorsed most of the conclusions of Corps '86. "General-purpose forces" were slightly redefined to delete the requirement that formations be able to form part of higher formation organization, which had resulted in their becoming larger to support an independent role. Instead, tasking and augmentation would be left to superior operational headquarters. The designation of a corps as the smallest complete combat system was endorsed, regardless of whether Canada could or would ever again field such a force. These concerns were dismissed as "irrelevant." Some analytical changes were made: the theoretical basis for combat tasks behind Corps '96 was constrained by the need to keep formation size smaller, and the list of combat functions was amended to conform to those in use by NATO.[80]

It was also thought that the size of the resulting formations could be controlled by the definition of the threat. The Combat Development Committee decided that the planners should work from a defensive mission in which the Canadian corps would be deployed after the initial attack of Warsaw Pact forces. In the selected scenario, either the Soviets would have failed to make a significant breach in NATO defences or NATO would have fallen back and established a new major defensive area. The attacking force was at the limit of what a corps-sized organization could cope with without being immediately overwhelmed: a Soviet tank army consisting of three tank divisions and one motor rifle division, plus an additional motor rifle division on the flank and a tank brigade in the second echelon. The corps was to include a light formation to conduct operations in urban or forested areas and "to provide a link to the reality of Canadian mobilization potential." In addition, the corps included an independent brigade group "to provide a logical link with the reality of the 4CMBG task."[81]

The combat development process thus rationalized a "steady as she goes" approach. The international situation appeared to be deteriorating and the Conservative government now appeared ready to support expanded armed forces. Although technical revisions had been made to the instructions given to staff in terms of how they were to delineate combat functions, and a somewhat less demanding scenario had been proposed for them to base studies on, the broad lines of previous "big army" studies were carried forward. The basis for study would continue to be the corps, whether or not such an organization was affordable. "General-purpose" – that is, heavy – forces were to be the standard model on which the army was based. Concerns regarding the links to the rest of the defence management process, industrial capability, and personnel resources were pushed aside. Although the Corps '96 studies would not be completed until 1991, the army was now prepared to support the government's ambitious 1987 Defence White Paper initiative.

The "Big Army" and the 1987 White Paper

During the 1984 federal election campaign, Brian Mulroney, who would soon be prime minister, said that the Canadian Forces would "go first class or stay at home."[82] After Erik Nielsen's brief and unsuccessful contemplation of light forces concentrated in Norway, his successor as defence minister, Perrin Beatty, focused on completing the promised Defence White Paper. Although some preliminary work had been done, this did not extend beyond an outline of possible content and the commissioning of staff "think pieces." According to some of those who participated in the process, Beatty wanted the White Paper completed quickly and without leaks that might prejudice his ability to get Cabinet's concurrence. Thus participation in the process was limited to a few, very senior officials: Chief of the Defence Staff Paul Manson, Deputy Minister Bev Dewar, Vice Chief of the Defence Staff Jack Vance, Assistant Deputy Minister (Policy) Robert Fowler, and Assistant Deputy Minister (Materiel) Ed Healey. The Command commanders were consulted through the headquarters committee system but, in the words of Lieutenant-General James Fox, the commander of Mobile Command, there was no "deep and wide discussion and input" from the army. Explicit mention of tanks – a significant force structure and budget issue – was added only at the last minute.[83]

When the White Paper, *Challenge and Commitment: A Defence Policy for Canada*, emerged in June 1987, it advanced a vision much more congenial to those who favoured a large mechanized army built around NATO's Central Front. It saw international affairs dominated by a struggle between East and West in which the other side, although perhaps not a completely evil empire, did not value personal freedom or the rule of law. Whatever the motivation of the East, the White Paper saw it as armed and dangerous. Although war was not inevitable, the West had no choice but to maintain a "rough balance" of conventional forces backed by nuclear arms. Moreover, Central Europe was "the geographic focus of the wider contest between East and West" and the "centre of gravity in the balance of power." The White Paper was complete with statistical charts and graphs portraying the quantitative advantage of the Warsaw Pact, and included polar projection maps depicting a large red Soviet bloc engulfing NATO and North America.[84]

The White Paper announced that, rather than focusing on Norway, Canada was dropping the Norwegian commitment. The forces formerly earmarked for CAST would be allocated to NATO's Central Front to turn Canada's contribution into a two-brigade division. The rationale for this was the difficulty in supporting two separate lines of communication and "severe" difficulties in deploying to Norway, which made timely deployment "questionable." Consolidation in southern Germany was regarded as a "more credible, effective and sustainable contribution to the common defence in Europe." The government said that it intended to pre-position a large portion of the division's equipment and supplies in Europe, acquire new tanks, increase airlift capability, and improve support resources. Canada would maintain the existing battalion group commitment to the ACE Mobile Force (Land) for service on the northern flank. At home, the government stated, existing forces were insufficient to guard vital points, conduct Arctic surveillance, or provide a quick-reaction force for the defence of Canada. The White Paper promised additional brigades, a minimally trained guard force, improvement to the Canadian Rangers, and establishment of a northern training centre.[85]

To meet the personnel requirements of this larger force, the government intended to expand the Reserves. It wished to reduce the distinction between Regulars and Reserves and to more fully implement the "total force" concept. The White Paper proposed mixed units of Regulars and Reserves, with varying proportions depending on the assigned mission and level of readiness. In the case of the army, the Militia would take on the defence of Canada and the guarding of vital points as its own tasks, as well as contribute to augmentation of the Regular Force. All this would require improvements to training and equipment that would be specified at a later date in a Reserve Force Development Plan. Altogether (navy, army, air force), the Reserves would expand to ninety thousand members.[86]

Challenge and Commitment pledged the government to provide the resources necessary to expand the army and the rest of the Canadian Forces. It famously promised the navy a fleet of ten to twelve nuclear-powered attack submarines. It also promised a five-year rolling funding plan through which Cabinet would adjust spending. Ominously, however, the government committed itself to only 2 percent annual real growth in the defence budget. Under the former Liberal government, 3 percent real growth had been achieved. The government presented this as a "floor" that would be exceeded from time to time as major projects temporarily placed greater demands on the budget.[87]

It must be noted that although the 1987 White Paper represented the high-water mark of political commitment to a big army on NATO's Central Front, it fell far short of the army's desire for a corps. The NATO contingent would amount to only an understrength division with two, rather than three, manoeuvre brigades. Critics were also quick to point out that it lacked adequate artillery and military engineering support. The White Paper said that mobilization would require "more attention," but the only specifics were with regard to emergency planning staffs in civil departments. As far as the army was concerned, however, the two biggest issues raised by the White Paper were the closely related subjects of the increase in the size and prominence of the Militia and the total cost of the government's program.[88]

The army estimated that to build the force required by the White Paper, a total military force of 80,209 personnel would be required. This necessitated increasing the Regular Force army from 22,500 to 30,329 and the Militia from 15,500 to 43,308, as well as adding an additional 6,492 from the Supplemental Ready Reserve, a list of retired Canadian Forces members who had agreed to serve again in an emergency. It was not clear that the Militia had the capacity to either triple its size or reach the higher levels of effectiveness required by the White Paper. None of its fundamental problems that had been identified since 1950 had been addressed. In 1987 it was scattered around the country in 131 units based on historical precedent rather than logic. It was absent from rapidly expanding urban areas such as Mississauga and Laval, but based in small towns such as Brockville and in rural areas. Militia units typically had a strength of about 150 but with the command structure of a full battalion of 800, complete with a lieutenant-colonel commanding, several majors, a regimental sergeant major, and an honorary colonel. Training took up no more than forty to forty-five days a year, and turnover was high. There were leadership shortages at all levels, with four Militia units being commanded by Regular Force officers, and a shortage of skilled tradesmen.[89] Departmental staff estimated that to grow by 40,000 the Reserves would have to recruit more than 200,000 individuals because of the 25 percent annual attrition. The army's share would be about three-quarters of the total. The number of eighteen- to twenty-four-year-olds was decreasing and former Regular Force members showed little inclination to join the Reserves. Of 69,000 individuals released from the Forces between 1974 and 1988 who were employable for further military service, only 1,400 joined the Primary Reserves.[90]

Regular and Reserve officers pointed to the considerable cultural problems that would have to be overcome to implement the White Paper's version of "total force." Colonel C.J. Addy pointed to the Regular Force's tendency to view the Militia as "untidy" and a politically necessary impediment to effectiveness. Regulars, he said, were "aghast at the lack of bureaucratic skills of the less-trained, part-time leadership" of the Militia, whereas they, on the other hand, had a highly developed, even exaggerated, sense of urgency and reacted well to "an autocratic hierarchical system." Regulars rotated through jobs every few years and tended not to consider the long-range implications of their decisions. The Militia for its part was local in spirit. The existence of regimental senates with the continued presence of old commanding officers and the importance of mess life added "an element of tribal conservatism which has persevered through a rough history of neglect by others and has ensured the enduring values of group loyalty, pride and dedication but which, on the other hand, dictates that any change is viewed very critically." From the Militia perspective, there was also skepticism that a major expansion would be achievable in fifteen years. They doubted their ability to quintuple the number of effectives in the Militia, especially given the current woeful state of Militia administration of recruitment and personnel management, which they found ridiculous and ineffective. They were well aware that retention was a huge problem, but thought that the army was not effective in recruiting the right people to begin with. The proposed Militia Training Centres were seen as problematic, because wherever they were placed they would be miles away from most units, requiring travel of a dozen hours to train for a couple of hours. The proposed composite units were also foreign to Militia mentality. Officers complained that units made up of companies from several Militia units would lack the sustaining power of the regimental system and would simply be collections of "foreigners," and that "the seams of disunity, mistrust, and the breakdown of cohesiveness would be shown."[91]

The government had no intention of amending the National Defence Act to protect reservists' jobs while they were training or deployed, or to make the release of reservists by civilian employers compulsory. Shortly before the White Paper was tabled, General Paul Manson, the chief of the defence staff, testified to the Standing Committee on National Defence that the department intended to rely on moral suasion:

> We must make the point with Canadian employers that reserve service is for the good of the country and that they themselves have an important part to play in permitting their employees who belong to the reserves to have time off for adequate training and wherever possible to provide compensation for lost pay as a result of reserve training as well.

Following publication of the White Paper, Beatty informed the same committee that the government was not thinking of offering employers tax incentives to allow reservists time off for training, but was asking employers to allow them two weeks off for training without prejudice to their vacation time and to top up Reserve pay whenever possible. There did not seem to be either an organizational or legal structure to back up the huge expansion of and reliance on the Militia that the government's policy depended upon.[92]

The greatest of all the practical impediments to expansion of the army was the shortage of money. The government's plan, even taken at face value, appeared to have only modest financial support in place for the program proposed by the White Paper. It totalled only 2.5 percent real growth each year, plus "bumps" of indeterminate size to cover major capital acquisitions. Even the reality of the growth was questionable. The Conservative government had abandoned the defence-specific deflator used to estimate the effect of inflation on military goods, and had instead adopted the Gross National Expenditure deflator, which was lower. According to analysts, this had led to an actual decrease in defence spending in 1987-88, rather than the 1.2 percent increase claimed by the government. There also did not appear to be adequate provision for the huge capital program being planned because it seemed unlikely that more than one project could be "bumped" at any one time, whereas the White Paper called for many concurrent projects. One commentator concluded: "The prospects are grim for attaining a level of equipment expenditure that will provide a credible military capability to meet current commitments. This in turn raises the question of the credibility of the policy itself."[93]

The most devastating critique of the policy's affordability came from Buzz Nixon, the former deputy minister of the department. Nixon wholeheartedly agreed with the direction the Conservative government had taken. To him, the "clarion call" of *Challenge and Commitment*'s recognition of security and defence as a primary responsibility of government was "the most profound CHANGE of the Defence White Paper." He feared, however, that the White Paper had actually increased the commitment/capability gap by increasing military commitments while providing inadequate resources. He noted that major army equipment projects had not been mentioned, notably the multi-billion dollar command, control, and communication system, the replacement of army helicopters, and the acquisition of an attack helicopter. The cost of increasing the Reserves to 90,000 was "the biggest sleeper." He estimated that to increase the Reserves, the Regular Force would also have to be increased by about 9,000 to provide instruction and administrative staff. The current budget for a Reserve Force of 22,000 was about $400 million, with only $62 million for capital equipment. Nixon estimated that a force of 90,000 would cost $1.6 billion, with a capital cost of $1 billion annually. Admitting that these sums might seem "outrageous," he explained that if the Reserves were to be ready – that is, trained and equipped – to be deployed on short notice, they would need the same equipment at the same scale of issue as the Regular Force. If the Regular Force needed 250 tanks, the Militia would need 1,000. The same logic would apply to other equipment as well. Nixon noted the actual decreases in the defence budget and estimated that to support the White Paper force, the defence budget would have to be $23 billion a year. This would require 5.3 percent real growth for fifteen years, making the total defence expenditure $240 billion over that period. This did not seem to relate to the rest of the government's budget, and he thought it would be extremely optimistic to expect greater than 4 percent real growth. Even this would require a cut of $25 billion in the implied spending plans. He did not think that the increase in the Reserve Force could possibly be met unless the National Defence Act was amended to provide call-out, obligatory training, job protection, and possibly a pension for reservists. The 16 percent annual growth in the Reserves projected by the White Paper would therefore prove unrealizable, but even a more realistic 8 percent expansion would be unaffordable, with personnel costs cannibalizing the capital equipment budget. Nixon's worst-case scenario was that the government would set out to implement its White Paper and would contract for the construction of the nuclear submarines. It would become evident that even 4 percent growth was unrealizable, but by that time abandoning the submarines would prove to be costly, a waste, and an embarrassment. All other capital projects would be constrained or eliminated, and Reserve programs would go by the board. "The managing of the defence program would then be absolute chaos."[94]

Nixon had overestimated the actual scope of the intended expenditure, at least in the case of the army. The army's personnel cost estimates grew steadily and levelled off at about $2 billion a year, Regular and Reserve. The Regular Force army was projected to grow from about 23,000 to just over 27,000. The Reserves would expand from 15,500 soldiers to almost 51,000. Ignoring the warnings of their staff, budget planners did not make any allowance for attrition in forecasting the cost of Militia expansion. The peak expenditure on Militia personnel was projected to be only $300 million a year. The army also did not intend to equip the Militia to anything like the same standard as the Regular

Force. Plans included 250 new tanks but no new tank was planned for the Militia, although the 114 Leopard tanks would be retained. Except for the new light armoured vehicle, it is not evident that the army intended to purchase much additional equipment for the Militia. Even so, the army forecast capital expenditures of over $20 billion over the fifteen-year planning period.[95]

The army's plan was therefore suspect. It depended on a massive expansion of the Militia to support the "big army," but the government had not provided the legislative or policy basis for a larger, much more ready Reserve. Nor were funds available to equip, or even recruit and retain, a much larger force. If the government had maintained its course, the Regular Force army would have emerged larger and better equipped, but the Militia would likely have persisted as a marginally trained, underequipped component. In any case, events intervened and the entire plan collapsed.

Government financial support for the program outlined in the White Paper had been weak from the outset. Dewar had been unable to get the Department of Finance to agree to a funding level of at least 4 percent real growth annually. In the end, Beatty had been forced to accept a vague financial position. By early 1989 the government was under considerable financial pressure and the defence budget became a major target for cuts. By then Bill McKnight had replaced Beatty as minister. The chief of the defence staff, General Paul Manson, presented options to the government ranging from zero growth in some years to 4 percent, but knew that the latter was wildly impossible given the circumstances. Canadian budgets are developed under strict secrecy, with few departmental officials involved. In this case, not even the Command commanders were brought into the loop. All three commanders were shocked and felt betrayed by the extent of the cuts.[96]

The effect of the April 1989 budget on the army was severe. The government attempted to cancel the division commitment to the Central Front, but was compelled to reverse the decision within two weeks because there had been no consultation with allies and the prime minister would have to face the wrath of NATO colleagues at a summit meeting in May. The tank project office established to purchase the tank authorized in the White Paper was disbanded. The command, control, and communications project originally intended to outfit an expeditionary division was severely curtailed to equip only 4CMBG and only with field radios, leaving the division without modern communications. The light armoured vehicle and related vehicle projects were cut back or placed on hold.[97]

The budgetary reverses were reinforced by policy shifts due to a dramatic change in the international climate. As with the shaky finances behind the White Paper, there had been numerous warnings of a major change in relations with the Soviet Union, where General Secretary Mikhail Gorbachev had begun a fundamental reform program of *glasnost* (openness), *perestroika* (restructuring), and *demokratizatsiya* (democratization) in 1985 with the announcement that the Soviet economy had stalled and reorganization was needed. In April that year, he suspended the deployment of SS-20 intermediate-range nuclear missiles in Europe, and in May he replaced Andrei Gromyko with Eduard Shevardnadze as minister of foreign affairs. In January 1986 he proposed the elimination of intermediate-range nuclear weapons in Europe and a strategy for eliminating all nuclear weapons by 2000. He also began to withdraw troops from Afghanistan and Mongolia. A few months after the Canadian White Paper was released, Gorbachev and President Reagan signed the Intermediate-Range Nuclear Forces Treaty. The policy of a "big army" had arrived just as the need for one dissipated.

Examining the situation, the Senate Special Committee on National Defence proposed radical solutions. The inability to fund the announced White Paper program and international changes that called into question the necessity for huge conventional forces seemed to the senators to be an "unexpected opportunity" to reconsider the Canadian contribution to NATO Europe. They proposed that the government consider restructuring the Canadian army as either a "defensive defence" formation that would have great anti-armour capability but limited mobility, or a more conventional air-mobile brigade. Either option would be cheaper than the White Paper force and would, they thought, make a significant contribution to NATO. The senators commented that National Defence was "in a state of confusion" and that they were concerned by the "apparent lack of coherence in current defence planning." They asked whether Canadians – or the government – were still persuaded that a major conflagration in Europe was in the offing.[98]

The army, however, clung to its plans as far as funding would allow. The 1 Canadian Division was activated in Germany on 30 November 1989. It was now modelled on a "Division '89" structure of 12,518 soldiers, not all of whom were stationed in Europe. It was to be a "come-as-you-are" division, with no planned growth, and remained as the Central Army Group reserve. The army was now aiming to create general-purpose forces at an "acceptable" level, which were "affordable" and which concentrated on "achievable" aims. This was known as the "Triple A Army."[99]

Corps '96 and the Collapse of Combat Development

For a few brief months, policy, concepts, and doctrine were all in alignment. This was the period from June 1987, when *Challenge and Commitment* was published, to April 1989, when the budget foreclosed any possibility that a big army would be constructed. In November 1987 the chief land doctrine and operations published *Land Formations in Battle,* one of the keystone manuals of the Canadian army. The manual dealt with the tactical handling of formations in battle and was naturally based on the corps as the fundamental organizational unit. It stated:

> Recently, the Canadian army instituted a combat development process to determine future organizations, equipment, and doctrine. This was a logical step given the absence of recent wartime experience to guide force development. As a result of the combat development process, it has been determined that land forces executing sustained operations against a sophisticated enemy must do so within the context of a corps organization, as it is at this level that all combat functions are satisfied. Thus one or more corps, supported by other formations and units as well as army level troops, will form the basis of forces committed to a future conflict. It is therefore imperative that professional officers have a thorough understanding of the planning and conduct of operations by corps, divisions, and brigades, as it is unlikely that there will be time to develop this expertise in a crisis, it is to this end that this publication has been written.[100]

The manual presented the NATO and US Army concept of concurrent engagement of all echelons of the attacking force and stated that the central concept was to detect and engage the enemy in depth. This would disrupt enemy plans and gain time to destroy their first echelon and follow-on forces. Following the Corps '86 concept, holding ground and attrition of the enemy were more prominent than manoeuvre. In defence, a commander must designate his vital ground – "that ground which if lost makes the defence untenable." He would then identify the main approaches and the key terrain that dominated or blocked them. Commanders would then select the terrain to be held and task their subordinates accordingly. This procedure would be carried out by all levels of command. "Vital ground must be held or, if lost, recaptured by forces of a higher formation." There was no discussion of own-force deep operations, even though this had seemed central to the overall concept. The battle was to be fought behind a barrier, usually a natural obstacle close to the forward edge of the battle area. The manual did allow for the corps commander to engage the enemy at the maximum distance, using battlefield air interdiction and long-range artillery.[101]

During the late 1980s, the army seemed resistant to making any changes in its concept and doctrine development processes. The Army Doctrine and Tactics Board rejected a proposal to actually conduct a field trial of tank-hunting doctrine that would generate hard data on the effectiveness of techniques and not be reliant on the professional judgment of participants. Rather than acquire or borrow laser designators that would allow fire to be actually registered on targets, the board decided that the Directorate of Land Operational Research should conduct a library search to see whether allies had done anything similar and prepare an article for the *Doctrine Bulletin*.[102] It was equally uninterested in reforming the management of the overall process. The army studied the US and British Army doctrine development systems and found that both of them were organized around a single senior commander who could ensure that teaching remained consistent with doctrinal developments while at the same time doctrine writers responded to the demands of the teachers. The paper reporting on the study proposed putting the Canadian process under the control of the commander of the Combat Training Centre at CFB Gagetown, New Brunswick, but no decision was made and the proposal died.[103]

The Corps '96 process thus proceeded untroubled, and was completed in the narrow window between policy approval and collapse. The Corps '96 system study was published in February 1987, but the close combat studies were not completed until October 1991, long after the policy that supported them had been abandoned.[104] The army planners had managed to keep their formations smaller than those of Corps '86 by creating an entire "echelon above corps" to provide logistic support to the deployed corps. This implied that the entire Canadian *army* could be sent overseas. If anything, it added to the unreality of the exercise.[105]

Corps '96 dealt with the concepts of the operational level of war and manoeuvre in a hesitant manner. The operational level was defined only as "the manoeuvre of large formations generally at army group/corps level to secure strategic goals within the NATO theatres."[106] The concept of planning campaigns to implement a series of operations to achieve strategic aims was only implicit. Moreover, the concept of "operations" was confined to large formations only, rather than being considered part of an "operational art" that might be relevant to small units. The concept was somewhat better (if not much more fully) defined in the later synopsis of the System Study as "the connecting link between strategy and tactics" and "the positioning or displacement of formations to attain military strategic objectives within a theatre of operations."[107]

Manoeuvre was an equally difficult topic for the Corps '96 planners. They acknowledged that NATO, being greatly outnumbered, could not win a battle of attrition and would have to disrupt a Soviet attack and then counterattack and go on the offensive by "offensive manoeuvre action against the enemy's depth." The ability to act faster than the enemy could respond was "of paramount importance," but how this was to be achieved was never discussed. The concept only said vaguely that "manoeuvre is generally characterized more by movement than by fire. At this level [the corps], the concept is based on a particular strategy, the application of principles of war and the specific relationship to a particular threat."

Corps '96 argued that even at the corps level, formations had to be structured as either offensive or defensive, but could not be both. It therefore chose to structure its corps around a defensive mission. Not coincidentally, this matched the army's bias towards attrition warfare.[108]

The combat organization that Corps '96 designed was a heavy mechanized infantry force with several layers of anti-armour weapons with which to absorb and defeat an assault by a Soviet operational manoeuvre group. As in Corps '86, the key concept of the battle for the main defensive area was to have infantry hold defensive positions while armoured forces manoeuvred. To do this, the infantry would have to be protected from newer Soviet ammunition, which could penetrate armoured personnel carriers. Corps '96 therefore proposed that armoured personnel carriers be entrenched and constructed with heavy overhead cover to provide protection during enemy preparatory bombardment. The infantry could dismount and fight from their positions when the cover lifted, assisted by heavy weapons fire from the entrenched vehicle. Movement would be achieved by providing high-speed entrenching equipment to prepare alternate positions.[109]

An "infantry manoeuvre vehicle" was recommended for transporting the infantry, who would fight dismounted and provide fire support against enemy infantry, light armoured vehicles, and attack helicopters. Corps '96 considered the infantry fighting vehicles operated by the Germans, British, and Americans but rejected them as too costly, too complex, carrying too few troops, and contributing to "an alarming degradation of fundamental infantry skills." The proposed vehicle, "APC 96," would have an engine and running gear that would enable it to manoeuvre with main battle tanks – a somewhat irrelevant requirement for a vehicle that would spend most of its time dug in. It would not be protected against tank fire, but would be sufficiently armoured so as not to be damaged by light armour vehicle kinetic energy rounds (about 30 mm cannon). It would be self-entrenching and nuclear/biological/chemical-protected, and would have a crew of ten. Its armament would be capable of defeating the Soviet BMP-2 infantry fighting vehicle's armour at six hundred metres. An illustration of the proposed vehicle was essentially an M113 with a bulldozer blade and a preposterously small turret, thus solving the main design conflict over trading armament for crew space in the rejected infantry fighting vehicle.

The System Study also proposed to equip the Canadian corps with a tank destroyer, as had Corps '86. This would free the tanks for mobile use. The tank destroyer would mount a 120 mm gun on a tank chassis. It would be retained as a formation resource and allocated to battle groups that were assumed to be on the main enemy axis of advance.[110]

Once again, the army had determined that it would fight with tactics and equipment quite different from those of any of Canada's allies, equipment that did not yet exist and for which no field trials or experiments had been conducted. Because the organizational units were arbitrarily designed around heavy and light divisions and an independent mechanized infantry brigade group, the prospect for reusing parts of the work appeared higher than for Corps '86. But the mismatch with allied doctrine and the construction of the core heavy infantry concept around non-existent equipment did not bode well.

The Corps '96 concept was not without its critics. The Canadian Land Force Command and Staff College published a paper that criticized Canadian doctrine for the defensive battle as exhibiting a "brick wall" mentality. It accused the army of being excessively infantry-oriented and lacking the "flexibility of mind" and mobility required to fight on a high-intensity battlefield. Even with the "excesses" of the large formations in Corps '86, Staff College exercises using Canadian doctrine had left commanders hard-pressed to retain adequate reserves with which to mount counterattacks. Without a change in doctrine, the Staff College argued that the Canadian army would become involved in "attrition warfare at best and defeat at worst."[111]

Reality did begin to impinge on the combat development process after the 1991 Gulf War. Major-General Gordon Reay, the chief land doctrine and operations, told the Army Doctrine and Tactics Board that although there had been a period when combat development was perceived as theory without application in the real world, "we are not at a stage where this is true and we have seen a perfect example with Op[eration] Desert Storm." As the army moved away from the Corps '86 and Corps '96 cycles and considered contingency operations, it would have to work out new doctrine, which would have to be joint in nature.[112] The army also decided to cancel a series of novel-like combat narratives intended to realistically portray a combat environment to junior officers because the Third World War scenario on the Central Front in Europe had been "overtaken by changing political realities." The next volume, describing the mobilization of the Canadian army in the 1990s to meet treaty obligations and for territorial defence was deemed to have "only a historical significance."[113]

It was not until May 1994, however, that the entire Corps project came to an end. The officer community finally revolted at the thirty-fifth meeting of the Army Doctrine and Tactics Board when it appeared that Corps '96 was going to move from an approved concept to a full set of doctrinal publications. The board openly criticized the current manuals, based on Corps '86, as unrealistic and irrelevant. Instead, it called for the wholesale adoption of US

Army operational doctrine and abandonment of Corps '96. If felt that basing Canadian doctrine on a formation of 186,000 personnel was nonsensical: "A generation of officers has had to memorize this fantastic, massive, conceptual formation, knowing that they would be working with completely different equipment and organizations in real life. Is it any wonder that doctrine has lost credibility?"[114] According to the board, Corps '86 did not reflect missions assigned to the Land Force, and basing the army's post–Cold War mission on the ability to defeat a Soviet combined arms army on a front of forty kilometres was questionable. Canadian doctrine did not recognize information-age technology (unlike the US Army), nor did it adequately deal with the operational level of war.

In fact, except for the combat development and doctrine development processes, the army had abandoned the corps concept and all that went with it by 1991. By then, new government policy and new structures were emerging that appeared more realistic and affordable.

The Army "Shirks"

What then are we to make of the army's twenty-year quest to be big? In the beginning, in the mid-1970s, it might have been construed as an attempt to provide legitimate professional advice and policy options to the political level. After the 1979 decision that the combat development process would not be constrained by either policy or resources but would be "pure," this claim became increasingly dubious. The army spent the balance of the time designing a force to please itself, not one designed to implement the policy elected officials had determined. During Perrin Beatty's tenure as minister, policy and combat development returned (mostly) into alignment. Even here, however, one can question whether the army had adequately discharged its professional duty to provide advice to the minister. The army supported plans that it should have known were completely unaffordable. Even if realized, the 1987 White Paper force would have been only distantly related to the conceptual designs. Moreover, the army appeared content to allow the government to adopt a force structure plan completely dependent on large numbers of reservists at a much higher state of training and readiness than had ever been achieved in practice. The available record does not provide a definitive answer to the question of whether the army counselled against this course, but it would appear that the army believed it could be like the "Little Engine Who Could," who made it up the hill with his train by chanting "I think I can, I think I can." To the extent that the army did not strongly warn the political level that building a "big army" would cost much more than was budgeted and require significant policy changes in the conditions of service of the Militia, it failed in its professional duty.

American political scientist Peter Feaver has proposed a theory of civil-military relations according to which civilian politicians are seen as "principals" and the military as their "agents." According to this theory, civilians "have a right to be wrong." In a democracy, it is unambiguous that the civil authority is supreme. According to Feaver, the poles of the civil-military relationship are "working" and "shirking." "Working is doing things the way civilians want, and shirking is doing things the way those in the military want."[115] There can be little doubt that the entire combat development process amounted to shirking.

Civilians must also bear some of the blame for two decades of wasted effort. The Defence Management Committee was well aware of what the army was doing and made it plain that it was not prepared to pay for the designs that the army was preparing. Yet none of the deputy ministers or ministers ever called the army to account, and NDHQ was apparently willing to let the army not only prepare plans but also educate its entire officer corps on the basis of a model that did not meet the needs of policy. The Management Review Group report had been the 1970s' response to armed services that were not heeding civilian direction. During the 1980s, the only discipline that was applied was the withholding of funds.

The army paid a price in the diversion of scarce staff resources to work on a theoretical problem that produced no practical result. In the interim, staff projects that were required to support real commitments in the real world were not given adequate resources. The price would be paid in the form of confused and even failed operations.

CHAPTER SEVEN

The Unified Staff and Operational Difficulties

WHEN THE ARMED SERVICES were unified in the mid-1960s, relatively little thought was given to the command and control of forces in the field or to expeditionary operations. This was perhaps not surprising because the dominant assumption was that Canadian forces abroad would invariably come under alliance control. The new organization evolved, rather than being designed from an explicit concept. To the extent that there was an implicit model behind the organization, it was that there would be a single, unified national headquarters directing different commands structured to plan and mount operations. The operational commands would be supported by integrated support services for communications, logistics, and personnel. Mobile Command, as designed by Major-General Roger Rowley and approved by Lieutenant-General J.V. Allard, conformed to this model.[1] Mobile Command was responsible for preparing plans and operational requirements; formulating, testing, and documenting tactical doctrine and operational procedures; planning, conducting, and analyzing assigned operations; and organizing, training, and equipping assigned land and air forces.

The evolutionary process did not produce organizations with robust operational staffs, however. Instead, the commands became pseudo-services that vied with National Defence Headquarters for national control of policy and resources. The three-star level of the different commanders gave them the appearance of service chiefs, and they were, in fact, the senior sailor, soldier, and aviator. Although the Task Force on Review of Unification of the Canadian Forces had discussed "command and control," the discussion revolved around the ability of the commanders to influence policy. The army complained about the lack of a "common, well-defined staff system," but this appeared to be more about a perception of excessive civilian control rather than any specific operational problem.[2] The planning and control of operations was simply not a major issue for the Canadian Forces as the major operational elements were directed by NATO and NORAD.

The integrated staff structures that evolved also focused on national-level issues rather than field operations. The early Materiel Command was merged with the NDHQ Chief of Logistics and Engineering, resulting in an organization that concentrated on procurement and distribution within the peacetime logistic support organization. Douglas Bland concluded in 1987 that there was "no high-level coordination aimed at designing a comprehensive consumer-oriented supply system for war."[3] Given the lack of political support for mobilization beyond rounding out standing forces, this was not a surprising result. Nevertheless, although the system that had evolved was sufficient to meet relatively static NATO commitments, it was not adequate for planning or controlling expeditionary operations, as events in the 1980s would demonstrate.

Cracks in the system became evident in the closing years of the 1970s. Mobile Command was dissatisfied with how the central personnel management system responded to mobilization requirements during the semi-annual NATO WINTEX exercises. It noted a "paralysis in the planning process" and was equally critical of overall government policy that was not supportive of the massive mobilization that it saw as necessary.[4] Additional concern was caused by RENDEZVOUS 81 (RV 81), a division-level Mobile Command exercise that had been delayed for two years because the Forces had lost the ability to conduct a strategic movement of forces within Canada, let alone an overseas deployment. An ad hoc organization had to be created to deploy Mobile Command units to Canadian Forces Base Gagetown, where the exercise took place.[5]

NDHQ toiled for the next two and a half years to develop a command-and-control policy, apparently hampered by legal considerations raised by the judge advocate general's staff that the chief of the defence staff's authority to command was unclear. Issues were not resolved until April 1983, when a final command-and-control policy was issued, clarifying the role of the CDS as the senior military adviser to the minister, who was responsible to the minister for the "effective conduct of operations" and for the readiness of the Canadian Forces. The policy explicitly stated that the CDS exercised command over the Forces and was permitted to delegate his command.[6]

The CDS, General C.G.E. Thériault, believed that he had two main responsibilities: to develop and maintain a system that matched people and technology to the operational needs of the forces, and to maintain workable operational plans. Unfortunately, it was apparent to him that unification had failed in that no staff or system had been created to support the CDS as a unified commander. This problem had been exacerbated by the resurgence of the service commands, which had blurred relationships. In Thériault's mind, there was no such thing as an "environmental command." Nevertheless, Mobile Command had strongly promoted the army and a command role for itself. Thériault regarded this as a bureaucratic ploy to justify the Command's existence as it had no clear operational role. He believed that "people were working to create commitments and to enhance their positions in divergence of the law and the reality of the position and resources of the CF."[7]

Continuing difficulties led Thériault to commission a study on the functions and organization of the Deputy Chief of the Defence Group at NDHQ. The study was led by newly retired Major-General Dan Loomis, who had recently served as chief of program. Loomis reviewed the problems encountered by the WINTEX exercises, which had identified deficiencies in NDHQ's ability to support the national government effectively in case of a NATO war. He also cited another national crisis management command post exercise, BOLD STEP '84.[8] According to him, attempting to manage a wartime crisis completely upset the internal operations of NDHQ, requiring the chief land doctrine and operations (CLDO) to take over organization and establishment issues from the assistant deputy minister (personnel). The DCDS Group overrode the vice chief and chief of program regarding resource allocation, and decisions normally made by the Program Control Board were made by the operational (and more junior) Battle Staff. Loomis concluded that these changes "bring into doubt the validity of our current organization. That is, if the peacetime organization is not valid in an emergency, then it should be changed so it can cope with an emergency."

Loomis also pointed to specific problems with the command and control of land forces: duplication of effort between Mobile Command HQ and NDHQ; Mobile Command's not being permitted to manage its own resources, resulting in problems in manning, equipping, and tasking land forces; abuse of the chain of command; and a feeling in Mobile Command that it was merely the custodian of army resources. The national supply system had bypassed Mobile Command and had not allowed the army to set controls or priorities in support of its operations and plans.

Loomis noted that under the forces-in-being concept, mobilization had not been an issue and the existing staff system had been adequate. However, with the expectation of expansion and prolonged sustainment of forces, the status quo no longer appeared viable. The key problem was that "most professionals in uniform" viewed the ranking officer (i.e., the command commanders) as "head of service," whereas NDHQ viewed itself not as a joint headquarters but as a unified headquarters exercising command over a single, unified force. No friend of unification, Loomis recommended that the role of commanders as heads of services be recognized. He was uneasy, however, that without an integrated staff agency overseeing the services, the three environmental commands would continue to present budget-busting plans and judge resource requirements on a service priority rather than national basis. (In a background paper, he had condemned the "parochialism" of the services' pursuit of their own programs to the detriment of the department's overall interests, and the resulting lack of credibility of defence plans throughout the government.[9]) Loomis therefore recommended a strong DCDS branch to control all war structures and plans.[10]

He also recommended a balance between environmental and central staffs in order to bring both enough service-specific expertise into NDHQ while ensuring that the CDS exercised effective control while avoiding the "retrograde step" of devolution to three separate services. This would require upgrading of the ranks of chiefs of maritime, land, and air operations within the headquarters and an effort to select and train officers who would have "the broader perspectives required" by service on a central staff.[11] Loomis tilted towards the central staff, stressing that environmental staff at NDHQ would only provide advice. His proposed terms of reference for the CLDO were somewhat ambiguous, however. This chief was termed the "senior army advisor in National Defence Headquarters for policy, training standards and doctrine" and was "responsive, where appropriate" to the commander of Mobile Command, implying that he was a Mobile Command official. It was clear, however, that he worked for the deputy chief of the defence staff and was responsible for preparing the army portion of the CDS's Operational Planning Directive to Commanders.[12]

The Loomis study did not resolve the problem of control of operations, and the contest between Mobile Command and NDHQ continued unabated. Familiar problems surfaced with the next major exercise, BRAVE LION, in 1986. BRAVE LION was the first live exercise actually deploying the Canadian Air-Sea Transportable (CAST) Brigade Group overseas to Norway, although previous exercises had been conducted in Canada and CAST had been a significant part of the WINTEX command post exercises. Planning this exercise, which tested a commitment on the books since 1968, took two years. During the planning phase, Mobile Command complained to NDHQ that the time had come to appoint a national exercise commander because there were significant decisions on hold. This sparked a rejoinder from the director general military plans and operations (DGMPO) at NDHQ that the DCDS was the officer controlling the exercise and therefore the "national exercise commander." The memo stated that Mobile Command had been represented throughout the planning by the chief of land doctrine and operations, implying that Mobile Command was the one that didn't have its act together. The DGMPO suggested that Mobile Command direct any additional questions through the CLDO, and twisted the knife further by adding that although NDHQ staff had offered to brief Mobile Command, the briefing "for various reasons" had not taken place. According to the DGMPO, Air Command had found this briefing very useful.[13]

The exercise identified a long list of planning and staff deficiencies. The existing contingency plan was rudimentary, and plans to support CAST with reinforcements, casualty evacuation, and logistics did not exist. An ad hoc logistics group was formed for the exercise, although the management of logistic support had been practised as part of the WINTEX command post exercises. The CF-5 fighter squadrons – the Rapid Reaction Squadrons – that were part of CAST were not integrated into the command structure, and even the helicopters were not integrated into the deployed brigade headquarters. Instead, a separate Aviation Wing (which did not include the CF-5 fighters) was set up and its headquarters co-located with that of the brigade. The post-exercise report commented that it would be "unwise to attempt to report on problems related to the overall organization and command and control at NDHQ and its relationship to commands," and that "weaknesses in methods by which the way NDHQ addresses crisis management are most important and can be dealt with discreetly." Sean Maloney has suggested that the discretion of the analysts was due to the fact that the CDS, General Thériault, was trying to move out of NATO's Central Region and concentrate the Canadian Forces on Norway during this period.[14]

The official pronouncements on BRAVE LION proclaimed that it was a success and that "remedial action should not be a major problem."[15] Nevertheless, the command-and-control structure remained fractured. Operation Bandit, a plan to extract from Haiti Canadian citizens who were threatened by the 1987 collapse of the Duvalier regime, ended in confusion. In the opinion of Vice-Admiral Charles Thomas, "NDHQ [did] not have the capability to plan a multidimensional operation ... Operation Bandit proved conclusively that the Canadian Forces does not have a [command, control and communications] system and future attempts to conduct similar operations will be severely hampered until this deficiency is resolved. Also, a system which activates the logistics network in response to short notice operational requirements must be developed."[16]

Operation Bandit also revealed a lack of coordination between the military and the political level. The CDS, Paul Manson, had attempted to quietly move Canadian troops to the Caribbean under cover of naval participation in a US Navy fleet exercise. Although Prime Minister Brian Mulroney and Defence Minister Perrin Beatty orally approved his actions, no official direction followed in writing, causing the suspension of any additional contingency preparations. External Affairs remained opposed to doing much at all, being "nervous" about press leaks, which were endemic throughout the operation. Overall, the politicians did not appear to have a clear appreciation of either the forces that would be required to extract Canadians from Haiti or the lead time that military preparations would require. In his diary Manson noted: "It was amazing to me that after 15 years we still do not have a good idea of how NDHQ would operate in war, nor with what resources. DM and I decided to commission a study (yet another!)."[17]

Similarly, the attempt to contribute a Canadian contingent to the United Nations Iran-Iraq Military Observer Group (UNIIMOG) in August 1988 revealed the degree of unpreparedness for contingency operations. The Special Service Force (SSF) Headquarters and Signal Squadron was selected for this assignment, but it received no statement of aim, no discussion of scope, no terrain analysis, and no maps. Apparently, SSF commanders and staff used a *National Geographic* map in their initial planning. The difficulties in planning this operation did lead to improvements at NDHQ, where the National Defence Operations Centre was strengthened.[18]

As noted, the frustrations of these operations resulted in yet another study: "The Functions and Organization of National Defence Headquarters in Emergencies and War," which was under the direction of the deputy minister and the chief of the defence staff, with Lieutenant-General John de Chastelain as the study director. The substantive work was carried out by Major-General W.E.R. Little and Mr. S.P. Hunter (hence the report was known as the "Little-Hunter" study). The study addressed the same problem as the Loomis study – who was in charge of operations – and also attempted to address resource management issues. The report appeared to be an uneasy balancing act between its authors, who appeared to favour de-unifying NDHQ, and its sponsors – de Chastelain and Deputy Minister Bev Dewar – who had ruled that out in the terms of reference. The authors suggested that de-unification would be a good thing by pointing out that although plans existed for NDHQ in war to some extent, these did not include the department. The authors also identified the support groups at NDHQ as problems. The Assistant Deputy Minister (Materiel) Group was found to have an unclear role in logistic support of deployed forces, while the Assistant Deputy Minister (Personnel) Group's proposal to create a recruiting and training command in war but not in peace was deemed problematic. The report complained that "there was a lack of precision" in the defence planning and force development process as it overlapped both policy formulation and program control, thus condemning both the assistant deputy minister (policy) and the vice chief of the defence staff by implication. The central dilemma identified by Loomis – that of the DCDS Group "try[ing] to represent each environment while trying to act as a unified staff" – was blamed squarely on the decision to maintain a unified NDHQ. Little and Hunter nevertheless concluded that there were no problems with the functions and structures of the existing organization that warranted drastic change, and dismissed problems between civil and military staff as "squabbles."

Little and Hunter did not think that the DCDS Group was effectively structured to offer the CDS "purple" or joint advice. Whereas the DM and the CDS needed "clear environmental advice," the team shied away from recommending that the Command commanders be installed at NDHQ. According to them, this would result in "probable overweighting on the environmental side," an "adverse effect" on the civil-military balance at NDHQ, and the weakening of command in the field, and would create both the risk of rank inflation and a perception of de-unification.

The study therefore recommended a "balanced" approach, in which the environmental staffs at NDHQ would become the representatives of the environmental commanders. The staff would be environmentally badged and would provide advice to the main decision-making committees at NDHQ. The DCDS would provide "purple advice," including advice on combined and joint operations, doctrine, and plans, and would also perform the functions of the principal operational staff officer at the headquarters.[19] The decision to adopt this arrangement represented another step in the re-emergence of the individual services and the rise of the commander of Mobile Command from a subordinate to a near-equal of the CDS.

The first test of the new staff system occurred during the Gulf War. The 2 August 1990 invasion of Kuwait by Iraq directly threatened not only world oil supplies but also the entire balance of power in the Middle East. An aggressive Iraq might not be sated by absorbing Kuwait, but might be tempted to swallow up Saudi Arabia, which, although larger, did not look much stronger. The UN swiftly passed Resolutions 660 and 661 calling for Iraqi withdrawal or the imposition of economic sanctions. Canada's initial response was to deploy a naval task group on 24 August, followed by a CF-18 squadron and a company of the Royal Canadian Regiment to act as its security detail. The United States launched its Operation Desert Shield, the British Operation Granby, and the French Opération Daguet, which moved four American divisions, one British armoured brigade, and one French light infantry division to Saudi Arabia by mid-September. Sometime around this date, Canadian officers at NATO headquarters were contacted by British Army representatives and asked whether Canada could provide a brigade under British control to form a Commonwealth Division in the Gulf.[20]

The Canadian army was cool to the idea of being under British command, but it seemed probable that the army could at least be asked to determine the feasibility of sending ground forces to the Gulf. Apparently, Mobile Command began an independent staff check or feasibility study on 26 October.[21] The DCDS completed his own staff check on 13 November, and informed the CDS that the army could man, deploy, and prepare an operationally ready brigade group, but that there were "problem areas." Interestingly, despite the recommendations of the Little-Hunter study, the DCDS contemplated giving the detailed planning task to Canadian Forces Europe rather than Mobile Command. This was based on the decision to employ 4CMBG as the basis of the brigade. The DCDS, however, recommended that Mobile Command be tasked with planning because Canadian Forces Europe was already heavily involved in the planning of Operation Friction, the naval and air deployment.

The DCDS staff check assumed that 4CMBG would be brought up to war establishment strength through the existing augmentation plan, Operation Pendant. A mechanized infantry battalion and a fourth tank squadron would be added to its strength. It would most likely be integrated into a multi- or bi-national force, but would operate as an entity. Planners assumed that it would be self-contained, with thirty days of combat supplies. They also assumed that third-line logistics and medical support organizations would be established, also based on existing plans.

The first problem area was the expected number of casualties. The Iraqi army was considered to be a battle-hardened, well-equipped force. Using NATO guidelines, planners estimated that the 11,000-personnel force would suffer 16,188 casualties, including 2,397 killed. Of the rest, 5,313 could be returned to action, so 10,875 replacements would be required. An operations research war game produced much lower estimates: 1,000 killed and 3,472 wounded, of which 1,416 could be returned to duty, resulting in a requirement for only 3,052 replacements.

Based on the expected number of casualties, a four-hundred-bed field hospital was required, but none existed in the Canadian Forces. The only available field hospital had only forty beds and could not be expanded to more than one hundred beds. There was not enough medical personnel, and legislation would have been required to call up reservists or civilians.

Other deficiencies included the lack of an intelligence platoon in the brigade, the lack of equipment for nuclear/chemical/biological warfare, a critical shortage of engines and major assembly items such that the brigade could not even be sustained until the end of its acclimatization period without major purchases, limited tank replacements, the need to charter airlift and sealift capacity, and the need for additional funds in the defence budget to pay for the operation.[22]

General de Chastelain followed through the next day, ordering Mobile Command to prepare a plan to assemble and deploy a mechanized brigade group to Saudi Arabia. The plan was to be submitted no later than 23 November. The order adopted the planning assumptions of the DCDS staff check and specified that the brigade be ready to embark forty-five days after the decision to deploy.[23]

The response from Lieutenant-General Kent Foster, the commander of Mobile Command, was positive but not entirely enthusiastic. It was his judgment that the Land Forces could assemble and deploy a brigade group if the assumptions made in his plan were accepted and the deficiencies in capability were made good. He stressed that the plan was nothing more than what had been requested: to assemble and deploy a brigade. According to Foster, the main deficiencies – namely, the need for a replacement tank and the establishment of a medical support group – had already been identified by the DCDS staff. The deployment would use all of the army's Leopard tanks, leaving none for training or sustainment. Foster advocated the procurement of new tanks and improved ammunition that would be capable of defeating the armour on the Iraqis' T-72 tanks. He also noted that the brigade's lack of medium-range anti-armour capability could be addressed by employing additional TOW Under Armour vehicles and improved .50 calibre ammunition that could penetrate the Iraqi BMP-1 infantry fighting vehicle at distances of over 200 metres. The brigade would also need a more capable low-level air defence such as the Javelin surface-to-air missile or the Air Defence Anti-Tank System (ADATS).

To address the deficiency in medical support, Mobile Command increased the requirement to a five-hundred-bed hospital. The plan noted that such a unit was not available in the Canadian Forces and that surgeons and anesthetists were also not available in sufficient numbers. Foster stated that he "remain[ed] very concerned about the lack of aviation in particular for medical evacuation and I am recommending the use of [the UTTH] squadron for medical evacuation at the third line level," even though there would be serious difficulties in sustaining the helicopters for more than fifteen days.

Based on a 35 percent voluntary turnout rate, Mobile Command planners estimated that the Reserves could generate only about 3,300 replacements, a number equal to the low-end casualty estimate. The high end would consume virtually the entire strength of the Militia.[24]

Operation Broadsword was never implemented and the army stayed home. General de Chastelain provided the government with a range of options, from a reinforced mechanized brigade group to units to protect the airfield. The government never provided a rationale for selecting a low level of land force involvement. However, given the high casualty estimates, the almost non-existent level of Canadian third-line medical support, the inadequacy of medevac aviation, and the probable difficulty in using the Militia to generate enough replacements, the decision appears sound. If the US Air Force had not destroyed Iraqi ground forces in one hundred hours, and had the Iraqis fought with reasonable efficiency, the low-end casualty estimates appear realistic. Although allies could have supplied new tanks and significant support to a Canadian brigade, no offers of medical support were made to Canadian planners, as the allies did not believe they possessed surplus capability.[25]

It is important to note that Mobile Command did not produce a complete plan, but more of a second staff check or appreciation of its capability. There is no evidence that the various staffs wasted time vying for control of the operation, as was the case with BRAVE LION. On the other hand, some contend that the staff collectively malfunctioned by loading the requirements with every bell and whistle they could think of, making the project look too immense, complex, and expensive to undertake. Task force operations were still not a matter of routine, and the chief of the defence staff was forced to ask the Australians how it was done.[26] As the army entered the 1990s, it was clear that it had improved its ability to plan expeditionary operations, but the full capability was not yet in place. There was no mature and adequately sized planning staff in place in either Ottawa or St. Hubert. Moreover, Operation Broadsword underlined the materiel deficiencies of the army, especially if the expectation was that it would operate outside of fixed NATO support structures. The "teeth" were not as sharp as they needed to be, and the "tail" had dangerously atrophied. Trying to fix things on the fly would create even greater risks in the coming decade.

The 1990s and the Increasing Pace of Operations

If the 1980s can be considered to be a decade of plans, then the 1990s should be known as the decade of operations. The army campaigned in Canada, Europe, and Africa, and supported minor operations elsewhere around the globe. Of the four major operations, only Oka – the domestic one – was both a tactical and political success. Canadian operations in the former republic of Yugoslavia were tactically successful but revealed shortcomings in personnel management that were politically costly to the army. The Somalia mission succeeded in its operational goals but was a political disaster. The intervention in Central Africa was both a professional and political embarrassment.

Oka

The Oka confrontation was sparked by the decision of the municipal government of Oka, Quebec, to allow the expansion of a golf course onto disputed First Nations land, but the sources of the conflict were more far-reaching and complex than this. Three important Mohawk reserves are clustered at or near the US-Canadian border: Akwesasne, with parts in Quebec, Ontario, and New York; Kanesatake, near the town of Oka; and Kahnawake, on the east side of the St. Lawrence River near Montreal. During the 1970s there had been violent incidents between the elected tribal councils and traditionalist factions; in addition, the Warrior Society advocated outright Mohawk sovereignty and violent confrontation. Mohawk lands straddled the international and provincial/state borders, and Mohawks themselves were exempt from many taxes. Organized crime attempted to profit from illegal cigarette and gasoline sales, which sovereigntists also supported as a way of resisting outside authorities. The New York state government's encouragement of legalized gambling on First Nations land created further division in the community. Elected leaders generally opposed the introduction of gambling facilities, but the Warrior Society supported it as an element of sovereignty. The struggle for community control resulted in violence, including the downing of a US National Guard helicopter. In early 1990 the Canadian army moved a mechanized infantry battalion to Cornwall, Ontario, in anticipation of a request for aid of the civil power that never materialized.[27]

The golf course debate thus took place in a highly volatile atmosphere. Residents of Kanesatake resisting the golf course were advised by the Warrior Society on how to conduct armed resistance. The Sûreté du Québec (provincial police) was called in by the municipality, and an ill-considered police assault on Mohawk positions led to the shooting death of a police corporal. Escalation was swift. Kahnawake residents blocked the Mercier bridge over the St. Lawrence, forcing commuters to make a three-hour detour into and out of Montreal. Weapons and Warrior Society reinforcements flowed into Kanesatake and Mohawk demands included nation-to-nation negotiations, return of Oka land, complete withdrawal of police, and the referral of all issues to the World Court.

The Quebec government refused to negotiate, but the provincial police were unable to handle the situation. There were an estimated two hundred insurgents at Kanesatake and four hundred at Kahnawake. They were equipped with assault rifles, .50 calibre sniper rifles, and light anti-armour weapons. The militants established a trench system, erected obstacles, and established a communications system among the three communities. The confrontation was clearly beyond the capacity of civilian police to contain and had even sparked non-native riots around the Mercier bridge and Kahnawake. On 6 August, the Attorney General of Quebec made a request for aid of the civil power under the National Defence Act.

Unlike all other situations, including war, where the chief of the defence staff is responsible to the minister of national defence, the aid of civil power provisions of the National Defence Act give the CDS the sole power to determine the appropriate military response to a request for aid of the civil power from a provincial government. The CDS is governed by Queen's Regulations and Orders (QR and O's), regulations under the National Defence Act that state, among other things: "The law, that no more force may be used than is necessary, applies at all times; lethal weapons must not be used to prevent or suppress minor disorders or offenses which are not serious, and in no case shall firearms be discharged if less extreme measures will suffice."[28]

The army's response was devised by Brigadier-General J.A. Roy, the commander of 5ᵉ Groupe-brigade méchanisé du Canada, in consultation with the commander of Mobile Command in St. Hubert. The army would respond with a massive display of force, not only to intimidate but also to be able to interpose itself between the various factions. It would take the initiative but would not use arms unless fired upon. In that case, the response would be immediate and "military in nature." The army also planned to use an extensive public relations campaign to keep the population informed.

The army moved 4,400 troops into place on 17 August and began patrolling and squeezing the militants through incremental advances backed by armoured vehicles. The relentless pressure forced the dismantling of barricades on the Mercier bridge on 2 September, and by 6 September the bridge was reopened. At Kanesatake, the perimeter held by the Warriors was continually reduced until all that was left was a single building. The remaining militants staged a riot that allowed several to escape, but fifty were arrested. The army had allowed the militants to withdraw most of their heavy weapons using light aircraft, and only 150 of an estimated 500 weapons were eventually seized.

The army's campaign was a complete success. The display of forceful but non-violent action resolved the situation without further loss of life and gained overwhelming public support for the army. The iconic image of the operation was a press photo of Private Patrick Cloutier in helmet and combat gear in a staring match with a masked Warrior. Press coverage acted as psychological warfare as well as public relations by demonstrating the extent of resources deployed, the resolve and patience of the army, and the futility of prolonging the confrontation in the hope that the army would do anything to increase public sympathy for the Warrior cause. Oka appeared to support the policy that mechanized infantry could play an effective peacekeeping role.

Yugoslavia

Canadian involvement in the stabilization of the former Yugoslavia was the military's longest and most expensive international commitment in the 1990s. The Canadian army began service in the former Yugoslavia in April 1992 as a member of the United Nations Protection Force (UNPROFOR), and continued to December 1995, becoming a member of the NATO Implementation Force (IFOR), which replaced UNPROFOR, until December 1996. Canada then became a member of the NATO Stabilization Force (SFOR) in Bosnia-Herzegovina from 1996 to 2004, and finally a member of the Kosovo Force (KFOR) in 1999.

During this period, over forty thousand Canadian Forces members served in the region. Between 1992 and 1995, eleven of the nine thousand Canadian troops who rotated through UNPROFOR were killed. The mission had considerable tactical success, especially during UNPROFOR, when it served as the force commander's reserve. But UNPROFOR also resulted in two boards of inquiry, a National Investigation Service (NIS) investigation, and two reviews of the NIS investigation. UNPROFOR demonstrated that the army had unresolved problems regarding the conduct of stabilization operations.

UNPROFOR's initial mandate was to disarm and protect the largely Serbian population of four UN Protected Areas in Croatia. The Canadian government supported this mission, not only for humanitarian reasons but also because it regarded involvement in Yugoslavia as part of its commitment to NATO and as a visible sign to NATO that, although Canada was withdrawing from Europe, it was not abandoning it. The 4 Canadian Mechanized Brigade in Lahr, Germany, was selected as the formation to provide the force. The reconnaissance came to the unsurprising conclusion that the several factions in Croatia were heavily armed with the complete range of Soviet equipment short of nuclear weapons, inherited from the Yugoslav National Army. The original plan of Canadian Forces Europe and 4CMB therefore called for a mechanized infantry battalion, including M113 armoured personnel carriers, TOW Under Armour anti-tank vehicles, and Leopard tanks. The UN had other ideas about how a "peacekeeping" force should be equipped, however, and rejected the idea of tanks and heavy equipment. In the end, the tanks were dropped from the force, which consisted of troops from the Royal Canadian Regiment and the Royal 22e Régiment. The force, known as CANBAT 1, was stationed in the UN's Sector West of Croatia.

Canada called its mission Operation Harmony, an example of wishful thinking at best and Orwellian usage at worst. The UN force was intended to ensure that both the Yugoslav National Army and Croatian forces withdrew and removed weapons from the demilitarized zones. There was supposed to be safe return of refugees and a return of the civilian police. It soon became clear, however, that none of these objectives had been met and that neither side was very supportive of an interposition force. The situation deteriorated when Slovenia and Croatia formally left Yugoslavia, virtually forcing Bosnia to declare independence also. This set off ethnic violence and terror in Bosnia-Herzegovina, including the siege of Sarajevo by the Serbs, who declared a Republika Srpska. A fierce contest ensued between Serbs, Croats, and Muslims for control of Sarajevo, a key transportation and political centre. CANBAT 1 was brought in to secure the Sarajevo airport and protect UN and non-governmental organization aid workers. The intervention was successful and CANBAT 1 returned to its original assignment.

Intensification of the war coincided with the replacement of 4CMB troops with a battalion from the Second Battalion of the Princess Patricia's Canadian Light Infantry (2PPCLI) from Winnipeg. Due to the restructuring of the army, 2PPCLI had only 320 soldiers out of its 860-soldier establishment. It was therefore topped up with Militia volunteers drawn from nearly seventy different units. The commanding officer, Lieutenant-Colonel Jim Calvin, put his composite unit through a demanding operational training program in the seventy-five days he had available. Militia soldiers arrived at the unit with basic weapons and physical fitness training but had little familiarity with heavy weapons, and only 385 of the 550 Militia volunteers were accepted by Calvin at the end of the training period.[29] This battalion ("ROTO 2" of CANBAT 1) would see the most intense action of the entire mission.

In June 1993 French Army Lieutenant-General Jean Cot took over as the UNPROFOR commander. His challenge was to restore the situation in the south, where the previous January six thousand Croatian troops had overrun UN forces in Dalmatia and seized the Maslenica Bridge, the airport of the coastal port of Zadar, and the hydroelectric dam at Peruca. Two French peacekeepers had been killed and thirteen wounded, and the French had withdrawn and refused to intervene further in the area. In response, the Serbs had reclaimed their heavy weapons from cantonments, with no interference from the French. Cot determined that the Canadian battalion would be the core of a force to be sent south to police the negotiated withdrawal of the Croatians. The Canadian battle group would be reinforced by two mechanized French companies. Cot's decision required Calvin to split his force of Canadians, thus breaking with Canadian doctrine that national formations were to be kept together. Calvin nevertheless obeyed the order and achieved his redeployment in thirty-six hours, a significant achievement as the less than welcoming Croatians had established numerous roadblocks.[30]

The Canadian troops soon found themselves in a dire situation. They came under mortar fire but could not respond. According to the unit chaplain, the company stationed near the Maslenica Bridge came close to mutiny and began talking about killing their own leadership.[31] They no longer understood what they were to accomplish. The 2PPCLI came under even greater pressure when the Croatians assaulted the village of Medak to eliminate a Serb salient and put their headquarters out of range of Serb gunners. The assault began just as the Canadians were moving up from Serb-held areas to begin implementing the ceasefire agreement. Under the Croatian barrage, they dug in and fortified their positions. Serb counterattacks and retaliatory artillery and missile strikes on Croatian urban areas brought the Croatian offensive to a close, and led to the "Medak Pocket Agreement," under which the Croatians would withdraw to their 9 September start line. The 2PPCLI and its associated French companies were to move forward and occupy the Croatian frontlines.[32]

When the Canadian and French troops attempted to implement the agreement on 15 September, they were met with Croatian small arms and machine gun fire. On the chance that the Croatians had mistaken the UN troops for Serbs, white APCs with large UN flags led the advance of the UN troops to their agreed positions. Croatian fire only increased. For the next fifteen hours the Croatians, using mortars and 20 mm cannon, engaged in a pitched battle with the UN troops. The latter held their positions but had neither the strength nor the mandate to go on the offensive and push the Croatians back, even when it became apparent that the Croatians were ethnically cleansing the Serb villages they had occupied. The UN troops could do little but wait and listen to the explosions and shooting in those villages. Even after the Croatians agreed to a withdrawal, roadblocks backed up by tanks prevented the Canadians from advancing. Calvin called a press conference in front of one of the roadblocks, denouncing the Croatians and demonstrating how they were blocking the UN. His actions caused the Croatians to withdraw – too late to save any Serbs but soon enough to prevent the Croatians from completely covering up what they had done. According to Colonel George Oehring, a Canadian officer who took over as commander of Sector South:

> Medak restored UNPROFOR's credibility resulting in renewed dialogue leading to a local informal cease-fire in November, a more formal and wider one at Christmas, and a "bilateral," universal cease-fire signed at Zagreb on 29 March 1994. Everybody hated us in September 1993. I was stoned and threatened during my first trip to Zadar to meet the Croat commander there. Medak changed all this. The Serbs, right up to my departure a year later, would spontaneously mention *the* resolute fairness of the Canadians at Medak, while the Croats, although grudgingly at first, came to respect the Canadians in Sector South.[33]

The UNPROFOR operations demonstrated that although the army's policy that general-purpose combat troops could handle stabilization operations was tactically correct, it was nevertheless inadequate. It became clear that many soldiers did not understand the government's or the UN's objectives or why they were placed in harm's way and not permitted to respond. Soldiers of all ranks were uncomfortable with a force structure that was too weak to enable them to enforce their will on combatants who were clearly killing civilians, and with rules of engagement that sometimes required them to passively accept being shot at and shelled. Writing after his term as CDS, General Rick Hillier also blamed NDHQ and the Canadian government:

> Those battle groups on the ground in Bosnia, in spite of being a UN mission without clarity, intent or purpose, still could have achieved so much if they had operated boldly. They were, however, enormously constrained in what they were able to do because of the risk-averse approach of both the government and the military in Ottawa ... we had promoted bureaucrats over combat leaders. We put battalions in place on the ground, but because of the nervousness in Ottawa, those units were, more often than not, reluctant to take on missions, slow to carry them out or unable to get approval for them, despite the fact the soldiers would see how necessary they were.

According to Hillier, the Canadian formations were known as "Can'tbat 1" and "Can'tbat 2."[34]

Although the actual record of Canadian units in UNPROFOR appears to belie Hillier's opinion (the 2PPCLI received a Commander-in-Chief's commendation for its Medak Pocket action and other units did not appear to be overly shy about engaging belligerent forces with TOW missiles and heavy weapons),[35] there is no doubt that soldiers of all ranks were uncomfortable about having trained as a combat force but not being allowed to engage in combat. There was also tension over civilian aspects of the mission. Some soldiers did not like non-combat assignments because it was "not what we trained for which was green."[36] Returning UNPROFOR veterans found that the government and the leadership of the department did not want to acknowledge the fact that they had been in combat. This was perhaps the result of a desire to maintain a low profile as the Somalia scandal was playing out (see the following section). Calvin recalled: "We were all very proud of what we did. But when we came home there was no recognition of what we had achieved even though if you talked to anybody in UNPROFOR at that time, they thought we were all bloody heroes. We came back here and it was just – you are done."[37]

There is little doubt that the troops felt that the government had paid them little attention. Upon stepping down as UNPROFOR's first deputy commander, Major-General Robert Gaudreau was quoted by the *Vancouver Sun* as saying: "As a soldier, as a peacekeeper, I felt abandoned by the [Canadian government] team that is supposed to provide us with political guidance." Gaudreau was referring to the lack of a senior Canadian diplomatic representative on the mission and the passive role Canada took regarding the direction of the mission.[38]

A large number of UNPROFOR veterans suffered from mysterious illnesses that they attributed to exposure to contaminated soil used in sandbags in their field fortifications. The Canadian Forces were unprepared to deal with these casualties, which arose from no specific trauma or definable injury. After years of public complaint by veterans who had been denied effective treatment or disability pensions, the Forces finally established a board of inquiry to look into the matter. The Croatia Board of Inquiry, headed by air force Brigadier-General G.E. Sharpe, determined that the cause of the injuries was not environmental contaminants but combat stress. The inquiry resulted in important changes to medical and personnel policy, including the recognition of operational stress as a legitimate illness.[39]

The Yugoslavia stabilization mission also raised questions about leadership style. The National Investigation Service examined the allegations of misconduct and leadership deficiencies in Croatia during Rotation 2. As mentioned earlier, one platoon engaged in mutinous acts, including putting naphtha gas in their warrant officer's coffee in the hope of incapacitating an NCO they found overly aggressive. The NIS investigation itself came into question: it was announced just as the Croatia Board of Inquiry was beginning and the warrant officer involved had been one of the main individuals alleging that the Canadian Forces were ignoring the plight of wounded veterans. The chief of the defence staff was compelled to conduct a special review of the NIS investigation. The review group found that traditional doctrine regarding operational imperatives contributed to the mutinous acts:

> In conventional combat operations it is accepted doctrine that the priority in descending order is mission, own troops, self. This presupposes a clearly understood mission supported not only by the chain of command but also to some extent the Government and ultimately the people of Canada [Clausewitz's social trinity] ... Given the issues presumed to be at stake during the Cold War the Canadian Forces trained to this standard for over 40 years. The difficulty is that during the types of operations to which the CF was committed in the 1990s missions were virtually never clear cut, the chain of command was not uniquely Canadian, Rules of Engagement were ambiguous and Canadian endorsement of the mission, either formally through the Government or in terms of Canadian public opinion, was often tenuous. [Equally important, no vital Canadian interests were at stake.] In these circumstances dogmatic adherence to war fighting doctrine remains inappropriate and unlikely to receive sustained support by subordinates.[40]

It took the rest of the decade for the army to work through the issues raised by stabilization missions, and even then many of them remained unresolved. These included not only the "mission, own troops, self" principle but also the need for greater knowledge of the languages and cultures of operational areas; the ethics of orders to treat belligerents evenhandedly while they were committing immoral or criminal acts; vague objectives and rules of engagement; and ambiguous political support both domestically and internationally.

The army's Yugoslavia problems did not end with CANBAT 1. CANBAT 2 (Operation Cavalier) also experienced difficulties with troop discipline and was the subject of several summary investigations and a board of inquiry. The breakdown occurred during the October 1993 to May 1994 rotation of a composite battle group from 5ᵉ Groupe-brigade mécanisé du Canada (5GBMC) based on 12ᵉ Régiment blindé du Canada (12RBC). The battle group contained A Company of the Royal 22ᵉ Régiment (R22ᵉR – the Van Doos). It was part of UNPROFOR's Bosnia-Herzegovina Command and was tasked with the security of the Muslim enclave of Srebrenica and security patrols around the city of Visoko. The 12RBC (like the PPCLI in CANBAT 1) found itself "*in* a war, but not *at* war." There was no ceasefire agreement until 23 February 1994, and soldiers were placed in dangerous situations providing assistance to humanitarian relief operations. They had to respond to hostage-taking incidents involving UN personnel, and even conducted a battle group blocking operation in Serb territory. UN troops were stretched thin. Canadian troops were stationed at detached locations where support and resupply were tenuous. Food consisted of hard rations, water was rationed, and leaves were infrequent. A Company of R22ᵉR was assigned to provide security to the Bakovici Mental Hospital, which was right on the confrontation line between Muslims and Croatians. The setting was horrific. Patients were dying of cold, neglect, and sniper fire, and the staff had fled. Canadian soldiers cleaned the hospital, buried the dead, and maintained security, escorting nurses and helping to feed patients.[41]

When 12RBC rotated out in May 1994, the incoming unit, Lord Strathcona's Horse (LdSH), heard accounts of questionable performance and misconduct at the Bakovici hospital, including misuse of alcohol, sexual misconduct, insubordination, violence, and black market activities. The outgoing commanding officer of the 12RBC ordered a military police investigation. The initial investigation was poorly conceived and executed, however, and was not supported by senior army commanders. Military police officials dismissed the allegations as minor and senior officers in the chain of command claimed they did not believe the allegations because of the good work of R22ᵉR at the hospital. The military police investigations dragged on without conclusion for over two years. In January 1996, when 5GBMC commander Brigadier-General Christian Couture issued a press release stating that nothing untoward had taken place at the Bakovici hospital, the regimental sergeant major came forward and challenged the conclusion, saying that unit personnel had not been interviewed by the MPs. Couture, however, told him to "slow down" and "mind your own business."[42]

NDHQ reopened the military police investigation and brought in a retired RCMP assistant commissioner to determine whether there had been a cover-up.

The chief of the defence staff instructed the commander of Land Force Command (formerly Mobile Command) to convene a board of inquiry to investigate the allegations. The board's report revealed a breadth of professional dysfunction underlying the misconduct at Bakovici.

The inquiry raised questions about the regimental system. Regimental exclusivism and pride had kept the command structure from operating appropriately. Members of R22^{e}R were reluctant to take problems to the commanding officer, who was not of their regiment. On the other hand, the commanding officer of 12RBC took a laissez-faire approach towards A Company because they were not part of his family. The units lived and worked apart, with headquarters exercising little control over the company. This was regarded as normal. One witness told the inquiry that "they were, after all, Van Doos and therefore not part of the 12[RBC] tribe per se." Soldiers accused of black marketeering were not charged but instead forced to put their illegal profits into the regimental fund. The commanding officer and sergeant major (from 12RBC) were not made aware of the issue, so the problem was contained within the Van Doos company. Similarly, soldiers testified that frequent drinking beyond the limits allowed by policy was not reported up the chain of command to preserve the good name of the regiment.[43] According to the board of inquiry:

> Criticisms of one's regiment, especially from an outsider, is tantamount to blasphemy and is not tolerated.
>
> Unfortunately for the Army this attitude has become so entrenched that even constructive criticism is deflected. Regiments become powerful entities unto themselves and the question of reform is seen with deep mistrust. Regiments are living breathing entities some of which have developed strong associations to act as their protectors. This is not bad per se. Where difficulties arise is when the good name of the regiment causes erosion of the chain of command and allows the Regiment to become more important than the Army itself.[44]

The inquiry also found the quality of leadership and discipline to be sadly lacking. Officers interpreted their responsibilities narrowly and concerned themselves with what the board called their own square on the checkerboard. Battle group officers with overall responsibility for the formation could not tell the board whether alcohol policy had been enforced because they had spent their work day in their office and the remainder of the day in the seclusion of their quarters. Officers saw their duties as administrative and emphasized bureaucracy over command. The NCO network was ineffective. Worse, officers had compromised discipline by visibly ignoring the alcohol policy of two beers a day and being drunk themselves. Dress and deportment went downhill and bandanas, backwards baseball caps, and T-shirts were worn at checkpoints where battledress, body armour, and helmets were required. It was not surprising that drunkenness on duty, inappropriate fraternization with locals, loss of weapons (including a .50 calibre machine gun), and falsification of records occurred.[45]

Breakdown in leadership and discipline was ascribed by the board to insufficient training. Although most of the leaders of CANBAT 2 had received the training required by their rank, the board believed that there was too little emphasis on leadership skills, and that for senior ranks what little training there was tended towards managerial skills. The result of "bureaucratic expediency and the desire to introduce more management training" was the loss of the army's leadership ability.

> However positive some of this may have been, it is clear that a great deal of this shift in attitudes ran counter to ideals within the regimental system. The consequent conflict in values seems to have in some cases left leaders adrift; not knowing whether to follow the age old principles espoused by the regimental system or accept a new way of doing business. In the resulting mix of old and new, some mistakes were made and inevitably it was the soldiers who suffered from a lack of firm leadership.

Similarly, the board complained that the Canadian Forces Ethics Program was directed solely at civilian employees and referred to soldiers as "clients" and senior members of the Forces as "senior management." The board believed that soldiers needed a program that was appropriate for their environment and that used military terminology in an operational setting.[46] The board thus attempted to transfer responsibility for the army's failure to civilian society. One wonders what civilian management model would have accommodated drunkenness on duty, ganglike clothing at work, theft and loss of company equipment, and assaults on customers.

Lieutenant-General J.M.G. Baril, the commander of Land Force Command, agreed with the board's report, including its conclusion that the desire to protect regimental reputation was one cause of the failures. He also accepted the conclusion that there had been an erosion of the personnel system, and although he was hesitant to point a finger at changes in society's values, he agreed that the increasing emphasis on management had sowed confusion as to what leadership was all about. Baril announced steps to review and define army culture, as well as specific corrective actions for particular failings.

Overall, the Yugoslavia missions showed that the army could deploy and sustain adequately trained troops in sufficient numbers to meet the government's objectives. The numbers peaked at about 2,500 in Yugoslavia and another 900 in Somalia. The deployment required a substantial number of reservists, but this was problematic only because of the inefficiency of the Militia, which had persisted since the end of the Second World War. Individual augmentees had to be brought together from a large number of Militia units, rather than as subunits who had trained together. Despite numerous complaints that the army was at a quantitative breaking point and that soldiers were being posted to back-to-back tours, the data are less than clear. The Auditor General of Canada reported that from 1990 to 1995 over 80 percent of those who had taken part in peacekeeping had had only one six-month tour of duty. There were, however, three thousand individuals who had had two or even three tours. These individuals tended to come from the army combat arms and combat service support occupations.[47]

The main challenge of stability operations was therefore mental rather than physical. Gaps appeared between the senior army leadership and the political level. The focus of the army on preserving itself as a general-purpose combat force resulted in considerable structural strain as the government accepted missions that employed combat troops but required them not to engage in combat. Leadership doctrine began to fray as it became more difficult for soldiers in the field to connect the dots between risking their lives and those of their subordinates and defending Canada or tangible Canadian interests. The army's regimental culture, built on the assumption that units would train and go into the field together, could not cope with the reality of composite units required by force downsizing and continuing deployments.

The war in Yugoslavia would mean the end of UNPROFOR as the Croatian military victory in Croatia in 1995 and Serb ethnic cleansing in Srebrenica caused NATO's Allied Rapid Reaction Corps to be brought in to prevent a collapse of NATO's position. With the signing of the Dayton Accords, NATO took over from the UN. Although Canada would continue to contribute troops to NATO missions until the end of the decade, the focus of the army would move elsewhere.

Somalia

The Somalia mission reprised many of the themes of Yugoslavia: stabilization versus "traditional peacekeeping," tactical successes, troop disenchantment, and lack of discipline. However, unlike the Bakovici hospital incident, which had been investigated by an internal board of inquiry, the Somalia mission ended with a full judicial inquiry that exposed the army's professional standards and regimental culture to minute and prolonged public scrutiny. The results would be devastating.

Somalia had been independent since 1960, when former Italian and British trust territories joined to form the Somali Republic. During the Cold War, Somalia became a zone of contention between the Soviet Union and the United States. In 1969 Major-General Mohammed Siad Barre, the commander-in-chief of the armed forces, seized power and established a socialist military dictatorship. He remained aligned with the Soviet Union until 1980, when the latter backed the Marxist government of Ethiopia during its Ogaden War with Somalia. Barre expelled the Soviets and sought aid from the United States. To protect its sea routes to the Persian Gulf, the United States took over the Soviet naval base at Berbera and gained access for its Central Command to military facilities in Somalia. During the period of Soviet support, arms had flowed into the country, making it the best-armed state in Black Africa. Barre's socialist government also attempted to suppress traditional clan society and clan mechanisms that resolved conflict.

The defeat of Somalia in the Ogaden War led to the collapse of the clan alliance that had supported Barre. It also created thousands of Ethiopian refugees, who poured over the border. They were supported by the Barre regime but opposed by the local population. Members of the local Isaaq clan formed the Somali National Movement, which began a guerrilla war against the Somali government. Barre was unable to defeat them militarily, but reprisals carried out by the government killed thousands of civilians in northern towns. Charges of genocide against the Barre government led both the United States and the Soviet Union to stop arms shipments to Somalia and Ethiopia between 1988 and 1991 and to encourage local reconciliation; by 1991, however, the entire south of Somalia was engulfed in civil war. In January 1991 United Somali Congress (USC) forces under General Mohammed Farrah Aidid took Mogadishu. Barre fled but the war continued, with various armed factions and looters fighting for power. Political negotiations to reconcile the various armed factions ended with the USC's naming of Mohammed Ali Mahdi as president. Aidid refused to recognize Mahdi and the central government dissolved into clan warfare.

Fighting damaged Mogadishu and the agricultural region in the south, which became a famine area. By March 1992 the International Committee of the Red Cross reported "horrifying" levels of malnutrition affecting 90 percent of the population. Only a third of the population of Mogadishu had access to clean water. Clan warfare and banditry prevented the distribution of food aid and Somalia collapsed into anarchy as an "economy of plunder" emerged.[48]

The national interests of Canada in Somalia were difficult to discern. There was an obvious need for humanitarian assistance, but the same could have been said about crises at the same time in Sudan, Sierra Leone, Afghanistan, and Sri

Lanka. Indeed, Canada was reluctant to commit personnel to the UN mission established in April 1992 because of concern for the adequate security of military personnel with the observer force. Moreover, the chief of the defence staff and the deputy minister advised the minister of national defence that the UN mission did not meet Canadian policy criteria for involvement: the mandate was unclear; agreements with the belligerents were doubtful given that Aidid had refused to accept a UN security detachment for the observer force; and safety concerns had been acknowledged by senior staff at the UN. The UN continued to press for a mission and for Canadian involvement. Secretary-General Boutros Boutros-Ghali was particularly vehement in urging intervention. On 23 July he delivered a tirade that the Security Council had been willing to intervene in Bosnia because it was a "rich man's war" and that he could name ten places that were worse off than the besieged Sarajevo. Continued media coverage was probably the decisive factor, with television networks such as CNN reporting continuously on the famine. The "CNN factor" motivated the Privy Council Office to advise Prime Minister Brian Mulroney on 18 August that "a Government statement on Canada's response to security and humanitarian needs in Somalia would be timely and well-received." Three days later Canada's commitment to the United Nations Operation in Somalia (UNOSOM) was announced.[49]

The military planning on which participation in UNOSOM was based was shaky at best. In anticipation of a formal UN request and Canadian involvement in the Somalia mission, Mobile Command Headquarters and NDHQ had undertaken analyses beginning around the end of July. Assuming that the request would be for a security battalion to safeguard fifty military observers based in Mogadishu, port and airport security, and escort to aid convoys, Mobile Command recommended a five-hundred-strong security unit of five companies. Taking into account Yugoslavia and other international operations, Mobile Command believed that it could support such an operation for a period not exceeding twelve months. It also noted that the Canadian Airborne Regiment (CAR) was the UN standby unit, but observed that finding qualified drivers for armoured vehicles within the CAR would be a problem. The Royal Canadian Dragoons (RCD) and 12e Régiment blindé du Canada (12RBC) were mentioned as alternatives. This estimate did not discuss either the proposed mission or the concept of operations, nor did it clarify the meaning of "security battalion" in operational terms. A five-hundred-soldier security unit composed of five companies was a novel concept not based on existing doctrine.

NDHQ did not question Mobile Command's estimate, and at the end of July the Command's commander, Lieutenant-General James Gervais, informed the

CDS that several units were available for the mission. It appears that the CDS, General de Chastelain, wanted the Canadian troops to be ready quickly and Mobile Command agreed that a "medium force" – that is, a reinforced CAR – could be ready to move within seven to thirty days. In spite of the assessment that the CAR was short of drivers and that the units that had them needed forty-five days to get ready, NDHQ staff concluded:

> The details of the situation in Somalia and the operational concept for the expanded UN involvement are unknown and therefore the capabilities needed to accomplish the tasks set out by [the Secretary-General] in his report to the [Security Council] of [24 July 1992] cannot be determined. Nonetheless the CF can provide and sustain a general purpose, combat capable force to provide security for this UN mission to provide humanitarian assistance in Somalia.

The Somalia Commission of Inquiry called this an "illogical summary" and a "corruption of the planning process."[50] The 1 Canadian Division Headquarters after-action report came to similar conclusions, stating: "The entire process of mounting this operation was rushed. Chains of command, lines of communication, delineation of responsibilities and most standard means established for doing business were perverted to get the mission accomplished in the limited time available. This was particularly unfortunate in light of the dangerous nature of the mission being under taken." Divisional headquarters staff pointed to the rush created by "political pressure" and to confusion regarding the roles of Mobile Command and NDHQ planners.[51]

During the month of August, the UN conducted additional reconnaissance in Somalia and concluded that two full infantry battalions would be required, with one-third of their combat strength in wheeled armoured personnel carriers. On 25 August the UN made an informal request for an infantry battalion of 750 soldiers to be assigned to Bossasso, which was considered the "most difficult" part of the mission. Based on this request, NDHQ ordered the various commands to prepare a contingency plan for Operation Cordon. The commander of Mobile Command was instructed to assemble and provide a battalion group for deployment to Bossasso to provide port security, aid convoy escort, and security for aid distribution centres. The force was to include engineers, second-line maintenance, logistic support troops, and some third-line medical support. The battalion was to be composed of rifle companies with a mix of wheeled armoured vehicles and trucks. This order had the effect of requiring the commander to change the normal composition of a field unit, and limited its combat arms element by requiring that combat support and combat service support requirements be taken out of a fixed number on strength. Gervais objected to this, regarding the mix of mechanized and motorized infantry as "professionally unsound." He objected to the cap of ten APCs per company in contrast to the army's minimum of fourteen. He pointed out the lack of a reconnaissance capability and concluded that the proposed force did not recognize standard cohesive fighting units. NDHQ should have defined the mission and ordered Mobile Command to recommend the force required. Instead, the CDS was micromanaging and specifying details while ignoring his own strategic responsibilities.

The Operation Cordon plan issued on 3 September 1992 was for a six-month to one-year deployment of a rifle battalion of 750, mounted on wheeled APCs with support elements included in the 750-soldier ceiling. Neither the mission nor the concept of operations had been clarified. Although Mobile Command assumed a can-do attitude, it engaged in a certain amount of handwringing, calling the force "lightly vehicled" and "austere." As orders moved from Mobile Command Headquarters through Land Force Central Area Headquarters to the Special Service Force and eventually to the CAR, little detail was added; in fact, the CAR never received a copy of the entire contingency plan. At the level of the Canadian Airborne Regiment there was no library of standard operating procedures for such routine tasks as arrest and detention, convoy escort, protection of aid distribution centres and base camps, crowd control, or mine protection, even though the regiment had been Canada's UN standby battalion for several years. Although Operation Cordon was never implemented, its plans were the basis for assuming that the army was ready to undertake the even more ambitious Operation Deliverance.[52]

The Canadian Airborne Regiment, to which the Somalia mission had been assigned, had been in existence since 1966 and had been part of the Special Service Force – a brigade-sized, quick-reaction force – since 1977. In 1979 it had been reorganized as a force of about 750 consisting of three "commandos," one drawn from each of the infantry regiments: the Princess Patricia's Canadian Light Infantry in Western Canada, the Royal Canadian Regiment from the anglophone East, and the Royal 22e Régiment from Quebec. Until 1992 each of the commandos had had the status of units and their heads that of commanding officers. The CAR itself had the status of a brigade and its commanding officer was a full colonel. This meant that the leadership of the CAR was more experienced and senior than that of a line battalion. The 1992 budget cuts resulted in the reduction of the size of the CAR and the loss of rank, status, and experience in its senior ranks.

The CAR also suffered from problems other than downsizing and reorganization. It had long-standing disciplinary problems that had never been resolved, and incidents on the eve of its departure for Somalia included disobedience to unit rules, socially unacceptable behaviour, and random criminal activity, including excessive aggression, damage to property, burning of the duty sergeant's car, unauthorized use of pyrotechnics, and drunkenness. In some cases, the offending individuals had had a long history of rule breaking and violence, but their parent regiments had never court-martialed them and had posted them to their commando in the CAR when they could put up with them no longer.[53] The regiment also had a culture that would prove problematic in a Third World stabilization operation. It thought of itself as an elite, aggressive unit. In particular, 2 Commando from the PPCLI cultivated an image as the most aggressive company and as "rebels." Their continued display of the Confederate Stars and Bars battle flag had been the subject of disciplinary action prior to deployment and would later raise questions of whether 2 Commando sheltered white supremacists.[54]

Lieutenant-Colonel Paul Morneault was appointed commanding officer of the CAR on 24 June 1992, just two months before the government committed it to Somalia. He had only a few weeks to train a unit struggling with disciplinary and internal cohesion problems without any real guidance from senior headquarters as to the nature of the mission and without doctrine on which to base a training plan. Moreover, he had to ensure that his light infantry unit assimilated light armoured vehicles, which meant knowing not only how to drive and service them but also how to change tactics to accommodate the vehicles. He quickly found himself in trouble with his superior, Brigadier-General Ernest Beno, the Special Service Force commander. Beno was dissatisfied with both Morneault's training plan and the actual conduct of the training, and he relieved Morneault on 21 October. Given the CAR's history of disciplinary problems, strong leadership was required, but the regiment whose turn it was to provide the commanding officer did not have a strong candidate. The most logical candidate was an anglophone PPCLI lieutenant-colonel who had already commanded the CAR. Not only was it the Royal 22e Régiment's turn at bat, however, but Canada's French-English relations were approaching a periodic crisis and army leadership was sensitive to the appearance of not being able to find a qualified francophone to command the senior francophone regiment. Mobile Command Headquarters preferred to take advice from La Régie (Senate) of R22^{e}R and appoint Lieutenant-Colonel Carol Mathieu, also of R22^{e}R.[55] Mathieu had no experience as a battalion commander, and no officer who recommended him for command vouched for his ability to turn around an unsteady unit within days. The same people who had recommended Morneault named Mathieu as his replacement.[56]

The Somalia Commission of Inquiry censured Mathieu for a long list of deficiencies, including not removing several subordinate officers who had either failed to curb ill discipline or actually been a party to it, failure to assess the readiness of his unit, failure to ensure that his unit was appropriately informed and trained in the mission rules of engagement, and failure to ensure that his unit was adequately trained and tested in the Laws of War.[57] It concluded:

> Land Force Command waived its own informal criteria in order to accommodate the parent regiments' nominees, even though candidates who met the requirements more fully were available, or could have been made available.
>
> Representatives of the regimental councils of the parent regiments, who are outside the chain of command and therefore unaccountable, had too much influence in the process. This is particularly problematic for the CAR, since these officers were virtually the only source of nominees from their regiments for postings to the CAR, and since any repercussions of a poor choice would be felt by the CAR and significantly less by their own regiments.
>
> In some cases, the chain of command allowed completely irrelevant factors, such as inter-regimental and national politics, to influence key appointment decisions.[58]

Events in Somalia also upset deployment plans. The situation continued to deteriorate and the United States offered to lead a peace enforcement mission. Boutros-Ghali argued that a peace enforcement action across the entire country under Chapter VII of the UN Charter was the preferred course of action. Canadian officials believed that the planned deployment to Bossasso could continue, but Boutros-Ghali was adamant that peace enforcement and peacekeeping had to be sequential. Canada therefore suspended Operation Cordon on 2 December and immediately decided to join the US-led United Nations Task Force in Somalia (UNITAF). UNITAF's mandate was "to use all necessary means" to establish a secure environment for relief operations in Somalia. Cabinet approved a nine-month deployment of nine hundred troops. Canadian Forces officials – from the chief of the defence staff down to Colonel Serge Labbé, the Joint Task Force commander designate – vigorously lobbied their US counterparts for a prominent role in the mission. The belief was that the CAR was immediately ready and anxious to go.

The assumption that the CAR was willing was well founded, as soldiers had been trained first for Operation Python, to police a truce in Morocco, and then Operation Cordon, both of which had been cancelled. The assumption that it was ready was less justified. In the early 1990s the Canadian Forces relied on the Operational Readiness and Effectiveness Reporting System to provide the chief of the defence staff with information on the ability of the military to meet missions and tasks. The system looked impressive but was in fact an empty shell.

Command headquarters (including Land Force Command) had not given units lists of essential equipment, personnel, or training. As a result commanders reported only deficiencies that they both knew of and considered important. These reports could be adjusted by higher headquarters, which often believed that deficiencies could be made up elsewhere. Land Force Command had no standards to use for assessing units. Field exercises were not validated, so the army had no way of knowing for sure that exercises tested operational requirements. The Auditor General found the whole thing subjective and could not determine the basis on which units were reported to be "ready."[59]

Mathieu was therefore able to declare the CAR "ready" only a few weeks after his predecessor, Morneault, had been relieved of his command for being unable to bring it up to standard. The Somalia Commission of Inquiry determined that the training Morneault had been able to conduct before embarkation was not significant or of a type on which a readiness declaration could be based because most of the unit's equipment was already packaged for shipment.[60] Both Mathieu and his boss, Special Service Force Commander Beno, were under pressure to declare the unit ready. Mathieu told the commission that if he had declared the unit not ready, "well, they would have said 'bye-bye' Mathieu, and brought in someone else."[61] Major-General Lewis MacKenzie, the area commander to whom Beno reported, frankly testified that "funny enough [readiness is] not a term we use ... within the Army; historically, it is a commander's responsibility to evaluate [readiness] according to his own standards."[62]

The Canadian Airborne Regiment Battle Group (CARBG) that was deployed to Somalia included A Squadron of the Royal Canadian Dragoons, the mortar platoon from 1 Battalion of the Royal Canadian Regiment, and 2 Combat Engineer Regiment. To command the battle group as well as Canadian air and naval assets assigned to the mission, NDHQ assigned Colonel Serge Labbé as commander and a headquarters staff from 1 Canadian Division in Kingston. Labbé was in Britain and learned of his appointment by telephone on 4 December. The divisional headquarters had been focused on Yugoslavia and did not even have a map of Somalia.[63] When Labbé arrived in Mogadishu with his advance party on 14 December, he had no idea what his troops would be expected to do. Directed by General de Chastelain to seek a high-profile mission, Labbé met with the US force commander, Lieutenant-General Robert B. Johnston on 15 December and proposed that the Canadian force be assigned to secure the Belet Huen Humanitarian Relief Sector. This proposal was accepted on 19 December and deployment to Belet Huen was set for 28 December.

In contrast to the relatively peaceful Bossasso, which had been the basis for the original planning of the mission, Belet Huen was a Wild West frontier town. Whereas Bossasso had a functioning government, local police force, and no clan violence, Belet Huen had been stripped by Barre's troops as they retreated to Mogadishu, leaving the area extremely vulnerable to famine. Clans fought for control of the highway, which was Somalia's major link to Ethiopia and a conduit for arms and manpower for General Aidid. The region was known for extortion and complicated clan politics. The climate was harsh. The temperature was often over 40°C and with humidity felt like 50°C. Fine dust quickly infiltrated clothing and machinery.[64]

The CARBG occupied Belet Huen by carrying out an air assault with the US 10th Mountain Division, deploying as though there were an opposing force and the airfield had to be captured. The Somali militia had already decamped, however, and had set up shop some thirty kilometres to the north. Canadian and US troops were met by welcoming crowds. The CARBG operated on a war footing, patrolling on a twenty-four-hour basis, and continued to assess the threat as high. For several weeks, troops lived in field entrenchments with no electricity, little water, no fresh food, and no washing facilities. When a permanent camp was set up, each commando went its own way and established a separate base for itself. The result was that instead of a concentrated, triangular base according to doctrine, the CARBG was strung out along the old Imperial Highway. The configuration meant that the camp was difficult to secure, a problem exacerbated by the fact that only enough barbed wire and construction materials had been shipped from Canada for a unified, triangular camp. The CAR in particular seemed to go out of their way to make themselves uncomfortable, living in the field in temporary bivouacs under canvas rather than in permanent structures. The three CAR commandos chose to adopt this manner of living in Belet Huen, even though there was no real reason to do so, despite shortages of material shipped from Canada. The Royal Canadian Dragoons chose to set up a triangular camp that was easily defended from thieves and infiltrators, and managed to scrounge furniture, a large-screen TV and VCR, and even a mini putting course for their common area.[65] Lack of planning for the specifics of the mission and a planning bias to reduce the number of support troops meant other gaps and shortages: a shortage of engineers to provide power, of clean water and storage, and of refrigeration and fuel storage. With no nearby harbour there were too few logistics personnel to unload ships and control the flow of personnel and supplies in Mogadishu. The Canadian force had no interpreters and was dependent on US forces to provide them; the nearest were 350 kilometres away. There was no base defence and security platoon, and the mortar platoon was given the job. Eventually forty-four additional troops were added for this duty. Initially, there was no civil affairs officer because, bizarrely, civil-military cooperation had not been identified as a requirement during planning. There were too few signallers and only a few cooks, leaving the force to live off hard rations, which quickly damaged morale.[66]

The CARBG settled into its mission of providing a secure environment for delivery of humanitarian relief by non-governmental organizations. This required programs of both military patrolling and seizure of weapons and also a hearts-and-minds campaign to gain the confidence of the local population. The goal was to restore the functioning of Somali civil society in the sector and consequently reduce the requirement for a military security presence. Colonel Labbé stated:

> We felt that if, during our time, our six-month period ... we could get those [local Somali civil] committees to demonstrate to the local population of people they served, in principle, that they were capable of making positive decisions, having a positive impact on the lives of residents of the Belet Huen area, not just Belet Huen, but the entire humanitarian relief sector for which we were responsible, 33,000 square miles of desert. We felt we might then have, upon our departure, established the seeds for further development of those institutions and put that region of Somalia back on the path to a normal lifestyle.[67]

The effectiveness of the CARBG in meeting its operational objectives is difficult to assess. Violence continued in the form of roadblocks and banditry. Aid was distributed but was often diverted through clan connections to benefit middlemen rather than the ultimate targets of the aid. An effective local police force was never developed. This is more properly a comment on the ambitious nature of the goal of restoring order with a small foreign force over such a large war-torn area than a criticism of the CARBG's inability to pacify the area and renew civil society in less than six months. If stabilization operations could have been so effective, they would undoubtedly have become more popular. Like the 2PPCLI in Yugoslavia, the Canadian Airborne Regiment became frustrated with being exposed to danger and harassment without being able to respond. Troops were stoned and had "*gallo*" (heathen) yelled at them on a routine basis. They lost their respect for Somalis and coined a derogatory term for them – "smoofties" – which no one really had a meaning for. Somalis were also referred to as "nig nogs," "jigaboos," "flip-flops," "Shomalians," and "gimmes" – the last referring to the troops' annoyance with Somali beggars.[68]

Frustration, especially with thieves who would infiltrate the Canadian base to steal anything that might be of value, resulted in breakdowns of discipline and at least two incidents in which Somalis were killed. Both incidents involved 2 Commando and individuals who had been identified as disciplinary problems prior to deployment but who had been included in the mission anyway. The first occurred on 4 March 1993, when Captain Michel Rainville, the reconnaissance platoon leader, set out bait to ambush thieves. An operation of dubious morality and value to begin with, Rainville's trap ended with two Somalis being shot in the back, one of them fatally. According to Major Barry Armstrong, the medical officer who examined the body, the dead man had been shot first in the back and then "dispatched" by a pair of shots to the head and neck. While Labbé and NDHQ were considering whether the Rainville incident required a military police investigation, a second Somali civilian was killed. On 16 March, Shidane Arone was captured by soldiers from 2 Commando in the abandoned US Seabees compound, which adjoined that of 2 Commando. That morning, Major Anthony Seward, the 2 Commando commander, had given orders that infiltrators were to be captured and "abused." Arone was taken to a bunker and over the course of several hours was beaten to death by members of 2 Commando. None of the company NCOs or officers present within thirty metres of the bunker intervened, although soldiers twice as far away heard screaming. The main perpetrator of the murder was arrested, but attempted suicide while in custody. On 19 March the DCDS, Vice-Admiral Larry Murray, ordered a military police investigation.[69] A military police investigation of the 4 March Rainville incident was not ordered until 15 April, after medical officer Armstrong made an allegation of murder.

The fallout from these two incidents would be a board of inquiry, a public inquiry under the Inquiries Act, several courts martial, and the disbandment of the Canadian Airborne Regiment. The "Somalia Affair" was not finished until 1997. These matters will be discussed in the section on the Somalia Inquiry in Chapter 8. From the point of view of operations, both Yugoslavia and Somalia illustrated the limitations of the army's policy that general-purpose combat forces were suitable for stabilization operations. Soldiers may have possessed the tactical skills to conduct operations, but they were not prepared for the difficulties of taking fire (in Yugoslavia) or for what they perceived to be continual disrespect and abuse (in Somalia). Troops indoctrinated to think of themselves as warriors and their job as combat had obvious difficulties in coping with the level of restraint required by these two operations.

Somalia revealed other weaknesses as well. The operational planning system still did not work. There were too many levels of headquarters involved. The chief of the defence staff effectively overrode the planning system and left Mobile Command to determine how to implement the resulting non-doctrinal organizations. Neither Mobile Command nor NDHQ had developed doctrine for the "new" peacekeeping or the old type. Each regiment did things its own way and lessons learned and procedures were passed on locally or not as staff rotated in and out of positions. It also became evident that NDHQ's central management processes for both personnel and readiness did not work. Both went against the grain of the army's culture and were ignored. Instead of an approach that favoured objective appraisal of personnel and unit performance, regimental politics and uncritical acceptance of the word of a fellow officer took over. All of these, together with a mentality that the senior officer present was not to be questioned and that bad news did not flow up the chain of command, made for a deadly combination.

Zaire: "The Bungle in the Jungle"

Operation Assurance deployed 354 Canadian personnel to Central Africa in the fall of 1996. It was the first UN multinational mission since 1956 – as well as the first Chapter VII operation – led by Canada. Operation Assurance showed that the army and the Canadian Forces still had significant weaknesses in staff systems, at both strategic and operational levels.

The mission was triggered by the 1 million Hutu refugees who fled Rwanda for Zaire in 1994 to escape retribution by the Tutsi army for the genocide perpetrated by Hutus. The Hutu refugees contained elements of the former Rwandan army and the Interhamwe militia that had been involved in the genocide. These elements naturally sought to control the refugee camps. The Rwandan Hutus displaced Zairian Tutsis, who began armed operations against them from bases in Rwanda, assisted by the Rwandan Tutsi army. The Zairian government declared the region south of Lake Kivu a war zone and gave the Tutsi insurgents a week to leave the country or be considered rebels. This precipitated an alliance between the Zairian Tutsis and a separate rebel group under Laurent Kabila, who had been at war with the Zairian government since the mid-1960s. Kabila escalated the violence and eventually all humanitarian assistance to the region was cut off. The fighting forced the Hutu refugees to move deeper into the Zairian jungle.[70]

The crisis led a number of countries, including Germany and France, to call for humanitarian military intervention. The Somalian experience had dampened the enthusiasm of the United States for such missions, and Canada also declined a request from the UN Secretary-General to send troops to secure the refugee camps, because such a mission lacked the support of neighbouring African states. As with Somalia, however, the international media and relief agencies continued paying attention to the crisis. The UN appointed the Canadian ambassador to the United States, Raymond Chrétien, as Special Envoy for the Great Lakes region of Africa. Subsequently, the UN and several European states organized a regional summit in Nairobi. The summit called for safe corridors and sanctuaries for refugees inside Zaire, renewed humanitarian aid, and steps to return the refugees to Rwanda. Rwanda and Zaire had their own agendas, however. Rwanda, not unnaturally, wanted to screen returning refugees for those who had participated in the genocide. Zaire wanted an intervention force to suppress its own rebellions.

On 6 November, Chrétien flew to Africa to attempt to resolve the crisis while the Joint Operations Staff at NDHQ began planning for a deployment on the assumption that Canada would contribute troops. On 9 November the UN Security Council approved a French resolution calling for a multinational force. The UN determined it would aid all the refugees and not attempt to sort out the armed elements. It was also apparent that neither France nor the United States would volunteer to lead the mission. In Canada, Prime Minister Jean Chrétien, Defence Minister Douglas Young, and Acting CDS Larry Murray acted on assurances from the United States and other countries that they would contribute to a Canadian-led mission. The Canadian government announced that it would lead a UN multinational force and appointed Lieutenant-General Maurice Baril as the force commander.

Baril was given the use of Kelly Barracks, the US European Command Headquarters, in Stuttgart, Germany, as the home of his forward planning cell. He also had use of US and British reconnaissance flights, satellite imagery from the United States and the Canadian RADARSAT, and information from various non-governmental organizations. NDHQ issued an implementation plan on 30 November, the same date that the Multi-National Force (MNF) Headquarters was activated in Entebbe, with liaison detachments at Kigali, Nairobi, Kinshasa, and Gisenyi. On 4 December the MNF HQ was moved to Kampala, where it was "integrated" with the Air Component Headquarters. The Canadian air force (Canadian Forces Air Command) did not accept "direct command" as planned by the Joint Force Headquarters planners. This meant that Baril had to liaise directly with a line commander for Air Component Command whenever an order or plan was produced. Canada had yet to achieve a "joint" headquarters.[71]

No other country actually assigned forces to the MNF, and Canada simply did not have troops available to meet the requirement while it already had forces in Bosnia, Croatia, and Haiti. It soon turned out that troops would not be required. Before the MNF had even managed to establish itself in Africa, intensified fighting between the Rwandan government and the Kabila forces pushed some 400,000 refugees back into Rwanda. Kabila wished to eliminate the refugee crisis to prevent an intervention force from constraining his own forces. Baril had difficulty determining exactly what the refugee situation was. On 21 November, Kabila forces began firing at low-flying reconnaissance aircraft. Zaire opposed air drops of relief supplies to the refugees, and Rwanda opposed the use of Entebbe by the MNF. Baril was able to negotiate a promise from Kabila not to fire on relief aircraft, but direct talks with Kabila created a problem with the Zairian government. Thus, the crisis had passed by the time the NDHQ implementation plan arrived.

By mid-December, there were still about 200,000 refugees somewhere in eastern Zaire but the MNF was no longer welcome in Rwanda. Baril recommended that the mission be terminated. This was proposed by the Canadian government on 13 December and accepted by the Security Council. The last elements left Entebbe on 31 December.

The Canadian Forces, particularly the army, did a thorough study of Operation Assurance. Long-standing flaws in the operational planning system were still evident. The joint operational planning process assumed that Canada would play the subordinate role of a troop provider, and thus made no provision for providing either strategic leadership or the physical infrastructure required by a multinational force. To the extent that the joint planning doctrine addressed mission strategy, it assumed that it would be developed by the government and handed to the operational planners. The reality was that the Department of Foreign Affairs and International Trade, the Privy Council Office, and Cabinet had no effective way of formatting or providing such direction.[72] Dependence on ad hoc processes meant that the government and NDHQ could not keep up with the pace of events, and the operational planners were left on their own.

Other weaknesses were also identified. No national assessment team had been dispatched to the theatre to support Canadian government decision making regarding the mission. The Canadian reconnaissance party was responsible only for operational-level issues in setting up the MNF. Both the government and the Canadian Forces had underestimated the requirements for force-level infrastructure, including logistics, medical, engineering, combat information systems, military police, finance, and other functions. The separate air component headquarters had not had enough staff to operate seven days a week, twenty-four hours a day. No provision had been made for a regional air management control centre, which in earlier missions had been supplied by NATO or the United States. Finally, the lack of intelligence had left the MNF vulnerable to misinformation by the media or NGOs.[73]

The Need for a New Staff System

Operations conducted in the 1990s revealed weaknesses that had been previously recognized but not effectively addressed as well as those that had been masked by the routine of predictable garrison duty in Europe under NATO. The army's conviction that general-purpose forces were suitable for the new peacekeeping appeared increasingly dubious. There was no doctrine at the army level for even common taskings such as convoys and checkpoints, and training did not prepare troops for the possibility of being ordered to do nothing while under fire or while witnessing atrocities committed by the belligerents. The soldier support system neither recognized nor was able to treat the resulting casualties.

Post-unification staff systems had resulted in a muddle. The Canadian Forces–wide central administrative systems that had been established to manage personnel and report on readiness were ineffectual and overridden by old-boy regimental politics. Just as important, linkages between the army and the government were broken. In both Somalia and Zaire, the government had made military commitments without any clear idea of the requirements and without coordinating military and diplomatic activities. Senior military leadership did not appear to have provided any restraining counsel in either case. In the case of Somalia, army commanders and the CDS (himself a soldier) simply assumed the Canadian Airborne Regiment to be appropriately trained and ready. In the case of Zaire, the requirements of leading a multinational force were underestimated. It was clear that old ways of doing business were no longer viable, but a new model had yet to emerge.

CHAPTER EIGHT

Reform and Constabulary Realism

For Canada, the focus in the 1990s was on domestic problems. Economic times were tough as the worst recession since the 1930s gripped the country. Three hundred thousand manufacturing jobs were lost in Ontario alone in the first years of the decade. Corporations downsized, and retailers lowered prices to such an extent that long-established firms went bankrupt and disappeared. The Atlantic fisheries collapsed, and British Columbia decided it would rather cut old-growth forests than see its lumber industry vanish. The country's slow-motion constitutional crisis continued with the unravelling of the Meech Lake Accord. The Mulroney government made a second attempt at constitutional reform with the Charlottetown Accord, but it too failed when it was rejected by voters in most provinces. Part of the fallout from economic and constitutional strains was the virtual disappearance of the Progressive Conservative Party in the 1993 election and the emergence of regional parties: the Reform Party in the West and the Bloc Québécois in Quebec. Jean Chrétien, the newly elected Liberal prime minister, inherited a $40 billion deficit and 1.4 million unemployed, along with the political and constitutional tangle. Foreign affairs, including the Gulf War in 1991, were merely a distraction to most Canadians.[1]

For the Canadian army, the 1990s marked the end of one era and the beginning of another. Trends that had become evident during the 1980s peaked in the 1990s. Chief of these was the decisive change in international politics as the Cold War ended and the Soviet Union and the Warsaw Pact unravelled. Canadian budgetary crises culminated in the 1994 austerity budget. All this was accompanied by the evident failure of the army's doctrine and combat development processes and the obvious failures of army discipline and professionalism in Croatia and Somalia. The 1990s became known as the "decade of darkness," a phrase used mostly to refer to the financial cuts and force reductions,[2] although there was much more to be concerned about than the budget.

Yet from failures of the old, new concepts of force structures and professionalism would emerge. The crisis of the "decade of darkness" would be an opportunity for the army to remake itself.

Post–Cold War Adjustment

Lieutenant-General D. Huddleston, the deputy chief of the defence staff, was profoundly skeptical of the Defence Department's ability to carry out meaningful reforms. In December 1990 he told his senior colleagues at National Defence Headquarters that his greatest concern was that the department would attack affordability problems by dealing with symptoms rather than causes. According to him, everyone knew "instinctively" that Canada was not getting the defence it should have for $12 billion a year.

> Whether the battle cry is "Reduce infrastructure!," "Dispose of aging, high-cost fleets!," or "Bring the Commanders to NDHQ!" we are avoiding the real issue, that DND is an extremely inefficient organization ... We have an enormously constipated administration and we have numerous and often competing constituencies striving to capture and spend dollars, not to ensure that they put the right weapon in the right hands ... How do we develop a plan to which people are actually committed? How do we mobilize our intellectual resources to something other than protecting rice-bowls and ensuring that nothing is conceded on our watch?

Huddleston believed that nothing would change unless the force commanders controlled their own support resources. Otherwise, the central materiel and personnel groups would protect their own resources at the commanders' expense. He had little faith in the Total Force policy:

> The navy puts the Reserves on little boats while the Regulars sail around in undermanned big boats claiming it's impossible to train Reservists beyond the spud-peeling level. The army creates 90/10 and 10/90 units, stretching the limits of Total Force credibility while it pleads the pressures of World War III and bemoans, for the fourth decade, the unfortunate imbalance of Militia units and the need for caution when dealing the Hon[orary] Col[onel]s and the CDA [Conference of Defence Associations].

There was little immediate response to this outpouring.[3]

The 1989 budget had left the army committed to a 12,500-soldier NATO division, although only 4 Canadian Mechanized Brigade (the word "Group" having been dropped from its title) remained stationed in Europe. The army hoped to preserve the status quo as much as possible. Lieutenant-General Kent Foster, the Land Force commander, wrote to army general officers that although force planners were under significant budget pressure, the army's plans remained rooted in the logic behind the 1987 White Paper. Although he thought it premature to share any details with his senior subordinates, he informed them that the army could no longer be justified by specific commitments and an identified threat. Instead, it had to be based on Canada's "fundamental need for an Army" and the army as a basic element of nationhood. The type of army needed was one based on general-purpose combat forces and structured as a "Total Force" with a large reserve element. He also intended to return to a regional command structure. The Militia, however, was not regarded as capable of doing much more than augmenting the Regular Force, because the characteristics of the reserves "do not permit them to meet the demanding and immediate requirements of many of the army's commitments." Nevertheless, the Militia was forecast to grow to target strength of 30,000 and receive improved individual and collective training. Foster also regarded the regimental system as an essential element of the restructured army; according to him, it had "proven to be a most effective means of recruiting, socializing and training individuals and imbuing them with the essential virtues of the military ethos and mutual commitment."[4]

The extent of the army's presence in Europe almost immediately became subject to budgetary review. According to Sean Maloney, the Department of National Defence considered both NORAD and the navy's commitments sacrosanct, leaving the army as the only source of significant savings. Because the Oka crisis and commitments to the United States for continental defence had made domestic cuts impossible, the only source was Canadian Forces Europe (CFE). National Defence proposed closing CFE completely, but the Department of External Affairs insisted that some presence was vital. A "Stationed Task Force" (STF) was therefore proposed.[5] As designed by Land Force Command (LFC), the task force would consist of two tank squadrons and two infantry companies with appropriate support, and was to be lodged on or near an allied base in Germany. In addition to the tanks, the STF was to be equipped with between eighteen and thirty-six TOW missiles, making the 1,200-soldier force a powerful battle group that the new Allied Command Europe (ACE) Rapid Reaction Corps would view favourably. The LFC design was criticized as imprudent by the chief of land doctrine and operations, who saw it as creating a non-doctrinal organization for a role that had not yet been determined. This drew a rejoinder from LFC that they were responsible for designing the STF and it had not been submitted for approval. Yet another LFC/NDHQ donnybrook might have ensued if further budget cuts had not killed the STF completely. With that decision, the army was based exclusively in Canada for the first time since the 1950s.[6]

Shifting priorities became public in September 1991, when Defence Minister Marcel Masse announced that the first priority was "defence, sovereignty and civil responsibilities in Canada," followed by collective defence and stability and peacekeeping operations. A subsequent internal Chief of the Defence Staff Force Development Guidance spelled out what this would mean for the armed forces. As mentioned above, the major reduction was to be the elimination of the brigade group in Europe. Readiness levels would be reduced and greater reliance placed on reserve forces. Although the government was aiming for 1.5 percent annual real growth in the defence budget, the budget would remain fixed until 1993. Personnel levels might fall as low as 73,000 of all ranks in the Regular Force. A general-purpose combat capability was still "policy fundamental" for the army, as was the Stationed Task Force and the ability to deploy a brigade for contingency operations.[7]

The next phase of planning, the Canadian Forces Development Plan (CFDP), made it plain how pressed the army would be in this new configuration. The CFDP admitted that the magnitude of change for the army would be "enormous." Although the Regular Force would be reduced, the Militia would grow to almost thirty thousand, requiring additional Regular Force trainers and imposing unfunded training costs. The army was opting to rely on "10/90 battalions" of 10 percent Regular Force personnel and 90 percent Militia soldiers, even though the concept was unproven. A significant portion of air defence would be turned over to the Militia. Third-line support troops would have to be taken from line units. The Leopard tanks and Cougar armoured fighting vehicles would have to be replaced within the fifteen-year planning period and all armoured personnel carriers directly thereafter. Under the heading of "Funding," the CFDP stated: "The funding and cash phasing of the Land Force Capital Equipment Program is a dynamic process which is updated on a continuing basis to reflect changing departmental priorities and financial resource allocations" – bureaucratese for "we intend to make things up as we go along."[8]

The policy was made public in a defence policy statement in April 1992. It was a new White Paper in everything but name. The policy statement cited cuts to the defence budget of $3.4 billion in 1989 and 1990, and additional cuts to planned spending of $2.2 billion in 1991 and 1992. Although the government aimed to increase the portion of the defence budget spent on capital and modernization, this was to be achieved by reducing personnel from 84,000 to 75,000 by 1995-96. In words that could have come from Pierre Trudeau's 1969 defence policy statement, the Conservative government placed considerable emphasis on the domestic roles of the armed services. Pointing out that there was no external threat unique to Canada, the policy statement noted:

> Canadians continue to suffer from the actions of those who disregard Canadian laws and jurisdictions. Problems of the 1990s facing governments include drug

> smuggling, a decaying environment and costly clean-ups, declining fish stocks, illegal immigration and terrorism. All demand national action. National Defence resources are required to detect and monitor potentially harmful activities and to support the enforcement activities of other government departments when their own capabilities are exceeded.

That said, the statement confirmed Canada's traditional support for collective security through NATO and the UN. However, it announced the cancellation of the Stationed Task Force and the end of Canadian Forces Europe. As for peacekeeping, the government forecast the need for new types of interventions, including non-military "preventative action" aimed at stabilizing a government and improving its security infrastructure, as well as armed actions to restore a legitimate government subverted by criminal elements or a neighbouring country.

The policy statement endorsed the army's restructuring plans for three similar brigade groups and a regional command structure. Army strength was set at 19,300 Regulars, 29,500 Militia, and 7,000 Supplementary Reservists. Although the army's heavy equipment – Leopard tanks, M109A1 self-propelled guns, and M113 armoured personnel carriers – were to be repatriated and distributed among the three brigade groups, the government did not intend to replace any of these systems. Announced re-equipment plans included only light armoured vehicles and light field guns. Tanks and infantry fighting vehicles were nowhere in evidence. The statement also announced the reduction of the Canadian Airborne Regiment to a battalion and the reduction of the 1 Canadian Division Headquarters to a task force headquarters for territorial defence and contingency operations.[9]

Even though the policy closely followed the army's own preferences, Land Force Command continued to have significant concerns regarding its affordability and achievability. The army hastened to remind the DCDS that the army in Canada had been at a relatively low level of readiness *before* the cutbacks and that the only high-readiness formation – CFE – had been eliminated. The army itself had proposed relying on the Militia to make up its deficit in numbers, but now reminded NDHQ central planners that without call-out legislation, rounding out the numbers in field force units that were held at about 60 percent strength could be done only by using Regulars. This would create problems of force generation and sustainment. The army also did not want to undertake any further personnel economies to pay for increases in capital funding, especially for the navy and air force. It also warned that bringing the heavy equipment home from Europe meant increased costs and that consequently central planners should not count on army operations and maintenance expenses to decrease.[10] Worse, even though the paid ceiling for the Militia had been increased, the Militia still could not generate enough soldiers to meet army requirements. The so-called paid ceiling of 29,700 was an accounting abstraction based on the assumption that all Militia service would be part-time. However, a significant number of full-time reservists were employed by the army. In addition, the army estimated that 17 percent, or about 5,000 soldiers, at any time were non-effectives. Of the 24,000 or so remaining, 20 to 30 percent were not sufficiently trained to be usable immediately. Thus, the army estimated that the Militia could generate only 17,000 to 19,000 troops at best. The army required about 12,000 troops to round out its peacetime strength, 11,000 military vital-point guards, and about 5,000 for replacements, reinforcement, and sustainment – a total of 28,000. Another 2,700 troops would be required if the army was forced to expand.[11]

The army's plan was less a bold new vision for itself than an attempt to fashion lifeboats and get as many of its passengers and crew as possible on board. The creation of three similar brigade groups, each with a mix of heavy tracked and lighter wheeled vehicles, meant that any major deployment would require the creation of composite formations. Indeed, rounding out units would require drawing out troops from other brigades. This would increase the complexity of planning and add to personnel turbulence as the tempo of operations increased. The preservation of general-purpose combat capability, and therefore tanks, self-propelled guns, and tracked carriers, was logical and defensible from a purely military point of view, as one could easily hypothesize deployments for which heavy equipment would be required. Yet heavy equipment was inconsistent with the government's priority of domestic defence and the ultimately optional nature of any overseas deployment. It also increased costs at a time when budgets were already in crisis and when the government had clearly indicated that it had no intention of replacing heavy equipment. The army also was engaging in wishful thinking when it suggested that legislation allowing it to call out reservists would be forthcoming. As well, it overestimated (or perhaps completely misunderstood) the effect of its regimental system on its culture and the army's links to Canadian society. According to force planners, the regimental system was "a product of historical evolution and it constitutes an essential link with the society which the Land Force represents." It would become plain as the Croatia and Somalia operations unfolded that the regimental system had become a sort of *émigration intérieure* with quite the opposite effect. At any rate, the requirement for composite units appeared to undercut the principles of the regimental system. Overall, the wisdom of embarking on a plan the planning instruction for which stated that "from the outset, it must be recognized that some of the structuring ideals will be unachievable" was questionable.[12] Huddleston's concerns about the protection of rice bowls had been prescient.

Towards Reform: The 1994 *White Paper on Defence*

The 1992 defence policy statement had decisively turned the page on the Cold War and set the army on a new path. It was going to be stationed in Canada, be more dependent on the Militia, and probably be more lightly armoured in the future, although existing heavy equipment would be kept. The continuing fiscal crisis, the need for budgetary restraint, and the election of a new Liberal government meant that a full defence review was required before further adjustments were made.

All three armed services would have preferred the status quo. General John de Chastelain, the chief of the defence staff, stated that "the emphasis on the need to counter the threat posed by the Soviet Union and its allies in Europe, and in the Atlantic and the Pacific [has been] replaced by the concept of general purpose combat capable armed forces, stationed in Canada for the most part, ready to deploy anywhere in the world in defence of Canada's interests." In the case of the army, this meant that the combined arms team (infantry, armour, and artillery) would be retained and the basic organizational unit would remain the brigade group.[13]

The alternative approach, proposed by various "peace groups," was an army that would be useful only for peacekeeping assignments where the principal task was truce enforcement and whose combat capabilities would be reduced to those required for self-defence.

A more sophisticated approach was advanced by the Canada 21 Council, a well-financed group with strong connections to the Liberal Party – more specifically, to the wing of the Liberal Party that had advocated a reduction of Canada's NATO commitment and a "small army" during the late 1960s and early 1970s, prominently including Ivan Head and Donald Macdonald. The Canada 21 Council's glossy report began by stating, "The Cold War is over." It put strong emphasis on using non-military means to take "preventative action" of aid and diplomacy, but was not so optimistic as to think that armed conflict could be eliminated or would even decline in the near future. In fact, it predicted a substantial increase in demand for Canadian peacekeeping troops, placing Canada for the first time in the position of having to refuse requests from the UN for participation. The Council believed, however, that Canada should be selective in the peacekeeping assignments it accepted, and should not participate in operations involving heavy armour or modern air power.

The Council took the view that Canada could support the Secretary-General's requests for troops to "enforce cease-fires" by being prepared to deploy two "light mechanized infantry battalions" with their associated logistic and signals components, or about 2,500 troops in all. This therefore resembled the two battle groups Canada had deployed to the former Yugoslavia. The Council also advocated the maintenance of additional capability to deploy 1,000 more troops for "traditional" peacekeeping operations. It believed that this capability could be affordable, but that the army did not need to be equipped for high-intensity operations against modern, heavily armoured forces. If policy did not change, "the result could be that Canada will have simply a miniature model of the traditional 'general purpose' military force – one with just a little of everything, but not enough of anything to be effective in any conceivable situation."

The force structure the Council proposed sharply reduced the navy to a coast guard plus three "peacekeeping support, multi-role replenishment ships from domestic shipyards," and would have cut the air force's fighter aircraft by two-thirds. The army, on the other hand, would be expanded to four brigades from three and would be equipped with "adequate" helicopters, modern armoured personnel carriers, and armoured vehicles. Tanks, on the other hand, would disappear.[14]

The Canada 21 Council report drew accusations from the defence community that it was a radical attempt to reduce the armed services to a constabulary, but its views regarding the army turned out to be surprisingly mainstream. Parliament reviewed defence policy through a Special Joint Committee of the Senate and the House of Commons. The Special Joint Committee toured the country and heard 275 witnesses at forty-seven meetings in Ottawa and most provincial capitals. Its report noted the breadth of views it had received – from those who wanted a decrease in Canadian commitments and capabilities to service-specific advocates who did not want the committee to lose sight of the contribution made by their arm. The committee came to many of the same conclusions as the Canada 21 Council, although it did not hold out hope that preventive action would be effective. Parliamentarians made it clear that they thought the day of the mass army was over: "We should not equip ourselves for the past – for a replay of World War II, or for Cold War contingencies that our allies have stopped worrying about." Forces to meet a nuclear threat were regarded as redundant, and the committee also warned against maintaining capabilities just because other countries did, because of history or as some international badge of honour. Most importantly – and not surprisingly, because the committee was dominated by government members – the report insisted that forces had to be affordable.[15]

The Joint Committee was content to leave the navy relatively untouched but, like the Canada 21 Council, it recommended reducing the air force and increasing the size of the army. Its recommended air force reduction was a more modest 25 percent, however. The army would be increased by 3,500 troops while the Canadian Forces as a whole would be reduced to 66,700. The army would be built around an expeditionary capability of two battle groups with appropriate logistic, medical, communications, and engineering support. Reacting to the overextension of current operations, the Joint Committee not only aimed lower in terms of expeditionary capability (two battle groups compared with the three deployed by the government) but also recommended a force structure with five formations for every one deployed. The committee wished to equip the army with new armoured personnel carriers and maintain a force equipped with artillery and light armour, but also agreed to maintain tank capability by modernizing the Leopard 1 tanks currently in the inventory.[16]

Parliamentarians stood behind the concept of a unified Canadian Forces and, again echoing the Canada 21 Council, declared that "the current, environmentally-based command structure of the Canadian Forces is not conducive to the most effective management of military forces in the new military environment of the 21st century." The three environmental command headquarters should therefore be disbanded and the "distinctive perspectives" of the three services represented by senior staff at NDHQ instead. The environmental staffs would be placed within a national Joint Staff. A new command structure that was "more geographic and functional," with a single officer in each region responsible for force generation and command of all three environments, would replace the environmental command, pseudo-service structure that had evolved since unification. In other words, the vision of Parliament was that land forces would be bigger and lighter, but the army would cease to exist as an institution.[17]

The government responded to these suggestions in its *1994 White Paper on Defence*. In rhetorical terms, the government position was the most conservative and apparently most supportive of the status quo. A "constabulary force" simply would not do. It would send a message of a lack of commitment to allies and would "betray our history and diminish our future." The government therefore intended to maintain "multi-purpose, combat-capable armed forces." A knowledgeable observer would note, however, that the forces would be "multi-purpose" rather than "general purpose," and indeed the government said that it was not necessary to maintain every type of capability in order to protect Canadian interests or to meet obligations to allies.

The government was prepared to deploy the Canadian Forces for a wide range of missions, including those beyond the range of traditional peacekeeping. Operations could be under multinational auspices, not only those of the UN or NATO. The new status quo, characterized by an increasing number of failed states, ethnic and religious conflict, and border tensions, was seen to require the maintenance of sufficient military resources to meet Canada's interest in maintaining stability.

The army designed by the government would also be larger, with an additional three thousand soldiers added to the field force. The cost of the increase in land forces would be paid for by reductions in headquarters and in the size of the Reserves, and by restructuring of the other services. The most notable reduction was a 25 percent cut in fighter aircraft through elimination of the obsolete and never very effective CF-5. The army would have the capability to deploy three separate battle groups or a brigade group within three months and "vanguard components" within three weeks. In addition, it would maintain an infantry battalion group for service as a standby force for either the UN or NATO. The only new equipment promised was a new armoured personnel carrier. The government noted that the Cougar direct-fire vehicles would "eventually" need to be replaced, but was silent about the future of the tank.

Unlike the Special Joint Committee, the government did not intend to abolish the army as a service through reorganization. It did, however, commit to reducing one layer of headquarters. It also threw a bone to the Reserves by adopting a new mobilization policy. The policy actually did little to change the status quo, as it implicitly regarded the Reserves as augmentees and did not propose to employ Reserves as formed units. Worse, from the perspective of Militia traditionalists, was the government's intent to re-examine the structure of the Militia to determine whether it should not be contributing a greater portion of support services – medical services, logistics, communications, and transport – rather than combat arms.[18]

The 1994 policy review appeared to have reached a consensus on the army. Stabilization operations were the major security requirement and so the army would have to grow, albeit modestly. Civilians generally did not envisage the need for heavy, mechanized infantry, although the requirement for combined arms was accepted. The litmus test for force structure was the tank. No one saw the need for a new one, although the Special Joint Committee would refurbish the existing ones. The concept of the Regular army as a nucleus for the mass army of the future was decisively rejected by everyone. The Regular army was the main force, to be supplemented by the Militia as augmentees or in support roles. Institutionally, "jointness" was preferred over an individual-service type of structure, but it was not at all clear where the elimination of one level of headquarters would lead. The continuity with the army force structure preferred by the Trudeau cabinet in the early 1970s was remarkable.

Internal Reform: Re-examining Doctrine

The collapse of the army's combat development process with the rejection of Corps '96 by the Army Doctrine and Tactics Board (ADTB) in May 1994 left the army without a blueprint for future development. The ADTB had recommended that the Canadian army should simply adopt the US Army's FM100-5 operations field manual as its own operational-level doctrine. The director general land force development, Brigadier-General N.B. Jeffries, objected to this, however. He argued that the Corps '96 project had already developed Canadian operational doctrine and that only those parts of American doctrine that were relevant and suitable should be adopted. He regarded American doctrine as largely unsuitable because of its emphasis on force projection, counter-insurgency, regime change, and reliance on technology "nonexistent in the Canadian Army." Jeffries also claimed that doctrine was culturally dependent and not transferable from one army to another:

> Canadian soldiers are highly respected and valued in both war and peace because they embody qualities that are unique to Canadian culture and society. Canadian soldiers carry no ideological baggage and are imbued with a natural sense of fair play and respect for others. These attributes combined with excellent fighting qualities enable us to carry out missions and tasks many other armies are incapable of.[19]

Notwithstanding these concerns, the Land Force Combat Development staff proceeded with efforts to integrate the FM100-5 concepts with Canadian doctrine. Although the army might have considered itself a paragon of virtue, it was clear that public support was waning and that unless the public understood the requirement for an army, it "risk[ed] irrelevance and ensures its continued underfunding and neglect by politicians." Combat development staff therefore proposed the development of doctrinal documents that would not only define the shape of the army but establish its raison d'être. This would be done through a top-level strategic doctrine manual, *CFP 300 – The Canadian Army*, which would be similar in format to the FM100-5 manual and would "establish that the Army is vital to the nation and always has been." Lower-level manuals would provide concepts at the operational and the tactical levels.[20] Lieutenant-General G.M. Reay, the commander of Land Force Command, accepted the proposal.[21]

Even before the ADTB scrapped Corps '96, some officers at the Canadian Land Force Command and Staff College had been anxious to reformulate army doctrine. Captain Ian Hope considered Corps '96 to be outdated in 1993, and noted that even though combat development staff were careful not to repudiate the Corps studies, they were already attempting to fill in gaps at the operational level. Hope contended that the army should leave behind its narrow mental outlook based on forty years of positional defence in Germany and adopt doctrine that would be applicable to a wider range of conflict. To him, this would be based on manoeuvre warfare theory and would adopt a decentralized command philosophy. Hope did not believe that the operational level of war was tethered to any particular size of force; in fact, in low-intensity conflict, "operations" could be planned and conducted by brigades, units, or even subunits. He forecast that Canada would deploy only units or small formations that would probably have to work independently. Lower-ranking officers would therefore have to function at the operational level – that is, to direct tactical activity in well thought out operations to achieve national objectives. According to Hope, Canadian commanders were "little served by the attrition-oriented ideas presented in the [then current] versions of CFPs 300 and 300(1)." Moreover, their subordinates "would have to work around the inclination for direct combat" embodied in lower-level doctrinal manuals. Hope believed that manoeuvre warfare theory would provide the required flexibility to maximize the use of limited resources in high-intensity operations and to avoid combative confrontation in low-intensity conflicts. It would also help achieve doctrinal compatibility with Canada's major allies, who had already "realized the folly of attritional warfare." He concluded: "We have two options; to adopt a modern approach to warfare and catch up with our allies, or to enter into the type of doctrinal slumbers we experienced in the 1930s which left us doctrinally bankrupt at the beginning of WWII."[22]

Hope had some allies outside Ottawa, such as Lieutenant-Colonel M.M. Fenrich, the Canadian Forces liaison officer to the US Army Combined Arms Center. Fenrich agreed that Canadian doctrine had been driven by a series of NATO plans and exercises in defensive contingency operations and was now out of touch with that of the allies. He also thought that Canadian doctrine had been driven by branch and corps competition for funding and resources, resulting in the Corps '96 paper.[23] Hope was opposed by NDHQ staff, who believed that adopting US doctrine would "once again see Canada as a kind of vassal or colonial state and our army a mere subsidiary or junior partner to the US Army, something clearly unacceptable to the majority of Canadians." They also argued that "manoeuvre warfare and direction [sic] control *(auftragstaktik)* [were] alien to the Canadian tradition of warfighting and the psyche and psychology of Canadian soldiers." To them, it was naïve to think that Canada could simply copy *auftragstaktik* (mission-type orders) from the Germans, operational manoeuvre from the Russians, or technology overmatch from the Americans. In the future, the Canadian army would possess little armour or mechanized forces, would focus on operations other than war, and would engage in only low- to mid-intensity conflict. It therefore required a doctrine appropriate to its reduced capabilities and limited employment roles. The last comments make it clear that Hope's position – that manoeuvre warfare principles could be employed by small formations of light forces – was either misunderstood or rejected.[24]

Brigadier-General Jim Cox, the director general land force development, did not share the conservatism of his staff and advocated a technology-based model of the future army that he called "the Third Millennium (3M) Soldier." Using digital technology, "the 3M Soldier [would] dominate the entire spectrum of conflict and its associated continuum of operations, including the lethal battle space, all of which together will be the Enabling Arena. The Enabling Method will be the Canadian form of manoeuvre warfare doctrine currently being developed." Cox's "Army 2000 Campaign Plan" was endorsed by the Land Force commander, Lieutenant-General J.M.G. Baril, but found few other supporters. Cox's plan was disliked for its rejection of tanks in the force structure, for Cox's lack of consultation of his own staff, and for its heavily Americanized jargon. Baril was forced to "clarify" Cox's paper at the Army Council, saying: "Let me be clear we are a warfighting army." He stated that the army would remain a general-purpose force (in spite of the prose of the White Paper) and that the current Leopard tank fleet would be retained in service to 2010 or beyond. Baril dodged the issue of whether the army could participate in high-intensity conflicts by noting the debate and saying that troops would be committed only when commanders believed them to be ready. He dropped the term "3M Soldier" and pledged that the Army Council would remain his "pre-eminent decision making body."[25]

When the new doctrinal manuals emerged in 1996, they were in the format suggested by Major James R. Near but the operational doctrine content was that of Captain Hope, although both men worked on drafting the document.[26] The new CFP 300, titled *Canada's Army: We Stand on Guard for Thee,* was solidly manoeuvrist in its orientation. It recognized the operational level of war as the link between the strategic and tactical levels, and although it defined the operational level as the level where campaigns were planned for theatres or areas of operation, it did not confine it to large formations. The securing of the Sarajevo Airport by the 1 Royal 22e Régiment Battle Group in the former Yugoslavia was cited as an example of the link between tactical actions and operational effect, because seizing the airport was of critical political and logistic importance. The companion CFP 300-1, *Conduct of Land Operations,* was explicit: the operational level was not defined by the number and size of forces or the echelon of headquarters involved.[27] Both documents adopted manoeuvre warfare principles. Command was to be decentralized and subordinate commanders were expected to act on their commander's intent rather than detailed orders or plans. Combat was aimed at destroying enemy cohesion and will, not necessarily physical destruction. To achieve this, pre-emption, dislocation, and disruption of the enemy on both the physical and moral planes of conflict were to be employed. Commanders were to strive to achieve *fingerspitzengefühl* (fingertip feeling) to quickly comprehend, evaluate, and synthesize all the elements of an operational environment.[28]

As Hope had suggested earlier, Canadian doctrine attempted to cut loose from the idea that military operations always involved combat – or that they should even involve combat. CFP 300 stated: "It should be emphasized that combat operations do not necessarily entail the application of violence." Outcomes could sometimes be achieved by convincing an adversary that if force were applied, he would lose. The Canadian army was intended to be able to conduct both combat and non-combat operations simultaneously, as had been the case in both Yugoslavia and Somalia.[29] This was elaborated in CFP 301 in a full chapter on "operations other than war." By definition, these included domestic operations, service-assisted and protected evacuations, peace-support operations, and humanitarian assistance. Peace support could include peace enforcement and was conceived of as tactically similar to warfighting, but with graduation of the level of force to match the political settlement desired. The aim of operations other than war was to seek de-escalation by controlling and preventing violence. CFP 301 stated in bold type: "In conflicts other than war ... the desired end-state is normally achieved through negotiation." Although Somalia and Yugoslavia were not cited as negative examples, CFP 301 stressed that inappropriate, unethical, or unprofessional conduct off duty would damage the legitimacy of the force and that credibility was based on operations conducted with "restraint, discipline, firmness and consistency, and always within the guidance of the rule of law."[30]

The 1990s thus ended with the army's publication of doctrine based on manoeuvre warfare theory. The key elements of the Canadian version of the concept were that: (1) small units could be actors at the operational level because they could significantly influence outcomes at the theatre level; (2) commanders at all levels must therefore be delegated resources and authority to carry out their commander's intent, and they must have the mental agility and courage to do this; and (3) "manoeuvre" worked on both the physical and moral or psychological levels, requiring a careful calibration of violence or, optimally, its total absence from some operations. Senior leaders recognized that this shift was as significant as the shift during the 1930s from trench warfare to blitzkrieg. At the process level, battle procedure would have to change to include new decision-making techniques such as intelligence preparation of the battlefield, synchronization of forces, and targeting and war-gaming in the sense that two or three courses of action should be developed and walked through during the planning process. The army would also have to move away from positive control to much more delegation to subordinate commanders.[31]

Faced with this challenge, there were deniers of both the ability of the officer corps to change and the appropriateness of asking them to do so. Major Howard Coombs was one of those who thought the officer corps unlikely to assimilate manoeuvre doctrine. In his US Army Command and General Staff College paper, Coombs stated:

> Canadian operational experience in peace and war over the last century has been characterized by: static warfare; attrition; lack of introspective thought; inadequate doctrine; centralized control and decentralized execution; rigid and uncompromising staff procedures as a result of a failure to develop and maintain an operationally capable general staff; and more recently, a neglect of warfighting due to the demands of peace support operations.

He considered it necessary for the Canadian army to "rid [itself] of [its] historical fixation with the methodical battle," but seemed to think this an unlikely prospect. The "heritage of the Land Forces" was "profound mistrust of a superior combined with enforced blind obedience to his every word." Coombs thought that CFP 300 was "admirable" but "at odds with [Canadian] military reality."[32]

The second branch of manoeuvre doctrine deniers – those who thought the concept inappropriate – was represented by Lieutenant-Colonel Roman Jarymowycz, the dean of the Militia Command and Staff Course at the Canadian Land Force Command and Staff College. Jarymowycz derided staff college manoeuvrists as "Jedi Knights" and dismissed the debate between attrition and manoeuvre as conceptually wrongheaded to begin with: "Manoeuvre, while applauded by the officer proletariat, will always be watched suspiciously by the attritionist old guard, tactical Trotskyites are invariably cast out as revisionists by our own attritionist Stalinists. Manoeuvre may be the *vox populi* of the staff college cadres, but it unnerves their bosses." Jarymowycz insisted that there was a cultural basis for doctrine and that in Canada it did not support manoeuvre warfare:

> The war-fighting doctrine developed in the Canadian Corps during the First and Second World Wars formed the basis, the doctrinal principles of what we are

> today. This basis is being eroded by a misinterpretation of foreign doctrines and a disquieting readiness to believe that others may be more professionally creative than we are. This is not completely true now, but may soon be. Caveat emptor.[33]

By the end of the decade, the army had achieved a revision of its doctrine on paper. Evidently, however, instilling the change in the hearts and heads of the officer corps would require more time.

Reform from Without: The Somalia Inquiry and Other Scandals

The 1990s turned out to be a "decade of darkness" for the army, not only because of severe and frequent budget cuts but also because of a succession of investigations, inquiries, revelations, and reports that undermined, if not completely destroyed, public confidence in the senior leadership of the army and of the Canadian Forces as a whole. The catalyst for this prolonged period of public scrutiny was the Somalia Inquiry.

Following the arrest and attempted suicide of Master Corporal Clayton Matchee, the primary accused in the death of the Somali prisoner Shidane Arone, military police from NDHQ arrived in Belet Huen to investigate Arone's torture and death. Charges were laid against five soldiers, ranging from murder to negligent performance of duty. Subsequently, charges were also laid against Captain Michel Rainville and Lieutenant-Colonel Carol Mathieu for the 4 March 1993 incident involving the baiting and ambush of infiltrators in which one Somali was killed and one wounded. In the case of Arone's death, all the accused were convicted of or pleaded guilty to at least some of the charges against them, except Matchee, who was found incompetent to stand trial. Both Rainville and Mathieu were acquitted (Mathieu by two courts martial). The trials kept the incidents before the public throughout 1993 and 1994.[34]

At the same time, Chief of the Defence Staff Admiral John Anderson convened a board of inquiry under Major-General Tom de Faye, commander of Land Force Western Area. Its mandate was to investigate the leadership, discipline, operations, actions, and procedures of the Canadian Airborne Regiment Battle Group. De Faye was hobbled, however, by the exclusion of any matters that were under military police investigation. This left the board of inquiry to work around the edges of the main problem. De Faye concluded that, except for the unfortunate incidents subject to the courts martial and flawed discipline in 2 Commando, nothing much was amiss. The board approved the layout of the camp, the screening of personnel, the selection of the CAR, and the adaptation of the regiment to cultural differences. General-purpose combat training was endorsed for peace support missions. The board concluded that "the outwardly alert posture of 2 Commando did not lead, in the Board's opinion, to any significant inappropriate behaviour or regrettable consequences within their area of responsibility in the town of Belet Huen. Nor did it prevent them from carrying out their mission of providing security to the citizens of Belet Huen in an extremely satisfactory manner, winning the respect of the authorities and the appreciation of the citizens of Belet Huen."[35]

It appeared that Somalia had been laid to rest by the courts martial and the de Faye board of inquiry, but a year after the report was issued, an internal review by Major-General Jean Boyle, the associate assistant deputy minister (policy and communications), indicated that it suffered from serious deficiencies and weaknesses, and that much of the information found in it that had not been publicly released would become public through the various courts martial. Boyle found, for example, that the conclusion that the CAR was well trained was not supported by the testimony heard by the board. He also questioned the leadership of the Canadian Joint Force Somalia (CJFS), referring to documents indicating that there had been "direct attempts to cover up the facts behind the 4 March incident [the baiting and shooting of two thieves, one fatally], which will no doubt be brought to light during the court proceedings. Also the 16 March incident [the death in custody of Shidane Arone] reveals a blatant attempt at the officer level to 'cover up' this incident. This will probably become public knowledge."[36]

Boyle's report was overtaken by events. In early 1994 a video made by CAR members in Somalia showed swastika-tattooed soldiers drinking and making racist comments about Somalis. This was followed in early 1995 by the broadcast of a second video, showing 1 Commando members participating in an initiation ritual that involved vomit, urine, and excrement. A third video, also of initiation rites, appeared that same year. Although some argued that the behaviour was "no worse than that in a college fraternity," the public was outraged. Defence Minister David Collenette took the extreme and unusual step of disbanding the Canadian Airborne Regiment on 5 March 1995. A few weeks later, the government appointed a Commission of Inquiry into the Deployment of Canadian Forces to Somalia. The commission was chaired by Judge Gilles Létourneau, with journalist Peter Desbarats and Judge Robert Rutherford as members. The commission's purview included not only the pre-deployment training and deployment of the CAR to Somalia but also the alleged post-deployment cover-ups.[37]

The commission's public hearings lasted for two years. The televised hearings were often confrontational, with commissioners clearly concerned the department was withholding evidence or even being dishonest in its representations. The public got a clear view of how regimental politics had affected the staffing of senior positions and how the army had no clear way of determining what it meant when it said that a unit was "ready." They also watched the most senior officers of the CAR's chain of command testify that they had no idea that the regiment indulged in initiation rituals, and saw General Boyle, now the CDS, shut down the entire Canadian Forces for a day for a "great Easter Egg hunt" to find missing records demanded by the commission. They also witnessed Major-General Brian Vernon's explanation of e-mails that could be construed as encouraging senior officers to collude in their testimony. Both Collenette and Boyle resigned in early October 1996. The new minister, Douglas Young, asked the commission to report by 31 March 1997. Despite the commission's complaints that it could not analyze the large number of documents that it had finally received late in the process or examine senior NDHQ officials, Young stuck to his deadline. The commission reported without coming to a conclusion on the issue of a cover-up.[38]

The Somalia Inquiry would have placed the army in a bad enough light even if it had taken place in isolation. As it turned out, the breakdown in discipline at the Bakovici hospital became known between September 1995 and July 1996 and provided another example of professional failure. Equally distressing was a string of allegations that senior army officers had abused their positions by lining their pockets through unjustified expense claims and by misusing government resources, such as executive aircraft, for their personal benefit. The extensive allegations filled a book, *Tarnished Brass: Crime and Corruption in the Canadian Military,* by Scott Taylor and Brian Nolan.[39]

The army's first reaction to evidence of professional failure was a combination of concern and denial. Colonel G.J. Oehring, the Land Force Command G1 (chief of staff for personnel) informed the commander in December 1994 that he had met with NDHQ staff to determine whether they could develop a method of judging "the pulse of the Army," and if so, whether they could then develop recommendations to address morale problems. Oehring saw the main issue as a "loss of confidence and trust" due to force reductions, loss of job security, increased commitments, frozen pay, rent increases for military housing, and denigration by the media. Especially problematic was the continuing malignment in the media over Somalia and the government's treatment of the troops as "costly disposables." Oehring called on senior leadership to acknowledge the crisis and on ministers and the prime minister to make public commitments and undertake an information campaign to change "public misconceptions." Oehring did not think the army responsible in any way for its predicament, however. He thought soldiers recognized that problems were beyond the control of senior leaders and that the NDHQ personnel system was at the root of "an increasingly *impotent military leadership and uncaring system.*" He did not hesitate to lay some of the blame on the troops themselves: "The Army's great system of paternal leadership and caring [had], alas, turned many of our troops into 'groupism junkies' and spoiled them for the routines of normal garrison and family life. *Leadership in a sense has thus created its own lasting problems*" (emphasis in original).[40]

In March 1995 Oehring claimed that a clear and coherent picture had emerged. The army was suffering from media denigration or neglect as a result of a social revolution "largely spearheaded by the Women's Movement, that brought changes so profound to family structures, human rights and sexual equality as to end much of the known way of military life; and which rushed in a dizzying and ever accelerating application of computer technologies to weapons." He asserted that many believed that morale was under attack from a greater number of "destructive agents" than at any time in the recent past. Chief among these agents was the media – "accountable to no one and capable of unlimited self defence," "predatory," and "exploitative." The government was also on the army's enemies list – able to "obliterate an entire regiment at a stroke of the pen when political futures seem threatened, yet these same powers cannot ease the hurt of thousands of soldiers and their families." Oehring proposed a freeze on prices on bases, temporary employment with base construction engineering for soldiers on leave or off duty, the granting of priority to soldiers' families for civilian jobs on bases, and a transfer of administrative jobs from NDHQ to isolated bases.[41]

Other officers were equally distressed, but not so inclined to exclude senior military officers from those responsible for the problem. In September 1996 Major-General Clive Addy, commander of Land Force Western Area, resigned, saying he was convinced that it was impossible to re-establish a bond of trust and understanding between the public, the government, and the armed forces from within the military. Addy cited abuses of power by senior military and civilian officials and said that "we must rid ourselves of the dual spectres of macho thuggery and bureaucratic careerism." He accused NDHQ of having confused policy with partisan politics, and civilian and military officials of having compromised the well-being and loyalty of soldiers for political peace or to divert criticism. He deplored the disbandment of the Canadian Airborne Regiment and requested that a Somalia campaign medal be issued.[42]

The crisis led the army to significantly change its plans for the contents of CFP 300, its fundamental doctrine manual. Initially, a significant portion was to have been devoted to justifying the army's existence to the public and to the political level. By 1996, this additional content had expanded considerably as part of a "campaign plan for army renewal." CFP 300 was redesigned to include material establishing the moral and ethical basis for army professionalism. The objective was to attack professional failings that had become visible and that cast doubt on the quality of army leadership. The publication could therefore be used as a principal tool in restoring the army's image. Doctrinal staff recognized that the army had real, deep problems that threatened its existence and that a lot more than a public relations exercise was required.[43]

In the end, CFP 300 became part operations manual, part public relations brief, and part sermon to the faithful. Only about a third of its pages were devoted to combat concepts and structures. It contained a complete chapter on professionalism and ethos but could not define precisely what it was, saying that "no single document can fully articulate this ethos, [yet] it is nonetheless implicit in the very nature of the profession of arms." Although it claimed that the ethos required honouring of Canadian values, it never spelled out what these values were. For the most part, the values spoken of were universally recognized virtues: duty, integrity, discipline, and honour. It did sermonize at times, warning that neglect of the military ethos encouraged soldiers to see their service as just a job and become self-serving, or that the military profession could take a "rogue form" and become focused on spurious concepts of elitism, either of which would result in a loss of public confidence and trust.[44]

Much of the remainder of the discussion of the military ethos was a defence of tradition. The "regimental system" – again, undefined – was lauded as "rich in comradeship and tradition, and which exudes shared values and unity of purpose." On the other hand, CFP 300 warned against taking regimentalism too far and allowing it to become more important than the good of the army as a whole or an impediment to promotion on the basis of merit. The preservation of "traditional symbols" such as dress, rank, and skill badges was held to be "equally important." CFP 300 occasionally veered into a creed that would not have been out of place in a minor English public school: "Good morale and *esprit de corps* are founded on and sustained by faith in leaders, maintenance of standards, a strong and warm sense of comradeship, having good matériel support, opportunities for sport and recreation and the desire to uphold the standards and traditions of those who have gone before." The army also made it clear that "management" was a function subordinate to command, and was "best effected by empathetic leadership." It admonished Defence Department managers to recognize the needs of individual soldiers and their families and to ensure continuing care and concern for the wounded and injured.[45]

The authors of CFP 300 claimed that it provided an image of what a professional army in a democratic society was supposed to be.[46] It had not, however, progressed much beyond the vision of a colonial British regimental culture advocated by Lieutenant-General J.J. Paradis in his submission to the Task Force on Review of Unification of the Canadian Forces in 1979. The army did understand that, post-Somalia, there was a dark side to its regimental culture but it was reluctant to let go. Major-General N.B. Jeffries's warning that the army must reject the view that it had been contaminated by societal values, and instead remain in step with Canadian society in order to retain legitimacy and public support, went largely unaddressed.[47] The Somalia Inquiry had opened the floodgates, however, and reform of the army was no longer under its control.

Towards Constabulary Realism

After terminating the Somalia Inquiry, Defence Minister Young was forced to provide a replacement. He initiated a study on the reform of military justice and commissioned four academics to report individually on what they thought was wrong with the Canadian Forces and what should be done about it. In March 1997 he used these studies as the basis of a report of his own – with a hundred recommendations – to Prime Minister Chrétien.

Young received a wide range of advice from the four academics. On the right, David J. Bercuson cautioned that a large-scale conventional war was still the most likely job for the army, citing the Korean, Six-Day, Yom Kippur, Falklands, and Gulf wars. Bercuson echoed many of the Task Force on Unification's criticisms, recommending the elimination of "Hellyer corporals" and the NDHQ personnel appraisal system. Jack Granatstein's perspective was even more pessimistic:

> Race, language, ethnicity, gender, sexual orientation – the list is endless. Our polity has been fragmented under the strain, and our political parties, or some of them, have become advocates for interest groups or regional causes. At the same time, there is rising crime, growing poverty and homelessness, a decline in educational standards, and an increase in marriage breakdown and the number of single-parent families. The spirit of the times is profoundly anti-elitist and unhealthy.

Like Bercuson, Granatstein recommended a mechanized army, but he went further, proposing a separate Canadian Forces headquarters with service chiefs having the right of access to the minister "in extraordinary circumstances and with the CDS' concurrence." The CDS would rule by "moral authority," and Granatstein appeared to favour a return to the old Chairman of the Chiefs of Staff system.

On the left, Albert Legault and Desmond Morton saw things somewhat differently. Legault considered the Somalia crisis to have been only the most recent one caused by the failure of the military to accept subordination to civilian authority. Morton considered the resistance to gender equality and ethnic balance misplaced, and rejected attempts to brand as careerists those officers who supported these values. The past traditionalists longed for was "either imaginary or, in contemporary Canada, improbable." Neither Legault nor Morton wanted to disassemble National Defence Headquarters into civil and military components – to reverse unification, as it were. Morton in particular rejected complaints that structures were the problem. It was true that ministers had not always accepted military advice, but "who would welcome advice that included exaggerated risk assessments, unresolved conflicts among competing interests and a measure of self-promotion by senior advisors." Like Legault, he saw the problem as stemming from a divergence in policy choices between politicians and soldiers, not from the structure of the Forces or the department. Although Morton recommended the retention of a heavily equipped army, arguing that the Srebrenica massacre put paid to the case for lightly armed peacekeepers who could only stand by and watch, he did not advocate a bigger force. His answer to the question "how much is enough?" was "as little as possible," and he believed that Canadian defence policy had "succeeded brilliantly" in this. Legault went much further, recommending a purely constabulary force.

What all the advisers had in common was the belief that the officer corps was undereducated and out of touch with Canadian society. According to Granatstein, the officer corps was "remarkably ill-educated ... surely one of the worst in the Western world." All agreed that a degreed officer corps was a requirement. There was also broad consensus that there was both a need and an opportunity for strategic rethinking of defence policy. Legault pointed out that the military was not solely responsible for failures of strategic direction or for the misemployment of forces in search of national prestige.[48]

Doug Young therefore had a wide range of advice to choose from. The path he picked was largely down the middle. He recognized that shifts in the global landscape and actual and pending cuts to the defence budget had significantly changed the environment of the Canadian Forces and the army. Although there was no direct or immediate threat to Canada, and although sovereignty and North American defence commitments came first, Canadians were "committed internationalists" and, within the limits of their resources, needed to be able to participate in multinational operations. He therefore endorsed the "multi-purpose, combat capable" force structure presented in the *1994 White Paper on Defence* as the appropriate course, while advocating stable and predictable funding levels in the future.

The minister tilted towards his advisers on the left in making it clear that the military must respect women's rights and reject discrimination based on race or sexual orientation. He recognized, moreover, that stabilization operations were extremely difficult and morally ambiguous, often forcing soldiers to choose between competing goods or evils under the glare of the media spotlight. He therefore instructed the Forces to produce a statement of values and beliefs to be incorporated in all recruiting, training, and professional development programs and personnel appraisals. He also rejected calls for separation of the civil and military components of National Defence Headquarters, and stated simply that the CDS had direct access to him and, when necessary, to the prime minister. He did, however, put in place measures to clarify civil and military accountabilities and to educate the officer corps regarding them.

Young also agreed with the consensus among the advisers that the regimental system had bred unhealthy rivalries and had overemphasized loyalty to the regiment at the expense of loyalty to the Canadian Forces as a whole. He therefore instructed the Forces to ensure that everyone appreciated the need for loyalty to the Forces as a whole, including ending regimental affiliations for officers above the rank of lieutenant-colonel and removing regimental affiliations from all army battle schools.

A series of reforms and improvements directed at operational missions were instituted. A Peace Support Training Centre was established at CFB Kingston and the Lester B. Pearson Canadian International Peacekeeping Centre at Cornwallis, Nova Scotia. There was greater emphasis on joint and combined training, more instruction to improve the handling of detainees and prisoners of war, and new restrictions on alcohol consumption.[49]

A major focus of Young's reforms was the re-examination of the officer education and professional development system. The reformed curriculum of the Royal Military College placed greater emphasis on the arts, humanities, and social sciences. The Canadian Forces College introduced major study components in national security studies and strategic studies, and eventually was able to offer a Master of Defence Studies degree. Within a decade, the officer corps would achieve Roger Rowley's goal of the baccalaureate degree as the basic educational qualification: in 2009, 90 percent of officers held an undergraduate degree and 50 percent had a graduate degree.[50] Formal education became a major factor in career advancement and command appointment.

A degreed officer corps was only a small part of the changes taking place, however. Young's initiative was carried forward by his successors. The post-Somalia reforms eventually led to a concept of Canadian Forces–wide military professionalism that included the key elements of the modernizers but also moved substantially beyond their vision to take into account post–Cold War realities. The reform process began with the appointment of Lieutenant-General

Romeo Dallaire as a special adviser to the chief of the defence staff, with a mandate to completely revise requirements for commissioned officers and for general officers. One of Dallaire's first steps was to launch a project called "Debrief the Leaders," which surveyed more than eight hundred officers on the challenges they had encountered in operations. The study included the Gulf War; UN Chapter VI operations such as the UN Protection Force (UNPROFOR) in the former Yugoslavia and the UN Operation in Somalia (UNOSOM); UN Chapter VII operations such as the NATO Stabilization Force (SFOR) and the Kosovo Force (KFOR); and domestic operations, including the confrontation with First Nations at Oka, Quebec, the Winnipeg flood, and the eastern Canada ice storm in 1998. The survey found that the Cold War "normal" of confrontation between states with similar weapons and reasonably well understood goals had been left behind by stability operations marked by high complexity, ambiguity, danger, and frustration. The report stated:

> C[anadian] F[orces] officers trained in the context of the Cold War and focused on the tactical level simply did not readily grasp the political, strategic and operational dimensions that have transformed how, when and to what purpose military force is used. The levels of frustration and stress generated by the contrast between conventional military philosophy, education and doctrine and real-world conditions were extremely high throughout the period.
>
> There is a growing unease with the inappropriateness of conventional paradigms and increasing awareness of the need for expanded officer training and education. That much is apparent from the evidence presented by the officers surveyed, based on their years of hard experience. A decisive paradigm shift is also required in the collective mind-set in terms of apprehending and integrating the utter transformation in the global security environment ...
>
> [The] conventional model of conflict, which assigns different functions, qualitatively and quantitatively, to the levels of strategy, operations and tactics, in fact retains a great deal of its coherence in the new global security environment. Now, however, strategic, operational and tactical levels, and indeed the whole military framework, are most often subordinated to diplomatic, economic, and even cultural factors. The potential for fighting is almost always present, but seldom predominates. And even if fighting is reverted to, the operation will be tightly controlled in pursuit of limited political/military objectives. In this context, the only way to be effective as leaders and commanders is "... by approaching the world as a globalist. That means always moving back and forth among the economic, national security, political, cultural, environmental and technological dimensions – assigning different weight to each in different contexts."[51]

The report predicted that officers of the future would need a military ethos that retained the concept of the soldier as a warrior while complementing it with the concepts of the soldier as a diplomat and a scholar. It quoted one senior officer who said that officers would have to redefine what professional job satisfaction meant by accepting the roles of humanitarian assistance and aid to the civil power in disasters or environmental crises, in addition to their traditional roles of war and deterrence. In summary, the objective of the profession "will be viable international relations, not a defeated opponent, stability and the cessation of violence, not the classic battlefield success."[52]

This new definition of professionalism thus closely paralleled what Morris Janowitz called the "constabulary force." Pointing to much the same dilemmas about the inapplicability of the traditional model – even during the Cold War – Janowitz called for a new set of military self-conceptions:

> The use of force in international relations has been so altered that it seems appropriate to speak of constabulary forces, rather than military forces. The constabulary concept provides continuity with past military experiences and traditions, but it also offers a basis for the radical adaptation of the profession. The military establishment becomes a constabulary force when it is continuously prepared to act, committed to the minimum use of force, and seeks viable international relations, rather than victory, because it has incorporated a protective military posture. The constabulary outlook is grounded in, and extends, pragmatic doctrine.[53]

The unpublished version of the officership reform project report, *Canadian Officership in the 21st Century*, did not pull any punches. The report found that although the armed services had high skills at the tactical level, they had failed to develop doctrine or skill at the operational and strategic levels. No adequate means existed to identify the competencies required or to test skills. Officer development had overemphasized "things" and practical skills, and what education was provided arrived too late in an officer's career. The Canadian Forces was not a "learning organization" and its culture inhibited organizational learning through "service parochialism, tribalism and stove-piping." Furthermore, the armed services needed to reintegrate with Canadian society and become a "career of choice."[54]

The final, published report did not contain any direct analysis or criticism of the status quo, but the analysis of the early versions had clearly been accepted. The "strategic objectives" of the officer professional development system included the development of the intellectual capacity of officers to command in complex, multidimensional operations with the objective of "the ordered application of military force" rather than victory. Understanding the "warrior ethos" was still part of the package, but not the centrepiece. Critical thinking (including critical analysis of the ethos), managing change, developing a learning organization, and making the military a career of choice all assumed much more prominent places in officer development.[55]

The process culminated in 2003 with the publication of *Duty with Honour: The Profession of Arms in Canada*, a work signed off by the chief of the defence staff and published by the Leadership Institute. It was the most complete and sophisticated statement of the military profession that the armed services had yet produced. It presented a theoretical underpinning for the military profession, showed how the military serves Canada in practice, and codified what it means to be a military professional. It went far beyond what the army had produced in CFP 300 five years earlier.[56]

Duty with Honour did not explicitly endorse the concept of the military as a constabulary force, but it appeared to lean in that direction. Although it noted both Huntington and Janowitz as "classic works," it drew nothing from either except the conclusion of both that "the essential function of the military profession is the ordered application of military force in defence of the state and its interests."[57] The model of professionalism was very much like that advocated by the Debrief the Leaders Project report. *Duty with Honour* called for the profession to maintain not only the abilities of the soldier warrior but also those of the soldier diplomat and the soldier scholar.[58] It pointed to the need for understanding "new forms of conflict" in which the actions taken by NCOs, warrant officers, and their subordinates can and do have consequences "up to and including the strategic and political level."[59] The concept made non-commissioned members of the profession and adopted the position taken by Rowley almost forty years earlier – that tactical leadership should be delegated to NCOs, leaving time for the officer corps to become proficient at the operational, strategic, and political/military levels.

Duty with Honour took great pains to explain both the legal structure for civilian control of the military and also the way in which the integrated civilian/military National Defence Headquarters worked. This appears to have been both a rebuttal of advocates of a standalone military headquarters and a response to the findings of the Debrief the Leaders survey that junior and mid-level officers did not understand how the national headquarters worked or why their mission objectives were often unclear, resulting in an "us-versus-them" mindset.[60] *Duty with Honour* defined the military profession as incorporating mainstream values but adding to them its own ethos based on unlimited liability, duty to obey lawful orders, and the "warrior's honour" of restraint and discipline.

The concept placed a great deal of stress on the theme of adherence to the law of armed conflict – not surprising given the origins of the project. It devoted a good deal of effort to underlining the importance of expertise, critical thinking, and lifelong learning. It acknowledged the importance of "history, heritage and traditions" to the maintenance of cohesion and esprit de corps, but disappointed some by not mentioning regimentalism at all.[61]

Overall, *Duty with Honour* would pass the test of being what most Canadians assume their military should be, and is. Traditionalists would find at least a minimum of their concerns addressed by the explicit recognition of unlimited liability and duty of obedience. The document, however, was strongly modernist in its orientation, and military professionals in the modernist camp would agree with nearly all of it.

A great deal of substance was given to the new model of professionalism. In 2002 the Canadian Forces established a Leadership Institute with a mandate to conduct research on all aspects of military leadership, and the entire military educational system was reorganized as the Canadian Defence Academy under a two-star officer. The Leadership Institute has been diligent in conducting research and publishing on both historical and current leadership issues. The growth in the number of degreed officers and the number of graduate degrees speaks for itself. The army has revived its Lessons Learned Centre, although the focus so far has been almost entirely on minor tactics.

Sixty years after Charles Foulkes articulated the need for a better-educated officer corps and one that was more integrated with Canadian society, his vision finally appeared to be taking shape across the Canadian Forces. The traditionalist paternal aristocratic model was in extremis, if not dead. The Forces officer corps, for the first time since the 1969 Rowley Report, had a coherent view of the profession, this time with far greater consensus and institutional support behind it. The extent to which the army embraced these changes was unclear, however, as evidenced by CFP 300.

The Reserves

With the abandonment of Corps '96, the withdrawal from permanent stationing of troops in Europe, and the reduction in size of the army, the mass army appeared to be no more. The *1994 White Paper on Defence* made it plain that there were no plans for using the Militia as the base for a big army, stating: "Reserve forces are intended as augmentation and sustainment for Regular Force units, and, in some cases, for tasks that are not performed by Regular Forces." It also stated that the government had "reconsidered the traditional approach to mobilization planning." The first two stages involved filling out the Regular Force. The third stage was envisaged to be the creation of a Korean War–type force and the fourth stage national mobilization for total war. Only "no-cost plans" were to be made for the final stage. Reserves were to be reduced in number, with special attention given to the Militia where the government observed that some units required "rejuvenation" to be more efficient and "better able to contribute to the Total Force concept." The government also said that consideration would be given to assigning more units to service support roles such as medical, logistics, communications, and transport functions. Finally, it warned that units that had diminished in size could be cut and that local communities must take more responsibility for sustaining Reserve traditions and activities.[62]

Given the poor state of the Militia in the early 1990s, this plan seemed logical. Attrition had remained high, at 23 percent annually for all the Primary Reserves, and training continued to be an "endless operation" of training new recruits to a minimum standard. According to the Auditor General of Canada, the Militia still could not conduct field operations above the subunit level. Training staff estimated that a large proportion of Militia soldiers would have to redo basic operational training before deployment. Militia commanding officers estimated that less than half of their soldiers would turn out voluntarily for a combat task. Indeed, actual experience was consistent with these dismal opinions. For example, the Militia had struggled to meet Lieutenant-Colonel Jim Calvin's requirement for 550 soldiers for ROTO 2 of CANBAT 1 in the former Yugoslavia. Volunteers came from seventy units and Calvin took only 385 of them overseas, where those selected performed extremely well. There were good soldiers in the Militia, but the organization was hopelessly inefficient at producing them.[63]

The Militia, however, had not given up on its notion of there being two armies – the Regular army and the Militia – or its ambitions to be Canada's mobilization base on which a big army could be reconstituted in an emergency. Fearing that there was a plan to halve its number of units and personnel, it mobilized its political resources to pressure Defence Minister Collenette to suspend Militia reorganization and establish a Special Commission on the Restructuring of the Reserves (SCRR). The agenda of the main Militia pressure group, which called itself "Reserves 2000," was a radical one. On the premise that the *1994 White Paper on Defence* had adopted mobilization as a national goal, it called for more than doubling the size of the Militia to 45,000, and for an independent governance structure that separated the Militia from the Regular army. Reserves 2000 solved the funding problem by assuming most of it away. Regarding purchasing equipment for an army three times the current size, it simply commented that "there will likely be some incremental cost."[64]

The SCRR was chaired by former Chief Justice of Canada Brian Dickson, who was joined by retired Lieutenant-General Charles Belzile, the former commander of Mobile Command, and prominent historian Jack Granatstein. It held extensive hearings across Canada, where it heard testimony regarding the poor state of the Militia. The SCRR adopted much of the Militia's view of the world as its own. Its report accepted the premise that the Militia was the army's "footprint" in society and a vital link to the wider community. It chided the government for its lack of planning for mass mobilization, which "seem[ed] very imprudent." It regarded detailed plans for Stages 3 and 4 of mobilization as a requirement to "reflect clearly defined roles for the ... Militia, as the basis for recruitment, training and the provision of formed units." The SCRR recommended that the Militia be tasked to provide subunits for overseas deployments, and that it be organized on the basis of a corps, with regional brigades. It did agree, however, with the department's plan to combine understrength units for training.[65]

The SCRR consulted with Reserves 2000 before releasing its report and obtained apparent support, but its recommendation that weaker units be combined with stronger ones drew the group's wrath. The minister's acceptance of the SCRR report also left the army with few good alternatives. A task force to examine mobilization recommended adoption of the twice-abandoned Corps '86 model as the organization of the Militia. The task force thought that the Militia should accept a lower standard of readiness to minimize the length of training required, rather than have some units at a higher level of readiness than others. NDHQ staff did not think much of the task force's plan, however. They condemned it as "shallow and ... more a collation of opinions than a well researched and rational study." The army had learned that its plans needed to start with defence policy. According to the director of army doctrine:

> The Militia cannot develop in a vacuum a structure to satisfy stages 3 and 4 of mobilization when there is not yet any DND/CF or Army plans. The Militia should be structured to fill holes in the actual structure to allow the deployment of a sustainable bde gp [brigade group] and BG [battle group] as required by our actual Defence Policy stated in the 1994 White Paper.

Moreover, the problems of forming a mass army that had become evident during the Corps '86 exercise were still fresh in the minds of army staff. There would be no equipment for the corps-sized force being planned, so training more soldiers did not make sense. Moreover, simply planning a corps-sized number of combat troops would be of little purpose unless communications zone and national infrastructure requirements were also met. Guarding vital points in

Canada might well require a large number of troops, but plans allowed for a full year to prepare for this mission and it was questionable whether any force in being was required to carry it out. Having all units at the same level of readiness was simply unaffordable.[66]

The department therefore did what many would accuse it of doing best: it engaged in bureaucratic delay. Rather than start work on an actual mobilization plan, the chief of the defence staff informed the House of Commons Standing Committee on National Defence and Veterans Affairs that the department would develop a "mobilization framework." The Minister's Monitoring Committee, a group of prominent persons appointed to ride herd on implementation of the Somalia Inquiry and other commitments, called this "a sparse framework of vague intentions ... inadequate ... and disappointing." In its final report a few months later, the Minister's Monitoring Committee found not only that no progress had been made on mobilization plans or on clarifying the role of the Militia but also that Militia strength had declined, training had been cut, and various other SCRR recommendations had been abandoned.[67]

Peace between the Militia and the Regular Force was not restored until the May 2001 appointment of Lieutenant-General Michael Jeffery as special adviser to the chief of the defence staff for Land Force reserve restructuring and as the designate chief of the land staff. Jeffery allocated more resources to Militia problems and established a project management office under a major-general to direct reforms. He intended to increase the Militia strength to 18,500 and integrate the Militia into the army's development plan. His concept for doing this was "managed readiness," which appeared more equitable by graduating the readiness levels of Regular Force units as well as those of the Militia. Reserves 2000 appeared to be mollified by Jeffery's program and by the promise that "hat badges" and unit identities would be retained, but the fundamental issue remained: there was no mobilization plan. And while the government had approved most of the SCRR recommendations, it never agreed to job protection legislation, a key enabler of any mobilization concept. By 2002 the government had brought in the Public Safety Act, which proposed to protect reservists' jobs if they were called out for an emergency, but not for training or non-emergency service. By 2005 regulations to effect even that much had not been promulgated. Ten years after the *1994 White Paper on Defence*, not much had changed.[68]

Assessing the 1990s

The 1990s certainly did turn out to be a "decade of darkness" – one that brought much turmoil and pain to the army through budget cuts, restructurings, command and staff failures, and internecine warfare between Regulars and Reserves. Nevertheless, the decade did set the army on a new trajectory in terms of its thinking. The army explicitly dropped its quest for bigness and began to recognize the contribution it could make as a small force. The "soldier-diplomat" and "soldier-scholar" attained at least some legitimacy alongside the "warrior" as complex stabilization missions demonstrated that general-purpose warfare skills were no longer sufficient and could not simply be downscaled to meet the needs of peace enforcement. Yet it would be wrong to conclude that the army had reformed, modernized, and attained unity with civil society. The army was still culturally chained to its British past even as Canadian society was becoming ever less anglo. The dispute between the Regular Force and the Militia demonstrated that the Reserves had not even progressed as far as the Regular Force and were mentally trapped in the 1940s, to which they were attempting to return.

Civilian leadership appeared to have coalesced around the concept of an army that could mount brigade-sized contingency forces for mid-intensity operations. Certainly, both Conservative and Liberal governments showed no hesitation in deploying forces for various types of stability operations under a wide range of conditions. Yet civilian leadership was less than sterling in several respects. It had neither the expertise to assess whether its piling on of missions in the early 1990s would result in overextension nor the will to question the army's can-do attitude very closely. When trouble arose, it followed a strategy of keeping a lid on problems, at least passively if not actively. It also allowed the army (and the other services) to drift into dubious practices of entitlement and privilege for senior officers instead of vigorously insisting on integrity when problems were first revealed. Civilian leadership had much to answer for in relation to the scandals that came to light during the decade. It also proved weak and irresolute when challenged. Reserves 2000 was able to force the government to abandon a mobilization concept that was consistent with foreign and defence policy as well as being affordable, in favour of a discarded approach that was both inconsistent with policy and beyond the government's means to implement. Even considering the fact that governments must always weigh the electoral costs and benefits of policy, the failure to resist Reserves 2000 was a costly mistake that would prolong the inefficiency and irrelevance of the Militia for another decade or more.

By the turn of the century, the army was on the road to becoming a national force but still a long way from its destination.

Conclusion

WRITING ABOUT THE CANADIAN Army's early history from 1860 to 1939, Stephen Harris concluded that "there appears to have been a consistent and fundamental disharmony between the requirements of maintaining a modern professional army in Canada and the way Canadian society has developed, influenced by its geographical isolation, its relatively small population, and its dependence first upon Great Britain, and then upon the United States as a defender of last resort."[1] The sources of disharmony may have changed somewhat over time, from political patronage in the Militia to competition for funding from social programs, but tension has continued into the twenty-first century.

The Policy Problem

The army's view of an appropriate national strategy and its role in it developed during the Second World War and changed little until the end of the Cold War. The army had suffered from lack of preparedness prior to the war and from deficits in professionalism caused by rapid wartime expansion. It did not want to return to being a small cadre force. Its postwar plan was for an army of two corps supported by universal military training. In light of the political crisis over the imposition of conscription during the war, these proposals appear to have been acutely out of touch with the reality of Canadian society. The army quickly discarded the concept of conscription but clung doggedly to its desire to be a large, heavy force. This was the core of the proposal sent by Lieutenant-General S.F. Clark to Defence Minister George Pearkes in 1958, which would have structured the army around three high-readiness brigades and a light brigade for continental defence and UN missions. It also underpinned the Corps '86 and Corps '96 projects, which drove army planning from the mid-1970s to the mid-1990s.

Implicit in the army's world view was that it was going to be part of an alliance force. Its early postwar plans envisaged a continuing association with the British

Army, and a more prominent role because of Britain's economic distress after the war. The army segued from Empire to NATO without effort or thought as NATO requirements became de facto Canadian requirements. Circumstances favoured the army's preferences during the early Cold War years as the war in Korea and the Soviet challenge in Europe motivated politicians to maintain what for Canada in peacetime were sizable ground forces. But there was little political enthusiasm for large overseas forces on a continuing basis.

The bias of the civil authorities is perhaps best summed up by Desmond Morton's comment to Defence Minister Douglas Young that the answer to "How much is enough?" had been "as little as possible" and that Canadian defence policy had "succeeded brilliantly" in this. Prime Minister Mackenzie King quickly reduced the 478,090-strong army of the Second World War to 19,000 Regular soldiers by 1947. Early Canadian plans for NATO designed by Chairman of the Chiefs of Staff Committee General Charles Foulkes were intended to insulate Canada from the unwanted expense of defending Europe. The Korean War and the crisis in Europe created by the Berlin blockade and the communist coup in Czechoslovakia led to the commitment of ground troops to Europe – but on the understanding that the Canadian brigade would be a token force and a temporary expedient until Western European economies revived sufficiently to support their own defence. Once the Soviet Union achieved a significant nuclear capability, politicians and civilian bureaucrats lost whatever belief they had had in the utility of land forces in Europe to provide anything more than a tripwire. Pearkes turned down Clark's proposed army of three ready mechanized brigades because he did not see how Europe could be reinforced once a war had gone nuclear. Civilians were of the view that the actual guarantor of peace was the nuclear second-strike capability of the United States, NATO's most effective deterrent force. Even NATO-skeptics in the Trudeau government like Ivan Head and Donald Macdonald supported spending on air defences that sheltered the US Air Force's Strategic Air Command. They did not, however, see much utility in a small Canadian land force in Europe that would not alter the strategic balance even if better armed and increased in size to a full division.

Much of the criticism of civilians by historians of the armed forces stems from an implicit acceptance of the army's strategic preferences. Bothwell and Granatstein disparage Trudeau for treating the senior military like college students, but by Lieutenant-General F.R. Sharp's own admission, the military had no ready answers to the prime minister's questions regarding the value of Canadian forces in Europe. Nor is it obvious that the civilian NATO-skeptics were wrong in their strategic appreciation of the situation. Indeed, Lieutenant-General Clark's Army Council paper on "The Nature of Future War" concluded that second-strike forces were the strategic key but attempted to argue that a large, ready mechanized army was itself a second-strike force.

The preference of the army was for heavy forces stationed in Central Europe. Pursuing this preference led Léo Cadieux and senior armed forces and departmental officials to thumb their noses at Cabinet direction to move the army from the Central Front. This is one of the most under-reported incidents of insubordination in Canadian civil-military relations. Neither Bothwell and Granatstein in *Pirouette* nor Bland in *The Administration of Defence Policy in Canada* discuss the connection of NATO policy to the Management Review Group. Yet both the defence minister and the prime minister were greatly upset to find that Cabinet direction had not been followed, and Trudeau instructed Macdonald to warn his senior officials that it was not to happen again. Coupled with the navy's non-compliance with Treasury Board direction regarding the construction of the DDH 280 destroyer, it is little wonder that Macdonald sought to strengthen controls over the military headquarters. The Management Review Group was not a poorly conceived attempt to force civilian management theories on the defence establishment or a triumph of administration over military operational priorities, but rather an attempt by the minister to bring a "shirking" military back under control. The creation of National Defence Headquarters, which merged Canadian Forces Headquarters with the civilian Department of National Defence, thus eliminating a separate national military headquarters, resulted in a generation of cultural warfare between the military and civilians in which the army played a prominent role. The army did not seem to recognize that it had been insubordinate or that its own actions had contributed to the imposition of greater civilian control.

Whether the defence policy pursued by civilians was in fact superior to that advocated by the army cannot be proven. What is certain is that the army presented no convincing policy proposals to the political leadership. Worse, when its preferences were rejected, it "shirked" by allying with those in Cabinet who wanted to keep the army on the Central Front and then spent almost two decades pursuing a force structure that was contrary to political direction, that grossly exceeded the funding voted by Parliament, and that would have required changes to the National Defence Act to support the Reserve force expansion advocated.

The Doctrinal Gap

To build an army requires not only a national strategy justifying why an army should be maintained but also a concept of how that army should be structured and would operate in the field. This is the domain of doctrine and combat development. Both doctrine and combat development should flow from, and inform, policy. Little capacity had been inherited from the British because Canada was a subordinate part of the British Imperial system and therefore did not need any independent doctrine or force development capability, and also because British Army culture relied on senior operational commanders to set their own doctrine. The Canadian army's first attempts in Exercises GOLD RUSH and FIRE-FLY were therefore driven by the chiefs of the general staff of the day, Guy Simonds and H.D. Graham. Neither exercise produced a practical product, although they did lead to a realization that a more disciplined approach was required.

The organization of a combat development staff and greater discipline in the doctrinal process enabled a more sophisticated approach to the problem of tactical nuclear warfare. But despite being internally coherent, neither the 1960 *Infantry Brigade Group in Battle* nor the 1961 *Canadian Army 1966-1970 Tactical and Logistic Concept* solved the tactical problems posed by battlefield nuclear weapons, and both defaulted to dependence on superior leadership. They were therefore faith-based systems. The final pre-unification attempt, led by Major-General Roger Rowley in his "Division 1965," was methodologically the best and would be regarded as a superior product even today. It blended operational field experiments, operations research, and systematic professional opinion to produce a force structure for the army. However, Rowley's division was not affordable within the army's existing budget. Unaffordable components were pushed off for further study.

The doctrine and force development products of the early 1960s should have raised questions at the policy level. There was no credible way to fight a tactical nuclear war in Central Europe, and even if the war remained at the conventional level, the army's best estimate was that it would be seriously underequipped. There is no evidence, however, that the army itself reconsidered its role on NATO's Central Front.

Paul Hellyer derailed the planning and development processes that had been so laboriously established and relied on a series of task forces to provide advice on force structure, the mobile force, and close air support. Moreover, he sought contradictory policy and force structure goals. He wanted a "mobile force" but at the same time completed the equipping of the brigade group in Europe as a heavy, nuclear-equipped force. He wanted air transportable but also highly capable combat forces. He interfered to an unwarranted extent in the selection of a close air support aircraft. The advice provided by the army was reasonable, given constraints, but biased towards heavy forces. The most serious error of the Hellyer period was the failure to clarify the relationship between the new Mobile Command and Canadian Forces Headquarters in Ottawa. Doctrine, force development, and operational planning capability withered as the two headquarters struggled to define their respective roles and contested for leadership. A combat development process would not be restored until 1976. Sorting out operational planning would take until the end of the century.

When the combat development process was finally restored, reaction had set in and the army was determined to follow its own path. Rejecting the government's policy of a modest, even token, force in Europe, it continued to fight against policy and planning guidance and pressed for mass mobilization while also pursuing its "big army" Corps '86 and Corps '96 force structure and doctrinal projects. The attempt to design an army so far removed from political and financial support and without the necessary industrial capacity can only be described as a bizarre (though prolonged) episode of magical thinking. It was as if by creating a plan the army could reverse policy, provide funding, and create industrial capacity. Methodologically, the Corps studies were a step backward from the rigorous, all-arms analysis of Division 1965. It was once again a case of decision makers who knew what they wanted and wanted staff only to work out the details. The government simply ignored the Corps exercises or was not even aware of them, and made only modest changes in response to the Task Force on Review of Unification and its concerns about civilianization.

The final doctrinal product of the twentieth century was CFP 300, *Canada's Army: We Stand on Guard for Thee*. It was more a statement of philosophy than a force structure analysis like the major studies that preceded it. It was remarkable primarily for its acceptance of the central principle of a constabulary force – that military operations do not necessarily entail the application of violence – and its recognition that, in stabilization operations, junior leaders were sometimes compelled to make decisions that could affect theatre-level objectives.

By the early 1960s, doctrine and force development had progressed from being dependent on the insight and biases of senior commanders to becoming a disciplined, relatively objective staff function. Unfortunately, Hellyer's interventions, the organizational turmoil of the integration of the armed services, and the military reaction to unification turned the clock back so that the Corps exercises were once again based on the preferences of senior officers, not analysis. Moreover, doctrine and force structure came to be regarded as a means of forcing on the government the army's preferred policy option of a large, heavily equipped force supported by mobilization. Predictably, it was a failure, and staff and the NDHQ bureaucracy had given plenty of warning. CFP 300 was a return to an approach that was much more consistent with government policy and the external environment.

The Intractability of the Militia

Related to both policy and force development was the Militia. The small standing army that the government considered essential did not require a large reserve. The low state of readiness that the Militia was able to achieve made the augmentation troops that it did provide expensive. The basic structural weaknesses had been recognized in the 1950s. Unless reservists received about a year of concentrated military training at the start of their service, they could not acquire or maintain the skills necessary to be useful. The geographically dispersed structure enabled the army to maintain a community footprint, but further compounded the training problem by maintaining too many small units that could not carry out effective collective training. It also increased overhead costs and led to rank inflation, with the many small units retaining senior officers and NCOs. Unfortunately, recognition of the problem did not lead to reform. The usual explanation is that the Militia's political power blocked attempts to rationalize the reserve force, although, as George Pearkes demonstrated, this power was often overestimated. Other forces were also at work. The Regular army had little incentive to rationalize the Militia as long as its goal was the creation of a big army. A corps-sized Militia, even of dubious effectiveness, gave substance to this aspiration. An underfunded shell was the result.

The strongest attempt to rebuild the Militia was the "Total Force" proposed by the 1987 White Paper *Challenge and Commitment: A Defence Policy for Canada,* but there was no attempt at legislative reform to protect reservists' jobs or make Militia soldiers more available in an emergency. Nor was there a realistic budget to support the size of force proposed by the White Paper. The *1994 White Paper on Defence* was more realistic, stressing that the main purpose of the Reserves was to augment and support deployed forces. It also stated the government's intent to review the Militia structure to determine whether it could play a larger role in support services. It promised a mobilization plan, but only in case of an emergency of Korean War magnitude would there be any real growth; only completely unfunded plans were proposed. Army staff could find no practical way to develop a mobilization plan and also lacked the motivation to keep working on the issue. The backlash from the Militia was predictable as its hopes had been raised only to be dashed. As the century ended, the Militia and its supporters appeared stuck in a time warp, insisting that the department fund an expensive mobilization base at huge expense to meet what the government considered the lowest of low-probability events.

The Army as a Profession

At the root of many of the army's problems lay its concept of professionalism. This had been inherited from the British Army in a largely unreflective manner.

The bias towards basing the officer corps on personal character rather than professional knowledge did not help the army develop the skills necessary to provide policy advice to the government or to keep in touch with a country that was rapidly becoming better educated. Indeed, by the early 1960s it appeared that the officer corps was having difficulty maintaining its core tactical expertise.

The army did have a "modernist moment" in the Officer Development Board of 1969. The officer corps as redesigned by General J.V. Allard and Major-General Roger Rowley would have been much better educated, and would have benefited from the establishment of a national security college that would have supported a strategic studies staff and a link to the civilian security bureaucracy and to the political level. However, the ink was barely dry on the board's report when both Allard and Rowley retired from the service. Those who followed did not share their enthusiasm for education and linkage to civil society. In fact, the 1970s saw the beginning of the dominance of reaction to the perceived "civilianization" of the military. The merger of the three historical armed services into the unified Canadian Forces had been bad enough, with the loss of heraldry, loss of a national army headquarters, and replacement of army service support branches by unified organizations. Worse was the creation of a National Defence Headquarters following the report of the Management Review Group, which ended an independent national military headquarters altogether. The army was at the forefront of those who proposed to the Task Force on Review of Unification of the Canadian Forces that the clock be turned back both organizationally and socially. Although they failed to achieve their organizational goals, traditionalists dominated the army officer corps until after the end of the Cold War. They fostered an atmosphere in which combat was seen as the only function of the army and in which simply ignoring civilian policy direction was regarded as legitimate. This, together with the reliance on regimental politics to fill key positions and the concurrent failure of central management systems to manage personnel and unit readiness, set the stage for failures in Croatia and Somalia.

The Somalia Inquiry and subsequent measures taken by the government to ensure that reform was being implemented led to the greatest changes ever in the army's concept of professionalism. Whereas unification had resulted in reaction, Somalia ended in reform. A degreed officer corps was accepted and implemented, and the army published new doctrine that recognized a constabulary role for itself as well as a combat mission. The concept of officership was extended to include the soldier-diplomat and the soldier-scholar alongside the combat arms officer.

Civilian Leadership

The other side of the civil-military relationship cannot be ignored. The role of ministers in managing the political/military relationship bears particular scrutiny. Between 1950 and 2001 there were twenty-seven ministers or acting ministers of national defence, but only a few of them had significant influence on the army. Overall, civilian leadership was, to say the least, inconsistent in the national strategy adopted and in the intended role of the army. Ministers with "big ideas" played a particularly disruptive role.

Paul Hellyer and Perrin Beatty stand close to the beginning and end of the half-century. Both had policy ideas that would have transformed the army, but neither had the unqualified support of Cabinet colleagues. Hellyer found that his Mobile Force did not have a role in the government's security policy, and that a mobile force that could defend itself, that could be transported, and that was affordable was impossible to design. Unification briefly opened the door to reformers like Allard and Rowley, but the reaction to unification and to disputes with subsequent ministers caused the reform moment to pass quickly. For the army, integration and unification occurred at the most inopportune moment, when it had just institutionalized its combat development function and given it a sounder basis for long-range planning.

Beatty's Total Force was in some ways a repeat performance of Hellyer's Mobile Force. Although the two policy visions were quite different from each other – one aimed at building a large, heavily equipped army on the Central Front, the other at building a mobile expeditionary force – both had weak Cabinet support and a budget that should have been seen as unrealistic from the start. Moreover, without policy changes to facilitate service in the Reserves by established tradespeople and professionals, the large Total Force could not be filled out. Both Hellyer and Beatty pushed the army into planning and force development that was only partly implemented before being scrapped. The fact that Hellyer was minister in the mid-1960s and Beatty in the late 1980s speaks volumes about the lack of development of a national strategy and policy for the army throughout the period.

In between, ministers provided widely varying policy direction to the army. Léo Cadieux encouraged and even colluded with the army to preserve its role as a heavy force on the NATO Central Front. His immediate successor and part of the same Trudeau government, Donald Macdonald, opposed the Central Front role and disciplined the armed services when they dragged their feet or thwarted his policies. James Richardson restored the air force as a pseudo-service by selling it in Cabinet as an economy measure that reduced the number of air headquarters, thus weakening unification and the concept of a mobile command. Allan McKinnon launched a more direct assault on unification with his task force to examine the issue, but achieved little other than further legitimizing reaction against "civilianization." Erik Nielsen's overenthusiasm spoiled the one chance light force advocates had of moving the army off the Central Front. Nielsen outdid Hellyer and Beatty: he not only lacked strong support for his initiative but failed to consult his Cabinet colleagues at all.

What remained constant on the civilian side of the equation was that Cabinets did not see any real use for a large army or in keeping the army on the Central Front. Nor did any Cabinet wish to amend the National Defence Act to allow the Reserves to be called out for service in peacetime or to protect reservists' jobs. This, and the conviction that spending more would not significantly increase Canada's security, meant that although individual ministers might be able to get agreement for plans on paper, they could not get money or legislation.

Civilians also bear a good deal of responsibility for the operational problems of the 1990s. The Hellyer unified force weakened staff planning systems by its lack of clarity as to what belonged to the Commands and what to the national headquarters. Civilian ministers failed to educate themselves regarding the uses and limitations of the military forces they maintained, and thus pushed for interventions that were beyond the capacity of the army to carry out without significant internal costs. Their military advisers might have served them better, but that is no excuse for insisting on missions with personnel and equipment establishments that were novel and smaller than requested, and for which no strong rationale or operational concept existed.

One minister whose contribution was largely positive was Douglas Young. Although he was minister for less than nine months in late 1996 and early 1997, his decision to terminate the Somalia Inquiry prevented it from reaching conclusions as to whether there had been an attempted cover-up, but it enabled the army and the Canadian Forces to turn the corner on the crisis and move from a destructive to a constructive phase. Young's wide-ranging report to the prime minister did not let the army off the hook or permit it to revert to its old ways. He endorsed the integrated civil-military headquarters and insisted on recognition of women's and minority rights within the Forces. Perhaps his biggest contribution was pushing the Forces towards constabulary realism in its orientation and towards an officer corps based on knowledge.

The Army and the State in Canada

This book began by challenging the view that the Canadian army reached its apogee in 1960 and then suffered decades of decline due to ill-conceived decisions by civilians – notably unification, the creation of a "civilianized" NDHQ, and perpetual underfunding of the NATO commitment to the Central Front. One must conclude, however, that this is, at the very least, an incomplete account. It might well be said that during the last half of the twentieth century there was an army in Canada but no Canadian army – that is, the army pursued its own goals with more vigour than it followed the direction of the political leadership of the country. The army was more attentive and responsive to allies than to its own government. There was an element of self-interest in this but also a strong belief in the usefulness of ground forces that exceeded the army's faith in the civilian leadership.

Belief in its own usefulness was accompanied by a blindness to national strategy at a higher level than the NATO requirement for land forces. If the army ever thought about trade-offs between the types of forces the country should maintain, its inevitable conclusion was that air and sea forces should be sacrificed for the army. Its vision became so narrow that even air forces required for joint operations such as close air support and air transport did not factor into army planning and were left to be tackled elsewhere.

The army appeared to have little appreciation for domestic politics. Its early advocacy of conscription was out of touch with the country's mood. It never seemed able to understand the limits of military funding. It regarded modern management and the expansion of rights enumerated in the Canadian Charter of Rights and Freedoms as unwelcome developments that undercut its ethos and military society. It was able to change only after coming under the combined pressure of the collapse of the Cold War international order, a domestic financial and fiscal crisis, and scandals involving its own behaviour.

On the civilian side, the attitude was often one of benign neglect. Attention paid to the army was often disruptive as ministers proposed and attempted to implement grand plans. It was also evident that civilians often lacked an appreciation of what the army was capable of doing. As the Cold War – "the war without battles" – ended and stabilization operations that could and did go "hot" took its place, the ability to understand the uses and limits of military force became a more relevant skill for civilian leaders.

The history of the Canadian army and the state during the last half of the twentieth century is therefore mainly a story of a troubled relationship, although one that was beginning to recover at the very end. It should prompt both civilians and members of the military to consider the connections between civil and military society. On the military side, officials must always bear in mind that their role is to be the *agent* of the state and that civilians do indeed have the right to be wrong. The military needs to be able to understand the state and society as a whole, not just the security elements of it. It also needs to recognize that it has a shared responsibility for building national security policy institutions that extend beyond the army, the Canadian Forces, and the Department of National Defence.

For their part, civilians must recognize that the role of *principal* is a demanding one. It means acquiring and maintaining at least a certain level of expertise in security matters. It also means that the political leadership needs to fully consider whether plans involving major changes to the military establishment are both financially viable and politically sustainable. Keeping Cabinet colleagues in the dark, freelancing, or hoping that Cabinet will pay a huge bill when it is finally rendered are tactics that fared badly during the twentieth century.

Institutional relationships and structures do matter. There are signs that the relationship between Canada's army and the state is better in the early twenty-first century than it was at the end of the twentieth. It will require significant understanding and effort from all parties to ensure that this progress endures.

Notes on Sources

Archival Sources

This book is based primarily on archival sources held by the Directorate of History and Heritage at the Department of National Defence and at Library and Archives Canada, both of which are in Ottawa. At National Defence, many files are "standalone" files indexed in the Card Catalogue, the Kardex, or both. These files are completely cited by record group in the notes to the text and are not listed here. Other documents are organized in collections. The principal Defence collections cited were:

Jean V. Allard fonds, RG 84/126
Catherine Allen fonds, RG 77/529
Claude Beauregard fonds, RG 96/30
Charles H. Belzile fonds, RG 2006/5
Canadian Army Staff College Library fonds, RG 99/11
Canadian Land Forces Command and Staff College fonds, RG 80/71
Chief of Defence Staff Study, 94/20
Romeo A. Dallaire fonds, RG 2001/25
Defence Management Committee fonds, RG 79/560
Deputy Chief of the Defence Staff fonds, RG 81/232
Director General Land Force Development fonds, RG 96/26
Charles J. Gauthier fonds, RG 92/288
Joint Staff fonds, RG 2002/17
Anthony Kellett fonds, RG 2001/5
George Lindsay fonds, RG 87/253
James Robert Near fonds, RG 2002/20
Personnel Management Policy Study Group Working Papers, RG 83/666
Robert Lewis Raymont fonds, RG 73/1223
Review Group on the Report of the Task Force on Unification of the Canadian Forces: Papers, 81/747

At Library and Archives Canada, the collections employed were:

Robert B. Bryce fonds, MG 31, E-59
Cabinet Conclusions, RG 2
Cabinet Defence Committee Minutes, R165-95-9-E
Department of External Affairs files, RG 25
Department of National Defence files, RG 24
John Diefenbaker fonds, Series XII
Arnold Danford Patrick Heeney fonds, MG 30, E 144
Paul T. Hellyer fonds, MG 32, B-33
Louis St-Laurent fonds, MG 26, L
Paul D. Manson fonds, R 11222
Lester B. Pearson fonds, MG 26, N-4
Norman A. Robertson fonds, MG 30, E 163
Gordon Smith papers, 1997-98/050 GAD
Pierre Elliott Trudeau fonds, MG 26, O-11

Researchers will find that the National Defence archives have prepared excellent finding aids for many of the record groups important to the late-twentieth-century army. Of particular note are the record groups of two headquarters secretaries: the Robert Lewis Raymont fonds (RG 73/1223) and the Charles J. Gauthier fonds (RG 92/288). From 1951 to 1989, these officers occupied various posts where they served the central decision-making committees and processes of the armed services and the Department of National Defence. As part of their papers, both Raymont and Gauthier also left book-length accounts of central decision making during their respective watches. These two record groups are important starting places for research on defence policy.

Library and Archives Canada has yet to catalogue much, if not most, of the material it has received from National Defence for the 1980s and 1990s. Finding aids for recent defence records are very basic or entirely absent. Consultation with subject matter expert archivists is essential.

Many documents important to this period are still classified. They may be reviewed and released under the Access to Information Act, but each file must be requested (and paid for) individually. Most requests are processed quickly, but review can take up to three years. More disconcerting are government-wide policies governing material released. Released documents are listed by department by date of release. There is no subject catalogue, much less full-text search capacity. Moreover, files released are deleted from Access databases after five years. Retrieving documents released to previous researchers can therefore prove impossible if they are cited only by the Access release number. Material released for this book is cited by archival reference whenever possible.

In addition to papers at the Directorate of History and Heritage and Library and Archives Canada, material related to army doctrine was consulted at the Fort Frontenac Library at Canadian Forces Base Kingston. Doctrinal documents and student papers held at the Canadian Forces College Library in Toronto were employed.

Interviews

Interviews were conducted of individuals mentioned or who played a prominent role in the events covered by the text. Not all subjects could be located, and not all those located consented to an interview. The following individuals generously agreed to meet with the author and provided their personal insights and sometimes access to personal papers:

Clive Addy
Kenneth Calder
Romeo Dallaire
Richard Evraire
James Fox
Robert Gaudreau
Paul Hellyer
Michael Jeffery
Lewis MacKenzie
Paul Manson
G.E. (Joe) Sharpe
Gordon Smith
Ramsay Withers
Douglas Young

General John de Chastelain (Retired) provided answers to author queries through a lengthy letter, and General Paul Manson (Retired) provided access to his papers at Library and Archives Canada. Lieutenant-General Richard Evraire (Retired) and Brigadier-General Joe Sharpe (Retired) also provided access to personal papers.

Notes

Introduction

1 Samuel Huntington, *The Soldier and the State: The Theory and Politics of Civil-Military Relations* (Cambridge, MA: Belknap Press, 1967), 61-72, 83-90.
2 Peter Feaver, *Armed Servants: Agency, Oversight, and Civil-Military Relations* (Cambridge, MA: Harvard University Press, 2003), 54-68.
3 J.L. Granatstein, *Canada's Army: Waging War and Keeping the Peace* (Toronto: University of Toronto Press, 2002).
4 Douglas Bland, *The Administration of Defence Policy in Canada, 1947 to 1985* (Kingston, ON: Ronald P. Frye, 1987).
5 John A. English, *Lament for an Army: The Decline of Canadian Military Professionalism* (Concord, ON: Irwin Publishing, 1998), 51-54.
6 David Bercuson, *Significant Incident: Canada's Army, the Airborne, and the Murder in Somalia* (Toronto: McClelland and Stewart, 1996), 241-42.

Chapter 1: The 1950s

1 Andrew Richter, *Avoiding Armageddon: Canadian Military Strategy and Nuclear Weapons, 1950-63* (Vancouver: UBC Press, 2002), 25-29.
2 James Eayrs, *In Defence of Canada: Peacemaking and Deterrence* (Toronto: University of Toronto Press, 1972), 324-72.
3 Desmond Morton, *A Short History of Canada* (Toronto: McClelland and Stewart, 1994), 228-44.
4 John A. English, *The Canadian Army and the Normandy Campaign: A Study of Failure in High Command* (New York: Praeger, 1991), 244-50; Sean Maloney, "General Charles Foulkes: A Primer on How to be CDS," in *Warrior Chiefs: Perspectives on Senior Canadian Military Leaders,* edited by LCol. Bernd Horn and Stephen Harris (Toronto: Dundurn Press, 2001), 220-21.
5 LGen. John H. Cushman, "Challenge and Response at the Operational and Tactical Levels, 1914-45," in *Military Effectiveness*, vol. 3, *The Second World War,* edited by Allan R. Millett and Williamson Murray (Boston: Unwin Hyman, 1990), 320-22.
6 J.P. Harris, *Men, Ideas and Tanks: British Military Thought and Armoured Forces, 1903-1939* (Manchester: Manchester University Press, 1995), 315-19; Williamson Murray, "British Military Effectiveness in the Second World War," in *Military Effectiveness,* vol. 3, *The Second World War,* edited by Allan R. Millett and Williamson Murray (Boston: Unwin Hyman,

1990), 107-14. See also Raymond Callahan, *Churchill and His Generals* (Lawrence: University of Kansas Press, 2007), 15.

7 David French, "Doctrine and Organization in the British Army, 1919-1932," *Historical Journal* 44, no. 2 (June 2001): 514-15.

8 Ibid., 513-14.

9 Colin McInnes, *Hot War Cold War: The British Army's Way in Warfare, 1945-95* (London: Brassey's, 1996), 30.

10 Stephen J. Harris, *Canadian Brass: The Making of a Professional Army, 1860-1939* (Toronto: University of Toronto Press, 1988), 203.

11 Quoted in ibid., 204.

12 Ibid.

13 Ibid., 208.

14 Canada, Army, Directorate of Staff Duties, Chief of the General Staff, *Canadian Army Manual of Training 1-36, Staff Procedures,* vol. 3, *Staff Duties in the Field* (Ottawa: Army Headquarters, 1963). This version promised a new edition with Canadian terminology by 1965.

15 Douglas E. Delaney, *Corps Commanders: Five British and Canadian Generals at War, 1939-45* (Vancouver: UBC Press, 2011), 9.

16 D.J. Goodspeed, *A History of the Defence Research Board of Canada* (Ottawa: Queen's Printer, 1958), 166-71.

17 David J. Bercuson, *Blood on the Hills: The Canadian Army in the Korean War* (Toronto: University of Toronto Press, 1999), 1-34.

18 Quoted in William Johnston, *A War of Patrols: Canadian Army Operations in Korea* (Vancouver: UBC Press, 2003). Given the concern expressed during the 1980s that civilianization had undermined the warrior spirit of the Canadian Forces, it is interesting to note that the decline started much, much earlier.

19 The major work on the Militia that discusses this period, T.C. Willett, *Canada's Militia: A Heritage at Risk* (Boulder, CO: Westview Press, 1990), simply notes in the chapter on history that the Militia were not involved in Korea.

20 Tamara A. Sherwin, "From Total War to Total Force: Civil-Military Relations and the Canadian Army Reserve (Militia)" (MA thesis, University of New Brunswick, 1997), 35.

21 Bercuson, *Blood on the Hills,* puts the start of "Notes" as the summer of 1951, 134.

22 Johnston, *War of Patrols,* 371-78. For the vignette regarding grenade polishing, see 271.

23 Robert A. Doughty, *The Evolution of US Army Tactical Doctrine, 1946-76,* Leavenworth Papers, no. 1 (Fort Leavenworth, KS: Combat Studies Institute, US Army Command and General Staff College, 1979), 12.

24 Johnston, *War of Patrols,* 25-26, 40.

25 G.G. Simonds, Canadian Contribution to the Integrated Force (Europe), HQTS 200-1 (SD1), 26 April 1951, Directorate of History and Heritage, Department of National Defence (DHH), RG 73/596.

26 Dominick Graham, *The Price of Command: A Biography of General Guy Simonds* (Toronto: Stoddart, 1993), 264.

27 Carl von Clausewitz, *On War,* edited and translated by Michael Howard and Peter Paret (Princeton, NJ: Princeton University Press, 1976), 593.

28 Quoted in Richard J. Walker, "The Revolt of the Canadian Generals, 1944: The Case for the Prosecution," in *The Insubordinate and the Noncompliant: Case Studies of Canadian Mutiny and Disobedience, 1920 to Present,* edited by Howard G. Coombs (Kingston, ON: Dundurn Group and Canadian Defence Academy Press, 2007), 61-62.

29 Ibid., 68-70, 84-90. The alternative point of view is in the official history, C.P. Stacey, *Arms, Men and Governments: The War Policies of Canada, 1939-1945* (Ottawa: Queen's Printer,

1970). Stacey claims that the minister had asked the army staff to put their opinion in writing and, therefore, the army "had exercised their constitutional function with complete propriety." Stacey is supported by Maurice Pope, the Military Secretary to the Cabinet War Committee, who argues in *The Memoirs of Lt.-Gen. Maurice A. Pope* (Toronto: University of Toronto Press, 1962) that he would have been aware if there had been a cabal and that the General Staff had behaved correctly. On the other hand, he clearly thinks that manpower policies were needlessly inefficient. Pope suggested to the Dominion Archivist that Jack Pickersgill and the Liberal Party started the rumours of a "palace revolution" to explain why the government had abandoned its promises and place the blame elsewhere (DHH, RG 89/97, Box 1, File 7).

30 Col. J.H. Jones, Strategic Situation Affecting Postwar Army, 19 June 1945, DHH, RG 2002/17, Box 128, File 16.

31 LGen. J.C. Murchie to Minister of National Defence, Post-War Army Organization, 12 August 1945, DHH, Joint Staff fonds, RG 2002/17, Box 128, File 20.

32 Speech by Douglas Abbott, Minister of National Defence, House of Commons, 16 October 1945, DHH, Kardex 112.3M2 (D286).

33 David A. Charters, "Five Lost Years: The Mobile Striking Force, 1946-1951," *Canadian Defence Quarterly* 7, no. 1 (Spring 1978): 45.

34 James Eayrs, *In Defence of Canada*, vol. 4, *Growing Up Allied* (Toronto: University of Toronto Press, 1980), 133-38. See also Douglas L. Bland, *The Military Committee of the North Atlantic Alliance: A Study of Structure and Strategy* (New York: Praeger, 1991), 115-46.

35 Eayrs, *Growing Up Allied*, 190-208.

36 Ibid., 208-10.

37 Minutes of the 503rd Meeting of the Chiefs of Staff Committee, 14 August 1951, Group of Canadian Forces in Europe, DHH, Kardex 112.3M2 (D296).

38 Ibid.

39 Ibid.

40 Col. C.H. Cook, DMO and P, to DCGS, Study of Ways and Means of Increasing Canadian Army Contribution to the Integrated Force in Europe by Two Divisions by D plus 30, 28 August 1951, DHH, Kardex 112.3M2 (D298).

41 Ingo Trauschweizer, *The Cold War US Army: Building Deterrence for Limited War* (Lawrence: University of Kansas Press, 2008), 24-35; Samuel P. Huntington, *The Common Defense* (New York: Columbia University Press, 1961), 66.

42 Sean M. Maloney, *Learning to Love the Bomb: Canada's Nuclear Weapons during the Cold War* (Washington, DC: Potomac Books, 2007), 39.

43 Ibid., 71-72.

44 Maloney, "General Charles Foulkes," 226.

45 Charles Foulkes, Reassessment of Canada's Defence Policy, Aims and Programmes for the Next Five Years, 1955-1960, 16 June 1955, DHH, Robert Lewis Raymont fonds, RG 73/1223, File 2558.

46 Exercise GOLD RUSH, Terms of Reference for a Study of the Organization of Field Formations to Meet Conditions of Future War, HQS 1200-G9 (ACS), 15 February 1955, DHH, RG 73/1299.

47 Simonds to MND, 14 March 1955, cited in Brief for the Chief of the General Staff, Exercise Gold Rush, HQS 2001-91/G9 (Ex GR), 12 June 1956, DHH, RG 73/1299.

48 Record of a meeting held in the office of the Chief of the General Staff on Wednesday, 19th Jan 1955 to discuss logistic support by aircraft in the forward area, ACS/M(55)1, 21 January 1955, DHH, RG 73/1299.

49 Exercise GOLD RUSH, Terms of Reference.

50 Army Council Secretariat, Record of a meeting to discuss the military characteristics of a light cargo aircraft, ACCS/M(55)5, 10 June 1955, DHH, RG 73/1299.

51 Ibid. Unfortunately, the actual working papers of the various study groups are yet to be located. At this point the complete findings of the study groups and their methodology are not known. The files reviewed include primarily those of the CGS's correspondence in reaction to the GOLD RUSH studies.

52 Disappeared from the planners' concept, but evidently not from the real world. De Havilland continued to develop the DHC-4 Caribou transport, which entered US Army service in 1962. The VSTOL Canadair CL-84 tilt-wing transport also seems to have been funded through this initiative. This aircraft first flew in 1965 and stayed in development into the early 1970s. Although prototypes were successful, it did not find a customer.

53 Brief for the Chief of the General Staff, Exercise Gold Rush, HQS 2001-91/G9 (Ex GR), 12 June 1956, DHH, RG 73/1299.

54 Record of a meeting to discuss both the tactical concept and the future of Exercise Gold Rush, ACS/M(56)11, 21 June 1956, DHH, RG 73/1299.

55 H.D. Graham to VCDS, 26 June 1956, DHH, RG 73/1299.

56 H.D. Graham to Minister of National Defence, 26 June 1956, DHH, RG 73/1299.

57 Exercise Gold Rush, HQS 2001-92/F15 (Ex GR), 3 July 1956, DHH, RG 73/1299.

58 Operation Fire-Fly, HQS 2001-91/F15 (Ex GR), 28 September 1956, DHH, RG 73/1299.

59 H.D. Graham to Brig. M.P. Bogert, Commandant, Canadian Army Staff College, Fort Frontenac, 27 November 1956, DHH, RG 73/1299.

60 Sean Maloney concludes that the development of Canadian tactical nuclear doctrine was "methodical," but he does not reference either GOLD RUSH or FIRE-FLY. Sean M. Maloney, "The Canadian Army and Tactical Nuclear Warfare Doctrine," *Canadian Defence Quarterly* 23, no. 2 (December 1993): 23-30.

61 Sean Maloney, *War without Battles: Canada's NATO Brigade in Germany, 1951-1993* (Whitby, ON: McGraw-Hill Ryerson, 1996), 499.

62 Ibid., 135.

63 Canadian Army Combat Development Guide, HQS 2100-2 (DCD), Annex "A," History of Combat Development in the Canadian Army, 1 June 1961, DHH, RG 72/722.

64 Land Combat in a Nuclear War, CAORE Working Paper 58/18, DHH, RG 73/1327.

65 MGen. J.V. Allard to all GOCs and Brigade Commanders, December 1958, DHH, RG 73/1327.

66 The Permanent Representative of Canada to the North Atlantic Council and the OEEC [Dana Wilgress] to the Secretary of State for External Affairs, The Present Position of NATO, 15 October 1957, Library and Archives Canada (LAC), John Diefenbaker fonds, Series XII, Reel M-9398.

67 Cited in J.L. Granatstein, *The Generals: The Canadian Army's Senior Commanders in the Second World War* (Toronto: Stoddart, 1993), 31-32.

68 S.F. Clark to the Minister, HQS 2000-1 TD 8266 (CGS), 29 December 1958, DHH, RG 73/311.

69 MGen. J.D.B. Smith to CGS, Role and Organization of the Army, 30 September 1958, DHH, RG 73/311.

70 MGen. J.D.B. Smith, The Nature of Future War, n.d., DHH, RG 73/311.

71 N.W. Morton to VCGS, 7 October 1958, DHH, RG 73/311. Morton anticipated Mobile Command by over a decade, and Rick Hillier's Transformation by about fifty years.

72 "The Nature of Future War," HQTS 2250-1 TD 8309, 23 December 1958, DHH, RG 73/311.

73 "The Organization of the Canadian Army," HQTS 2000-1 TD 8287, 23 December 1958, DHH, RG 73/311. Clark had been allowed to see a copy of LGen. Graham's report to Cabinet on civil defence in early December.

74 George Pearkes to CGS, 9 January 1959, DHH, RG 73/311.
75 S.F. Clark to Minister of National Defence, HQS 2000-1 8266 (CGS), 22 January 1959; George R. Pearkes to CGS, 23 January 1959, DHH, RG 73/311.
76 S.F. Clark to Minister of National Defence, 4 March 1959, DHH, Robert Lewis Raymont fonds, RG 73/1223, Ser. V, File 2550, Army Equipment.
77 Trauschweizer, *The Cold War US Army*, 70-75.
78 Ibid., 77.
79 R.L. Raymont, Background of the Suggested Change in Role of the Canadian Brigade in Europe as Proposed by General Speidel, 17 June 1969, DHH, RG 73/1223, File 2526A. Raymont drafted this account for the CDS when the issue recurred a decade later. He attached original source documents to substantiate his account. The bulk of the account that follows is from Raymont.
80 Willett, *Canada's Militia*, 73.
81 Put together, three brigades approximate a single division.
82 Quoted in Desmond Morton, *Ministers and Generals: Politics and the Canadian Militia, 1868-1904* (Toronto: University of Toronto Press, 1970), 18.
83 George Mackenzie Urquhart, "The Changing Role of the Canadian Militia, 1945-1975" (MA thesis, University of Victoria, 1977), 27-31.
84 Ibid., 39-43.
85 G. Simonds, Reorganization of the Canadian Army Reserve Force, 4 September 1952, DHH, RG 73/606.
86 Simonds to GOCs, 3 September 1952, DHH, RG 73/606.
87 MGen. Chris Vokes to CGS, 9 September 1952, DHH, RG 73/606.
88 Brigadier Bennett in MGen. N.E. Rodger, GOC Prairie Command to CGS, 4 January 1954, DHH, RG 73/606.
89 Memorandum to Cabinet Defence Committee, Formation of a Canadian Army Regular Reserve, Cabinet Defence Committee, Ninety-seventh meeting, 2 December 1953, LAC, Cabinet Conclusions, RG 2, 2752.
90 MGen. H.A. Sparling, VGCS, Reorganization of the Reserve Force, HQS 2001-3/1 D 81 (SD 1), 2 April 1954, DHH, RG 73/294.
91 Sherwin, "From Total War to Total Force," 26-53.
92 Cabinet Defence Committee, Ninety-ninth meeting, 13 April 1954, Organization of Canadian Army (Reserve Force), LAC, Cabinet Conclusions, RG 2, 2749.
93 Charles Foulkes to Frank Miller, 17 July 1956, DHH, Robert Lewis Raymont fonds, 73/1223, Ser. V, File 2550, Army Equipment.
94 Sherwin, "From Total War to Total Force," 71.
95 W.A.B. Anderson, A Report on the Organization, Equipment and Training of the Canadian Army (Militia), April 1957, DHH, RG 73/612.
96 Ibid., 78-79.
97 J. Mackay Hitsman, "The Canadian Army's Role in Survival Operations," Report 96, Historical Section (G.S.), Army Headquarters, 29 October 1962, DHH.
98 Ibid., 27, 31.
99 Brigadier M.S. Dunn, Report on the Operation of the Canadian Army (Militia), 14 October 1959, DHH, RG 73/613.
100 J. Granatstein, *Canada's Army: Waging War and Keeping the Peace* (Toronto: University of Toronto Press, 2002), 350-51.
101 Sherwin, "From Total War to Total Force," 114.
102 Urquhart, "The Changing Role of the Canadian Militia," 81.
103 Willett, *Canada's Militia*, 76-77.
104 Urquhart, "The Changing Role of the Canadian Militia," 85.

105 Richard A. Preston, *Canada's RMC: A History of the Royal Military College* (Toronto: University of Toronto Press, 1969), 329.

106 Guy Simonds to Secretary, Chief of Staff, Officer Production, 23 April 1951, DHH, RG 73/306; Guy Simonds to Secretary, Chief of Staff, Production of Officers, The Service Colleges, 26 April 1951, DHH, RG 73/306.

107 Minutes of a Special Meeting, Chiefs of Staff Committee, 3 May 1951, DHH, RG 73/306.

108 LCol. H.F. Wood, "Man Management, Part 1," *Canadian Army Journal* 10, no. 3 (July 1956): 22-31.

109 Col. G.M.C. Sprung, *The Soldier in Our Time: An Essay* (Philadelphia: Dorrance and Company, 1960), 99. Col. Sprung held a PhD from the University of Berlin and had been a wartime intelligence staff officer. He was Canadian Army Director of History from 1961 to 1964.

110 Charles Foulkes to Chiefs of Staff, CSC 1231.1, Officer Production, 15 March 1952, DHH, RG 73/306.

111 BGen. D.R. Agnew, Commandant, RMC to Brooke Claxton, 26 October 1953, DHH, RG 73/306; Guy Simonds to Brooke Claxton, HQC 3590-1 (CGS), 14 May 1954, DHH, RG 73/306.

112 Marcel Chaput, *Analysis of Results of Canadian Army Staff College Entrance Examinations*, Canadian Army Operations Research Establishment Working Paper 59/3, December 1959, DHH, RG 81/249.

113 John A. English, *Lament for an Army: The Decline of Canadian Military Professionalism* (Concord, ON: Irwin Publishing, 1998), 48-49; Roger Rowley to DGMT, Canadian Army Staff College – Policy, 10 June 1958, DHH, RG 76/157; Army Tactical Symposium – 1962, October 1962, DHH, RG 73/1314.

Chapter 2: Soldiers, Civilians, and Nuclear Warfare in the 1960s

1 Ingo Trauschweizer, *The Cold War US Army: Building Deterrence for Limited War* (Lawrence: University of Kansas Press, 2008), 70-75; Sean M. Maloney, *War without Battles: Canada's NATO Brigade in Germany, 1951-1993* (Whitby, ON: McGraw-Hill Ryerson, 1996), 128.

2 Canada, Army Headquarters, Director Military Training, *Canadian Army Manual of Training, CAMT1-8, The Infantry Brigade Group in Battle, Part 1 – Tactics*, 1960, Directorate of History and Heritage, Department of National Defence (DHH), RG 81/344.

3 Canada, Army Headquarters, Director Military Training, *Canadian Army Manual of Training, CAMT1-11, The Infantry Brigade Group in Battle, Part 2 – Administration*, 1960, DHH, RG 81/345.

4 *The Canadian Army 1966-70 Tactical and Logistic Concept*, Third Draft, CDY 59-2-1, HQS 2100-2-1 (DCD), 8 August 1961, DHH, RG 81/616.

5 How this would have been achieved prior to the invention of the Global Positioning System (GPS) is unclear, especially since the signals part of the concept already expressed concerns about channel capacity. Nevertheless, the concept postulated "vehicle navigation aid," a "simple hook-up to the rear link radio set," and a display with "three dials showing a six-figure map reference."

6 21st Meeting, Land/Air Warfare Committee, 6 April 1961, DHH, Kardex 112.3M3.003 (D4).

7 Canadian Army Operations Research Establishment, Leadership Requirements Tactical Concept 1966-70, Report 120, July 1961, DHH, RG 81/5.

8 Canada, Army Headquarters, Directorate of Combat Development, *The Canadian Army Post-1970 Operational Study*, 11 August 1961, DHH, RG 81/615.

9 "The Tasks and Problems of the Canadian Army: CGS' Talk to National Defence College," 12 July 1961, DHH, RG 81/674, 2, quoted in Sean M. Maloney, "'Global Mobile': Flexible Response, Peacekeeping and the Origins of the Forces Mobile Command, 1958-1964," in *Army Doctrine and Training Bulletin* 1, no. 1 (Spring 2000): 24.
10 MGen. J.P.E. Bernatchez, VCGS to GOCs and Branch Heads, Army Manpower, 18 September 1961, DHH, Kardex 112.352 (D44).
11 LGen. G. Walsh, CGS to HQ Commands and Branch Heads, Headquarters 1st Canadian Infantry Division (HQ 1 CDN Inf Div), Reactivation and Terms of Reference, 20 July 1962, DHH, Kardex 112.352 (D44); LGen. G. Walsh, CGS, SD 1 Letter 62, Army Tactics and Organization Board, Activation and Terms of Reference, 17 July 1962, DHH, Kardex 112.352 (D44).
12 Army Tactical Symposium, October 1962, DHH, RG 73/1314.
13 MGen. J.P.E. Bernatchez to Command Commanders and AHQ Branch Heads, Follow-up Paper on Army Tactical Symposium 1962 for Discussion at the First Meeting of the CDTDC, 25 October 1962, DHH, RG 81/272.
14 Army Tactics and Organization Board, Final Report [Rowley Report], ATOB 1963 Activities, DHH, RG 87/165, 1-24.
15 Army Tactics and Organization Board, Co-ordinating Conference 1, 25 February – 1 March 1963, Digest of Presentations and Record of Discussions, DHH, RG 80/234.
16 Ibid.
17 Minutes of 63/3 Meeting of the CDTDC, 30 August 1963, DHH, RG 81/272.
18 Robert A. Doughty, *The Evolution of US Army Tactical Doctrine, 1946-76*, Leavenworth Paper 1 (Fort Leavenworth, KS; Combat Studies Institute, US Army Command and General Staff College, 1979), 21; Trauschweizer, *The Cold War US Army*, 114.
19 Minutes of 64/1 Meeting of the CDTDC, ABC Armies Operational Concept 1971-80, 21 January 1964, DHH, RG 81/272.
20 Trauschweizer, *The Cold War US Army*, 145.
21 L.J. Byrne and A.G. Clifton, *A Study of the Defensive Battle in Nuclear War (U), II*, CAORE Report 135, February 1963, DHH, RG 81/66.
22 Paper for VCGS, Optimum Canadian Divisional Organization, 31 May 1962, DHH, RG 73/1307.
23 Ross Fetterly, "The Influence of the Environment on the 1964 Defence White Paper," *Canadian Military Journal* 5, no. 4 (Winter 2004-05), http://www.journal.forces.gc.ca/.
24 Canada, Royal Commission on Government Organization (Glassco Commission), *Report*, vol. 4, *Special Areas of Administration* (Ottawa: Queen's Printer, 1963), 59-83.
25 Andrew Richter, *Avoiding Armageddon: Canadian Military Strategy and Nuclear Weapons, 1950-63* (Vancouver: UBC Press, 2002), 81-88.
26 Ibid., 90-91.
27 Ibid., 100-2; J.L. Granatstein, *A Man of Influence: Norman A. Robertson and Canadian Statecraft, 1929-68* (Ottawa: Deneau Publishers, 1981), 338-46.
28 Dewar would become deputy minister of national defence from 1982 to 1989 and subsequently deputy clerk of the Privy Council.
29 D. Bev Dewar, The Defence Problem, 7 January 1960, DHH, Robert Lewis Raymont fonds, RG 73/1223, File 767.
30 Ibid.
31 Comments of Privy Council Office Paper "The Defence Problem" by Mr. D.B. Dewar on 7 January 1960, n.d., DHH, Robert Lewis Raymont fonds, RG 73/1223, File 767.
32 R.L. Raymont, annotation on file, n.d., DHH, Robert Lewis Raymont fonds, RG 73/1223, File 767.

33 R.B. Bryce, Policy Problems Arising from Major Weapons, 1 March 1960, Library and Archives Canada (LAC), Robert B. Bryce fonds, MG 31, E-59, 9; R.B. Bryce, notes for a letter to NAR [Norman A. Robertson] to be shown to PM, n.d., LAC, R.B. Bryce fonds, MG 31, E-59, 9.

34 *Calgary Herald,* 29 August to 3 September 1960, DHH, Robert Lewis Raymont fonds, RG 73/1223, File 767.

35 Cabinet Meeting, Berlin Situation, 17 August 1961; Cabinet Meeting, Berlin Situation, 21 August 1961; Cabinet Meeting, Possible defence measures arising out of Berlin situation, 22 August 1961; Cabinet Meeting, Militia Training Plan, 28 August 1961, LAC, Cabinet Conclusions, RG 2, 6177.

36 Denis Smith, *Rogue Tory: The Life and Legend of John G. Diefenbaker* (Toronto: Macfarlane Walter and Ross, 1995), 452-88.

37 John Gellner, Proposals for a Liberal Defence Policy, n.d. [December 1962], LAC, Paul T. Hellyer fonds, MG 32, B-33, 72; Extract from the Liberal Programme, General Election – 1962, 30 April 1962, LAC, Paul T. Hellyer fonds, MG 32, B-33, 72; Smith, *Rogue Tory,* 468-69.

Chapter 3: The Army and the Unified Force, 1963-67

1 Quoted in Sean M. Maloney, *Learning to Love the Bomb: Canada's Nuclear Weapons during the Cold War* (Washington, DC: Potomac Books, 2007), 46.

2 Kenneth J. Clifford, *Progress and Purpose: A Developmental History of the United States Marine Corps, 1900-1970* (Washington, DC: History and Museums Division, Headquarters, United States Marine Corps, 1973), 109-11. The USMC was a most enthusiastic supporter of helicopters and "vertical envelopment."

3 Canada, House of Commons, *1963 Special Committee on Defence: Minutes of Proceedings and Evidence, October 17, 1963,* 439-77; Sean M. Maloney, "'Global Mobile': Flexible Response, Peacekeeping and the Origins of the Forces Mobile Command, 1958-1964," in *Army Doctrine and Training Bulletin* 1, no. 1 (Spring 2000): 27.

4 *1963 Special Committee on Defence,* 498, 505, 593-94.

5 R.L. Raymont, handwritten note on file, n.d., Directorate of History and Heritage, Department of National Defence (DHH), Robert Lewis Raymont fonds, RG 73/1223, File 3275.

6 In his memoirs, Hellyer would accuse Sutherland of being a pedestrian thinker, unable to rise to the conceptual heights he expected, and discounted the influence of the committee. Hellyer's main complaint seems to have been that the committee did not support service unification, which became the most controversial part of his reforms. However, his 1964 *White Paper on Defence* would reflect almost all the advice given by Sutherland's committee. Paul Hellyer, *Damn the Torpedoes: My Fight to Unify Canada's Armed Forces* (Toronto: McClelland and Stewart, 1990), 36.

7 Report of the Ad Hoc Committee on Defence Policy, 30 September 1963, DHH, RG 72/153, 7, 30-33.

8 Ibid., 29.

9 Ibid., 80-87.

10 Ibid., 91.

11 Ibid., 94-102.

12 Ibid., 102-4.

13 Ibid., 106-16.

14 Ibid., 120-21.

15 Ibid., 136-38.

16 Ibid., 140-41.

17 Ibid., 146-58.
18 Ibid., 159.
19 Ibid., 159-60.
20 Paul Hellyer to Chiefs of Staff Committee, 27 August 1963, Library and Archives Canada (LAC), Department of National Defence files, RG 24, Box 20, File 1200 M4, Army Planning Group, Committees, Mobile Force Study.
21 Minutes of the 9th Meeting of the Joint Service Study Group to Study a Plan for a Mobile Force, Discussion with the Minister and the CCOS, First Report of the Mobile Study Group, 3 October 1963, LAC, Department of National Defence files, RG 24, Box 20, File 1200 M4.
22 Paul Hellyer, letter to author, 27 October 2012.
23 Col. E.W. Henselwood, Army Planning Group, to Brig. H.W. Love, Chairman, Ad Hoc Mobile Force Study Group, Ground Component – Mobile Force, 18 October 1963, LAC, Department of National Defence files, RG 24, Box 20, File 1220 M4.
24 Army Planning Group – Mobile Force Study, 22 October 1963, LAC, R Department of National Defence files, RG 24, Box 20, File 1220 M4.
25 Brig. H.W. Love, Chairman, Joint Service Study Group, to Planning Group, Army Division – Mobile Force, 24 October 1963, LAC, Department of National Defence files, RG 24, Box 20, File 1220 M4.
26 Army Council, Minutes, 31 October 1963, DHH, Robert Lewis Raymont fonds, RG 73/1223, File 1718.
27 A Study of the Composition and Cost of a Mobile Force, Interim Study, 15 November 1963, DHH, Kardex 184.009 (D1). The report was termed "interim" because final details of the table of organization and equipment remained to be worked out. No later report was completed. Sean Maloney, "'Global Mobile,'" 29, argues that force planners had been "intellectually honest" in their approach, but the interim report exhibits mental gymnastics of the highest order, although the problem is defined clearly enough.
28 A Study of the Composition and Cost of a Mobile Force, Interim Study, 15 November 1963.
29 Army Council, Minutes of the 63/58 Meeting, 2 December 1963, DHH, Robert Lewis Raymont fonds, RG 73/1223, File 1728.
30 Sean Maloney, "'Global Mobile,'" 30-31; Department of National Defence, *White Paper on Defence* (Ottawa: Queen's Printer, 1964), 11, 15.
31 *White Paper,* 13.
32 Ibid., 21-24.
33 Tom Axworthy, "Soldiers without Enemies: A Political Analysis of Canadian Defence Policy 1945-1975" (PhD dissertation, Queen's University, 1978), 395-96, LAC, Paul T. Hellyer fonds, MG 32, B-33, 67; Paul Hellyer, interview with the author. Hellyer cannot recall this meeting, but he reviewed Axworthy's text without comment in 1978.
34 Minutes of a meeting of the Cabinet Committee on External Affairs and National Defence, *White Paper on Defence,* 24 March 1964, LAC, Paul T. Hellyer fonds, MG 32, B-33, 84; Paul Hellyer, interview with the author.
35 Vernon J. Kronenberg, *All Together Now: The Organization of the Department of National Defence in Canada 1964-1972,* Wellesley Papers 3/1973 (Toronto: Canadian Institute of International Affairs, 1973), 29-53.
36 Report of the Ad Hoc Committee on Defence Policy, 30 September 1963, DHH, RG 72/153.
37 A Study of the Composition and Cost of a Mobile Force, 15 November 1963, DHH, Kardex 184.009 (D1).
38 Jean V. Allard with Serge Bernier, *The Memoirs of Jean V. Allard* (Vancouver: UBC Press, 1988), 227-29.

39 Allard and Bernier, *Memoirs*, 231-33; Sean Maloney, "'Global Mobile II': The Development of Forces Mobile Command, 1965-1972," *Army Doctrine and Training Bulletin* 4, no. 2 (Summer 2001): 8-9.
40 Appreciation and Proposed Options for the Structure of the Canadian Army Field Force, 1965-70 Period, ATOB, 5 April 1965, DHH, RG 95/2, Series 1, Box 1.
41 Ibid.
42 R.J. Sutherland to VCDS, ACE Mobile Force, 20 October 1965, DHH, Kardex 184.009 (D1).
43 Minutes of Chief of Defence Staff – Staff Meeting 37/65, 30 November 1965, DHH, RG 73/1223, File 1559.
44 The Defence Plan 1966-76, 25 February 1966, DHH, Robert Lewis Raymont fonds, RG 73/1223, File 1572.
45 Ibid.
46 Air Marshal Sharp, Memorandum to CDS for Consideration at CDS Staff Meeting, Optional Contributions to NATO, 14 June 1967, DHH, Robert Lewis Raymont fonds, RG 73/1223, File 2525; see also RG 73/1223, File 1612.
47 Brig. N.H. Ross, Acting Deputy Chief Operations, to Deputy Chief Plans, Optional Contributions to NATO, 14 July 1967, DHH, Robert Lewis Raymont fonds, RG 73/1223, File 2525.
48 Minutes of Chief of Defence Staff – Staff Meeting 16/67, Optional Contributions to NATO, 19 July 1967, DHH, Robert Lewis Raymont fonds, RG 73/1223, File 1612.
49 Mobile Command Headquarters Organization Book (Draft), 27 August 1965, DHH, Jean V. Allard fonds, RG 84/126.
50 LGen. J.V. Allard, Commander Mobile Command, to CDS, Mobile Command Implementation –Problems Encountered, 5 November 1965, DHH, Robert Lewis Raymont fonds, RG 73/1223, File 3200.
51 Ibid.
52 ACM Miller, CDS, to Command Mobile Command Headquarters, Mobile Command – Problems Encountered, 11 January 1966, DHH, Robert Lewis Raymont fonds, RG 73/1223, File 3200.
53 CFP 165, *The Conduct of Land Operations*, Art. 110, CFHQ, 1 January 1967, DHH, RG 82/236. See also Maloney, "'Global Mobile II,'" 11-12.
54 CFP 165, Art. 1705.
55 See, for example, Sir Robert Thompson, *Defeating Communist Insurgency* (New York: Frederick A. Praeger, 1966).
56 CFP 165, chs. 15 and 16; Combat Development and Tactical Doctrine Committee, Minutes of 64/1 Meeting, ABC Armies Operational Concept 1971-80, 21 January 1964, DHH, RG 81/272.
57 CFP 165, Arts. 232-35.
58 Hellyer, *Damn the Torpedoes*, 73-75.
59 Maloney, "'Global Mobile II,'" 13, 16.
60 Maj. D.C. Johnson, *A Study of the Deployment of a Canadian Task Force of Battalion Group Size to Mozambique (South East Africa)*, Directorate of Land Operational Research, Staff Note 27, August 1967, DHH, RG 80/590.
61 LGen. J.V. Allard to CDS, Airlift Capability – Augmentation, 14 January 1966, DHH, Robert Lewis Raymont fonds, RG 73/1223, File 3200.
62 VCDS to CDS, Status Report – Ministers Planning Guidance Memorandum Dated 23 March 1967, 29 June 1967, DHH, Robert Lewis Raymont fonds, RG 73/1223, File 2100; Minutes of CDS – Staff Meeting 6/67, Strategic Mobility, 15 March 1967, DHH, RG 73/1223, File 1601; Minutes of CDS – Advisory Committee Meeting 29/68, Review of 69/70 Defence

Programme, 13 September 1968, DHH, Robert Lewis Raymont fonds, RG 73/1223, File 1637.

63 Minutes of CDS – Staff Meeting 8/67, Mobile Command – Aviation Force Structure Study, 29 March 1967, DHH, RG 73/1223, File 1601A; VCDS to CDS, Status Report – Ministers Planning Guidance Memorandum Dated 23 March 1967, 29 June 1967, DHH, Robert Lewis Raymont fonds, RG 73/1223, File 2100.

64 *White Paper,* 22.

65 A Study in the Composition and Cost of a Mobile Force, 15 November 1963.

66 There is a form of military analysis known as an "appreciation of the situation." "Situating the appreciation" is a phrase meant to convey a dishonest analysis that begins with the desired answer and works backwards. Ray Stouffer, "Cold War Air Power Choices for the RCAF: Paul Hellyer and the Selection of the CF-5 Freedom Fighter," *Canadian Military Journal* 7, no. 3 (Autumn 2006), 63-74, speculates that Hellyer was driven partly by his personal association with Northrop Aircraft, which began when he studied at the Northrop Aeronautical Institute, and partly by his own beliefs about the appropriate uses of airpower.

67 Paul Hellyer to CDS, RE: Aircraft Requirements, 4 August 1964, DHH, Kardex 184.009 (D1).

68 ACM F.R. Miller to Minister of National Defence, Aircraft Requirements, 14 September 1964, DHH, Kardex 184.009 (D1); Paul Hellyer, interview with the author.

69 ACM F.R. Miller to the Minister, Tactical Aircraft, 7 June 1965, DHH, Kardex 184.009 (D1).

70 CF-5 Tactical Aircraft Program, Memorandum to Defence Council [from CDS], 17 August 1965, DHH, Robert Lewis Raymont fonds, RG 73/1223, File 1548A.

71 Col. W.H. Casley, Project Manager, CF-5 History of Events 1964-1971, DHH, Robert Lewis Raymont fonds, RG 73/1223, File 2505.

72 Summary Record of Decisions of Defence Council Meetings, 156th Meeting, 25 August 1965, DHH, Robert Lewis Raymont fonds, RG 73/1223, File 1472.

73 CDS – Staff Meeting 9/67, Briefing on Project 530 – Northrop Proposal for Follow-on Aircraft, 3 May 1967, DHH, Robert Lewis Raymont fonds, RG 73/1223, File 1603; Memorandum for the Chief of Defence Staff from Vice Chief of the Defence Staff, Canadian Advanced Multi-Role Aircraft (CAMRA) – Northrop P530 Proposal, 1 May 1967, DHH, Robert Lewis Raymont fonds, RG 73/1223, File 1603. The P530 project evolved into the YF-17 and eventually into the F/A-18, which was acquired to replace the CF-101 and CF-104, but not the CF-5. The air force never warmed to the ground support mission.

74 George Mackenzie Urquhart, "The Changing Role of the Canadian Militia, 1945-1975" (MA thesis, University of Victoria, 1977), 102-5. See also Tamara A. Sherwin, "From Total War to Total Force: Civil-Military Relations and the Canadian Army Reserve (Militia)" (MA thesis, University of New Brunswick, 1997), 84-86.

75 Army Council, Minutes, Five Year Programme, 29 July 1963, DHH, Robert Lewis Raymont fonds, RG 73/1223, File 1725.

76 Canadian Army Manning Plan 1963 (Updated 8 April 1964), DHH, RG 74/738.

77 Sherwin, "From Total War to Total Force," 92-94; Urquhart, "The Changing Role of the Canadian Militia," 108.

78 *White Paper,* 24-25.

79 Paul Hellyer, interview with the author; Urquhart, "The Changing Role of the Canadian Militia," 131; Sherwin, "From Total War to Total Force," 98-100.

80 Sherwin, ibid., 103.

81 A "subunit" is a squadron (armour), battery (artillery), or company (infantry), the size of which varies according to the type of unit and organizational doctrine of the day.

82 Kronenberg, *All Together Now,* 90-91.
83 *White Paper,* 19.
84 Kronenberg, *All Together Now,* 78.
85 Defence Council, December 1965, quoted in J.L. Granatstein, *Canada's Army: Waging War and Keeping the Peace* (Toronto: University of Toronto Press, 2002), 365. Moncel seemed to blow hot and cold as a preservationist of service tradition. At one point he tried to sell Hellyer on the concept of reorganizing the infantry into a single regiment with numbered battalions, thus wiping out all the existing regimental names at one blow. Paul Hellyer, *Damn the Torpedoes,* 160.
86 Canada, House of Commons, Standing Committee on Defence, Minutes of Proceedings and Evidence, 20 February 1967.
87 MGen. (Ret'd.) George Kitching to Lester B. Pearson, 18 July 1966, LAC, Lester B. Pearson fonds, MG 26, N-4, 37, File 100.82, Policy.
88 Allard with Bernier, *Memoirs,* 250.
89 Hellyer, *Damn the Torpedoes,* 247-48, quotes MGen. F.F. Worthington's report of the reaction of soldiers in the NATO brigade group to his new green uniform.

Chapter 4: Trudeau and the Crisis in Civil-Military Relations

1 Cabinet Minutes, White Paper on Defence, 25 March 1964, Library and Archives Canada (LAC), Cabinet Conclusions, RG 2, 6264; Canada, Royal Commission on Government Organization (Glassco Commission), *Report,* vol. 4, *Special Areas of Administration* (Ottawa: Queen's Printer, 1963), 2125-36.
2 R.J. Sutherland to The Minister, 8 November 1963, LAC, Paul T. Hellyer fonds, MG 32, B-33, 68; R.J. Sutherland to The Minister, 2 December 1963; E.B. Armstrong, Deputy Minister, to The Minister, Possible Force Structure, 1963-1973, 19 December 1963, LAC, Paul T. Hellyer fonds, MG 32, B-33, 84.
3 Vernon J. Kronenberg, *All Together Now: The Organization of the Department of National Defence in Canada 1964-1972,* Wellesley Papers 3/1973 (Toronto: Canadian Institute of International Affairs, 1973), 110-11; J.L. Granatstein, *Canada's Army: Waging War and Keeping the Peace* (Toronto: University of Toronto Press, 2002), 354.
4 A/M F.R. Sharp, Memorandum to CDS for Consideration at CDS Staff Meeting, Status Report – Minister Planning Guidance Memorandum, 29 June 1967, Directorate of History and Heritage, Department of National Defence (DHH), Robert Lewis Raymont fonds, RG 73/1223, File 1610.
5 Minutes of Chief of Defence Staff – Special Staff Meeting, Mobile Command Major Equipment Programs, 17 July 1967, DHH, Robert Lewis Raymont fonds, RG 73/1223, File 1611.
6 Gen. J.V. Allard, Introduction to the Purpose and Rationale for Defence Forces, Special CDS Conference, Kingston, Ontario, 29 August 1967, DHH, Robert Lewis Raymont fonds, RG 73/1223, File 832.
7 Rationale for Canadian Defence Forces (draft), 17 August 1967, DHH, RG 81/39.
8 Léo Cadieux to CDS, Chairman Defence Research Board, Deputy Minister, Policy Guidance – 1968/1974, 8 February 1968, DHH, Robert Lewis Raymont fonds, RG 73/1223, File 2101.
9 MGen. N.G. Wilson-Smith to CDS, Discussions Concerning Role and Re-location of Canadian Force Europe, 26 March 1968, DHH, Robert Lewis Raymont fonds, RG 73/1223, File 2531.
10 J.V. Allard, Brief for Major-General Wilson-Smith's Discussions with SACEUR, 12 March 1968, DHH, Robert Lewis Raymont fonds, RG 73/1223, File 2531.

11 MGen. N.G. Wilson-Smith to CDS, Discussions Concerning the Role and Re-location of Canadian Force Europe, 26 March 1968, DHH, Robert Lewis Raymont fonds, RG 73/1223, File 2531; SACEUR to CDS, Future Role and Location of 4 CIBG and 1 Air Division Canadian Armed Forces, 12 April 1968, DHH, Robert Lewis Raymont fonds, RG 73/1223, File 2531.

12 Rationale for Canadian Defence Forces, CFP 243, n.d. [never officially issued], DHH, RG 90/452.

13 R.L. Raymont to Allard, handwritten note, 1 April 1968? [date partially illegible], DHH, Robert Lewis Raymont fonds, RG 73/1223, File 832.

14 Allard to Cadieux, Rationale for Canadian Defence Forces, 31 May 1968, DHH, Robert Lewis Raymont fonds, RG 73/1223, File 832; Brig. H.E.T. Doucet, Executive Assistant to the Minister of National Defence to Allard, Rationale for Canadian Defence Forces, 5 June 1968, DHH, Robert Lewis Raymont fonds, RG 73/1223, File 832.

15 Memorandum to Cabinet, Defence Review, 30 April 1968, DHH, Robert Lewis Raymont fonds, RG 73/1223, File 2101.

16 Trudeau's views have been set out clearly in J.L. Granatstein and Robert Bothwell, *Pirouette: Pierre Trudeau and Canadian Foreign Policy* (Toronto: University of Toronto Press, 1990), 1-35.

17 Ibid., 14.

18 Defence Policy Review, Draft, 2 July 1968, DHH, Robert Lewis Raymont fonds, RG 73/1223, File 2101. No copy of the final draft of 8 July could be located.

19 MGen. (Ret.) Charles J. Gauthier, "The Formulation of Defence Policy from 1970 to 1990" (unpublished paper for the Directorate of History, Department of National Defence, Ottawa, n.d.), 16-7, DHH, Charles J. Gauthier fonds, RG 92/288, File 53. Gauthier had served as the executive assistant to the CDS in 1973 and served in increasingly senior positions at CFHQ and NDHQ after that, always in a policy advisory position, rising to the rank of major-general and continuing as a civilian executive after retirement from the military. When he left the department, the Directorate of History commissioned him to write a multi-volume study of defence policy. This work is required reading for those interested in the period.

20 Ibid., 17.

21 The Prime Minister's Remarks at the December 9th Meeting, DHH, Robert Lewis Raymont fonds, RG 73/1223, File 2104.

22 LGen. F.R. Sharp to the Minister, 20 December 1968, DHH, Robert Lewis Raymont fonds, RG 73/1223, File 2104.

23 Granatstein and Bothwell, *Pirouette,* 5, 385.

24 Canadian Defence Policy: A Study, n.d., LAC, Pierre Elliott Trudeau fonds, MG 26, O-11, 2.

25 Gauthier, "Formulation of Defence Policy," 22-3; The Defence Policy Review, February 1969, DHH, Robert Lewis Raymont fonds, RG 73/1223, File 2105; also at LAC, Pierre Elliott Trudeau fonds, MG 26, O-11, 2, File 100.8.

26 Cabinet Minutes, Meetings of 29 March, 30 March, 1 April, and 3 April 1969, The Defence Policy Review and the Report of the Special Task Force on Europe, LAC, Cabinet Conclusions, RG 2, 6340. A full account of the Cabinet meeting and the negotiations around it can be found in Granatstein and Bothwell, *Pirouette,* 1-35.

27 Chronological Résumé Concerning Canadian Force Commitments to NATO Europe Including the Air/Sea Transportable Combat Group to AFNORTH, n.d., DHH, Robert Lewis Raymont fonds, RG 73/1223, File 2530.

28 Aide-mémoire, Policy Decisions Regarding Canadian Forces Europe Period May 1968 to September 1971, Prepared by DGP, 20 September 1972, DHH, Robert Lewis Raymont fonds, RG 73/1223, File 2530.

29 Granatstein and Bothwell, *Pirouette,* 28.
30 The Carl Gustav is an 84 mm recoilless rifle effective against moving armour at about 400 m and stationary targets at 700 m.
31 Proposals for Canadian Force Reduction – NATO Force Presentation by Rear-Admiral R.W. Timbrell, Deputy Chief Plans, to SHAPE, 29 May 1969, DHH, Robert Lewis Raymont fonds, RG 73/1223, File 2519.
32 First Draft, Operational Equipment Requirement, OER L-14/66, Direct Fire Support Vehicle (DFSV), 1971-80, May 1968, LAC, Department of National Defence files, RG 24, 3500-L14/66.
33 Preliminary Report, Project BRONZE NIMBUS, Directorate of Land Operational Research, 31 July 1969, DHH, Jean V. Allard fonds, RG 84/126, File 105.
34 Gen. Goodpaster to Léo Cadieux, 3 August 1969, DHH, Robert Lewis Raymont fonds, RG 73/1223, File 2530.
35 SACEUR to DND Canada, Canadian Proposal to Reduce the Size of Its Forces in Europe – SHAPE Alternative Proposal, 3 August 1969, DHH, Robert Lewis Raymont fonds, RG 73/1223, File 2530.
36 MGen. M.R. Dare to CDS, Summary of SACEUR Proposal Canadian Forces Europe, 12 August 1969, DHH, Robert Lewis Raymont fonds, RG 73/1223, File 2530.
37 Chronological Résumé, DHH, Robert Lewis Raymont fonds, RG 73/1223, File 2530.
38 Cabinet Minutes, Canadian Nato Force Proposals, 13 August 1969, LAC, Cabinet Conclusions, RG 2, 6340.
39 Extract from Record of DPC Ministerial Session, 3 December 1969, DHH, Robert Lewis Raymont fonds, RG 73/1223, File 2530.
40 Canadian Forces Headquarters, "CFP 200: Defence Planning Guidance," 15 September 1970, DHH, Robert Lewis Raymont fonds, RG 73/1223, File 2098. Although termed a "planning guidance," the document actually provided little direction and was more of a summary of the dilemmas faced by defence policy makers and force planners than anything else.
41 Granatstein and Bothwell, *Pirouette,* 236.
42 Gauthier, "The Formulation of Defence Policy," ch. 1, "Implementing Defence Policy," 28-29, DHH, Charles J. Gauthier fonds, RG 92/228, File 53.
43 Ibid., 30; Col. F.T. Harris, Director Combat Development, CLFCSC Presentation, Future Concepts, 10 March 1971, DHH, RG 80/499.
44 Gauthier, "The Formulation of Defence Policy," 31.
45 Macdonald to CDS and DM, 12 January 1971, DHH, Robert Lewis Raymont fonds, RG 73/1223, File 2530.
46 Gen. F.R. Sharp to Minister of National Defence, Canadian Force Commitments to NATO Europe Including the Air/Sea Transportable Group to AFNORTH, 1 February 1971, Robert Lewis Raymont fonds, DHH RG 73/1223, File 2530; Gauthier, "The Formulation of Defence Policy," 32.
47 Telephone interview, Gordon Smith, 4 October 2012; Granatstein and Bothwell, *Pirouette,* 237.
48 Donald S. Macdonald, Comments on Mar. 12th draft, handwritten note, n.d., LAC, Gordon Smith papers, 1997-98/050 GAD.
49 Gauthier, "The Formulation of Defence Policy," 40-42, 51; Gordon Smith to Donald Macdonald, Force Structure and Budgets, 26 March 1971, LAC, Gordon Smith papers, 1997-98/050 GAD.
50 Donald S. Macdonald to Pierre Trudeau, 16 March 1971, LAC, Pierre Elliott Trudeau fonds, MG 26, O-11, 2; Pierre Trudeau to Donald S. Macdonald, 22 March 1971, LAC, Pierre Elliott Trudeau fonds, MG 26, O-11, 2. See also LAC, Gordon Smith Papers, 1997-98/050 GAD.

51 Donald S. Macdonald to Pierre Trudeau, Role of the Canadian Land Forces Stationed in Europe: Assignment to ACE Mobile Force (Land), 30 April 1971, LAC, Pierre Elliott Trudeau fonds, MG 26, O-11, 2.
52 Pierre Trudeau to Donald S. Macdonald, 13 May 1971, LAC, Pierre Elliott Trudeau fonds, MG 26, O-11, 2; Donald S. Macdonald, Notes on the Meeting of Cabinet on the Evening of Thursday, July 22, 1971, on the Subject of the DEFENCE WHITE PAPER, LAC, Gordon Smith Papers, 1997-98/050 GAD.
53 Granatstein and Bothwell, *Pirouette,* 237.
54 Cabinet Minutes, The White Paper on Defence, 22 July 1971, LAC, Cabinet Conclusions, RG 2, 6381.
55 Department of National Defence, *Defence in the 70s: White Paper on Defence* (Ottawa: Information Canada, 1971), 35-36.
56 Ibid., 32, 41.
57 Colin S. Gray, "Defence in the Seventies: A White Paper for All Seasons," *Canadian Defence Quarterly* 1, no. 4 (Spring 1972): 30-34.
58 Gauthier, "The Formulation of Defence Policy," 57-61.
59 Mobile Command Headquarters, Historical Report 1973, Doctrine Section, Fort Frontenac Library, Kingston, ON.
60 Mobile Command Headquarters, Historical Report 1979, Deputy Chief of Staff Combat Development, Fort Frontenac Library, Kingston, ON. One wonders how successful this division of duties was when one notes that the Mobile Command office of primary interest was called "Combat Development" even though the function was supposed to be the purview of NDHQ.
61 Col. P.A. Neatby, Deputy Commander, Mobile Command, Doctrine Discussion FMC, 19 July 1973, DHH, Director General Land Force Development fonds, RG 96/26, Box 1.
62 Land Doctrine Study – Publication Presentation, n.d. [annotated December 1974], DHH, Director General Land Force Development fonds, RG 96/26, Box 1; CFP 165, *The Conduct of Land Operations,* 30 October 1973, DDH, RG 82/366.
63 Col. J.A. Fox, Director Land Plans, to Chief Land Operations, Doctrine – Status Report, 9 September 1975, DHH, Director General Land Force Development fonds, RG 96/26, Box 1.
64 MGen. J.J. Paradis to CFC, CLFCSC, FMCHQ, HQ CFE, Land Staff Training, 16 September 1975, DHH, Director General Land Force Development fonds, RG 96/26, Box 1.
65 L. Denis Hudson, Memorandum for the Prime Minister, Configuration of the Canadian Land Forces in Europe, 20 March 1973, LAC, Pierre Elliott Trudeau fonds, MG-26, O-11; Ivan L. Head, Memorandum for the Prime Minister, Configuration of the Canadian Land Forces in Europe, 4 April 1973, LAC, Pierre Elliott Trudeau fonds, MG 26, O-11; P.E. Trudeau to James Richardson, 12 April 1973, LAC, Pierre Elliott Trudeau fonds, MG 26, O-11.
66 Memorandum to Cabinet [draft], Land Force Policy, 6 September 1974, DHH, Director General Land Force Development fonds, RG 96/26, Box 1.
67 MGen. W.C. Leonard, Commander, Canadian Forces Europe, Commander CFE Introductory Remarks to Joint Attack Helicopter Instrumented Evaluation Steering Committee, 10 July 1973, LAC, RG 24, 23842, File 3500-2, Pt. 1, Cobra Trial, 1972-73; Capt. B.A. Muelaner, "The Search for the Best Anti-tank Defence," *Canadian Defence Quarterly* 3, no. 4 (Spring 1974): 24-30; Wayne D. Ralph, "The Bell AH-1Q TOW Cobra: Operational Experience and Field Trials," *Canadian Defence Quarterly* 4, no. 2 (Autumn 1974), 24-27. The argument that the attack helicopter was "too expensive" to replace the tank was not supported by the trials. While the helicopter cost more to purchase and more to operate, its effectiveness more than compensated (in good weather). The often-quoted $300 million to $400 million to re-equip the army as a light force would appear to have been arrived at

by including all the equipment needed to modernize the army, including TOW missiles and low-level air defence missiles that were required whether the force was based on tanks or helicopters.

68 Memorandum to Cabinet [draft], Land Force Policy, 6 September 1974, DHH, Director General Land Force Development fonds, RG 96/26, Box 1.

69 Capt. W.L. Pickering, "Has the Tank a Place on Today's Battlefield? Australian and Israeli Experience," *Armoured Review* 8 (April 1973): 4-5.

70 Royal Canadian Armoured Corps Association, "Position Paper on Main Battle Tank Retention, Defence in the 70s and the Main Battle Tank," *Armoured Review* 8 (1973): 11.

71 Col. (Ret'd.) J.M.E. Clarkson, "Spark at Yom Kippur: Many Surprises in an Eighteen-Day War," *Canadian Defence Quarterly* 3, no. 4 (Spring 1974): 21.

72 Gauthier, "The Formulation of Defence Policy," ch. 3, "Funding the Defence Program from 1970 to 1975."

73 Ibid., 108, 137-40; Memorandum to Cabinet, Financing the Defence Program for 1975-76 to 1979-80, 13 October 1974, DHH, George Lindsay fonds, RG 87/253-II-14.4.

74 Memorandum to Cabinet [draft], The Defence Program – The Tasks, 15 January 1975, DHH, George Lindsay fonds, RG 87/253-II-14.3.

75 Sylvain Cloutier to P.M. Pitfield, Clerk of the Privy Council, 24 January 1975, DHH, George Lindsay fonds, RG 87/253-II-14.3.

76 Item 4, The Defence Program: Tasks, 21 February 1975, DHH, George Lindsay fonds, RG 87/253-II-14.3. Interestingly, Pitfield cautioned Trudeau not to refer to an attached PCO aide-mémoire but only to the main DND paper, probably recalling the blow-up when Cadieux had discovered Ivan Head's study on the table at the same time as his memorandum to Cabinet in 1968.

77 Gauthier, "The Formulation of Defence Policy," 156, 167.

78 VAdm. R.H. Falls, VCDS, to Deputy Minister, Chief of Defence Staff, Chief of Operations Research and Analysis Establishment, Defence Structure Review – Phase II, 26 May 1975, DHH, George Lindsay fonds, RG 87/253; Memorandum to Cabinet [draft], The Defence Program – Force Models and Effectiveness, 25 June 1975, DHH, George Lindsay fonds, RG 87/253.

79 Granatstein and Bothwell, *Pirouette,* 254-55.

80 CFP 311 (1), *The Tactical Air Wing in Battle,* 24 April 1970, DHH, RG 80/278.

81 The story of the rise of Air Command is best told in Catherine Eyre, "The Organization of Air Command, 1973-1976," unpublished study (Directorate of History, 1976), DHH, Catherine Allen fonds, RG 77/529.

82 Col. W.E.J. Hutchinson, DLP4, and LCol. T.M. Marshaw, SSO Doc FMC HQ, Doctrine and Publications Report, Land Forces Combat Development Committee, First Conference, 26 July 1976, LAC, Department of National Defence files, RG 24, File CFBV 3189-1-1, vol. 1.

83 Col. J.A. Fox, DLP, *Combat Development Guide,* Land Forces Combat Development Committee, First Conference, 26 July 1976, LAC, Department of National Defence files, RG 24, File CFBV 3189-1-1, vol. 1.

84 Ibid.

85 Ibid.

86 Dr. J.J. Conn, DLOR, Operational Research, Land Force Combat Development Committee, First Conference, 26 July 1976; Minutes, First Meeting of the Land Forces Combat Development Committee, Land Forces Combat Development Committee, 1-2 June 1976, LAC, Department of National Defence files, RG 24, File CFBV 3189-1-1, vol. 1.

87 LCol. G.C.F. McQuaid and LCol. W.E.J. Hutchinson, Presentation on Research War Game BRONZE RAMPART to the Defence Symposium, 24 January 1977, DLOR Staff Note 77/3, LAC, Department of National Defence files, RG 24, File CFBV 3189-3-12, vol. 1; see also ORAE Project Report 61, Preliminary Report, BRONZE RAMPART, July 1977, DHH, RG 81/115.

88 Douglas Bland, *The Administration of Defence Policy in Canada* (Kingston, ON: Ronald P. Frye and Company, 1987), 61.

Chapter 5: Reform, Regimentalism, and Reaction

1 J.L. Granatstein, *Canada's Army: Waging War and Keeping the Peace* (Toronto: University of Toronto Press, 2002), 353-58.

2 Edward Cardwell, the British Secretary of State for War (1868-74), undertook the reform of the British Army. One aspect of this was the reorganization of all line infantry regiments into two battalions sharing a depot and recruiting area. One battalion would serve overseas while its counterpart was at home training.

3 Col. (Ret.) John Joly, quoted in Commission of Inquiry into the Deployment of Canadian Forces to Somalia, *Dishonoured Legacy: The Lessons of the Somalia Affair,* vol. 1 (Ottawa: Public Works and Government Services Canada, 1997), 164-65.

4 Anthony Kellett, *The Canadian Regimental System,* Director General Policy Planning Discussion Paper as input to the Minister of National Defence's Report to the Prime Minister on Leadership and Management of the Canadian Forces, 25 March 1997, Directorate of History and Heritage, Department of National Defence (DHH), Anthony Kellett fonds, RG 2001/5, File 5; Anthony Kellett, *Regimental Executive, Advisory and Representative Bodies,* Director Social Economic Analysis, Staff Note 12/85, August 1985, DHH, Anthony Kellett fonds, RG 2001/5, File 9.

5 Frederic Thompson, "The Profession of Arms in Canada, 1945-1970," prepared for the Chief of the Defence Staff, April 1970, DHH, Robert Lewis Raymont fonds, RG 73/1223, Ser. 9, File 3156. P.E. Coulombe, "The Changing Military Career in Canada," in *On Military Ideology: Studies Presented at Varna International Sociological Association Conference 1970, Part II,* edited by Morris Janowitz and Jacques Van Doorn (Rotterdam: Rotterdam University Press, 1971), 187.

6 Cmdre. R.L. Hennessy, Bolte Report, Staffing of the Minister's Manpower Study Officers (1964), 11 December 1964, DHH, Personnel Management Policy Study Group Working Papers, RG 83/666, V, 132, Folder 14.

7 Defence Council Extract of Minutes, P1151-4110/D1 (A Sec [CP]), Report of the Minister's Manpower Study, 14 July 1965, DHH, Personnel Management Policy Study Group Working Papers, RG 83/666, V, 132, Folder 14; NDHQ Comments on the Report of the Minister's Manpower Study (Officers), August 1965, DHH, RG 75/519.

8 Gen. J.V. Allard, Foreword, Report of the Officer Development Board, March 1969, DHH, RG 82/140 (hereafter cited as ODB Report).

9 ODB Report, ch. 2, "The Emergence of Military Professionalism and the Military Ethic."

10 ODB Report, ch. 3, "The Officer Corps in Canada to the End of the Second World War."

11 ODB Report, ch. 5, "Economic, Sociological, Political and Military Change."

12 It is interesting to note that the 2010 recruiting campaign of the Canadian Forces, "Fight with the Canadian Forces," followed much along these lines, showing the armed forces rescuing airliner crash survivors in the Arctic, interdicting drug smugglers on the high seas, and rescuing hostages someplace hot and dry overseas.

13 ODB Report, ch. 6, "Precepts of Officer Development."
14 Department of National Defence, "Canadian Officership in the 21st Century: Strategic Guidance for the CF Officer Corps and the Officer Professional Development System, September 2000," Version 3.2, 5 July 2000, DHH, Romeo A. Dallaire fonds, RG 2001/25, Box 3.
15 R.B. Byers, "Defence and Foreign Policy in the 1970s: The Demise of the Trudeau Doctrine," *International Journal* 32, no. 2 (Spring 1978): 320.
16 Department of National Defence, *White Paper on Defence* (Ottawa: Queen's Printer, 1964), 23.
17 Richard Mayne, "Its Own Worst Enemy: Ship Advocacy in the RCN, 1963-64," *Canadian Naval Review* 2, no. 3 (Fall 2006): 24-28.
18 Marc Milner, *Canada's Navy: The First Century* (Toronto: University of Toronto Press, 1999), 248.
19 Details of Request to the Honourable the Treasury Board, 19 February 1965, DHH, RG 87/34.
20 DHH Programme, Ship Construction Contracting, 31 August 1965, DHH, RG 87/34.
21 L. Cadieux to the Treasury Board, Additional Funds for the Construction of the Four Ships of the DDH 280 Programme, 10 November 1967, DHH, RG 87/34.
22 Sylvain Cloutier, Acting Secretary to the Treasury Board, to E.B. Armstrong, Deputy Minister, TB685745, 11 February 1969, DHH, RG 87/34.
23 Management Review Group, Staff Report E – Research, Engineering and Procurement (Including Special Problems in Ship Procurement), July 1972, DHH, RG 84/32, 2.
24 LGen. M.R. Dare, VCDS, to CDS, The White Paper, 5 February 1971, Library and Archives Canada (LAC), Gordon Smith papers, 1997-98/050 GAD; Douglas Bland, *The Administration of Defence Policy in Canada, 1947-1985* (Kingston, ON: Ronald P. Frye, 1987), 59-63.
25 Management Review Group, Report to the Minister of National Defence on the Management of Defence in Canada, July 1972, DHH, RG 84/32, Folder 1, 1-14.
26 Ibid., 14-16.
27 Ibid., 19.
28 MGen. (Ret.) Charles J. Gauthier, "The Formulation of Defence Policy from 1970 to 1990" (unpublished paper for the Directorate of History, Department of National Defence, Ottawa, n.d.), ch. 1, "Implementing Defence Policy," 58.
29 Management Review Group, Report, 38-39.
30 Ibid., 39-40.
31 Ibid., 41-43.
32 J.B. Pennefather to the Minister of National Defence, MRG Interim Report and DND Management Structure, 29 October 1971, LAC, Gordon Smith Papers, 1997-98/050 GAD.
33 Confusion and rivalry between the deputy minister and the chief of the defence staff had been built in by legislation. The National Defence Act assigned "management and direction" of the Canadian Forces to the minister and "control and administration" of the Forces to the chief of the defence staff without defining any of the terms. In Canada, deputy ministers have all the powers of their minister, except the power to make regulations, through the Interpretation Act.
34 Sylvain Cloutier to MND [Macdonald], handwritten note, 5 November 1971, LAC, Gordon Smith Papers, 1997-98/050 GAD; J.L. Granatstein, "Making the Department of National Defence Work in the 1970s: The Deputy Minister and the CDS Remember," *Canadian Military History* 20, no. 2 (Spring 2011): 60-62; Bland, *The Administration of Defence Policy in Canada*, 70-85.

35 Desmond Morton, *A Short History of Canada* (Toronto: McClelland and Stewart, 1994), 274.
36 Deborah Cowen, *Military Workfare: The Soldier and Social Citizenship* (Toronto: University of Toronto Press, 2008), 136, 151, 168-76.
37 Charles A. Cotton, Rodney K. Crook, and Frank C. Pinch, "Canada's Professional Military: The Limits of Civilianization," *Armed Forces and Society* 4, no. 3 (May 1978): 365-89.
38 Charles A. Cotton, *Military Attitudes and Values of the Army in Canada* (Toronto: Canadian Forces Applied Research Unit, December 1979).
39 Ibid.
40 BGen. D.G. Loomis, "The Regimental System," *Mobile Command Letter, Special Supplement,* 29 July 1975, DHH, RG 79/39. It is interesting that while most advocates of regimentalism, including Loomis, claimed that the greatest advantage was combat cohesion, Loomis would criticize the "industrial" system for producing ... combat cohesion!
41 Ibid.
42 Col. J.E. Neelin and Col. L.M. Pederson, "The Administrative Structure of the Canadian Armed Forces: Over-Centralized, Overly Staff-Ridden," *Canadian Defence Quarterly* 4, no. 2 (Autumn 1974): 33-40.
43 Douglas Bland, *Chiefs of Defence: Government and the Unified Command of the Canadian Armed Forces* (Toronto: Brown Book, 1995), 101-4.
44 LGen. J.J. Paradis, Speech given by LGen. Paradis on Unification, 14 November 1979, DHH, Review Group on the Report of the Task Force on Unification of the Canadian Forces: Papers, RG 81/747, Folder 10.
45 Annex C to Mobile Command Brief to Unification Review Task Force, SO3 Pers (P and D) Brief for Unification Task Force, Civilianization of the Forces, 26 October 1979, DHH, Review Group on the Report of the Task Force on Unification of the Canadian Forces: Papers, RG 81/747, Folder 10.
46 William Johnston, *A War of Patrols: Canadian Army Operations in Korea* (Vancouver: UBC Press, 2003), 371-77.
47 Anthony Kellett, *Motivation and Behaviour: The Influence of the Regimental System, Part I – Esprit de Corps,* Operations Research and Analysis Establishment, Directorate of Social and Economic Analysis, ORAE Report R109, June 1991.
48 Col. Gardam to DGCPOR, Task Force on Unification – Personal Views – Part 2, 19 June 1980, DHH, Review Group on the Report of the Task Force on Unification of the Canadian Forces: Papers, RG 81/747, Folder 19.
49 LGen. James C. Smith, ADM(Per) to Commander Mobile Command, Delegation of Authority to Commanding Officers, 29 November 1979, DHH, Review Group on the Report of the Task Force on Unification of the Canadian Forces: Papers, RG81/747, Folder 24.
50 Task Force on the Review of Unification of the Canadian Forces, *Final Report,* 15 March 1980, 39-41, 52.
51 Ibid., 42.
52 Ibid., 65-66, 70, 77.
53 Bland, *Chiefs of Defence,* 111.
54 Review Group on the Report of the Task Force on Unification of the Canadian Forces, *Report,* 31 August 1980, 18 (in author's possession).
55 Ibid., 19.
56 "Personnel Concept," Canadian Forces, May 1983 (in author's possession).
57 C.R. Nixon, Notes for Presentation by Mr. C.R. Nixon, Deputy Minister of the Department of National Defence, at the Canadian Forces Staff College, Toronto, 9 September 1981, "Role of the Deputy Minister in the Department of National Defence" (in author's possession).

58 LGen. (Ret'd) Richard Evraire, interview with the author; Richard Evraire, "General and Senior Officer Professional Development in the Canadian Forces," ISP-MPA Master's Project, Queen's University, Kingston, ON, n.d., 19, 29-31, 84-86.
59 LGen. J.J. Paradis, Speech given by LGen. Paradis on Unification, 14 November 1979, DHH, Review Group on the Report of the Task Force on Unification of the Canadian Forces: Papers, RG 81/747, Folder 10.

Chapter 6: The Plan for a "Big Army"

1 Robert Close, *Europe without Defense? 48 Hours that Could Change the Face of the World* (New York: Pergamon Press, 1979).
2 Canadian Land Forces Staff Course 1980, GEN/2/LDE, Lecture-Demonstration – Operations General, Directorate of History and Heritage, Department of National Defence (DHH), Canadian Land Forces Command and Staff College fonds, RG 80/71, Folder 464.
3 Canadian Land Forces Staff Course 1980, GEN/1/P, Precis – Operations General, and GEN/21/P, Anti-Armour Aspects of Operations, DHH, Canadian Land Forces Command and Staff College fonds, RG 80/71, Folder 464.
4 MGen. René Gutknecht, Chief Land Doctrine and Operations, to NDHQ staff, FMC and 4CMBG, 22 June 1979, DHH, RG 80/493.
5 NDHQ Policy Directive P16 – DND Procurement Policy, 13 February 1976, DHH, Director General Land Force Development fonds, RG 96/26, Box 10, File 4.
6 NDHQ Policy Directive P26 – The Development and Employment of the Primary Reserve and the Supplementary List, 11 June 1978, DHH, Director General Land Force Development fonds, RG 96/26, Box 2.
7 Adm. R.H. Falls to Command Commanders and NDHQ Group Principals, Guidance for the Development of Mobilization and Readiness Plans, 22 August 1978, DHH, Director General Land Force Development fonds, RG 96/26, Box 10, File 4.
8 BGen. H.G. Trower, DGMPO to DCDS, Mobilization Planning, 1 April 1976, DHH, Director General Land Force Development fonds, RG 96/26, Box 1, Mobilization Planning, 1.
9 MGen. P.A. Neatby, Deputy Commander, to ADM(Per), Personnel Management – War, 16 September 1977, DHH, Director General Land Force Development fonds, RG 96/26, Box 1, Mobilization Planning, 1; LCol. J.E.P. Lalonde, Brief for Commander FMC, A Wartime Personnel Doctrine, 10 November 1977, DHH, Director General Land Force Development fonds, RG 96/26, Box 1, Mobilization Planning, 1.
10 BGen. R.G. Thériault, DGRC, to DCDS, Mobilization Planning, 8 June 1976, DHH, Director General Land Force Development fonds, RG 96/26, Box 1, Mobilization Planning, 1.
11 DMMD [Director Military Manpower and Distribution], CF Emergency Manning Plan, 1st Draft, August 1978, DHH, Director General Land Force Development fonds, RG 96/26, Box 10, File 4, vol. 1; MGen. J.A.R. Gutknecht, CLDO, to DGMPO, Emergency Manning Plan First Draft CLDO Comments, 3 November 1978, DHH, Director General Land Force Development fonds, RG 96/26, Box 10, File 4.
12 LCol. E. Exley, DLP2 [Director Land Plans 2], Army Structure for War: An Examination of Current Land Force Structure Difficulties, 16 May 1979, DHH, Director General Land Force Development fonds, RG 96/26, Box 10, File 4.
13 BGen. R. Michaud, DGRC, to CLDO, Primary Reserve Establishment for the Militia, 31 May 1979; LGen. G.C.E. Thériault, DCDS, to PCB members, PDP P-2895, The Development

and Employment of the Primary and Supplementary Reserves, 18 April 1979, DHH, Director General Land Force Development fonds, RG 96/26, Box 3.

14 LGen. J.J. Paradis, Commander FMC, to DCDS, FMC Readiness and Mobilization Planning, 4 June 1979, DHH, Director General Land Force Development fonds, RG 96/26, Box 10, File 4.

15 [DLP?], FMC Perception, Initial Manning Requirement, n.d., DHH, Director General Land Force Development fonds, RG 92/26, Box 10, File 4.

16 LGen. J.J. Paradis, Commander FMC, to VCDS, Procurement Policy for the Army, 4 July 1979, DHH, Director General Land Force Development fonds, RG 96/26, Box 10, File 4.

17 LGen. R.M. Withers to Commander Mobile Command, Procurement Policy, 24 July 1979, DHH, Director General Land Force Development fonds, RG 96/26, Box 10, File 4.

18 Col. J.K. Dangerfield, DLP, to A/CLDO, Mobilization and Readiness Planning, 30 July 1979, DHH, Director General Land Force Development fonds, RG 96/26, Box 10, File 4.

19 Record of Meeting, A/CLDO/COMD FMC, Exclusive for A/CLDO, Not for Float or File, 2 August 1979, DHH, Director General Land Force Development fonds, RG 96/26, Box 1, Mobilization Planning, 2.

20 Minutes of a Meeting on Mobilization and Readiness Planning Held in Conference Room B on 8 August 1979, DHH, Director General Land Force Development fonds, RG 96/26, Box 1, Mobilization Planning, 2.

21 Col. J. K. Dangerfield, Director Land Plans, to CLDO, Army Mobilization Preparatory Notes for Discussion CLDO/FMC/MPTF, 9 April 1980, DHH, Director General Land Force Development fonds, RG 96/26, Box 11, File 4.

22 Canadian Land Forces Staff Course 1980, TRG/1/P, Precis – Mobilization Planning and Training, n.d., DHH, Canadian Land Forces Command and Staff College fonds, RG 80/71, Folder 475.

23 Report of the Mobilization Planning Task Force, May 1981, Library and Archives Canada (LAC), Department of National Defence files, RG 24 Acc 2004-01315-X, Box 1.

24 Canada, Parliament, House of Commons, Statement Presented by the Minister of National Defence to the Standing Committee on External Affairs and National Defence, 12 June 1980.

25 Canada, Parliament, House of Commons, J. Gilles Lamontagne, Statement to the Standing Committee on External Affairs and National Defence, The 1981-82 Estimates for the Department of National Defence, 26 March 1981.

26 Canada, Parliament, House of Commons, Standing Committee on External Affairs and National Defence, Seventh Report, First Session, Thirty-second Parliament, *Action for the Reserves,* 18 December 1981, 28, 49-55, 62-63.

27 Canada, Parliament, House of Commons, Standing Committee on External Affairs and National Defence, Minutes of Proceedings and Evidence, First Session, Thirty-second Parliament, 1980-82, Issue 73, 18 May 1982, 6-11.

28 Canada, Parliament, House of Commons, Standing Committee on External Affairs and National Defence, Minutes of Proceedings and Evidence, First Session, Thirty-second Parliament, 1980-83, Issue 84, 17 March 1983, 14.

29 Canada, Parliament, House of Commons, Standing Committee on External Affairs and National Defence, Minister's Statement, Defence Estimates 1983/84, Appendix EAND-66, 21.

30 Mobilization Planning, NDHQ Instruction DCDS 12/83, 16 August 1983, DHH, Deputy Chief of the Defence Staff fonds, RG 81/232, Box 2.

31 Canada, Parliament, House of Commons, Standing Committee on External Affairs and National Defence, Minutes of Proceedings and Evidence, First Session, Thirty-second Parliament, 1980-83, Issue 92, 12 May 1983, 10.
32 T.H. Goodfellow, *Reserve Force Study*, ORAE Report R61 (Ottawa: Department of National Defence, September 1976), 3-10, Fort Frontenac Library.
33 Col. D.A. Nicholson, Commander's Conference, Militia Problems – First Report – April 1980, DHH, Director General Land Force Development fonds, RG 96/26, Box 2.
34 Canada, Parliament, House of Commons, Sub-committee of the Standing Committee on External Affairs and National Defence on Armed Forces Reserves, Report Presented by the Conference of Defence Associations of Canada, Appendix "RFFR-E," First Session, Thirty-second Parliament, 1980-81, 27 October 1981, 3A-15-3A-20.
35 George Mackenzie Urquhart, "The Changing Role of the Canadian Militia, 1945-1975" (MA thesis, University of Victoria, 1977), 206. Urquhart has done the most in-depth analysis of Militia strength available. However, he may have been overly kind. In 1979 the deputy chief of the defence staff estimated that only 30 percent of the Militia was effective (LGen. G.C.E. Thériault to Program Control Board members, 18 April 1979, DHH, Director General Land Force Development fonds, RG 96/26, Box 3).
36 D.B. Dewar to VCDS, Normative Defence Services Program, 12 September 1983, LAC, RG 24 Acc 2004-01315-X, Box 1.
37 Army Combat Development Guide (Second Draft), DHH, RG 81/135.
38 "The Combat Development Process," *Canadian Army Doctrine Bulletin* 3 (September 1981): 15-18.
39 Defence Management Committee, Summary of 283rd Meeting, 23 October 1978, DHH, Defence Management Committee fonds, RG 79/560.
40 Col. J.F.T.A. Liston, DCOS Combat Development and Training Development, FMC HQ to Distribution List [DG-level NDHQ staff and army formation commanders], 27 March 1979, DHH, Canadian Army Staff College Library fonds, RG 99/11. The logic was blindingly false because the army was designing a corps that was two levels greater than the under-strength brigade group that the budget weakly supported. Even allowing for modest brigades, a corps would require troops at both the division and corps level, such as heavy artillery and aviation, not found within a brigade.
41 It is interesting to compare Liston's plan with what his boss, the commander of Mobile Command, was pressing for under his mobilization initiative. Although Liston's plan would have doubled the size of the army, it was about one-quarter of what the mobilization planners were calling for. It was also based on tasks actually assigned by the government.
42 Constraints: Their Application to Force Structuring and the Combat Development Process, A Discussion Paper for the 1979 Combat Development Committee, n.d., DHH, Canadian Army Staff College Library fonds, RG 99/11.
43 Minutes, Fifth Meeting of Land Forces Combat Development Committee, 23-27 April 1979, DHH, RG 80/539.
44 MGen. René Gutknecht, Chief Land Doctrine and Operations, to NDHQ staff, FMC, 4CMBG, 22 June 1979, DHH, RG 80/493.
45 Land Force Combat Development Study, LFCDS 77-8-1, The Canadian Infantry: 1986-1995, 1 March 1978, 7-8, DHH, RG 81/46 (hereafter cited as The Canadian Infantry).
46 Minutes of the Second Meeting of the Canadian Infantry Study Team, 26-29 September 1977, DHH, RG 81/38.
47 The Canadian Infantry, 2.
48 Ibid., 82.
49 Ibid., 76-77, 94-95.
50 Ibid., 112-23, 197-204.

51 Ibid., 96-99.
52 Ibid., 221.
53 Ibid., 221-28.
54 Armour, 1986-1999, 1, General, December 1979, DHH RG 80/488.
55 Land Forces Combat Development Study, Air Support 1986-1995, 8 November 1978, DHH, RG 80/490.
56 ORAE Project Number 96242, BRONZE TALON 3 Report, 13 November 1981 (see especially Indirect Fire – Question 8, 1-4), DHH, Director General Land Force Development fonds, RG 96/26, Box 11, File 5.
57 Ibid., Part 2, Section 3, 5.
58 Ibid., Part 2, Section 2, 2.
59 "The Combat System Study," *Canadian Army Doctrine Bulletin* 4 (June 1982): 26-27.
60 Ingo Trauschweizer, *The Cold War US Army: Building Deterrence for Limited War* (Lawrence: University of Kansas Press, 2008), 196-208; Robert H. Scales, *Certain Victory: The US Army in the Gulf War* (Washington, DC: Brassey's, 1994), 10, 12-15.
61 "Canada–United States Army Tactical Doctrine Seminar," *Canadian Army Doctrine Bulletin* 2 (March 1981): 65-66.
62 "Canadian-German Army Tactical Doctrine Seminar," *Canadian Army Doctrine Bulletin* 4 (June 1982): 91-94.
63 Corps '86 Staff Data (for Study Purpose Only), B-GL-303-004/FP-Z01, 12 August 1987, Canadian Forces College Library, Toronto.
64 The new version of FM100-5 was published in 1982.
65 Minutes of the Fourth Meeting of the Army Doctrine and Tactics Board Working Group, 13-15 April 1981; Minutes of the Sixth Meeting of the Army Doctrine and Tactics Board Working Group, 20-21 October 1981; Minutes of the Seventh Meeting of the Army Doctrine and Tactics Board Working Group, 10 February 1982; Minutes of the Eighth Meeting of the Army Doctrine and Tactics Board Working Group, 29 March 1982, DHH, RG 93/418.
66 CLDO/DLCD, System Study 1996-2005, The Corps Model Part 1 – Concept and Structuring Guidance, December 1986, 1-2, DHH, Director General Land Force Development fonds, RG 96/26, Box 12, File 6.
67 Army Doctrine and Tactics Board, 16th Meeting, Report on the Concepts and Organization Board and CD Sub-Committee Meetings, December 1984 – February 1985, 18 April 1985, DHH, RG 93/418.
68 BGen. Terrence Liston, "The Development of Canada's Land Forces: A Problem of Policy and Expenditure Management" (unpublished student paper, École nationale d'administration publique, April 1984), 97-114, 118.
69 Major C.B. Bradley, "Breaking the Mirrors and Removing the Smoke: A Primer for Canadian Army Combat Development" (MA thesis, Royal Military College, 1988), provides a good assessment of the deficiencies of the doctrine produced by the Corps '86 process.
70 General Thériault, Transcript from Tape, 5 March 1992, DHH, Chief of Defence Staff Study, RG 94/20; Douglas Bland, *Chiefs of Defence: Government and the Unified Command of the Canadian Armed Forces* (Toronto: Brown Book, 1995), 245-52. Bland's account is based on this interview and others. The only other detailed account is by Peter Langille, "In Pursuit of Strategic Flexibility," *Peace Magazine*, April-May 1989, 19, which also relies on confidential interviews for key data. Thériault made at least part of his version of events public at a Canadian Institute of International Affairs conference ("General Fears N-subs May Be Extravagant," *Ottawa Citizen*, 28 March 1988).
71 Chief of Land Development and Operations, Land Force Combat Development Guide, 1996-2005, October 1985, DHH, Director General Land Force Development fonds, RG

96/26, Box 6, Land Force Development Guide (hereafter cited as Land Force Combat Development Guide).

72 Minutes of a Meeting of the Army Doctrine and Tactics Board Working Group, 28-29 May 1986, DHH, RG 93/418.

73 Land Force Combat Development Guide, 3-1 to 3-4.

74 Ibid., 3-4 to 3-7.

75 Ibid., 1-3.

76 Ibid., 1-6.

77 Ibid., 2-3.

78 VAdm. N.D. Brodeur, DCDS, to Distribution List [Associate ADM (Policy), Associate ADM (Materiel), Chief Personnel Development, and senior DCDS staff], NDHQ Instruction DCDS 13/85, Canadian Forces Concept of Expansion, 3 October 1985, LAC, Department of National Defence files, RG 24 Acc 2004-01315-X, Box 1.

79 Land Force Combat Development Guide, 2-6 to 2-7.

80 Ibid., 2-8.

81 Ibid., 6-11 to 6-14.

82 John Willis, "Defence Spending, 1988-89," *Canadian Defence Quarterly* 18, no. 1 (Summer 1988): 53.

83 Gen. (Ret'd) Paul Manson, LGen. (Ret'd) Jim Fox, LGen. (Ret'd) Richard Evraire, interviews with the author. Paul D. Manson, diary, entries 9 October 1985 to 18 June 1986, LAC, Paul D. Manson fonds, R 11222, Box 12, File 12.7.

84 Department of National Defence, *Challenge and Commitment: A Defence Policy for Canada* (Ottawa: Supply and Services Canada, 1987), 1-6, 9, 21, 53.

85 Ibid., 60-64.

86 Ibid., 65-66.

87 Ibid., 67.

88 Col. Brian S. MacDonald, "The White Paper, the Army Reserve and Army Reform – 1987-2002," *Canadian Defence Quarterly* 17, no. 4 (Spring 1988): 10; *Challenge and Commitment*, 71.

89 General Purpose Land Force Development Plan, 1988, DHH, Director General Land Force Development fonds, RG 96/26, Box 5; Col. James S.H. Kempling, "Brave New Army: The Militia of 2002," *Canadian Defence Quarterly* 17, no. 3 (Winter 1988): 34-36.

90 G.A. Bossenmaier and T.A. Ewashko, "The Reserve Force Component of the Total Force Concept: Resources, Attrition, and Policy Considerations," Staff Note 6/89, Operational Research and Analysis Establishment, Directorate of Manpower Analysis, Ottawa, September 1989, 4-19.

91 Col. C.J. Addy, "The Military Future of an Unmilitary People: Total Force, an Operational Army Presence in Canadian Society" (unpublished student paper, National Defence College, May 1988), 9-13; Maj. D.R. Gagné, "Armée 2002: La perception d'un réserviste," *Armour Bulletin / Bulletin des Blindés* (Été 1989): 20-22; Capt. D.J. Banks, "Army 2002 and the Militia Regimental System," *Infantry Journal* 18 (Spring 1989): 30-32.

92 Canada, Parliament, House of Commons, Standing Committee on National Defence, Minutes of Proceedings and Evidence, Second Session, Thirty-third Parliament, 1986-87, Issue 9, April 1987, 16; Issue 17, 26 November 1987, 11.

93 John Willis, "Defence Spending in 1988-89," *Canadian Defence Quarterly* 18, no. 1 (Summer 1988): 52-53.

94 C.R. Nixon, Defence White Paper Review: The Changes, the Situation, the Outlook, n.d. [1987], DHH, C.R. Nixon fonds, RG 98/64, File III.22. Nixon sent his paper to Paul Manson, the CDS, and copied the VCDS, ADM (Pol), ADM (Mat), and ADM(Fin), C.R. Nixon to P.D. Manson, 17 July 1987, LAC, Paul D. Manson fonds, R 11222, Box 4, File 4.7.

95 Army input to CFTFDP [Canadian Forces Total Force Development Plan], 6 May 1988, DHH, Director General Land Force Development fonds, RG 96/26, Box 5.
96 Bland, *Chiefs of Defence*, 255-56.
97 Canada, Senate, Special Committee of the Senate on National Defence, *Canada's Land Forces* (Ottawa: Supply and Services Canada, October 1989), 87-94.
98 Ibid., 65-69, 96, 101-2.
99 MGen. J. K. Dangerfield, "The 1st Canadian Division: Enigma, Contradiction or Requirement?" *Canadian Defence Quarterly* 19, no. 5 (April 1990): 7-14.
100 B/GL-301/FP-001, Land Formations in Battle, 1, Land and Tactical Air Operations, 26 November 1987, 1-1-7.
101 Ibid., 13-1-1 to 13-4-1.
102 LCol. W.J.H. Stutt, A/G3 Tactics, Field Trial – Tank Hunting Doctrine, 24 March 1988, DHH, RG 93/418; Minutes of a Meeting of the Army Doctrine and Tactics Board Working Group, 1 June 1988, DHH, RG 93/418.
103 Supporting Paper for Agenda Item V, 24th ADTB Meeting, 21-22 June 1989, Doctrine Reduction Study, DHH, RG 93/418.
104 MGen. R.J. Evraire, Letter of Promulgation, System Study 1996-2005, The Corps Model, Part I, 23 February 1987, DHH, RG 92/26, Box 12, File 6; System Study 1996-2005, The Corps Model, Part 2 – Combat Function Study, October 1991, DHH, Director General Land Force Development fonds, RG 92/26, Box 13, Files 8-9.
105 System Study 1996-2005, The Corps Model, Part 2 – Combat Function Study, The Echelon Above Corps. The Canadian Army Overseas, 1st Draft, 17 April 1988, DHH, Director General Land Force Development fonds, RG 92/26, Box 12, File 7.
106 System Study 1996-2005, The Corps Model, Part 1, 6-2.
107 System Study, 1996-2005, Synopsis of: Part 1 – Concept and Structuring Guidance; Part 2 – Combat Function Studies, October 1991, 1-8, Canadian Forces College Library.
108 System Study 1996-2005, The Corps Model, Part 1, 6-7, 6-11; System Study 1996-2005, Synopsis, 1-8.
109 System Study 1996-2005, The Corps Model, Part 2, XS-5 to XS-8.
110 Ibid., 4-8 to 4-13.
111 LCol. W.M. Holmes, A Discussion Paper on Canadian Army Defence Doctrine Prepared for the Army Doctrine and Tactics Board, 3 July 1990, LAC, Department of National Defence files, RG 24, 1180-13 (ADTB), 3.
112 Minutes of 30th Meeting of the Army Doctrine and Tactics Board, 20 June 1991, DHH, RG 93/418, 17.
113 Brief for ADTB Concerning the Status of CFP 301(4), Fourth Clash, April 1991, DHH, RG 93/418, 17.
114 Maj. M.D. Kampman, "Getting Our Doctrine Back on Line" (unpublished student paper, Canadian Forces College, Toronto, 3 April 1995), 22-23.
115 Peter Feaver, *Armed Servants: Agency, Oversight and Civil-Military Relations* (Cambridge, MA: Harvard University Press, 2003), 54-68.

Chapter 7: The Unified Staff and Operational Difficulties

1 Vernon J. Kronenberg, *All Together Now: The Organization of the Department of National Defence in Canada 1964-1972*, Wellesley Papers 3/1973 (Toronto: Canadian Institute of International Affairs, 1973), 68-78; Mobile Forces Headquarters Organization Book, 27 August 1965, Directorate of History and Heritage, Department of National Defence (DHH), RG 73/1322.

2 Task Force on Review of Unification of the Canadian Forces, *Final Report* (15 March 1980), 39-40 (in author's possession).
3 Douglas Bland, *The Administration of Defence Policy in Canada, 1947 to 1985* (Kingston, ON: Ronald P. Frye, 1987), 138.
4 Canadian Land Forces Staff Course, 1980, TRG/1/P, Precis – Mobilization Planning and Training, n.d., DHH, Canadian Land Forces Command and Staff College fonds, RG 80/71, Folder 475; LCol. J.E.P. Lalonde, Brief for Commander FMC, A Wartime Personnel Doctrine, 10 November 1977, DHH, RG 92/26, Box 1, Mobilization Planning, 1. Just how badly the system performed is open to question. Sean Maloney agrees with the Mobile Command assessment (see note 5) based on interview data concerning WINTEX 79. This exercise report could not be located. However, nothing so dire appears in either the WINTEX 77 or WINTEX 81 post-exercise reports, Library and Archives Canada (LAC), Department of External Affairs files, RG 25, Files MF 5990, 27-24-6-2-4, and MF 5988, 27-24-6-2-4.
5 Sean M. Maloney, "Purple Haze: Joint Planning in the Canadian Forces from Mobile Command to J-Staff, 1975-1991 (Part 1)," *Army Doctrine and Training Bulletin* 5, no. 4 (Winter 2002-03): 61.
6 Ibid.
7 Gen. G.C.E. Thériault, Transcript from Notes, 7 December 1992, 7 January 1992, 20 February 1992, DHH, Chief of Defence Staff Study, RG 94/20. It seems likely that the January and February interviews were actually done in 1993.
8 BOLD STEP '84, IECC First Impression Report, 8 March 1984, LAC, Department of External Affairs files, RG 25, MF5995, File 27-24-6-1. Interestingly, there is no DND annex to this government-wide report. The only extant source is Loomis.
9 D.G. Loomis, The Impact of Integration, Unification and Restructuring on the Functions and Structure of National Defence Headquarters (A Supporting Paper to the NDHQ Study S1/85 Report), 31 July 1985, DHH, Director General Land Force Development fonds, RG 96/26, Box 4, 1985, 131.
10 NDHQ Study Directive S1/85, Functions and Organization of DCDS Group, 31 January 1985, DHH, Charles J. Gauthier fonds, RG 92/228, File 110.
11 Interim Report on NDHQ Study S1/85, n.d. [31 March 1985], 238-42, DHH, Charles J. Gauthier fonds, RG 92/228, File 107.
12 Chief of Land Doctrine and Operations, Annex E to NDHQ Study S1/85, 31 March 1985, DHH, Charles J. Gauthier fonds, RG 92/228, File 106.
13 Telex, Appt of a National Ex Comd, From FMC HQ, To DGMPO, 012040Z Aug 85, LAC, RG 24, File 2265-L58-B4, Part 2; Telex, Exercise BRAVE LION Planning, From NDHQ, To FMC HQ COS Ops, 070750Z Aug 85, LAC, Department of National Defence files, RG 24, File 2265-L58-B4, Part 2.
14 Maloney, "Purple Haze," 63-64. Maloney cites the BRAVE LION post-exercise report and related documents that he obtained through Access to Information, but these documents are no longer available. The Access to Information office destroys its holdings after five years and a renewed request through DND access channels turned up nothing in departmental files. The report may eventually surface when Library and Archives Canada finishes cataloguing the mass of documents it has received from National Defence relating to the 1980s and '90s.
15 LCol. G.D. Hunt, "Reinforcing the NATO North Flank: The Canadian Experience," *Canadian Defence Quarterly* 16, no. 4 (Spring 1987): 36.
16 Maloney, "Purple Haze," 66.
17 Gen. Paul D. Manson, diary entries 31 December 1987 to 1 February 1988, LAC, Paul D. Manson fonds, R11222, Box 13, File 13.2.

18 Maloney, "Purple Haze," 67-68.
19 The Functions and Organization of National Defence Headquarters in Emergencies and War: Final Report, 10 February 1989, DHH, Charles J. Gauthier fonds, RG 92/228, Files 101 and 102; reprinted in its entirety in Douglas L. Bland, ed., *Canada's National Defence*, vol. 2, *Defence Organization* (Kingston, ON: Queen's University, 1998), 411-501. See also Douglas Bland, *Chiefs of Defence: Government and the Unified Command of the Canadian Armed Forces* (Toronto: Brown Book, 1995), 191-95, and Maloney, "Purple Haze," 69-70.
20 Sean Maloney, "'Missed Opportunity' Operation BROADSWORD, 4 Brigade and the Gulf War, 1990-91," *Army Doctrine and Training Bulletin* 5, no. 1 (Spring 2002): 25. Maloney's is the most detailed account of Operation Broadsword available, and appears to be based on both interviews and documentation.
21 Ibid., 26.
22 Resume Staff Check Op Broadsword Bde Gp Option, enclosure to LGen. D. Huddleston, DCDS to CDS, Provision of Mech Bde Gp to Saudi Arabia – Staff Check, 2250-165/OPB (DCDS), 13 November 1990, Access to Information Request A0314382-1 (in author's possession).
23 141400Z Nov 90, NDHQ Ottawa [signed by Gen. de Chastelain] to FMCHQ ST HUBERT/COMD, CDS Tasking Instruction, Op Broadsword Preparatory Planning, LAC, Department of National Defence files, RG 24, File 3350-165/B231. Note that Maloney says that 1 Canadian Division was tasked rather than Mobile Command.
24 LGen. K.R. Foster, Commander to DCDS, Contingency Planning – Op Broadsword, 23 November 1990; FMC Contingency Plan 1, Operation Broadsword, November 1990, LAC, Department of National Defence files, RG 24, File 3350-165/B231.
25 Supplementary Assessment, Level Three Medical Support – Operation Broadsword, DCDS to CDS, Provision of Mech Bde Gp to Saudi Arabia – Staff Check, 2250-165/OPB (DCDS), 13 November 1990, Access to Information Request A0314382-1 (in author's possession); John de Chastelain, communication with the author, 30 May 2012.
26 Bland, *Chiefs of Defence,* 201.
27 Sean M. Maloney, "Domestic Operations: The Canadian Approach," *Parameters* 27 (Autumn 1997): 8-9.
28 Quoted in Claude Beauregard, "The Military Intervention in Oka: Strategy, Communications and Press Coverage," *Canadian Military History* 2, no. 1 (1997): 27.
29 Croatia Board of Inquiry, 16 September 1999, VII, 16-18 (in author's possession); Carol Off, *The Ghosts of the Medak Pocket: The Story of Canada's Secret War* (Toronto: Vintage Canada, 2004): 81-90.
30 Croatia Board of Inquiry, 16 September 1999, VII, 53-57; Off, *The Ghosts of the Medak Pocket,* 118-22; Lee Windsor, "Professionalism under Fire: Canadian Implementation of the Medak Pocket Agreement, Croatia 1993," *Canadian Military History* 9, no. 3 (Summer 2000): 28; Donna Winslow, "Canadian Warriors in Peacekeeping: Points of Tension in Complex Cultural Encounters," PWGSC Contract W7711-8-7486 on behalf of the Department of National Defence, Defence and Civil Institute of Environmental Medicine, Toronto, November 1999, 14-15.
31 Off, *The Ghosts of the Medak Pocket,* 148.
32 Croatia Board of Inquiry, 16 September 1999, VII, 87-118; Windsor, "Professionalism under Fire," 28-29.
33 Windsor, ibid., 34.
34 Rick Hillier, *A Soldier First: Bullets, Bureaucrats and the Politics of War* (Toronto: HarperCollins, 2009), 157-59; MGen. Lewis Mackenzie shares Gen. Hillier's view that NDHQ restrained vigorous action by field commanders (interview with the author, 16 May 2012).

35 John Marteinson and Michael R. McNorgan, *The Royal Canadian Armoured Corps: An Illustrated History* (Toronto: Royal Canadian Armoured Corps Association, 2000), 403-8.
36 Winslow, "Canadian Warriors in Peacekeeping," 10.
37 Quoted in G.E. (Joe) Sharpe, *Croatia Board of Inquiry: Leadership (and Other) Lessons Learned* (Winnipeg: Canadian Forces Training Material Production Centre, 2002), 4.
38 Quoted in Off, *The Ghosts of the Medak Pocket*, 113; MGen. (Ret'd) Robert Gaudreau, interview with the author, 15 May 2012.
39 Executive Summary, Final Report, Board of Inquiry – Croatia, n.p., 19 January 2000 (in author's possession); News Release, Chief of the Defence Staff Responds to Sharpe Interim Report, NR – 99.125, 16 December 1999, http://www.forces.gc.ca/.
40 Quoted in Karol W.J. Wenek, "Looking Back: Canadian Forces Leadership Problems and Challenges Identified in Recent Reports and Studies," Canadian Forces Leadership Institute Report, June 2002, 22 (in author's possession).
41 Department of National Defence, Board of Inquiry, Command, Control and Leadership in CANBAT 2, *The Board Report*, 15 November 1996, 1-4, 1-14 to 1-18, LAC, ACC2008-00757-X, Boxes 4 and 5, Access to Information release A-2011-00286.
42 Department of National Defence, *The Thomas Report: Investigation of Delay in Investigating the Allegations of Misconduct/Poor Performance of Canadian Forces Members at the Bakovici Hospital, Bosnia-Herzegovina*, prepared by Lowell E. Thomas, Assistant Commissioner, Royal Canadian Mounted Police (Retired), 8 November 1996, 13-25, LAC, ACC2008-00757-X, Boxes 4 and 5, Access to Information release A-2011-00286.
43 Donna Winslow, "Misplaced Loyalties: The Role of Military Culture in the Breakdown of Discipline in Two Peace Operations," *Journal of Military and Strategic Studies* 6, no. 3 (Winter 2004): 8-11.
44 Department of National Defence, Board of Inquiry, *The Board Report*, 7-7 to 7-8.
45 Ibid., 4-5, 4-8, 4-11, 4-16, 6-10.
46 Ibid., 5-12, 7-2, 7-3 to 7-4.
47 Auditor General of Canada, *1996 May Report of the Auditor General of Canada*, ch. 7, Peacekeeping – National Defence, paras. 7.37-7.56, http://www.oag-bvg.gc.ca/internet/English/.
48 Commission of Inquiry into the Deployment of Canadian Forces to Somalia, *Dishonoured Legacy: The Lessons of the Somalia Affair*, vol. 1 (Ottawa: Public Works and Government Services Canada, 1997), 217-26.
49 Ibid., 3: 721-22; Louis A. Delvoie, "Canada and International Security Operations: The Search for Policy Rationales," *Canadian Military Journal* 1 (Summer 2000): 23.
50 Commission of Inquiry, *Dishonoured Legacy*, 3: 809-14.
51 Annex A to 3350-52 (G3 Plans), After Action Report – Op Deliverance, 25 February 1993, LAC, Department of National Defence files, Ban2000-01333-3, Box 3, Somalia Manual, After Action Report and Briefing.
52 Ibid., 818-20, 822-28.
53 Commission of Inquiry, *Dishonoured Legacy*, 1: 242-49.
54 Donna Winslow, *The Canadian Airborne Regiment in Somalia: A Socio-Cultural Inquiry* (Ottawa: Canadian Government Publishing, 1997), 85-140.
55 Commission of Inquiry, *Dishonoured Legacy*, 2: 511.
56 Ibid., 2: 689.
57 Ibid., 4: 1017-27.
58 Ibid., 2: 522.
59 Auditor General of Canada, *1994 Report of the Auditor General of Canada*, ch. 24, National Defence – Defence Management Systems, http://www.oag-bvg.gc.ca/internet/English/, paras. 24.81-24.92.

60 Commission of Inquiry, *Dishonoured Legacy*, 2: 623.
61 Ibid., 4: 1021. See also 1: 260.
62 Ibid., 2: 697.
63 Ibid., 3: 838-39.
64 Ibid., 1: 228-29.
65 Winslow, *The Canadian Airborne Regiment in Somalia*, 206-7.
66 Commission of Inquiry, *Dishonoured Legacy*, 3: 856-58.
67 Ibid., 1: 276.
68 Winslow, *The Canadian Airborne Regiment in Somalia*, 236, 252.
69 Commission of Inquiry, *Dishonoured Legacy*, 1: 320-26.
70 The following account is taken from Michael A. Hennessy, "Operation 'Assurance': Planning a Multi-National Force for Rwanda/Zaire," *Canadian Military Journal* 2 (Spring 2001): 11-20. Hennessy's account is based on after-action and lessons learned reports secured under Access to Information. These records are no longer available from DND because Access files are kept for only five years. Documents held by Library and Archives Canada have not been screened or released.
71 M. Hennessy, Operation Assurance Case Study, Canadian Forces College, 19 (in author's possession).
72 J3 Lessons Learned, Proposed Follow-on Plan, Issue 5 – Crisis Management (in author's possession).
73 Speaking Notes for Lieutenant-General Leach, Commander Land Force Command for His Appearance before the Conference of American Armies, Operation Assurance: Lessons Learned from a Military/Governmental Perspective, n.d. (in author's possession).

Chapter 8: Reform and Constabulary Realism

1 Desmond Morton, *A Short History of Canada* (Toronto: McClelland and Stewart, 1994), 320-32.
2 The term "decade of darkness" was coined by LGen. Al DeQuetteville (Retired) in an interview with BGen. G.E. Sharpe and Alan English: G.E. Sharpe and Alan English, "CFLI Project Paper – The Decade of Darkness," n.p., n.d., in author's possession.
3 LGen. D. Huddleston, DCDS to VCDS, Force Restructuring, 3 January 1991, Directorate of History and Heritage, Department of National Defence (DHH), Director General Land Force Development fonds, RG 96/26, Box 13, File 3.
4 LGen. Kent Foster, Commander Land Force Command, to Distribution List [Land Force general officers], Land Force Policy Themes – The Way Ahead, 14 December 1990; Canadian Land Force Structuring Philosophy, 15 June 1990; The Employment of the Militia in the Restructured Army, 15 June 1990, DHH, James Robert Near fonds, RG 2002/20, Box 3, File 3.6.
5 Sean Maloney, *War without Battles: Canada's NATO Brigade in Germany, 1951-1993* (Whitby, ON: McGraw-Hill Ryerson, 1996), 481-82. Maloney does not cite his sources and the book is unfootnoted, making this account unverifiable.
6 Canadian Force Europe (CFE) Disbandment, Restructure of Force Mobile Command (FMC) Personnel and Materiel, Concept of Operations and Support, 5 February 1992; MGen. Paul Addy, CLDO, to DComdr FMC HQ, Stationed Task Force (STF) Organization, 12 February 1992; FMCHQ DCOMD to NDHQ/CLDO, 20 February 1992, STF Org, DHH, Director General Land Force Development fonds, RG 96/26, Box 7, CLDO 1992.
7 Chief of the Defence Staff, Force Development Guidance, 1991, 20 December 1991, DHH, Director General Land Force Development fonds, RG 96/26, Box 13, File 3.

8 Canadian Forces Development Plan 1992 (U), Draft, June 1992, 5-8 to 5-11, 7-43 to 7-44, DHH, Director General Land Force Development fonds, RG 96/26, Box 13, File 3.
9 Department of National Defence, *Canadian Defence Policy* (n.p., April 1992).
10 Col. N.B. Jeffries, Director General Land Force Development, to Distribution List [DCDS FPD for action], July 1992, DHH, Director General Land Force Development fonds, RG 96/26, Box 13, File 3.
11 MGen. P.G. Addy, CLDO, to Distribution List [principal NDHQ staff], Land Force Development Plan, Elaboration of Concepts (Draft), May 1992, DHH, Director General Land Force Development fonds, RG 96/26, Box 13, File 3.
12 Land Force Development Guide, 1992, 5-5, DHH, Director General Land Force Development fonds, RG 96/26, Box 14, File 2.
13 Quoted in Joseph T. Jockel, *The Canadian Forces: Hard Choices, Soft Power* (Toronto: Canadian Institute of Strategic Studies, 1999), 31.
14 Ivan Head, *Canada 21: Canada and Common Security in the Twenty-First Century* (Toronto: University of Toronto Press, 1994), 11, 34-35, 53-57, 62-64, 80.
15 Canada, Parliament, Special Joint Committee of the Senate and the House of Commons on Canada's Defence Policy, *Security in a Changing World: The Report of the Special Joint Committee on Canada's Defence Policy,* Issue 32 (n.p.: Parliamentary Publications Directorate, 1994), 13-15, 19-22.
16 Ibid., 31-36.
17 Ibid., 46.
18 Department of National Defence, *1994 White Paper on Defence,* http://www.forces.gc.ca/admpol/.
19 Maj. J.R. Near, Position Paper for the 36th ADTB Meeting, "Proposal for Developing Canadian Army Doctrine at the Strategic, Operational and Tactical Levels," 7 October 1994, DHH, Director General Land Force Development fonds, RG 96/26, Box 15, File 12.
20 Ibid.
21 LGen. G.M. Reay to Distribution List [LF Area commanders and equivalents], Strategic and Operational Doctrine, 31 January 1995, DHH, Director General Land Force Development fonds, RG 96/26, Box 15, File 12.
22 Captain Ian Hope, Changing a Military Culture: Manoeuvre Warfare and a Canadian Operational Doctrine, Canadian Land Force Command and Staff College, November 1993, DHH, James Robert Near fonds, RG 2002/20, Box 1, Folder 1.5.
23 LCol. M.M. Fenrich, Sharpening Land Force Vision, 1994, 21 February 1994, DHH, James Robert Near fonds, RG 2002/20, Box 1, Folder 1.5.
24 Maj. J.R. Near, Updating Canadian Army Doctrine, 25 April 1994, DHH, James Robert Near fonds, RG 2002/20, Box 1, Folder 1.5.
25 Army Campaign Plan 2000, 27 March 1996; Maj. D.M. Bergstrand, DLFD4-4, to DGLFD, Army 2000 Campaign Plan, n.d.; LGen. J.M.G. Baril to Area Cdrs, COS, Reserve Advisor, Army 2000 Campaign Plan, June 1996, DHH, James Robert Near fonds, RG 2002/20, File 3.06.
26 Maj. Howard G. Coombs, *Canada's Army and the Concept of Maneuver Warfare: The Legacy of the Twentieth Century (1899-1998)* (Fort Leavenworth, KS: US Army Command and General Staff College, n.d.), 41.
27 Department of National Defence, *Canada's Army: We Stand on Guard for Thee,* B-GL-300-000/FP-000 (n.p.: 1998), 79-80; Department of National Defence, *Conduct of Land Operations – Operational Level Doctrine for the Canadian* Army, B-GL-300-001/FP-000 (n.p.: 1996), 1-3. These documents will be referred to as CFP 300 and CFP 301 rather than the more cumbersome document numbers adopted by National Defence in the 1990s.
28 CFP 300, 100-3; CFP 301, 2-1 to 2-6.

29 CFP 300, 74-75.
30 CFP 301, 10-1 to 10-4.
31 Gen. Stephenson/Gen. Archibald, DGLFD/COS JT Brief to LFDC, 25 April 1995, Library and Archives Canada (LAC), Department of National Defence files, RG 24, 1996-97/1063, Box 2, File 1 – Land Force Dev C.
32 Coombs, *Canada's Army and the Concept of Maneuver Warfare*, 29, 38, 40-41.
33 Roman Jarymowycz, "Doctrine and Canada's Army – Seduction by Foreign Dogma: Coming to Terms with Who We Are," *Army Doctrine and Training Bulletin* 2, no. 3 (August 1999): 48-52.
34 Commission of Inquiry into the Deployment of Canadian Forces to Somalia, *Dishonoured Legacy: The Lessons of the Somalia Affair*, vol. 1 (Ottawa: Public Works and Government Services Canada, 1997), 335-40.
35 Ibid., 1: 342-45; Department of National Defence, Board of Inquiry, *Canadian Airborne Regiment Battle Group, Phase 1 Volume XI*, 28 August 1993, K-5, LAC, National Defence fonds, RG 24-G-9, Box 1 to 5, BAN 2008-0757-X, 098-1024 OFRC.
36 Commission of Inquiry, *Dishonoured Legacy*, 1: 348-49.
37 J.L. Granatstein, *Canada's Army: Waging War and Keeping the Peace* (Toronto: University of Toronto Press, 2002), 407-8.
38 Commission of Inquiry, *Dishonoured Legacy*, 1: 350-58; Vernon testimony, Somalia Inquiry, 18 June 1996, LAC, *Information Legacy*, 80; Somalia Inquiry Commission, Document Book Series, Registrar's Loose Exhibits, General – P-160-P-197, LAC, ACC 1998-00701-4, Box 76, File 4002-1, Part 6.
39 Scott Taylor and Brian Nolan, *Tarnished Brass: Crime and Corruption in the Canadian Military* (Toronto: Lester Publishing, 1996). See especially Chapter 4, "The Generals: There's No Life Like It."
40 Col. G.J. Oehring, G1, to Comd, Morale in the Army, 5 December 1994, DHH, James Robert Near fonds, RG 2002/20, Box 2, File 2.2.
41 Col. G.J. Oehring, G1, Morale in the Army: Fact and Solution Finding Project, 1 March 1995, DHH, James Robert Near fonds, RG 2002/20, Box 2, File 2.2.
42 Address by MGen. (Ret'd) C.J. (Clive) Addy, 9 September 1996, DHH, James Robert Near fonds, RG 2002/20, Box 2, File 2.2.
43 Maj. J.R. Near, Position Paper for the 36th ADTB Meeting, "Proposal for Developing Canadian Army Doctrine at the Strategic, Operational and Tactical Levels," 7 October 1994, DHH, Director General Land Force Development fonds, RG 96/26, Box 15, File 12; Maj. J.R. Near to DLFD, Proposal for Campaign Plan for Army Renewal, 31 May 1996, DHH, Director General Land Force Development fonds, RG 96/26, Box 15, File 12.
44 CFP 300, 34-36.
45 Ibid., 37, 41, 43-44.
46 Maj. J.R. Near, The Army's Self Image – Actual and Potential, Presentation to CTC Professional Development Seminar "The Army and the Nation," 1-2 October 1998, DHH, James Robert Near fonds, RG 2002/20, Box 5, File 5.8.
47 MGen. N.B. Jeffries to Distribution List [not on file], CFP 300 – Canada's Army, Third Draft – Comments, 27 January 1997, DHH, Director General Land Force Development fonds, RG 96/26, Box 15, File 12.
48 D.J. Bercuson, J.L. Granatstein, Albert Legault, Desmond Morton, "A Paper Prepared for the Minister of National Defence," 25 March 1997 [four separate papers with the same title and date], DHH, Claude Beauregard fonds, RG 96/30, Series 9, Box 11, Files 21-4.
49 Hon. Douglas Young, Report to the Prime Minister on the Leadership and Management of the Canadian Forces, 25 March 1997, DHH, Claude Beauregard fonds, RG 96/30, Series 9, Box 11, File 20.

50 David J. Bercuson, "Up from the Ashes: The Re-Professionalization of the Canadian Forces after the Somalia Affair," *Canadian Military Journal* 9, no. 3 (2009): 31-39, http://www.journal.forces.gc.ca/.

51 Department of National Defence, *The Debrief the Leaders Project (Officers)* (n.p., May 2001), 20-22.

52 Ibid., i, 23.

53 Morris Janowitz, *The Professional Soldier* (New York: Free Press, 1971), 418. Interestingly, neither this definition nor Janowitz's book is referenced in the *Debrief the Leaders Project* report.

54 LGen. Dallaire left the project because of health problems in January 2000 and was replaced by BGen. Charles Lemieux. The project was then assigned to VAdm. Lynn Mason (Retired) in May 2000. *Canadian Officership in the 21st Century: Strategic Guidance for the CF Officer Corps and the Officer Professional Development System, September 2000,* Version 3.2, July 2000, DHH, Romeo A. Dallaire fonds, RG 2001/25, Box 3.

55 Department of National Defence, *Canadian Officership in the 21st Century (Officership 2020): Strategic Guidance for the Canadian Forces Officer Corps and the Officer Professional Development System* (n.p.: February 2001).

56 Department of National Defence, *Duty with Honour: The Profession of Arms in Canada* (n.p.: Canadian Defence Academy – Canadian Forces Leadership Institute, 2003).

57 Ibid., 7. Although referencing Huntington and Janowitz, this formulation appears to be based on General Sir John Hackett's definition in *The Profession of Arms* (London: Sidgwick and Jackson, 1983), 9, that "the function of the profession of arms is the ordered application of force in the resolution of a social problem."

58 Ibid., 18.

59 Ibid., 64.

60 Department of National Defence, *Debrief the Leaders Project,* 13.

61 David J. Bercuson, *The Fighting Canadians: Our Regimental History* (Toronto: HarperCollins, 2008), 20.

62 Department of National Defence, *1994 White Paper.*

63 J. Berryman, DG Compensation and Benefits, to Jean Thivierge, Assistant Secretary, Personnel Policy Branch, Treasury Board Secretariat, 11 June 1991, LAC, Department of National Defence files, ACC 2000-01285-X, Box 23, File 5794-4, Part 1; Auditor General of Canada, *1992 Report,* 18.132-18.140, at http://www.oag-bvg.gc.ca/.

64 Reserves 2000, *Canada's Army of the Future: Militia Component Staffing and Funding* (Toronto: n.p., 1999), 4; Reserves 2000, *Canada's Army of the Future: Leadership and Militia Command and Control* (Toronto: n.p., 1999); Peter W. Hunter, Co-Chair of Reserves 2000, "Special Commission on the Restructuring of the Reserves: 10 Years Later – Selected Conference Speaking Notes," *Journal of Military and Strategic Studies* 8, no. 2 (Winter 2005-06): 1-10.

65 Quoted in J.L. Granatstein, "The Search for an Efficient, Effective Land Force Reserve," *Canadian Military Journal* 3 (Summer 2002): 7.

66 Col. J.J. Moreau, DAD [Directeur – Analyse de défense], to Cmdt CLFCSC, LFRR Mobilization Study – DAD Comments, 27 July 1998; LCol. J. Hamel, A/DAD, to Cmdt CLFCSC, LFRR Mobilization Study – DAD Comments, 26 July 1998, LAC, Department of National Defence files, RG 24, 3290-1, vol. 1.

67 Department of National Defence, Minister's Monitoring Committee on Change in the Department of National Defence and the Canadian Forces, *Interim Report – 1999,* Chapter 8; Department of National Defence, Minister's Monitoring Committee on Change in the Department of National Defence and the Canadian Forces, *Final Report – 1999.*

68 J.L. Granatstein, *The Special Commission on the Restructuring of the Reserves, 1995: Ten Years Later* (Calgary: Canadian Defence and Foreign Affairs Institute, 2005), 7-10, 18-20, 28-34; Granatstein, "The Search for an Efficient, Effective Land Reserve Force," 8; Hunter, "Special Commission on the Restructuring of the Reserves: 10 Years Later – Selected Conference Speaking Notes," 4-5.

Conclusion

1 Stephen J. Harris, *Canadian Brass: The Making of a Professional Army, 1860-1939* (Toronto: University of Toronto Press, 1988), 220-21.

Bibliography

Addy, Col. C.J. "The Military Future of an Unmilitary People: Total Force, an Operational Army Presence in Canadian Society." Student paper, National Defence College, 2008.

Allard, Jean V., and Serge Bernier. *The Memoirs of Jean V. Allard.* Vancouver: UBC Press, 1988.

Banks, D.J. "Army 2002 and the Militia Regimental System." *Infantry Journal* 18 (Spring 1989): 29-35.

Beauregard, Claude. "The Military Intervention in Oka: Strategy, Communications and Press Coverage." *Canadian Military History* 2, no. 1 (1997): 23-47.

Bercuson, David J. *Blood on the Hills: The Canadian Army in the Korean War.* Toronto: University of Toronto Press, 1999.

–. *The Fighting Canadians: Our Regimental History.* Toronto: HarperCollins, 2008.

–. *Significant Incident: Canada's Army, the Airborne, and the Murder in Somalia.* Toronto: McClelland and Stewart, 1996.

–. "Up from the Ashes: The Re-Professionalization of the Canadian Forces after the Somalia Affair." *Canadian Military Journal* 9, no. 3 (2009): 31-39. http://www.journal.forces.gc.ca/.

Bland, Douglas L. *The Administration of Defence Policy in Canada.* Kingston, ON: Ronald P. Frye, 1987.

–. *Canada's National Defence.* Vol. 2, *Defence Organization.* Kingston, ON: Queen's University, 1998.

–. *Chiefs of Defence: Government and the Unified Command of the Canadian Armed Forces.* Toronto: Brown Book Company, 1995.

–. *The Military Committee of the North Atlantic Alliance: A Study of Structure and Strategy.* New York: Praeger, 1991.

Bradley, Maj. C.B. "Breaking the Mirrors and Removing the Smoke: A Primer for Canadian Army Combat Development." MA thesis, Royal Military College, 1988.

Byers, R.B. "Defence and Foreign Policy in the 1970s: The Demise of the Trudeau Doctrine." *International Journal* 32, no. 2 (Spring 1978): 312-38.

Callahan, Raymond. *Churchill and His Generals.* Lawrence: University of Kansas Press, 2007.

Canada, Auditor General of Canada. *1994 Report of the Auditor General of Canada.* Ottawa, 1994.

–. *1996 May Report of the Auditor General of Canada.* Ottawa, 1996.

Canada, Canadian Forces. *Personnel Concept.* n.p., 1983.

Canada, Commission of Inquiry into the Deployment of Canadian Forces to Somalia. *Dishonoured Legacy: The Lessons of the Somalia Affair.* Ottawa: Public Works and Government Services Canada, 1997.

Canada, Department of National Defence. *1994 White Paper on Defence*. n.p., 1994.
–. *Canada's Army: We Stand on Guard for Thee*. B-GL-300-000/FP-000. n.p., 1996.
–. *Canadian Defence Policy*. n.p., 1992.
–. *Canadian Officership in the 21st Century (Officership 2020): Strategic Guidance for the Canadian Forces Officer Corps and the Officer Professional Development System*. n.p., 2001.
–. *Challenge and Commitment: A Defence Policy for Canada*. Ottawa: Supply and Services Canada, 1987.
–. *Conduct of Land Operations – Operational Level Doctrine for the Canadian Army*. B-GL-3-001/FP-000. n.p., 1996.
–. *Corps '86 Staff Data (for Study Purpose Only)*. B-GL-303-004/FP-Z01. n.p., 1987.
–. *The Debrief the Leaders Project (Officers)*. n.p., 2001.
–. *Defence in the 70s: White Paper on Defence*. Ottawa: Information Canada, 1971.
–. *Duty with Honour: The Profession of Arms in Canada*. n.p.: Canadian Defence Academy – Canadian Forces Leadership Institute, 2003.
–. *The Thomas Report: Investigation of Delay in Investigating the Allegations of Misconduct/Poor Performance of Canadian Forces Members at the Bakovici Hospital, Bosnia-Herzegovina*. n.p., 1996.
–. *White Paper on Defence*. Ottawa: Queen's Printer, 1964.
Canada, Department of National Defence, Board of Inquiry. *Canadian Airborne Battle Group*. n.p., 1993.
–. *Command, Control and Leadership in CANBAT2: The Board Report*. n.p., 1996.
Canada, Department of National Defence, Board of Inquiry – Croatia. *Provisional Report*. n.p., 15 December 1999.
Canada, Department of National Defence, Minister's Monitoring Committee on Change in the Department of National Defence and the Canadian Forces. *Final Report – 1999*. n.p., n.d.
–. *Final Report – 2003: Land Force Reserve Restructure, Professional Development, Education and Leadership*. Ottawa, 2003.
–. *Interim Report – 1999*. n.p., n.d.
Canada, Department of National Defence, Task Force on Review of Unification. *Final Report*. n.p., 1980.
Canada, House of Commons, Special Committee on Defence. *1963 Special Committee on Defence: Minutes of Proceedings and Evidence*. Ottawa, 1963.
Canada, House of Commons, Standing Committee on External Affairs and National Defence. *Action for the Reserves*. Ottawa, 1981.
–. *Minutes of Proceedings and Evidence*. Ottawa, 1980-84.
Canada, House of Commons, Standing Committee on National Defence. *Minutes of Proceedings and Evidence*. 1966-67.
–. *Minutes of Proceedings and Evidence*. 1984-86.
Canada, Parliament, Special Joint Committee of the Senate and the House of Commons on Canada's Defence Policy, Security in a Changing World. *The Report of the Special Joint Committee on Canada's Defence Policy*. n.p.: Parliamentary Publications Directorate, 1994.
Canada, Royal Commission on Government Organization [Glassco Commission]. *Report*. Vol. 4, *Special Areas of Administration*. Ottawa: Queen's Printer, 1963.
"Canada–United States Army Tactical Doctrine Seminar." *Canadian Army Doctrine Bulletin* 2 (March 1981): 65-67.
"Canadian–German Army Tactical Doctrine Seminar." *Canadian Army Doctrine Bulletin* 4 (June 1982): 91-94.

Charters, David A. "Five Lost Years: The Mobile Striking Force, 1946-1951." *Canadian Defence Quarterly* 7, no. 1 (Spring 1978): 44-47.

Clarkson, Col. (Ret'd.) J.M.E. "Spark at Yom Kippur: Many Surprises in an Eighteen-Day War." *Canadian Defence Quarterly* 3, no. 4 (Spring 1974): 9-22.

Clausewitz, Carl von. *On War,* edited and translated by Michael Howard and Peter Paret. Princeton, NJ: Princeton University Press, 1976.

Clifford, Kenneth J. 1973. *Progress and Purpose: A Developmental History of the United States Marine Corps, 1900-1970.* Washington, DC: History and Museums Division, Headquarters, United States Marine Corps.

"The Combat Development Process." *Canadian Army Doctrine Bulletin* 3 (September 1981): 15-20.

"The Combat System Study." *Canadian Army Doctrine Bulletin* 4 (June 1982): 25-42.

Close, Robert. *Europe without Defence? 48 Hours that Could Change the Face of the World.* New York: Pergamon Press, 1979.

Coombs, Maj. Howard G. "Canada's Army and the Concept of Maneuver Warfare: The Legacy of the Twentieth Century (1899-1998)." Student paper, US Army Command and General Staff College, n.d.

Cotton, Charles A. *Military Attitudes and Values of the Army in Canada.* Toronto: Canadian Forces Applied Research Unit, 1979.

Cotton, Charles A., Rodney K. Crook, and Frank C. Pinch. "Canada's Professional Military: The Limits of Civilianization." *Armed Forces and Society* 4, no. 3 (May 1978): 365-89.

Coulombe, P.E. "The Changing Military Career in Canada." In *On Military Ideology: Studies Presented at Varna International Sociological Association Conference, 1970, Part II,* edited by Morris Janowitz and Jacques Van Doorn. Rotterdam: Rotterdam University Press, 1971.

Cowen, Deborah. *Military Workfare: The Soldier and Social Citizenship.* Toronto: University of Toronto Press, 2008.

Cushman, LGen. John H. 1990. "Challenge and Response at the Operational and Tactical Levels, 1914-45." In *Military Effectiveness.* Vol. 3, *The Second World War,* edited by Allan R. Millet and Williamson Murray. Boston: Unwin Hyman, 1990.

Dangerfield, MGen. J.K. "The 1st Canadian Division: Enigma, Contradiction or Requirement?" *Canadian Defence Quarterly* 19, no. 5 (April 1990): 7-14.

Delaney, Douglas E. *Corps Commanders: Five British and Canadian Generals at War, 1939-45.* Vancouver: UBC Press, 2011.

Delvoie, Louis. "Canada and International Security Operations: The Search for Policy Rationales." *Canadian Military Journal* 1 (Summer 2000): 13-24.

Doughty, Robert A. *The Evolution of US Army Tactical Doctrine, 1946-1976.* Fort Leavenworth, KS: Combat Studies Institute, US Army Command and General Staff College, 1979.

Eayrs, James. *In Defence of Canada.* Vol. 3, *Peacemaking and Deterrence.* Toronto: University of Toronto Press, 1972.

–. *In Defence of Canada.* Vol. 4, *Growing Up Allied.* Toronto: University of Toronto Press, 1980.

English, John A. *The Canadian Army and the Normandy Campaign: A Study of Failure in High Command.* New York: Praeger, 1991.

–. *Lament for an Army: The Decline of Canadian Military Professionalism.* Concord, ON: Irwin Publishing, 1998.

Evraire, Richard. "General and Senior Officer Professional Development in the Canadian Forces." ISP-MPA Master's project, Queen's University, n.d.

Feaver, Peter. *Armed Servants: Agency, Oversight and Civil-Military Relations.* Cambridge, MA: Harvard University Press, 2003.

Fetterly, Ross. "The Influence of the Environment on the 1964 Defence White Paper." *Canadian Military Journal* 5, no. 4 (Winter, 2004-05). http://www.journal.forces.gc.ca/.

French, David. "Doctrine and Organization in the British Army, 1919-1932." *Historical Journal* 44, no. 2 (June 2001): 497-515.

Gagné, Maj. D.R. "Armée 2002: La perception d'un réserviste." *Armour Bulletin/Bulletin des Blindés* (Été 1989): 20-22.

Goodspeed, D.J. *A History of the Defence Research Board of Canada.* Ottawa: Queen's Printer, 1958.

Graham, Dominick. *The Price of Command: A Biography of General Guy Simonds.* Toronto: Stoddart, 1993.

Granatstein, J.L. *Canada's Army: Waging War and Keeping the Peace.* Toronto: University of Toronto Press, 2002.

–. *The Generals: The Canadian Army's Senior Commanders in the Second World War.* Toronto: Stoddart, 1993.

–. "Making the Department of National Defence Work in the 1970s: The Deputy Minister and the CDS Remember." *Canadian Military History* 20, no. 2 (Spring 2011): 59-64.

–. *A Man of Influence: Norman A. Robertson and Canadian Statecraft, 1929-68.* Ottawa: Deneau Publishers, 1981.

–. "The Search for an Efficient, Effective Land Force Reserve." *Canadian Military Journal* 3 (Summer 2002): 5-12.

–. *The Special Commission on Restructuring of the Reserves, 1995: Ten Years Later.* Calgary: Canadian Defence and Foreign Affairs Institute, 2005.

Granatstein, J.L., and Robert Bothwell. *Pirouette: Pierre Trudeau and Canadian Foreign Policy.* Toronto: University of Toronto Press, 1990.

Gray, Colin S. "Defence in the Seventies: A White Paper for All Seasons." *Canadian Defence Quarterly* 1, no. 4 (Spring 1972): 30-34.

Hackett, General Sir John. *The Profession of Arms.* London: Sidgwick and Jackson, 1983.

Harris, J.P. *Men, Ideas and Tanks: British Military Thought and Armoured Forces, 1903-1939.* Manchester, UK: Manchester University Press, 1995.

Harris, Stephen J. *Canadian Brass: The Making of a Professional Army, 1860-1939.* Toronto: University of Toronto Press, 1988.

Head, Ivan. *Canada 21: Canada and Common Security in the Twenty-First Century.* Toronto: University of Toronto Press, 1994.

Hellyer, Paul. *Damn the Torpedoes: My Fight to Unify Canada's Armed Forces.* Toronto: McClelland and Stewart, 1990.

Hennessy, Michael A. "Operation 'Assurance': Planning a Multi-National Force for Rwanda/Zaire." *Canadian Military Journal* 2 (Spring 2001): 11-20.

Hillier, Rick. *A Soldier First: Bullets, Bureaucrats and the Politics of War.* Toronto: HarperCollins, 2009.

Hunt, G.D. "Reinforcing the NATO North Flank: The Canadian Experience." *Canadian Defence Quarterly* 16, no. 4 (Spring 1987): 31-35.

Hunter, Peter W. "Special Commission on the Restructuring of the Reserves: 10 Years Later – Selected Conference Speaking Notes." *Journal of Military and Strategic Studies* 8, no. 2 (Winter 2005-06): 1-10.

Huntington, Samuel P. *The Common Defence.* New York: Columbia University Press, 1961.

–. *The Soldier and the State: The Theory and Politics of Civil-Military Relations.* Cambridge, MA: Belknap Press, 1967.

Janowitz, Morris. *The Professional Soldier.* New York: Free Press, 1971.
Jarymowycz, Roman. "Doctrine and Canada's Army – Seduction by Foreign Dogma: Coming to Terms with Who We Are." *Army Doctrine and Training Bulletin* 2, no. 3 (August 1999): 48-52.
Jockel, Joseph T. *The Canadian Forces: Hard Choices, Soft Power.* Toronto: Canadian Institute of Strategic Studies, 1999.
Johnston, William. *A War of Patrols: Canadian Army Operations in Korea.* Vancouver: UBC Press, 2003.
Kampman, Maj. M.D. "Getting Our Doctrine Back on Line." Student paper, Canadian Forces Command and Staff College, 1995.
Kellett, Anthony. *Motivation and Behaviour: The Influence of the Regimental System. Part 1 – Esprit de Corps.* Operations Research and Analysis Establishment, Directorate of Social and Economic Analysis, ORAE Report No. R109. Ottawa, June 1991.
Kempling, Col. James S.H. "Brave New Army: The Militia of 2002." *Canadian Defence Quarterly* 17, no. 3 (Winter 1988): 31-38.
Kronenberg, Vernon J. *All Together Now: The Organization of the Department of National Defence in Canada, 1964-1972.* Wellesley Papers 3/1973. Toronto: Canadian Institute of International Affairs, 1973.
Langille, Peter. 1989. "In Pursuit of Strategic Flexibility." *Peace Magazine,* April-May 1989, 19.
Liston, BGen. Terrence. "The Development of Canada's Land Forces: A Problem of Policy and Expenditure Management." Student paper, École nationale d'administration publique, 1984.
Macdonald, Col. Brian S. "The White Paper, the Army Reserve and Army Reform – 1987-2002." *Canadian Defence Quarterly* 17, no. 4 (Spring 1988): 9-20.
Maloney, Sean M. "The Canadian Army and Tactical Nuclear Warfare Doctrine." *Canadian Defence Quarterly* 23, no. 2 (December 1993): 23-30.
–. "Domestic Operations: The Canadian Approach." *Parameters* 27 (Autumn 1997): 135-52.
–. "General Charles Foulkes: A Primer in How to Be CDS." In *Warrior Chiefs: Perspectives on Senior Canadian Military Leaders,* edited by Bernd Horn and Stephen Harris. Toronto: Dundurn Press, 2001.
–. "'Global Mobile': Flexible Response, Peacekeeping and the Origins of Forces Mobile Command, 1958-1964." *Army Doctrine and Training Bulletin* 1, no. 1 (Spring 2000): 20-34.
–. "'Global Mobile II': The Development of Forces Mobile Command, 1965-1972." *Army Doctrine and Training Bulletin* 4, no. 2 (Summer 2001): 7-21.
–. *Learning to Love the Bomb: Canada's Nuclear Weapons during the Cold War.* Washington, DC: Potomac Books, 2007.
–. "'Missed Opportunity': Operation Broadsword, 4 Brigade and the Gulf War, 1990-91." *Army Doctrine and Training Bulletin* 5, no. 1 (Spring 2002): 24-31.
–. "Purple Haze: Joint Planning in the Canadian Forces from Mobile Command to J-Staff, 1975-1991 (Part 1)." *Army Doctrine and Training Bulletin* 5, no. 4 (Winter 2002-03): 57-72.
–. *War without Battles: Canada's NATO Brigade in Germany, 1951-1993.* Whitby, ON: McGraw-Hill Ryerson, 1996.
Marteinson, John, and Michael R. McNorgan. *The Royal Canadian Armoured Corps: An Illustrated History.* Toronto: Royal Canadian Armoured Corps Association, 2000.
Mayne, Richard. "Its Own Worst Enemy: Ship Advocacy in the RCN, 1963-64." *Canadian Naval Review* 2, no. 3 (Fall 2006): 24-28.

McInnes, Colin. *Hot War Cold War: The British Way in Warfare, 1945-95.* London: Brassey's, 1996.
Milner, Marc. *Canada's Navy: The First Century.* Toronto: University of Toronto Press, 1999.
Morton, Desmond. *Ministers and Generals: Politics and the Canadian Militia, 1868-1904.* Toronto: University of Toronto Press, 1970.
–. *A Short History of Canada.* Toronto: McClelland and Stewart, 1994.
Muelaner, Capt. B.A. "The Search for the Best Anti-tank Defence." *Canadian Defence Quarterly* 3, no. 4 (Spring 1974): 24-30.
Neelin, Col. J.E., and Col. L.M. Pederson. "The Administrative Structure of the Canadian Armed Forces: Over-Centralized, Overly Staff-Ridden." *Canadian Defence Quarterly* 4, no. 2 (Autumn 1974): 33-40.
Off, Carol. 2004. *The Ghosts of the Medak Pocket: The Story of Canada's Secret War.* Toronto: Vintage Canada, 2004.
Pickering, Capt. W.L. "Has the Tank a Place on Today's Battlefield? Australian and Israeli Experience." *Armoured Review* 8 (April 1973): 4-5.
Pope, Maurice. *The Memoirs of Lt.-Gen. Maurice A. Pope.* Toronto: University of Toronto Press, 1962.
Preston, Richard A. *Canada's RMC: A History of the Royal Military College.* Toronto: University of Toronto Press, 1969.
Ralph, Wayne D. "The Bell AH-1Q TOW Cobra: Operational Experience and Field Trials." *Canadian Defence Quarterly* 4, no. 2 (Autumn 1974): 24-27.
Reserves 2000. 1999. *Canada's Army of the Future: Leadership and Militia Command and Control.* Toronto, 1999.
–. *Canada's Army of the Future: Militia Component Staffing and Funding.* Toronto, 1999.
Richter, Andrew. *Avoiding Armageddon: Canadian Military Strategy and Nuclear Weapons, 1950-63.* Vancouver: UBC Press, 2002.
Royal Canadian Armoured Association. "Position Paper on Main Battle Tank Retention, Defence in the 70s and the Main Battle Tank." *Armoured Review* 8 (April 1973): 10-11.
Scales, Robert H. *Certain Victory: The US Army in the Gulf War.* Washington, DC: Brassey's, 1994.
Sharpe, G.E. *Croatia Board of Inquiry: Leadership (and Other) Lessons Learned.* Winnipeg: Canadian Forces Training Material Production Centre, 2002.
Sharpe, BGen. G.E., and Alan English. "CFLI Project Paper – The Decade of Darkness." n.p., n.d.
Sherwin, Tamara. "From Total War to Total Force: Civil-Military Relations and the Canadian Army Reserve (Militia)." MA thesis, University of New Brunswick, 1997.
Smith, Denis. *Rogue Tory: The Life and Legend of John G. Diefenbaker.* Toronto: Macfarlane Walter and Ross, 1995.
Sprung, G.M.C. *The Soldier in Our Time: An Essay.* Philadelphia: Dorrance and Company, 1960.
Stacey, C.P. *Arms, Men and Governments: The War Policies of Canada, 1939-45.* Ottawa: Queen's Printer, 1970.
Stouffer, Ray. "Cold War Air Power Choices for the RCAF: Paul Hellyer and the Selection of the CF-5 *Freedom Fighter.*" *Canadian Military Journal* 7, no. 3 (Autumn 2006): 63-74.
Taylor, Scott, and Brian Nolan. *Tarnished Brass: Crime and Corruption in the Canadian Military.* Toronto: Lester Publishing, 1996.
Thompson, Sir Robert. *Defeating Communist Insurgency.* New York: Frederick A. Praeger, 1966.

Trauschweizer, Ingo. *The Cold War US Army: Building Deterrence for Limited War.* Lawrence: University of Kansas Press, 2008.

Urquhart, George Mackenzie. "The Changing Role of the Canadian Militia, 1945-1975." MA thesis, University of Victoria, 1977.

Walker, Richard J. "The Revolt of the Canadian Generals, 1944: The Case for the Prosecution." In *The Insubordinate and the Noncompliant: Case Studies of Canadian Mutiny and Disobedience, 1920 to Present*, edited by Howard B. Coombs. Kingston, ON: Dundurn Group and Canadian Defence Academy Press, 2007.

Wenek, Karol W.J. "Looking Back: Canadian Forces Leadership Problems and Challenges Identified in Recent Reports and Studies." n.p.: Canadian Forces Leadership Institute, 2002.

Willett, T.C. *Canada's Militia: A Heritage at Risk.* Boulder, CO: Westview Press, 1990.

Willis, John. "Defence Spending, 1988-89." *Canadian Defence Quarterly* 18, no. 1 (Summer 1988): 48-53.

Windsor, Lee. "Professionalism under Fire: Canadian Implementation of the Medak Pocket Agreement, Croatia 1993." *Canadian Military History* 9, no. 3 (Summer 2000): 23-35.

Winslow, Donna. *The Canadian Airborne Regiment in Somalia: A Socio-Cultural Inquiry.* Ottawa: Canadian Government Publishing, 1997.

–. "Canadian Warriors in Peacekeeping: Points of Tension in Complex Cultural Encounters." Toronto: Defence and Civil Institute of Environmental Medicine, 1999.

–. "Misplaced Loyalties: The Role of Military Culture in the Breakdown of Discipline in Two Peace Operations." *Journal of Military and Strategic Studies* 6, no. 3 (Winter 2004): 345-67.

Index

Canadian War Museum · Musée canadien de la guerre

STUDIES IN CANADIAN MILITARY HISTORY

John Griffith Armstrong, *The Halifax Explosion and the Royal Canadian Navy: Inquiry and Intrigue*

Andrew Richter, *Avoiding Armageddon: Canadian Military Strategy and Nuclear Weapons, 1950-63*

William Johnston, *A War of Patrols: Canadian Army Operations in Korea*

Julian Gwyn, *Frigates and Foremasts: The North American Squadron in Nova Scotia Waters, 1745-1815*

Jeffrey A. Keshen, *Saints, Sinners, and Soldiers: Canada's Second World War*

Desmond Morton, *Fight or Pay: Soldiers' Families in the Great War*

Douglas E. Delaney, *The Soldiers' General: Bert Hoffmeister at War*

Michael Whitby, ed., *Commanding Canadians: The Second World War Diaries of A.F.C. Layard*

Martin Auger, *Prisoners of the Home Front: German POWs and "Enemy Aliens" in Southern Quebec, 1940-46*

Tim Cook, *Clio's Warriors: Canadian Historians and the Writing of the World Wars*

Serge Marc Durflinger, *Fighting from Home: The Second World War in Verdun, Quebec*

Richard O. Mayne, *Betrayed: Scandal, Politics, and Canadian Naval Leadership*

P. Whitney Lackenbauer, *Battle Grounds: The Canadian Military and Aboriginal Lands*

Cynthia Toman, *An Officer and a Lady: Canadian Military Nursing and the Second World War*

Michael Petrou, *Renegades: Canadians in the Spanish Civil War*

Amy J. Shaw, *Crisis of Conscience: Conscientious Objection in Canada during the First World War*

Serge Marc Durflinger, *Veterans with a Vision: Canada's War Blinded in Peace and War*

James G. Fergusson, *Canada and Ballistic Missile Defence, 1954-2009: Déjà Vu All Over Again*

Benjamin Isitt, *From Victoria to Vladivostok: Canada's Siberian Expedition, 1917-19*

James Wood, *Militia Myths: Ideas of the Canadian Citizen Soldier, 1896-1921*

Timothy Balzer, *The Information Front: The Canadian Army and News Management during the Second World War*

Andrew Godefroy, *Defence and Discovery: Canada's Military Space Program, 1945-74*

Douglas E. Delaney, *Corps Commanders: Five British and Canadian Generals at War, 1939-45*

Timothy Wilford, *Canada's Road to the Pacific War: Intelligence, Strategy, and the Far East Crisis*

Randall Wakelam, *Cold War Fighters: Canadian Aircraft Procurement, 1945-54*

Andrew Burtch, *Give Me Shelter: The Failure of Canada's Cold War Civil Defence*

Wendy Cuthbertson, *Labour Goes to War: The CIO and the Construction of a New Social Order, 1939-45*

P. Whitney Lackenbauer, *The Canadian Rangers: A Living History*

Teresa Iacobelli, *Death or Deliverance: Canadian Courts Martial in the Great War*

Graham Broad, *A Small Price to Pay: Consumer Culture on the Canadian Home Front, 1939-45*

Isabel Campbell, *Unlikely Diplomats: The Canadian Brigade in Germany, 1951-64*

Printed and bound in Canada by Friesens

Set in Helvetica Condensed and Minion
by Artegraphica Design Co. Ltd.

Copy editor: Francis Chow

Proofreader: Lana Okerlund